COUNTERCURRENTS

Études d'histoire du Québec / Studies on the History of Quebec

Magda Fahrni et/and Jarrett Rudy
Directeurs de la collection / Series Editors

COUNTERCURRENTS

Women's Movements in Postwar Montreal

AMANDA RICCI

McGill-Queen's University Press
Montreal & Kingston • London • Chicago

ISBN 978-0-2280-1727-1 (cloth)
ISBN 978-0-2280-1728-8 (paper)
ISBN 978-0-2280-1823-0 (ePDF)
ISBN 978-0-2280-1824-7 (ePUB)

Legal deposit second quarter 2023
Bibliothèque nationale du Québec

Printed in Canada on acid-free paper that is 100% ancient forest free
(100% post-consumer recycled), processed chlorine free

This book has been published with the help of a grant from the Canadian
Federation for the Humanities and Social Sciences, through the Awards
to Scholarly Publications Program, using funds provided by the Social
Sciences and Humanities Research Council of Canada.

Funded by the Financé par le
Government gouvernement
of Canada du Canada

Canada

Canada Council Conseil des arts
for the Arts du Canada

We acknowledge the support of the Canada Council for the Arts.
Nous remercions le Conseil des arts du Canada de son soutien.

Library and Archives Canada Cataloguing in Publication

Title: Countercurrents : women's movements in postwar Montreal /
   Amanda Ricci.
Names: Ricci, Amanda, author.
Series: Studies on the history of Quebec ; 42.
Description: Series statement: Études d'histoire du Québec / Studies on
   the History of Quebec ; 42 | Includes bibliographical references and
   index.
Identifiers: Canadiana (print) 20230143105 | Canadiana (ebook)
   20230143148 | ISBN 9780228017288 (paper) | ISBN 9780228017271 (cloth) |
   ISBN 9780228018230 (ePDF) | ISBN 9780228018247 (ePUB)
Subjects: LCSH: Women—Political activity—Québec (Province)—Mon-
   tréal—History—20th century. | LCSH: Feminism—Québec (Province)—
   Montréal—History—20th century. | LCSH: Social movements—Québec
   (Province)—Montréal—History—20th century.
Classification: LCC HQ1460.M65 R53 2023 | DDC 305.409714/2809045—dc23

Contents

Acknowledgments

I begin by acknowledging my wonderful doctoral advisors, Suzanne Morton and John Zucchi, for their excellent mentorship, guidance, and patience. I could not have asked for more generous graduate supervision. Their assistance and encouragement made the project and my academic career possible. I could not possibly thank them enough.

My postdoctoral advisors, Steven High at Concordia's Centre for Oral History and Digital Storytelling and Ian McKay at McMaster's Wilson Institute for Canadian History, provided me with an academic home at a critical juncture in my career. The Social Sciences and Humanities Research Council of Canada, the Montreal History Group, and the Department of History at McGill University provided financial support during my years as a graduate student, for which I am very grateful. Sean Mills has been a key mentor and friend over the years, and his assistance and conversations about academia have been invaluable.

The current and former members of the Montreal History Group showed me the ropes and took an interest in my work. I also thank them for the camaraderie, as well as their generosity to younger scholars and graduate students. Like so many others, I keenly feel the absence of the incomparably kind and enthusiastic Jarrett Rudy.

I also express my gratitude to Jonathan Crago, Magda Fahrni, Robert Lewis, and the rest of the staff at McGill-Queen's University Press for all their help bringing the book to completion, as well as the anonymous reviewers of the manuscript for their constructive and rigorous comments. Licia Canton and Decio Cusmano lent a hand with editing, proofing, and translation.

People who have read and reread parts of the manuscript offered critical advice, for which I am greatly indebted: Lana Povitz, Sean Mills, Suzanne Morton, Laura Madokoro, Franca Iacovetta, Adele Perry, Nancy Janovicek, Colin Grittner, Rachel Sandwell, Brian Gettler, Myra Bloom, Magda Fahrni, Martin Messika, and Lilia Topouzova. My writing group – Sarah Schulman, Lana Povitz, Jeanette Estruth, and Nick Juravich – offered incisive comments and much-needed feedback early in the writing process.

All mistakes are, of course, my own.

I am grateful to all my lovely colleagues and students at Glendon, as well as my fellow graduate students at McGill – too many to name here – who have made coming to work a pleasure.

The warm hospitality and friendship of Jessica Carpinone, Lana Povitz, Carolynn McNally, Rachel Sandwell and Gavin Walker, Marie-Luise Ermisch, Hodan Ismail, Erika Nielsen, Claire Garnier, Émilie Tanniou and Mehdi Dallali, Lilia Topouzova and William Nelson, Hilary Chan and Alison Harvey, Gemma Albanese, Alicia Caravalho, Laura Madokoro, Kelly Roberts, my brunch club, and my high school friends have also kept me going over the years. I would never have finished this book without the help of my friends and Glendon and York colleagues, all of whom selflessly put up with my neuroses and provided invaluable encouragement.

Last but certainly not least, I thank my parents, my brother, cousins, and entire family for roots and wings.

Abbreviations

AFAQ	Association des femmes autochtones du Québec
BANQ	Bibliothèque et Archives nationales du Québec
CSF	Conseil du statut de la femme
CWC	Coloured Women's Club of Montreal
FFQ	Fédération des femmes du Québec
FLF	Front de libération des femmes du Québec
FLQ	Front de libération du Québec
IFC	Indian Film Crew
IQA	Indians of Quebec Association
LAC	Library and Archives Canada
LFAS	Ligue féminine d'action sociale
NCC	Negro Community Centre
NFB	National Film Board of Canada
NIB	National Indian Brotherhood
PAC	Pan-African Congress
PQ	Parti Québécois
QNWA	Quebec Native Women's Association
RAFA	Rassemblement des femmes haïtiennes
RCSW	Royal Commission on the Status of Women
RFQ	Regroupement des femmes québécoises
UNIA	Universal Negro Improvement Association
VANWS	Voice of Alberta Native Women's Society

COUNTERCURRENTS

Introduction

"A Nation Is Not Broken until Its Women Are Down"

In the summer and fall of 1990, the international community turned its attention to Kahnawà:ke and Kanehsatà:ke, two Kanien'kehá:ka (or Mohawk) communities near Montreal, located in Quebec, Canada's only predominantly French-speaking province. The most easterly nations of the Haudenosaunee Confederacy, they were engaged in a contentious battle for land, showing the world that the colonization of Indigenous peoples of the Americas was an incomplete, and ultimately botched, endeavour. Women occupied a conspicuous place during the seventy-eight-day standoff between these collectivities and the Quebec and Canadian governments, putting their lives on the line to show everyone who controlled the territory. Since the beginning of the resistance movement, pan-Indigenous political ties have been reactivated, bolstering local actions and reigniting grassroots politics. Journeying across the country, the participants in the Grandmothers Walk in Solidarity with Mohawk Clan Mothers, who consisted of Métis, Plains Cree, and Cree-Ojibway women, as well as one non-Indigenous woman, made it clear to the federal and provincial governments in a communiqué that "the Mohawk, like all Indian nations in the Americas, never gave up their right to self-determination and sovereignty; our land is sacred and we will not stop until our claims are justly dealt with … We support the actions of our young people who defend our lands and rights to self-determination. We say further that if Mohawk blood is shed, you had better be prepared to shed the blood of aboriginal grandmothers, women and

children because, A NATION IS NOT BROKEN UNTIL ITS WOMEN ARE
DOWN."[1] To the clan mothers, grandmothers, and women on the ground,
they said, "You are not alone ... We will not stop our trek until we reach
Mohawk country, or until Ellen Gabriel publicly states that your crisis is
over."[2] Acting as spokesperson for the self-described "people of the pines,"
Gabriel called for nation-to-nation talks with the prime minister of Canada.
A soft-spoken artist and future Quebec Native Women's Association president from Kanehsatà:ke, Gabriel spoke French reasonably well, so she was
chosen to go before television cameras and microphones to explain Mohawk
demands to a francophone Quebec public. Within a day, pictures of the
young woman had been beamed all over the world, making her a symbol
of the struggle.[3]

Describing her decision to remain behind the barricades despite the dangers, Gabriel stressed her obligations to her nation and community. As she
explained, "Iroquois culture dictates that women are the titleholders to the
land, just as they are titleholders to chieftainships, the rationale being that,
like Mother Earth, women give life and nurture it."[4] Indeed, scholars such
as Susan Hill highlight the role of Haudenosaunee epics and forms of governance in informing women's behaviour. With these lessons, women are
"taught to respect the earth and recognize the kindred spirit they share with
her as the bearers of new life."[5] Their potential and ability to sustain hu-
mankind are affirmed in ceremony, even today.[6] Women are instructed to
honour their special connection to their territory through the Great Law
of Peace, a constitution that still holds sway. They are thus holders of the
land under the law and duty-bound to protect it for the benefit of future
generations. Since identity and land are closely connected in Haudenosaunee culture, maternal lines determine national belonging.[7] This notion of responsibility to the land, to the nation, and to the community has
been a defining feature of women's politics.[8]

Using the past to counteract injustices in the present, community leaders
frequently evoke the powerful role that women played in Haudenosaunee
communities prior to colonization. Relative to European women, they
wielded significant political, diplomatic, and cultural sway.[9] As Gabriel
writes, "Modern feminism and the fight for women's equality owes its birth
to Indigenous women. Prior to contact, Indigenous women had a significant

role in the decision-making processes, cultural heritage, good governance, the health and well-being of nations, and retained equal rights with those of men. But, the role and importance of Indigenous women in contemporary life changed dramatically with the onslaught of colonization."[10] Colonization and settlement structured their lives and their politics: they had no choice but to resist the theft and exploitation of their lands, as well as the racist myths embedded in settler cultures. Haudenosaunee women grappled with the Indian Act as well, first instituted in 1876. Governing the lives of First Nations peoples, the Indian Act introduced patrilineality and patriarchy as the benchmark for allocating Indian status. Section 12(1)(b) determined that if a woman chose to marry a non-Indian man, she and her children would lose their status.[11] Settler colonialism undoubtedly affected both Indigenous men and women but not identically.[12]

Reflecting a shared social location, Indigenous women from various nations acted together politically. In the late 1960s and 1970s, they formed new women's organizations to debate, discuss, and overcome issues of common concern. Pan-Indigenous and multilingual, the Quebec Native Women's Association (QNWA) was officially founded in 1974. With no more than moderate funds, its founders travelled across Quebec and Canada to increase their collective power. They also travelled internationally, using moral suasion to speak independently on the world stage as citizens of sovereign nations.[13] Over time, the QNWA earned a reputation as one of the most dynamic Indigenous women's organizations in the country. In a 2008 interview with Kim Anderson, Gabriel attributed the association's vitality to the dedication of its members and to its leadership. She also mentioned the specificity of the Quebec context, clarifying that "the French-English situation has caused us to struggle more than other provinces to maintain our identity." The QNWA benefited from some "interesting allies along the way," helping its movement to become well established.[14] The association's supporters ranged from well-connected Québécois feminists to African-descended Montrealers. Black women's organizations moved mostly in parallel to the QNWA; nevertheless, they declared their solidarity, as well as occasionally came together, with their Indigenous counterparts.

Despite the rich political tradition of Indigenous women, scholars note their ambivalence toward feminism as an ideology stereotypically associated with middle-class white women. "Political identities are not straightforward," as historian Sarah Nickel explains. The reticence among some grassroots organizers and community leaders to adopt the label "feminist" reflects, in part, "a general anxiety around the term itself" and the "tendency for outsiders to ascribe identities to individuals they themselves might not always embrace."[15] Rather than directly assigning a label to women's politics, this study looks at their actions and their analyses. Women-led political movements, or "Indigenous feminisms," as Nickel argues, "have the potential to expose and destabilize patriarchal gender roles and the structures that sustain and promote continued Indigenous dispossession and disempowerment through colonialism."[16] For Indigenous peoples in general, their connection to and alienation from their land remain major political factors.[17]

Competing Feminist Nationalisms

In the decades following the Second World War, women from all walks of life became increasingly frustrated with the world around them. Drawing on longstanding political traditions, they bound together – sometimes on their own, other times with men – to revolutionize social norms and to contest myriad forms of gender inequality. Taken as a whole, this generation's political project was expansive: it touched on women's place in the family, in the workforce, in broader Quebec and Canadian society, and in the international political economy. The infrastructure that this cohort of activist women established was equally impressive. Women's centres and community organizations, socialized daycare, anti-racist education initiatives, human rights legislation, improved access to contraception and abortion, Indian Act amendments, and other legal gains irrevocably changed Quebec.

The women's movement, however, did not exist in a vacuum. No longer content to accept previous generations' hierarchies and conventions, young people challenged the status quo. Red Power, Black Power, global anti-colonialism, the Quebec liberation movement, and the student movement, among so many other social movements, defined and influenced these decades. Due in part to these overlapping social justice projects, some of the women in this study rejected the term "feminist" or remained hesitant to use the terminology. Other women wholeheartedly embraced the label, centring it as a key component of their political identities. This book incorporates both types of women activists, arguing that a broader definition of "feminism" is necessary in order to write against Quebec's and Canada's "narratives of exclusion" – historical writing that privileges the descendants of French and English settlers while erasing the contributions of Indigenous, African-descended, and other diasporic women. To ignore grassroots organizers' ambiguous rapport with the language of feminism, or for that matter, with each other, would be to downplay the full scale of women's oppositional politics during this period.[18]

Women's choice of tactics reflected their social location. For example, the Quebec Native Women's Association, with close ties to Kahnawà:ke, a predominantly Mohawk community close to Montreal, sought to reclaim Indian status for exogamous women who had lost their Indian status after out-marriage. This was far from the QNWA's only concern; it was equally critical of the colonial aspects of the education and health systems and was a proponent of self-determination. Members of the Montreal chapter of the Congress of Black Women of Canada and various Haitian women's groups tackled racially exclusionary school curricula, eased the transition of newcomers to the city, participated in numerous international conferences dedicated to overcoming racial oppression, and contributed to the overseas struggle to end the dictatorship of François Duvalier (1957–71) and Jean-Claude Duvalier (1971–86) as well as South African apartheid (1948–94). The Front de libération des femmes du Québec adopted the slogan "No liberation of women without the liberation of Quebec! No liberation of Quebec without the liberation of women!" to express its sense of dual oppression. Founded in the early 1980s, the Collectif des femmes immigrantes du Québec sought to build bridges among various immigrant women organizers. These are only a few of the many organizations in Montreal and nearby Kahnawà:ke that were led by a generation of activist women in the postwar period.

Although well known within their respective political scenes, many of these grassroots organizers have been overlooked by Quebec historians or portrayed strictly in the context of their own nations or communities. Taking a different approach, this study examines these activists alongside each other to broaden the parameters of feminist histories.[19] More specifically, *Countercurrents* includes two types of politicized women in its analysis: feminists, whose critique of male supremacy was overt and explicit; and activists, who professed a communal consciousness. Both groups of women engaged in self-assertions in political spaces on behalf of themselves, even if women in the second category did so in "solidarity with men and women of the same group, local or global."[20] By examining these two groups of women together, and considering them equally relevant for feminist genealogies, the book traces the roots of the broad-based explosion of feminist activity in Montreal in the postwar period to Black and Red Power ideologies, two movements with a strong collectivist ethos, a grassroots approach to social change, and inspirational ideas of freedom.[21] Members of these expansive, transnational movements for self-determination contested their contemporaries' understandings of social justice. Community organizers close to these political movements simultaneously forced the more self-identified feminist women to contend with ideas of "multiple" or "interlocking oppressions," as they were called by the second half of the 1970s. They did so in a province where the francophone majority considered itself dominated by an English-speaking minority as well as by the Canadian federation. From the 1970s into the 1990s, when this study ends, the women's movement evolved considerably: white women could no longer claim ownership over feminism, even if the impact of this shift had yet to be fully felt on the ground. Moreover, the intensification of neo-liberalism and incidences of overt backlash against feminism reshaped the women's movement, giving rise to new questions and to new paradigms for understanding gender oppression. The book thus ends there.

By pondering the origins, actions, and tactics of all these organizations, *Countercurrents* considers the ways that the various feminist or women-centred political projects interacted and changed each other over time. In this sense, the study understands intersectionality "as a constellation of knowledge projects that change in relation to one another in tandem with changes in the interpretative communities that advance them."[22] The main focuses of this study are Montreal and Kahnawà:ke, two different, albeit interconnected, locations with entangled histories. The product of a double colonization, first by the French and then by the English, Montreal has been a site of overlapping national projects, multiple languages, and hybrid cultures since its foundation in the 1600s. Diasporic and immigrant peoples entered into this unique intercultural dynamic and added to it, carving out a place for themselves. These communities participated in the city's polyvocal conversation as "a third partner," inserting their own definitions of belonging into a settler colonial space.[23]

Mere kilometres away, Kahnawà:ke had taken on a predominantly Mohawk character shortly after its establishment as a multi-ethnic Indigenous collectivity in the 1660s. Politically, economically, and geographically linked to Montreal, Kahnawà:ke's territorial integrity was and is constantly under threat by the building of bridges, railroads, and canals.[24] Significantly, a faction of the community refuses to recognize Quebec or Canada and has remained steadfast in its commitment to autonomy in all facets of life. Kahnawà:ke is part of the Haudenosaunee Confederacy, a centuries-old political federation that has been held together by the Kaianere'kò:wa (Great Law of Peace). Under this law, women are recognized as leaders of the Confederacy in partnership with their male relatives.[25] With the goal of allowing people to live together harmoniously, the Kaianere'kò:wa lays out the legal framework for managing territories, interacting with others based on kinship responsibilities, and choosing leaders.[26] In other words, despite the influences of the metropolis across the river, Mohawk people had their own political traditions and agendas. The latter included cultivating pan-Indigenous ties with other nations across North America.

In the years and decades following the Second World War, when European empires crumbled and youth revolted against their elders' values and traditions, Montreal and Kahnawà:ke were junctures for energetic cosmopolitan political movements. Activist women from these two places fostered political ties with like-minded people that spanned the continent and, in some cases, the world. They purposefully met with women in other locales to increase their power and authority. For example, Indigenous and Black women were especially well represented at the conferences of the United Nations Decade for Women, held in Mexico City (1975), Copenhagen (1980), and Nairobi (1985). They attended or organized other international conferences as well, such as "Women under Apartheid," a hemispheric conference on women in southern Africa that was hosted by Montreal in 1980. As organizers and attendees of these gatherings, activists in this study criticized Quebec and Canadian policies and worked to develop new frameworks. *Countercurrents* takes seriously these transnational actions and analyses, fleshing out protagonists' notions of the collective and, by extension, their ideas of political subjecthood. By acting on the world stage, grassroots organizers were able to subvert their marginalized status at home and expand their political network. The women's movement became a node for new visions of citizenship, crafted to overcome marginalization by the nation-state, by their own imagined community, and by the broader women's movement.

The chapters that follow explore these specificities, grounded in the necessary cultural context. Grassroots organizers aspired for belonging and full equality in multiple political communities simultaneously.[27] In this study, citizenship, nationhood, and nationalism are in turn defined rather expansively, severed from an exclusive rapport with the state to instead encompass people's memberships in a variety of collectivities – local, ethnic, national, and transnational.[28] Indeed, "the boundaries of nations," as sociologist Nira Yuval-Davis explains, "virtually never coincide with those of nation-states." There are always individuals or communities living in societies and states who are not considered to be, or who do not regard themselves as, supporters of the nation. There are members of national collectivities who live in other countries, and there are nations that have never had a state or that are divided across several states.[29] Whatever the circumstances, feminist scholars stress the gendered nature of nations and nationalisms where women have been viewed as the biological and cultural reproducers of the people, a resource requiring not only protection but also tight control. Their sexuality and private lives do not belong to themselves but to the collective. In minority or colonized contexts, moreover, nationalism has frequently been conceived as an effort to revive the dignity of an "emasculated nation" that has been degraded by foreign penetration, occupation, and domination.[30]

That nationalism is Janus-faced is well known. One side reveals a frightening reality: xenophobia, expansionism, aggression, and genocide. The other reveals a relatively positive outcome: community, belonging, sovereignty, territorial integrity, and in some cases, pluralism.[31] Nationalisms can divide women with conflicting nationalist aspirations, all the more so in settler society contexts where multiple sovereignties conflict with each other in the same geographical area. A site of two colonizing powers of unequal weight, Quebec is a unique setting in which to consider these questions. For many women in this study, the problem was not whether to join their respective national liberation struggles but how to address the patriarchal assumptions of their male colleagues.[32] Over time, they managed to assert their own demands under a broader nationalist framework, fearful that if sovereignty was achieved, they would be left out of the nation-building process. Thus women activists created new women-centred or feminist national liberation projects in postwar Montreal and Kahnawà:ke, albeit not easily, not absent tension with their male counterparts, or not in agreement with all quarters of the women's movement. Since the political projects under study do not map easily onto liberal, socialist, or radical definitions of feminism, the book, in sum, steps outside of these frameworks, continuing a tradition in Quebec scholarship of thinking about feminism and nationalism at the same time.[33]

Setting the Scene

People around the world were beginning to challenge institutions of authority after the Second World War, and Quebecers were no exception. Citizens of Canada's only predominantly French-speaking, Catholic province found themselves once again ruled by the authoritarian Maurice Duplessis. Premier of the province from 1936 to 1939, Duplessis was re-elected from 1944 to 1959.[34] Through an adept use of patronage, populist rhetoric, and close ties to the Catholic Church, Duplessis was voted in again and again, even as he ceded control of the Quebec economy to American and Anglo-Canadian capital.[35] But beneath the surface, change was brewing. Women's workplace behaviour, in the form of strikes, hinted at social changes to come.[36] Simultaneously, the mythical French Canadian family of ten or twelve children was just that, a myth: birth rates had declined. As francophone women were considered mothers of the nation – a notion that later generations would repudiate – their bodies were surveilled by priests and nationalistic commentators promoting cultural continuity. To their chagrin, women had already found ways to exercise a measure of control over their family life.[37] Buttressed by the slow but steady decline of the Catholic Church and the increasing demands placed on the state by civil society, Quebec was on the cusp of redefinition.

The election of 1960 symbolized the birth of a new era, the beginning of what historians refer to as the Quiet Revolution. Jean Lesage's Liberal Party sought to reclaim control over the Quebec economy through a state-directed evolution that was intended to benefit the francophone majority rather than the English-speaking minority.[38] Excitement was in the air, and neo-nationalists were centre stage. The members of a rising francophone intelligentsia became the loudest voices and main drivers promoting the modernization of Quebec society. Although not completely neutral – as we will see, several politicians opposed access to abortion into the 1970s – the provincial government secularized the state.[39] The pace of change was dizzying but welcomed by francophone Quebecers, the idea being to use an expanding state in order to promote French speakers' social mobility and to territorialize the Quebec identity, the latter of which would have consequences for Indigenous communities, as Indian-Crown relations were normally under federal jurisdiction. The provincial state sought to extend its reach to cover the whole territory, including the northernmost regions.[40]

Quebec women made political gains as well, adding to the positive momentum that accompanied their rising education levels and workforce participation rates. In 1964, married women finally acquired the right under the province's civil code to act independently of their husbands in a legal capacity.[41] The elimination of married women's subordination under the law accompanied the emergence of women's organizations, such as the communist Ligue des femmes du Québec in 1958, the pacifist Voix des femmes/Voice of Women in 1961, and the reformist Fédération des femmes du Québec (FFQ) in 1966, all of which together altered the political sphere.[42] Even if decidedly middle-class or bourgeois in orientation, the FFQ was a steady presence in feminist circles and remains so to this day.

Both reformist and leftist women were eager to participate in the period's sweeping changes. Bringing together some of the major women's organizations of its time, the FFQ was instrumental in establishing the Royal Commission on the Status of Women in 1967 as well as the Conseil du statut de la femme and the federal Canadian Advisory Council on the Status of Women in 1973. Officially secular and nonpartisan, the FFQ was open to all and sought to bring feminist women together, as indicated in the first article of its constitution: "Group together women and associations, wishing to coordinate their activities in the field of social action, without distinguishing race, ethnic origin, colour or creed."[43] Although the FFQ did not fully represent Montreal or Quebec – in fact, in the mid-1970s, the FFQ's president commented on the underrepresentation of Indigenous and immigrant women – the organization's makeup was never entirely homogenous.[44]

The FFQ was also intergenerational. Since most women in Quebec were granted the vote at the provincial level only in 1940, more than two decades later than other jurisdictions in Canada, there was significant overlap between pre- and post-suffrage women's movements; notably, First Nations women had to wait until 1960 to cast a ballet federally and until 1969 to do so provincially.[45] Thérèse Casgrain is one example of a feminist whose activism spanned the two movements. Born into a wealthy family, Casgrain joined the Co-operative Commonwealth Federation (now the New Democratic Party) in 1946. In 1961, the now-seasoned activist established a Quebec branch of the Voix des femmes/Voice of Women, whose members attended international peace conferences in opposition to the proliferation of nuclear weapons. Finally, in 1966, Casgrain became one of the founding members of the FFQ and later the honorary president.

Historians describe the 1960s and 1970s as a time of "mental liberation," a complete shift in mindset, during which an "expansive politicizing climate was spreading throughout Québécois society."[46] Political life held an indisputable intensity, perhaps especially for women who were contending simultaneously with the metropolis's ebullient mood and with the burn of exclusion. For example, the young editors and writers of the journal *Parti pris*, "who had just arrived in university when the provincial Liberals came to power in 1960," as historian Sean Mills explains, "worked to imagine new forms of democracy for the province."[47] Their political project pushed for secularization, independence, and socialism, the journal's task being to help "the budding revolutionary class to achieve self-consciousness."[48] They discussed francophone Quebecers' alienation, their dehumanization, and their need for an authentic culture of resistance, as well as the material and psychological consequences of colonialism at the hands of English Canada and the American Empire. But even these young male activists "emerged out of a patriarchal society that systematically minimized and devalued women's roles as political actors, and in many ways, they reproduced these structures within their own organizations and texts."[49] In the literature of resistance, women were strictly symbols, sometimes celebrated as bastions of culture and *survivance* and other times killed or raped as symbols of anglophone domination.[50] Like so many other nationalist projects in this book, then,

the one undertaken by male activists in the 1960s was in part based on a reclaiming of manhood.

Grassroots organizers' politics were directly informed by their socio-
economic status. Although the postwar period was a time of unprecedented
economic prosperity for Quebec and Canada, not everyone fared equally
well in the labour market or saw their material conditions improve dramatically. In Montreal, one-fifth of the population lived below the poverty
line in the 1960s.[51] French Canadians, single mothers and large families, immigrant communities, and First Nations peoples faced the greatest economic marginalization. English speakers were the most affluent, whereas
Indigenous people in Montreal, who numbered 3,125 in 1971, were at the
bottom of the socio-economic ladder. Nearby Kahnawà:ke also faced
conditions of hardship. Colonial domination had destroyed the previously
vibrant economies of the Confederacy, forcing Indigenous people surrounding Montreal into a position of economic dependency and migration to other urban centres such as Brooklyn, New York, in search of work
and better opportunities. With a declining land base and increasingly limited access to natural resources, Mohawk people were forced to develop
capital-based projects in order to acquire some economic self-sufficiency.[52]
The combination of sexism with other forms of discrimination made Montreal an even tougher place for women than it was for men. First Nations
women, followed by Black women, then Italian women, and then French
Canadian women, were the most likely to live in poverty, measured in terms
of their wages.[53] If the women's movement was a meeting point for grassroots activists, they came at the question of gender equality from different
social locations. Since their fight, to varying degrees, was always multifaceted, they demanded full citizenship in multiple imagined communities
at once.

Interventions

The book makes three main interventions. First, in arguing that Montreal
and Kahnawà:ke were sites of competing feminist nationalisms, the book
offers a framework that links differing political priorities and disagreements
among feminists to broader structural questions related to, for example,
settler colonialism, anglophone domination, the state, or patriarchy. Strong

expressions of feminist nationalisms were what was specific about the Quebec context, where most grassroots organizers acted and thought in terms of the nation or community, broadly defined. There were very real tensions among activist women in Montreal and Kahnawà:ke, yet whether Mohawk, diasporic, or Québécois, the book's protagonists mobilized an activism that sought the simultaneous promotion of two collectivities: women and a broader imagined community. Women activists all fashioned liberation movements that comprised self-determination, whether for Indigenous and African-descended peoples, for francophone Quebecers, or for immigrant communities in search of genuine inclusion. They did so, however, from a place that both endorsed women's equality and often critiqued patriarchal versions of nationalism or leftist social movements. Activist women thus contributed to a broader diffusion of power in Montreal and its surroundings, where liberation was no longer the sole purview of white men or, as this book contends, white women. In varied ways, organizations such as the bilingual Congress of Black Women, the Quebec Native Women's Association, and the Collectif des femmes immigrantes du Québec critiqued socioeconomic disparities in Montreal and Kahnawà:ke. They advanced their social justice agendas in the city and beyond in a manner that reflected their memberships' respective needs.

By intervening in the period's political debates, feminists and other politically active women challenged their contemporaries' understanding of inequality. On the left, the conversation around social inequality was unique in Quebec during the period under study. Scholars have analyzed white Québécois people's unique positionality as both colonized and colonizer, racialized and white, minority and majority. When Great Britain defeated France on the Plains of Abraham in Quebec City in 1759, French colonialists and their descendants became, according to literary scholar Corrie Scott, both the object and the subject of racialized discourses. Not unlike Jewish or Irish people, French Canadians have been portrayed as Others.[54] With the advent of the 1960s, activists and intellectuals contested Québécois marginalization, relying on an anti-colonial and gendered language. Identifying with the "wretched of the earth," to borrow the phrasing of anti-colonial thinker Frantz Fanon,[55] francophone Quebecers were inspired by the likes of Albert Memmi and Aimé Césaire, using their writings to better understand their own oppression within the Canadian federation. Poet

Michèle Lalonde's "Speak White" (1968) not only contained a moving critique of English speakers' debasement of francophones using highly racialized language but also positioned Québécois people in solidarity with global decolonization and civil rights movements.[56] However tenuous, feminist radicals adopted anti-colonial thinking in the late 1960s and early 1970s as part of their understanding of their own gender oppression, developing an identity that diverged from those of other white women in the Global North. By calling themselves "the slaves of the slaves," Québécois women tapped into Black Power ideologies as well, applying them to their own condition. It was a way of thinking that was rife with contradictions. Most significantly, the white, Quebec-based writers who pushed these ideas into the mainstream neglected to include Indigenous and African-descended Quebecers in their analyses (and indeed, among their ranks). This book is therefore, in part, an inquiry into the limits of white women's radical politics.[57]

Second, *Countercurrents* emphasizes activists' distinct priorities, showing how political projects existing in the same space evolved in different ways. Although each organization had its own goals, certain commonalities and divergences are worth highlighting. If feminists of this generation have been stereotyped as disregarding the family, the reverse was true for many of the case studies here. Most protagonists in fact prioritized intergenerational ties, directing considerable energy toward an older or a younger generation and often invoking the idiom of family or motherhood. For instance, the QNWA, the Congress of Black Women, and the Maison d'Haïti all had children in mind when conceiving their political work. In a context where white elites denigrated Black and Indigenous mothering, these women's organizations boosted parents, especially mothers, highlighting their valuable role in making sure that the next generation was connected to its culture of origin and thus revitalization. Activists sometimes relied on ideas of revolutionary motherhood to counteract harmful state and social practices, such as within the judicial and school systems.[58] Without a doubt, anti-racist and decolonial education for young people was a priority for this cohort of women activists, and they were willing to go to great lengths to critique as well as complement the existing formal system.

Similarly, these community leaders cultivated linkages with, or referenced, their elders, looking to them as foremothers in the struggle for social justice. The Centro Donne Italiane di Montreal, for example, provided key services to unilingual women, serving as a reference point for first-generation immigrants. The founders of the women's centres, rather than focusing on their maternal responsibilities, primarily reached out to their mothers' generation, aiming to provide services to an older, mostly unilingual, working-class group of women. Their focus on first-generation immigrants spoke volumes about the place of southern Europeans in broader Quebec society. Without the burden of racial discrimination, community organizers did not have to worry about racist teachers or school curricula. Instead, they could focus on easing the transition of allophone newcomers, a stance that nevertheless brought them into contact with other organizations professing similar goals. Whether maternal or filial, the self-assertions of most grassroots organizers in this study were never strictly about themselves, even if their community-oriented visions varied cross-culturally.

Central to this history is women's creation of new political knowledge. By pushing for access to abortion, founding women's centres, and attending women's conferences, feminists in Montreal, the book argues, developed a way of thinking about gender oppression that aimed to democratize relations among women and men, *as well as* among women of different social locations. Implicit in radical Québécois women's politics was the desire for genuine equality between the French and English in Quebec and Canada. This framing in turn influenced how Indigenous and diasporic women articulated their own claims for social justice. They advocated for complete equality in a way that addressed their unequal place in multiple collectivities, including Quebec. In this heightened political atmosphere, feminist leaders sought to bring women of their communities *into* politics on a fair footing with both the women and the men of (more) dominant cultures by trying to create the conditions whereby they could fully participate in all factions of society and political life. By taking on leadership roles at the grassroots level, activist women facilitated the exercise of social and political citizenship through, for example, French-language classes – contrary to popular belief, allophone women wanted to learn French – Indian status, access to birth control, and anti-racist education.

In short, the upsurge of women's activism in the postwar era changed the political dynamic in the city, where new political actors and issues came to the fore and fought for the limelight. As a cohort, women's activists of this era created new social thought, large parts of which remain with us today. By the 1980s, women of diverse backgrounds were more likely to be in the same room with one another. Feminists were consequently forced to contend with issues of social and political difference under the umbrella of the women's movement. This shift in consciousness, however incomplete among Euro-Québécois women and middle-class women more generally, would not have been possible without the nearly two decades of political work on the part of Indigenous, Black, and other diasporic activists.

Third, the book argues that feminism is best understood when explicitly studied in relation to other political projects. The book addresses a historical moment in women's activism when the intensity of the conversations around social and gender injustice led to a shift in community organizing. A true plethora of women's organizations, many of which are still in operation, were founded during this period. Grassroots organizers, however, tapped into more than just women-only social and political networks. For instance, historians and geographers have portrayed Montreal as a centre for Black radical thought and community organizing from the times of enslavement until today.[59] The Congress of Black Women of Canada can trace its origins to, among others, Caribbean anti-colonial and pan-African thinking, civil rights struggles in the United States as well as Canada, Garveyism, and the Coloured Women's Club of Montreal, established at the turn of the twentieth century. Its membership remained active within other community organizations and initiatives, as well as the global anti-apartheid movement, throughout the period under study. Evoking the legacies of slavery and colonization, Congress members built on a longstanding tradition of global Black organizing and resistance.[60] Haitian Montrealers, many of whom attended Congress events, were part of parallel, primarily Haitian feminist organizations. They were also among the founding members of the Maison d'Haïti, which, from the early 1970s until today, has played an integral role in the community and has contributed to the international women's movement by attending conferences all over the world. Bringing these experiences back with them to Montreal and into predominantly female political spaces, grassroots organizers infused the broader women's movement with new energies and ideas.

By stressing the importance of overlapping social movements, the book joins the growing historiography challenging the "wave" metaphor of feminist activism, a paradigm that often promotes the notion that Black,

Indigenous, and diasporic women were latecomers to feminism. In this common periodization of women's movements in North America, the "first wave" of feminist activism refers to women's quest for voting rights starting at the turn of twentieth century, whereas the "second wave" surged in the mid-to-late 1960s and sought to call into question women's limited social roles through, for example, access to contraception and increased workforce participation. According to the authors of "Is It Time to Jump Ship? Historians Rethink the Waves Metaphor," the metaphor centres the politics and experiences of "privileged, white heterosexual women," focusing on when they were most active in the public sphere. "The multidimensional aspects of feminism too often are excluded" in this interpretation, where "women of color, working-class women, women with disabilities, lesbians, and older women who engaged in activism that responded to overlapping forms of oppression, including sexism, have rarely been incorporated into waves narratives in their own right."[61] When marginalized women are included, as these historians remind us, their involvement is evoked to demonstrate either sisterhood or tensions between women. Critiques of wave-related agendas by scholars and activists are then "used to demonstrate the race, class, and other biases of 'feminism,' presuming feminism to be always white and middle class."[62] Labour historian Dorothy Sue Cobble rhetorically raises the question, "If, for example, we take race and class to be as important as gender in restricting women's freedom, then are not the movements organized around ending these discriminations" as important?[63] Put simply, as historian Julie Gallagher states, the metaphor tends to centre "the priorities of relatively elite women," who often have the luxury of appraising the world in primarily gendered terms, pre-emptively excluding other social movements from feminist accounts.[64]

This study includes women's activism in mixed-gender settings alongside explicitly self-described feminist efforts in order to portray Indigenous and Black women's own prioritizing of anti-racist and anti-colonial struggles within the context of gender politics. Inspired by African American historiography, the book argues that "feminist" practice existed in these spaces, even if the label was not necessarily used.[65] The paths to equality that these leaders envisioned encompassed the well-being of their entire community. Their vision for a better future not only included a more equal role for women but also focused on the undoing of the daily injustices faced by men and children. Black and Indigenous women had urgencies that necessitated leadership outside of autonomous women's organizations, and these urgencies influenced their organizing style and priorities. This situation does not mean, however, that they were complacent about sexism or that they were disinterested in women's liberationist principles.[66] As US historian Robyn Spencer explains, "Battles for national liberation all too often reinscribed patriarchy by analyzing gender contradictions as a secondary consideration."[67] As we will see, Indigenous and Black women were strong and, in many ways, uncompromising leaders who often pushed back against the patriarchal dictates of their male comrades.[68] With all this in mind, the book understands all women's agency as politically valid, regardless of whether or when they chose to organize in women-only spaces. This study also emphasizes Black and Indigenous women's contributions to mixed spaces[69] at a time when, for some women, national liberation and women's liberation were mutually reinforcing concepts.[70]

Given the wide-ranging and, in some cases, diverging priorities of activist women in Quebec's metropolis, the study necessarily embraces an expansive definition of feminism. Following historian Premilla Nadasen, the book understands feminism as "a political program working to empower women, to ensure them autonomy and control over their lives in a way that does not impede the autonomy or contribute to the exploitation of other women."[71] This broad definition allows for analytical room to include women who did not self-identity as feminist. "Feminism" as a term carries a great deal of baggage due in large part to its association with white middle-class women of the Global North. Many actors, from white working-class women to women of colour, have distanced themselves from the word. Scholars Mishuana Goeman and Jennifer Nez Denetdale, for example, outline Indigenous women's ambiguous relationship with the term "feminism" as a thought and practice "long held to be in purview of white rule." Goeman and Denetdale still "affirm the usefulness of Native feminism's analysis," however, and declare that "Native feminist analysis is crucial if we are determined to decolonize as Native peoples."[72] The term, at least initially, failed to resonate among Black women as well. As Spencer writes, "Scholars of black feminism have argued that '[in] combination [the] pressure to maintain (at least outwardly) racial solidarity with Black men and [the] alienation from the agenda of the predominantly White, middle-class women's movement account, historically, for Black women's reluctance to identify as feminists."[73] This reticence did not mean that their politics ignored women's needs or that they never challenged men for leadership roles.

A Comparative Feminist Framework

The book adopts a comparative feminist framework as "a way to theorize a complex relational understanding of experience, location, and history."[74] At the heart of this notion lies the concept of "relationality rather than separation."[75] Thus the book puts Indigenous, diasporic and immigration, and Quebec histories in the same analytical frame, drawing inspiration from historians working in those fields.[76] Mary Jane McCallum, for example, critiques the "habitual isolation of Aboriginal (Indigenous) history from broader inquiries," an approach that "tends to limit its wider relevance." As McCallum puts it, "There is currently no professional understanding in Canada that 'good' history must also be good Aboriginal history or that Aboriginal history can radically alter the entire profession of history itself." Although focused on the English-speaking professional community, Mc-Callum's conclusions can certainly be applied to its French-language counterpart.[77] Historian Lisa Rose Mar similarly opposes historians' overemphasis on "white practices of racial exclusion," explaining that "the belief that Chinese Canadian history is so estranged from the rest of Canada that it is a separate, specialized topic is a profound erasure."[78] The same could be said for African Canadian histories. Canada – and for that matter, Quebec – to cite geographer Katherine McKittrick, "is a nation that has and is still defining its history as Euro-white, or nonblack,"[79] where "narratives of erasure and domination ... make the possibility of black Canada surprising and unexpected."[80] As a result, Black Montrealers are an "absented presence" in nation-centric historiographies.[81] With McCallum's, Mar's, and McKittrick's ideas in mind, *Countercurrents* is enriched by an entire generation of feminist historians who have thought very seriously about how gender intersects with other categories of social difference.

Relying on feminist newsletters and conference proceedings, personal archives, community-based archives and newspapers, and oral histories,

Countercurrents introduces a new cast of characters to the history of the women's movement in Montreal and expands the archive on women's activism in Quebec and Canada. Although the book makes good use of the Canadian Women's Movement Archives Collection, located at the University of Ottawa, and the easily identifiably feminist fonds at the Bibliothèque et Archives nationales du Québec in Montreal, most of the material in the manuscript was found in other archival fonds or classified separately. Further, I include the sources of community-based organizations led by both women and men alongside those of women's organizations in order to reflect the book's expansive definition of feminism.

Importantly, I also examine materials from prominent, predominantly white, women's groups as one means to look for points of contact among different feminists while also thinking critically about the ways that some women were invisible to their counterparts or socially distant. Therefore, I include the most read French-language feminist sources, such as those published by the Fédération des femmes du Québec, throughout the manuscript. By doing so, I point to unexpected presences, notably Indigenous women in the orbit of the FFQ, as well as to absences and the ways that feminists from different backgrounds – not only Québécois – erased one another, excluded one another, or failed to take each other into account. The sources in this study are thus read comparatively. If feminist papers have been rightfully credited with creating new political networks, inciting debate, and forging an "imagined feminist community," they were not the only sites of critical analysis relevant to women's lives.[82] Women authored a great deal of material, much of which remains outside of the feminist archive.

This book has its limitations, leaving much more to be written. As a white settler currently based in Toronto, I am an outsider to most of these histories. I have tried to minimize violent language, but readers will notice inconsistencies. When the speaker or writer is Black, for example, I have left the original language in the text, honouring the person's word choice. I have also aimed for clarity when referring to book titles or names of organizations. My main purpose in writing this book is to help open the door for more cross-cultural or community-based studies. Notwithstanding the important feminist credo that "the personal is political," readers should note that *Countercurrents* is more about feminists and community organizers as political and intellectual actors than it is about women's experiences or innermost lives. Although psychological and emotional questions are not entirely absent, my emphasis is on women's public personas. By the 1980s, queer women's omnipresence within social movements was obvious, a fact addressed only sporadically in this book, and more research needs to be conducted on queer women, particularly queer women of colour, two-spirited women, and transfeminists, just as future historians could more overtly address homophobia within the women's movement.[83] Finally, I have chosen to focus on select women's or community-based organizations, to the exclusion of unions or communist and socialist groups. Women played important roles in these spaces, and it would be worthwhile to study the extent of their contributions and impact, as well as the reciprocal impact of these organizations on women's politics. Such a study could have important implications for the historical and present-day priorities of working-class women of all backgrounds. But my focus here is on the intersections between feminisms and nationalisms in order to reflect on the continued significance of nations and nation-states *and* their transcendence by women's movements.[84]

Organization of the Book

Countercurrents points to new political genealogies and sites of feminist activism. Chapters 1 and 2 focus respectively on the universes surrounding the Quebec Native Women's Association and the Congress of Black Women of Canada. Drawing on traditional forms of governance, on their own role as mothers, and in some cases, on feminist-inspired discourse, Mohawk and other Indigenous women engaged in multiple forms of grassroots organizing in the postwar period, from defending land to reclaiming Indian status. Despite the ongoing existence of the Great Law of Peace, a constitution that asserts the matriliny and matrilocality of the Haudenosaunee Confederacy, out-married women lost their right to membership under section 12(1)(b) of the federal Indian Act. The largest Indigenous community in Canada when these laws were being introduced at the end of the nineteenth century, Kahnawà:ke would play a key role in this debate until section 12(1)(b)'s removal in 1985. Kanien'kehá:ka women's organizing was inherently transnational; their political imaginary ignored the existence of colonial borders. During the bridge blockade near Cornwall, Ontario, in 1968, for instance, they defended their right to freely traverse the Canada-US border duty-free, evoking the jurisdiction of the Confederacy. The movement for Red Power across North America gained political momentum after this incident. Mohawk women were also part of a broader movement of pan-Indigenous organizing in the late 1960s and early 1970s. Building on previous work by the Indian Homemakers' Clubs, many of which were founded in the 1930s, the organizers of the 1971 First National Native Women's Conference in Edmonton fostered the type of international ties among Indigenous women that paved the way for the Quebec Native Women's Association. Officially established in 1974, the QNWA was a multilingual, multinational platform for advocacy, a political space where women could address their unique concerns as women and make the appropriate strategic linkages to advance their agendas.

The Congress of Black Women similarly enabled Black Montrealers of various national provenances to get to know one another in a predominantly female space. It, too, had much deeper roots, reflecting the history of Black political and community life in Quebec. By the end of the nineteenth century, railway porters and their families had set up a vibrant institutional network, establishing, for example, a branch of the Universal Negro Improvement Association and the Coloured Women's Club of Montreal. Bolstered by successive waves of immigration from the Caribbean, these organizations set the stage for postwar instances of civil rights organizing and expressions of pan-Africanism and Black Power.[85] Although English-speaking women got the Congress of Black Women off the ground in the early 1970s, they quickly built bridges with French-speaking Haitian women at a time when Montreal demographics were changing. When Canada dropped its racially exclusive immigration law in favour of a points system in 1967 and Quebec put into place its own Ministère de l'immigration in 1968 to attract immigrants from the Francophonie, the city welcomed newcomers from the Caribbean, East Asia, South America, and North Africa.[86]

Women from the QNWA and the Congress travelled far and wide to advance their political goals, from the inaugural United Nations World Conference on Women, held in Mexico City in 1975, to the Sixth Pan-African Congress, hosted by Dar es Salaam, Tanzania, in 1974. Although distinct, both organizations' memberships expanded notions of citizenship to bypass the nation-state in order to foster more expansive ideas of social justice and, ultimately, women's liberation. They wanted to ensure that women would have a place in a self-determined future, where they, too, would have a say in building institutions and in defining collective notions of belonging.

Important not only in and of themselves, the Red and Black Power movements, with their roots in the 1940s and 1950s or earlier, also paved the way, in part, for the Front de libération des femmes du Québec (FLF) and for the Centre des femmes, the focus of chapter 3. The impact of the Black Power and other national liberation movements on Québécois organizers was profound. Black Power rhetoric infused FLF writings, illustrating its broad reach. FLF members were also inspired by Indigenous freedom fighters, showing the ways that some North Americans romanticized the "Third World," as well as the Haudenosaunee matriarchy, supposedly part of a distant past. Despite organizing autonomously, radical francophones remained dedicated to promoting the well-being of all Québécois women and men, who, in their minds, were colonized by English Canadian and American imperialist capitalists. They developed a feminism that tried to speak to working-class francophone people. By building on Marxist ideas and the Quebec liberation movement, they not only helped to give the Quiet Revolution its "second wind" but also challenged patriarchal versions of neo-nationalism.[87] In short, Québécois feminists on the left connected their fate to that of Quebec. Their commitment to sovereignty coloured their relationships with anglophone feminists in Montreal and in other parts of Canada. By virtue of their race and, to a degree, their class privilege, FLF members were able to garner media and scholarly attention. However, contrary to simplistic understandings of this period of feminist activism, they did not see the world strictly through the lens of gender. Socialist and other forms of leftist critical analysis inspired their political work.[88]

The next two chapters are organized both chronologically and thematically. Chapter 4 enters the vibrant world of the Haitian diaspora, discussing women's integral role in opposing the Duvalier dictatorship and in defending the rights of new arrivals to Quebec, such as by founding the Maison d'Haïti in the early 1970s. By the mid-1970s, more immigrants were arriving in Quebec from Haiti than any other country.[89] Whereas the first wave of Haitian migrants consisted of middle-class professionals, the second wave came out of the working classes and thus experienced more trouble integrating economically. Supporting the rising international women's movement, Haitian Montrealers were active participants in the events of the UN Decade for Women (1975–85) as well. This chapter paints a grassroots picture of transnational feminism – that is, of movement building across borders. Women organizing from within the growing Haitian community in Montreal took insights from longstanding political traditions and applied them to their new setting, such as by critiquing racial and class biases in the education system and tying them to Quebec's colonial past. Diasporic Haitians asserted their right to first-class citizenship in Montreal, in the global community, and in Haiti, the latter especially relevant for those who returned to the country after the fall of the dictatorship. For Haitian Montrealers, these political spheres were interconnected.

Chapter 5 examines the Centro Donne Italiane di Montreal, founded in 1978. The Italian community ballooned after the Second World War, making Italian the third most spoken language after French and English by 1961. The Centro Donne was one of seventy women's centres founded in Quebec over a span of ten years. Largely through service provision, the Centro Donne filled in for a state that could not account for women whose lives were lived outside the official languages. Spearheaded by younger women, the centre served as a reference point for a socially disenfranchised older generation, many of whose members worked in the garment industry.[90] Italian Montrealers did not propose to alter conventional understandings of citizenship. Their contributions to the Centro Donne reflected their desire for pluralistic forms of belonging to Quebec society and better services for allophone newcomers. Relying on mostly Italian-language sources, the chapter connects the history of the community to progressive social movements, further belying stereotypes regarding foreign-born women's supposed passivity.

By the 1980s, immigrant women were increasingly entering into coalitions with one another, such as by organizing the 1982 conference "Femmes immigrées, à nous la parole!" and founding the Collectif des femmes immigrantes du Québec. The collective was established in August 1983 by seventy-five women working within various immigrant organizations, including the Maison d'Haïti and the Centro Donne. Chapter 5 concludes with an analysis of the 1992 conference "Un Québec féminin pluriel," which was in part a response to tensions within the women's movement. On the one hand, Euro-Quebecers were more likely to pay lip service to intersectional frameworks by the 1990s, but on the other hand, some feminists' condonement of remnants of ethnic nationalism as well as unaddressed questions regarding territorial dispossession and systemic racism hampered genuine solidarity politics in predominantly female spaces.

If this period of feminist activism has been considered one of the most successful in advancing gender equality, much of this triumph can be explained by the strategies and tactics adopted by the women in this study. In Montreal and Kahnawà:ke, grassroots organizers stayed close to the ground, as evidenced by the proliferation of women's organizations, women's centres, and other political groups where women's needs were taken into consideration. As a result, women were anchored in more than just feminist contexts through their "nationalism." With deep roots in earlier movements, which will be explored in the relevant chapters, postwar women's movements were successful in mainstreaming the conversation of gender equality from the mid-1970s through the 1990s. Community organizers responded and adapted to the needs of their communities as they arose, doing so by means of either women-only or mixed associations.

Their leadership's (and my own) evocation of community, however, was and is strategic. Communities are fraught, porous, and evolving. They are made rather than being a given. They can be homophobic, sexist, classist, racist, and so many other things. Yet many women chose to work within these spaces. They did so while developing personal and professional ties outside of the communities where they worked, making Montreal the metropolis that it is today. Although they occurred roughly at the same time, these women's movements were autonomous and had distinct political goals, many of which have yet to be fully realized. Territorial dispossession, systemic racism, poverty, homophobia, and myriad forms of violence remain a grim reality for so many women. Even if this generation of women achieved incredible accomplishments that benefited all women to some degree, the gains landed unevenly. By locating the origins of this period of feminism in the Black and Red Power movements, as well as examining the effects of the proliferation of feminist radicalism across a wide range of contexts, the book seeks new ways of defining feminist priorities and thus imagining feminist futures. It also hopes to open additional ways of exploring women's politics, both within and beyond feminism.

1

Guardians of the Nation
Kahnawà:ke Women's Activism

One of the most well-known figures of her generation, as well as a steady presence in Kahnawà:ke and Montreal in the 1960s, Kahentinetha Horn was an impassioned advocate involved in a blockade of the International Bridge near Ahkwesáhsne in 1968. Invoking the Jay Treaty of 1794, Horn and the other people involved in the protest made public their refusal of the legitimacy and laws of Quebec and Ontario, Canada, and the United States. They blocked the bridge to stress that international borders were meaningless for Haudenosaunee and other Indigenous peoples. Horn promoted a return to traditional forms of governance, ones that, as thinkers consistently note, contain a large and important place for women.[1] As she stated in an interview, "May I sum up what I stand for: return and reinstatement of the legal Indian government – the Six Nations Iroquois Confederacy. Return of self-respect, poise, courage, and determination for Indians so they can stand, be masters of their own lives – by guarding our land, developing our communities, improving our housing, reforming our medical care, training in suitable and useful skills, controlling our education."[2]

With locations in Quebec, Ontario, and upstate New York, Kanien'-kehá:ka communities recognize the Kaianere'kò:wa (Great Law of Peace). Like other constitutions, the Kaianere'kò:wa outlines the objectives of the main institutions of government, delineates the division of power among these bodies, and provides a definition of the relationship between governments and the peoples. These principles are rooted in treaties such as the Guswantah (Two Row Wampum Treaty) that the Haudenosaunee Confederacy signed with the Dutch, English, and French. Based on friendship,

peace, and mutual respect, the treaty mandated that each nation would retain its respective laws and constitution, that they would deal with each
other as equals, and that they would respect each other's jurisdiction and
sovereignty. The Haudenosaunee have never ceded their title to the lands
on either side of the colonial border.[3] To this day, the Kahnawa'kehró:non
are among the most strident in defending their territory. Their flag has become known all over the world, recognized by marginalized peoples in far-
flung locales and hoisted as a symbol of Indigenous resistance, of which
women such as Horn were no small part.

Mary Two-Axe Earley was another leader of national and international
renown from Kahnawà:ke. She rose to prominence in the 1960s and 1970s
after she contested section 12(1)(b) of the federal Indian Act, arguing that
its universal imposition of patrilineal band membership on First Nations
communities across Canada was detrimental to women, their children, and
their respective nations.[4] After the 1951 revisions, exogamous women lost
not only their Indian status but also their band rights and privileges, including the right to own property within their community. They could no
longer take part in band business and were prevented from returning to live
with their families even when in need. They were also refused burial on the
territory of their ancestors, and the children of these partnerships were not
recognized as Indians under the law. In contrast, non-Indigenous women
who married Indian men acquired status and band rights under section
11(1)(f). In 1956, the Indian Act was further amended to allow members of
Indian reserves to contest the legitimacy of children, questioning whether
the father was a status Indian. From then on, as Martin Cannon explains,
"Indian women's status, in the legal sense, meant nothing, since only men
could bestow legitimacy on their children."[5]

By contesting their exclusion from membership lists, Kanien'kehá:ka
women opposed the sexism and racism of the Indian Act.[6] In 1975, Two-
Axe Earley took her campaign all the way to the United Nations World
Conference on Women, held in Mexico City during International Women's
Year. In Mexico, she encountered other Indigenous and anti-colonial activists. There, she spoke out against Canada's colonial policies on the world
stage and explained exactly why they targeted women. The tragic irony was
that Haudenosaunee peoples had been matrilineal and matrifocal for most
of their history, with land and identity passing through the maternal line.

Further, clan mothers were the ones who adopted and integrated outsiders into the community so that they had "responsibilities to something larger than themselves,"[7] and to this day, women are the ones who assign children their names in the Kanien'kehá:ka language during certain ceremonial festivals.[8] Feminine pronouns – she, one, someone – are used for persons of unspecified gender and for the collective term "people" in Mohawk, signifying women's inherent importance.[9]

The membership question in Kahnawà:ke continues to be a fraught and emotional issue, one that needs to be put into a much larger framework. The central problem for exogamous women was not simply inequality under the Indian Act or patriarchy. Rather, their disempowerment was directly related to the consequences of settler colonialism, specifically a shrinking land base. Kahnawà:ke's land loss from the seventieth through the nineteenth centuries was profound. The Haudenosaunee lived and hunted in the St Lawrence Valley for centuries, but the first people to form the village arrived in the mid-seventeenth century.[10] In 1680, King Louis XIV formally established the community with a seigneurial land grant. The original land grant was for forty-five thousand acres and included two islands, islets, and shoals. Due to mismanagement and illegal land concessions by the Jesuits, much of its original territory was whittled down over the years. British agents continued the pattern of profiting from the sale of Kanien'kehá:ka lands to settlers, encouraging the encroachment of neighbouring farmers of European extraction. Moreover, the village's proximity to Montreal – Quebec's and Canada's primary metropolis for most of the twentieth century – meant that its territorial integrity was constantly under threat. In the late 1800s, Kahnawà:ke experienced the aftershocks of the city's rapid urban development and spectacular population growth due to rural exodus and immigration, namely the unwanted presence of bridges, railroads, and canals. The federal government also surrendered land to create rights-of-way for Hydro-Québec and Bell Telephone, all of which occurred in the core residential and agricultural areas of the reserve.[11] Today, the land base of Kahnawà:ke consists of less than 13,000 acres.[12]

In this specific context of land loss, one that came with geographical proximity to a large urban centre, the presence of outsiders could threaten Kahnawà:ke's very existence. With resources strained, who, but more importantly *how*, people belonged was of the utmost importance. As potential voters and property owners, white men who married into the community posed the greatest menace. To pre-empt a takeover and to ration dwindling space, the community condoned the legal exclusion of out-married women in the latter half of the nineteenth century. By that time, Kahnawà:ke was the most populous Indigenous community in Quebec and Canada. These measures were then codified in section 12(1)(b) of the Indian Act, remaining there until 1985, when an estimated 127,000 people had their status restored.[13]

Launched in the late 1960s, the campaign to overturn section 12(1)(b) of the Indian Act was a long, collective struggle, one that left a complex legacy. Women from Kahnawà:ke travelled all over the continent to make links with other Indigenous organizers and to fight for their right to national belonging. They then brought this pan-Indigenous political ethos back home, founding – alongside other Indigenous women – the Quebec Native Women's Association (QNWA) in 1974. The association focused on a range of issues, including racism in the education system, employment prospects, and out-adoption, while also confronting the implications of section 12(1)(b). The QNWA was a multinational, multilingual group. It brought together, and was open to, women from all the Indigenous nations in Quebec. Due to geography, the legacy of residential schooling, and colonial histories, Indigenous communities in the province spoke a combination of their mother tongues and one or two colonial languages. The Kanien'kehá:ka, for example, favoured English. In select instances, the QNWA made strategic linkages with well-resourced, well-connected, and mostly white women's groups, notably the Fédération des femmes du Québec; however, its ultimate raison d'être was focused elsewhere. Not unlike Kahentinetha Horn, the members of the Quebec Native Women's Association were primarily concerned with the survival and flourishing of their respective nations. Despite the inevitable divergences, women's grassroots organizing shared two common goals: to empower their communities and to defend their land. These priorities formed integral components of women's political movements. Thus this chapter further territorializes and localizes questions of land loss and membership, putting these activist fronts in the same analytical frame. Many of these issues are ongoing.

A Basis for Leadership

Whether or not they self-identified as feminists, Indigenous women's per-
severance in transmitting their culture provided a basis for leadership. As
Lenape scholar Joanne Barker writes, "Feminism is shown to have multiple
intellectual and political genealogies within Indigenous communities that
need to be remembered, not for the sake of feminism, but for the sake of
Indigenous knowledge and the relationships and responsibilities it de-
fines."[14] Haudenosaunee women wielded, and continue to exercise, significant and meaningful forms of power within their communities. The
creation story, which serves as the basis for contemporary Haudenosaunee
philosophy, contains a female-centred narrative, shaping women's ongoing
relationship and responsibilities to the land.[15] In one retelling, Sky Woman
contributes a seed to the water world, "making her own contribution, as the
grandmother of all humans, to creation." As historian Lisa Brooks explains,
"rather than being planted in a void by a divine male creator, the earth requires the conduit of a woman's body and mind."[16] The Great Law of Peace
further codified women's clout by guaranteeing them a special role in the
consensus-building process as well as the power to recall nominal leaders
and to veto any decision deemed against the interest of the community.[17]
Under this constitution, individuals were defined by the territory to which
they belonged, a connection determined by their family identification and,
more specifically, by maternal bloodlines.[18] Article (wampum) 44 ensured
that Haudenosaunee peoples were matrilineal and matrilocal, clearly stating, "The lineal descent of the people of the Five Fires (the Iroquois Nations)
shall run in the female line. Women shall be considered the progenitors of
the Nation. They shall own the land and the soil. Men and women shall
follow the status of their mothers."[19] The role of women within Haudenosaunee enclaves shifted with colonization. The Haudenosaunee Confederacy's thinkers nevertheless regarded the Great Law of Peace as a living
tradition into the twenty-first century, and its wampums are viewed as communal narratives.[20]

   To provide the necessary background for understanding twentieth-
century debates, the next few paragraphs outline some basic historical context. After Europeans settled in the northern Americas and the fur trade
economy accelerated, Indigenous women frequently married traders, at

their own initiative, and served as cultural brokers, "ensuring sustenance and survival for both their people and the Europeans in an era increasingly complicated by the demands of Western intrusion." As historian Brenda Child argues, they "were often positioned as political, social, and economic intermediaries between their people and the newcomers."[21] Initially, colonialists were almost entirely dependent on these intermarriages. If fur-trading husbands were held to a high standard by their newfound relatives, entering into a broader social network that emphasized reciprocity,[22] their wives' labour, food production, language skills, and political acumen contributed to the expansion of this market and indeed the entire North American economy.[23] Despite the "many tender ties" holding intercultural families together, the dynamics among peoples started to shift as settlement accelerated, especially with the arrival of larger groups of European women.[24] Up until the 1670s, colonial authorities in New France took a permissive view of intermarriage on the condition that it was blessed by a priest, contributed to the increase of the population, and "civilized" the Indigenous spouse – an undertaking that proved impossible.[25] In 1663, Louis XIV sent some 770 young girls – the *filles du roi*, or king's daughters – to New France, intending for them to marry and have children with French men. Within a mere twenty years, the European population had increased more than threefold, going from 3,000 in 1663 to around 10,000 in 1681. By the end of the French regime, the St Lawrence Valley contained between 65,000 and 75,000 inhabitants, the vast majority of whom could trace their lineage to the *filles du roi*.[26] This colonial tactic to increase the settler population, combined with a rise in racial thinking and the skittishness of the Catholic hierarchy about intermarriage, started to malign Indigenous women.[27]

For Kahnawà:ke, anxiety around intermarriage arose during a time of land loss, a reality that would only accelerate after the building of the Lake St Louis and Province Line Railroad in 1852.[28] By the mid-nineteenth century, the colonial government was bombarded with petitions from Indigenous communities demanding protection from settler incursion. The 1850 Act for the Better Protection of the Lands and Property of the Indians in Lower Canada aimed to stop the encroachment on Indian land by farmers and loggers, but it also gave the Crown the authority to manage those lands and legalized the category "Indian." Besides establishing the legal precedent that Indians ultimately had no say in who would be considered a member of the nation or community, this document specified that status was transferrable to and from both male and female spouses. After an outcry from several First Nations, the law was changed so that non-Indigenous men would not be able to gain access to Indian resources and land through marriage.[29]

In Kahnawà:ke – at the time, the most populous First Nations community in Quebec and Canada, with 1,500 residents[30] – some people advocated excluding out-married women and their husbands from its membership list while leaving, conversely, non-Indian women on the register. The latter would have been perceived as less threatening than non-Indian men, as they wielded less power in a colonial society intent on annexing territory for commercial development and settlement. As anthropologist Audra Simpson argues, "The extinguishment of the rights of Mohawk women, therefore, was less an attempt at discriminating against their own people than an attempt to protect the community from a possible takeover by non-Indian men."[31] In the years that followed the founding of Canada, "state-sanctioned gender discrimination within the field of Indian policy would escalate dramatically."[32] The Gradual Enfranchisement Act of 1869 unilaterally altered Indigenous political frameworks, putting the federally prescribed band council system into place and further codifying the exclusion of out-married women. All these provisions were then incorporated into the Indian Act, first enacted in 1876.[33] Whereas belonging and acceptance had been "situational" in previous decades rather than structural, race and gender were now meaningful categories, used to determine membership.[34]

Women and Land Defence

Women consistently tried to combat intrusion. In 1897, eighty-eight women from Kahnawà:ke lobbied for a return to traditional governance, maintaining that the band council system had exacerbated and caused disputes.[35] This resistance to settler laws only increased in the twentieth century. Although political, cultural, and spiritual perspectives within Kahnawà:ke remained diverse, women were, again, among those driving this rejection of colonial institutions and engaging in these overt forms of land defence.

Born in 1940 in Brooklyn, New York, Kahentinetha Horn, for example, became a well-known, if controversial, figure in Kahnawà:ke and Montreal in the 1960s. A one-time model, Horn may have been one of the "first modern-day Indigenous celebrities," according to Kahente Horn-Miller.[36] Using her presence in urban spaces to try to change them, Horn gave an address at McGill University's Redpath Museum in April 1964. Located in the heart of downtown Montreal, McGill was a symbol of the city's entrenched anglophone elite.[37] Its founder, James McGill, his fortune made during the fur trade era of the late 1700s, had owned enslaved Indigenous and Black people,[38] and its museum carried the name of Peter and Grace Redpath, who had donated family money earned in part through refining sugar grown and harvested by enslaved Afro-Cubans.[39] On this spring afternoon in 1964, however, Horn advocated for a Department of Indian Studies, or "better still, a Department of Indian Life." (As a youngster, while attending the United Church Indian School, Horn had been told that she was part of a "dying race.")[40] As a rallying point for Indigenous knowledges and specialists, the department would contribute to communities' economic and political sovereignty. It would train the next generation of leaders as well as teach the world about North America's past. "We Indians," she told the audience, "are always displeased to read that Cartier, or Champlain or someone like that 'discovered' Canada or the St. Lawrence. This is ridiculous."[41] Part of the rising Red Power movement, Horn was vehement in her anti-assimilationism, seeking to transform majority white institutions rather than adapting to them.

Like her counterparts, Kahentinetha Horn was tied to her family's and community's political traditions and history. The daughter of an ironworker and a homemaker, Horn spent her formative years with her mother's parents on their farm near the St Lawrence River, hearing and speaking Mohawk as well as being exposed to the Longhouse traditions. She grew up watching her grandparents trying to stop the St Lawrence Seaway project. Despite protracted opposition, the seaway was built on Kanien'kehá:ka territory in 1957. Her grandfather Diabo had to be carried away from his home just before it was dynamited.[42] Interviewed by the *Montreal Gazette* in the early 1960s, Horn recalled, with sadness,

Large ferryboats used to run between the reservation and Lachine. These great white boats took the tourists and fishermen to and fro. Hundreds of cars were to be seen waiting their turn to get on the ferry. Dozens of small shops lined the approach to the ferry, where Indians

sold their handicrafts. On the shoreline of the lake scores of row-
boats were rented for $1.00 a day to tourists who wanted to go fishing.
Among the islands, two or three hundred yards offshore, good bass
was to be found. Indian guides would take you farther out into the
river for the big muskies. In the autumn there was good duck shooting.
All of this has changed. The great bridge has taken the automobile
traffic. Where the cars once stood waiting for the ferry there are now
broken bits of asphalt, stunted trees, bits of grass and desolation. The
St. Lawrence Seaway has cut through the Caughnawaga shoreline, leaving the shoreline a hundred feet or so of shallow, brackish, stagnant
water. The islands are gone. There is no longer any fishing. There are
no guides. Progress has to come. But when progress has its victims,
something should be done for them.[43]

Due to the seaway, Kahnawà:ke lost its traditional connection to the Lachine Rapids.[44] Not only did the St Lawrence Seaway Authority seize 1,260
acres of riverfront land to build a canal, but the company's actions also cut
through an "important site of economic and cultural activity." The riverfront was a vibrant site of community and family life. Swimming and fishing spots, as well as the historic village and homes, were lost to the seaway,
only to be replaced by huge noisy ships and uprooted families.[45] When it
was clear that the St Lawrence Seaway Authority had ignored Kahnawà:ke's
wishes, the community hired three prominent McGill law professors and
launched an appeal to the Canadian courts and the United Nations, in
which the band council railed against the company's and the government's
actions: "We Indians are the primordial inhabitants placed here by the Great
Spirit and universally recognized as the only true Citizens of North America. Humanity blushes at the events of this period of Colonial History and
Dictatorship, and Usurpation."[46] This flagrant disrespect for Kahnawà:ke's
political will by the federal government put a match to the hay stack.

   Scholars argue that Kahnawà:ke's turn to Red Power began in the aftermath of the land seizure.[47] The interplay of land loss, federal disregard for
Mohawks' ability to control development, and a renewed interest in traditional political culture led to new forms of nationalism. The legacy of the
seaway betrayal was thus an intensified assertion of independence.[48] In the
1960s, francophone Quebecers were also using an anti-colonial language to

demand self-determination. A full-length study on the connections and disjunctures among Kahnawà:ke and Québécois neo-nationalisms still needs to be completed, but for Kahentinetha Horn, Quebec was included in her notion of "refusal."[49] In 1965, she contested the idea that French Canadians were a colonized people at the public hearings on the Royal Commission on Bilingualism and Biculturalism. She instead named them "the first invading race." As Horn argued, "this would be more appropriate, and then the English could be the second invading race." By participating in the preliminary hearings, the Kahnawà:ke resident advanced perspectives that were, in her words, "suppressed, suppressed in the history books, suppressed everywhere." As she asserted, "I am not a citizen of Canada. I am a private citizen of the Six Nations Iroquois Confederacy." Horn advanced a Haudenosaunee national narrative and history. Referring to the Confederacy, she reminded her audience, "We still follow the treaties, and we still follow our constitution of our nation, which was developed in the year 900 A.D., and we still follow a constitution which is one thousand years old and the United Nations follows that constitution because they adopted the principles of our constitution in the year 1950. Now, we are a separate sovereign nation."[50] Multiple sovereignties did not coexist equally.

Although they refused to recognize Quebec or Canada, Kahnawà:ke did not, of course, exist in a vacuum. According to philosopher Gerald Taiaiake Alfred, Quebec served as "an instigator of conflictual processes that increased the intensity of the Mohawks' nationalist assertions."[51] With the rise of a more assertive, territorial-based Quebec nationalism in the 1960s and 1970s, the provincial government aimed to increase its presence within Indigenous communities, forcing a collision of sovereignties.[52] Band councillors founded the Indians of Quebec Association (IQA) in 1965 when, to quote the association's publication *Our Land, Our People, Our Future* (1974), "the province's native population became increasingly aware of the need to form a common front to handle negotiations with the provincial government."[53] (Kahentinetha Horn was not a member of the association.) The IQA's objectives were vast, as its leaders sought to defend Indigenous nations' inherent rights, to improve their material conditions, and to protect hunting and fishing privileges. The organization would later serve as a key interlocutor between the provincial government and Indigenous groups after the Robert Bourassa administration launched the James Bay hydroelectric project in 1971.[54] With the Quebec government's eyes on northern Quebec in particular, the IQA pushed back. As the president, Chief Andrew Delisle, reminded readers, "The Indian and Inuit People have never surrendered, ceded, or relinquished their lands – and never will ... Our history and our allegiance is to this Land – and to no other. Today we still live in this land that belonged to our forefathers – that still belongs to us – and we will pass this Land on to our children and our children yet unborn."[55] Attempts at pan-Indigenous organizing in Quebec can be traced back to the Council of the Tribes, established in 1913 in Cleveland, Ohio, and to the League of Indians of Canada (1919–32). The Quiet Revolution context accelerated, yet did not define, political matters for Haudenosaunee and other Indigenous communities, whose relationship with their territory had long been embedded in their political consciousness and thus provided a basis for pan-Indigenous politics.[56]

In December 1968, Kahentinetha Horn, alongside about sixty women, men, and teenagers from both Ahkwesáhsne and Kahnawà:ke, blocked the International Bridge at Cornwall, Ontario, to protest duties levied on all items, including groceries, worth over five dollars. Ahkwesáhsne is a predominantly Mohawk community of about 13,000 bordering Ontario and Quebec as well as the State of New York. When Haudenosaunee people were asked to pay a fee to cross the bridge, they immediately invoked the Jay Treaty of 1794, known for its provision allowing North American Indians to live and work freely in the United States as well as to cross the colonial border without a Canadian or American passport.[57] Kahentinetha Horn consequently stressed, "We are not breaking the law. We are doing what is right. The world is looking at us. The whole world is looking at us right here and now." She asked the crowd, rhetorically, "Are we going to give up? Or are we going to send out a call to our brothers and sisters all over North America to come and help us?"[58] The Royal Canadian Mounted Police arrested forty-one people, including Horn, who was charged with concealing an "offensive weapon." Along with the other people involved, she was later acquitted after a well-publicized trial attended by Six Nations chiefs, clan mothers, and family members, as well as representatives of the Cree, Blackfeet, and Mi'kmaq Nations.[59] Portrayed in the National Film Board of Canada (NFB) documentary *You Are on Indian Land* (1969), the debacle drew global attention to the Indigenous struggle in Quebec and Canada.

Released in 1969, it was one of the most influential and widely distributed films made by the Indian Film Crew (IFC), the first all-Indigenous unit at the NFB. The IFC sought to use cinema as a tool for organizing social activism and did so to great effect. *You Are on Indian Land*, most notably, was shown at the 1970 Occupation of Alcatraz.[60] According to the pre-eminent Sioux philosopher and theologian Vine Deloria Jr, "Pressure began to build in Indian country following the Cornwall Bridge Incident."[61]

Although she took on a leadership role, Horn did not self-identify as a feminist. Rather, she prioritized Kanien'kehá:ka sovereignty, land defence, and culturally specific ideas of complementarity in terms of gender roles.[62] In an interview with *Maclean's Magazine* in 1964, Horn asserted an oppositional identity, claiming that Mohawk women were superior to white women: "I'm sorry if this upsets some people … I just happen to be able to judge the women I meet in the world – in New York, on reserves, in television, magazines, businesses – and the women of my reserve, for example, impress me as being mentally superior and physically as having fewer aches and pains and more energy. I just happen to believe that Indian women have a higher standard of intelligence than other women."[63] As she stated in the same interview, building on her use of strategic essentialism, "The only kind of integration we can accept is an integration that means freedom to live, breathe, move, develop our culture within the framework of the whole community. We can't accept integration if it means that all Indians become white, or all whites can become Indians."[64]

Horn was not alone as an Indigenous woman active in politics. Chief of the Innu band in Schefferville from 1965 to 1967, An Antane Kapesh published her landmark *Je suis une maudite sauvagesse: Indiennes d'Amérique du Nord* in Innu-aimun in 1976, arguing that "we were already civilized long before a single White man came here to our territory."[65] In a scathing critique of the Euro-Québécois education, justice, and health care systems, Kapesh stressed the need for self-government. "And if the White man doesn't want to understand that, then it's up to him to keep quiet," she wrote. "He's the one who should go back to where he came from."[66] Kapesh never used the word "feminist." However, she did invoke her status as a mother: "The thing that I worry a lot about now, and will worry about for the rest of my life, is that the White man messed up my kids."[67] She advocated complete linguistic immersion at the grade school level and a land-based education to reclaim language skills. As she wrote, appealing to a francophone audience, "I believe that if the government had shown as much respect for our Indian language as it did for its own French language, when it started giving a White education to Indian children, it would probably have made. serious efforts to avoid killing their Indian language."[68] Worried for her children's economic and cultural future, Kapesh also feared for their well-being at the hands of the police, especially when it came to her son.[69] What Kapesh and Horn thought privately about gender inequality remains to be seen, but they were uncompromising in their dedication to their respective nations.

The federal government, however, purposefully ignored the Red Power movement, instead advocating for assimilation. More commonly referred to as the White Paper of 1969, *The Statement of the Government of Canada on Indian Policy* proposed to transfer the responsibilities for First Nations from the federal government to the provinces, abolish the Indian Act, terminate all treaties, and eliminate special status and recognition. Although presented using the language of equality, policymakers ignored the impact of colonialism and racism as well as Indigenous understandings of treaties and self-governance.[70] Shocked by its heavy-handedness, organizations such as the Indians of Quebec Association came together under the fledging National Indian Brotherhood (NIB) to contest the policy.[71] Perhaps the most well-known advocate for scrapping the White Paper was the NIB's president and author of *The Unjust Society* (1969), Harold Cardinal, who penned *Citizens Plus* in 1970, known as the Red Paper.[72] *Citizens Plus* drew from recommendations made in 1966 by anthropologist Harry B. Hawthorn that, as "charter members," First Nation peoples should have additional rights beyond those accorded by Canadian citizenship and that treaty rights should be protected in perpetuity.[73] Although the White Paper was eventually withdrawn in 1971, its legacy haunted conversations regarding the Indian Act. Male-dominated organizations such as the NIB were conditioned by the events to refute state-directed measures enacted under Indian legislation. Thus, when nonstatus women sought to reclaim membership by invoking gender discrimination, they found themselves on shaky ground. The language of formal equality had been "used as a wrecking ball" in recent memory, prolonging conversations on legal change well past 1969.[74]

Indigenous Women's Nation Building

Trying to reverse a discourse that pitted the individual against the collective, Kanien'kehá:ka women consistently argued that their reinstatement would bolster their nation. Arguing that the elimination of section 12(1)(b) would be good for them and for their community, they put forward a revamped understanding of Mohawk citizenship. Born in Kahnawà:ke in 1911, Mary Two-Axe Earley was one of the foremost defenders of nonstatus people, becoming "a national symbol for the plight of Indigenous women."[75] After growing up in Brooklyn, New York, Two-Axe Earley married an Irish American in 1938, and when her husband passed away, she wanted to return to her birthplace but was blocked by the Indian Act's provisions. She lived in a house bequeathed to her by grandparents, and still the band council only tolerated her presence. In the late 1960s, a friend of hers died of a heart attack, which Two-Axe Earley believed was due to the stress of eviction from Kahnawà:ke.[76] The activist's own experiences, as well as those of her friends, led her to challenge the legislation.[77] Two-Axe Earley and others like her paid a price for their outspokenness. Women waited until sundown to go to each other's houses in order to examine the ramifications of the Indian Act. If someone did not come to a meeting, Two-Axe Earley would go to her home, tell her what they had discussed at the meeting, and then try to convince her to come to the next one. "We missed you," is what she would say. "This is what we were talking about." Since women were frightened, Two-Axe Earley and her counterparts organized in a kind and gentle manner. Thus they treaded carefully. They also got mail from Indigenous women all over the country.[78]

Mary Two-Axe Earley and other nonstatus women first entered the spotlight in the late 1960s. After years of lobbying by the Committee for Women's Equality, Prime Minister Lester B. Pearson's Liberal government set up the Royal Commission on the Status of Women (RCSW) in 1967, a body that would command the country's attention for over six months.[79] In total, Indigenous women presented nine briefs, detailing for the first time "the extent of the discrimination" that they faced.[80] In 1968, Two-Axe Earley and thirty other women of Kahnawà:ke, encouraged by the Fédération des femmes du Québec's Thérèse Casgrain, made the consequences of section 12(1)(b) known to Quebec and Canadian society.[81] Its authors began with the following, nodding to the broader women's movement: "In the last several decades, the Caucasian women of our hemisphere have earned equal rights with men in regards to the following: inheritance, equal voting rights, equal employment opportunities, equal educational benefits and other inalienable rights. As North American Indian women residing in the same hemisphere, we ask that many of these rights be shared with us."[82] The Canadian Citizenship Act, for example, ensured that marriage would have no impact on a woman's citizenship. Although First Nations met the category of birthright citizenship, they were not mentioned in this landmark piece of legislation, enacted on 1 January 1947.[83] The rest of the RCSW brief, however, addresses the ramifications of women's loss of Indian status, not only for exogamous women but also for Kahnawà:ke, specifically.

By the late 1960s, the presence of "outsiders" was having a worrisome impact on Mohawk life. Due to its proximity to Montreal, Kahnawà:ke's land was constantly under threat, and housing was an ever-more-pressing issue. Women as well as men were increasingly sensitive to the presence of non-Indian people in the community, especially as intermarriage rates had risen significantly since the 1950s.[84] The authors of the RCSW brief were by no means in disagreement with the importance of thinking in terms of the common good; in fact, they primarily wanted to assert their own and their children's belonging and ability to contribute to the collective. At the time, there were over two hundred male members of the band married to non-Indian women of various backgrounds. The population of voting age was roughly 2,000 people, and since women with Indian status could vote and run for office in band council elections after the 1951 revisions to the Indian Act, non-Indigenous women's clout was palpable. The list included women from the following backgrounds: Danish, Irish, Jewish, French, Black, German, Italian, Polish, and English.[85] Scholars know relatively little about these relationships, but they certainly speak to a certain level of contact among communities.

Out-married women wanted the right to vote in elections and other matters "since our experience in the environment of our reservation should enlighten us on those matters of greatest concern for the best interest of the Indian people." They also demanded Indian rights for the children of mothers who had lost status. The authors of the brief claimed that they had "properly instructed" their progeny in the "ways of our ancestors." Pointing to a belief in the power of Indigenous mothering, the children of non-Indian women, in contrast, were sometimes "raised with the language, customs, mores, beliefs and values of a non-Indian." They in turn demanded Indian rights for their own children, as well as for people who "are a proven one-quarter or more Indian." The authors also demanded – for themselves, their children, and all children of one-quarter "Indian blood" – full educational benefits at all levels, like those enjoyed by status Indians. They also, importantly, demanded that their children not be bused to faraway schools. Lastly, they wanted to retain their right to their inherited property, suggesting that "any Indian woman should have the right to keep or dispose of inherited properties as she feels fit as long as the property stays among the people of one-quarter or more Indian ancestry."[86] Conscious of the ramifications of enlarging membership, the authors advocated for a careful inclusion of exogamous women and their descendants.

Soon after the RCSW, nonstatus women from Kahnawà:ke started to organize politically. In 1967, Two-Axe Earley co-founded Equal Rights for Indian Women (later incorporated as Indian Rights for Indian Women in 1970),[87] the first organization dedicated to the repeal of section 12(1)(b). Then, in 1973, the National Organization of Indian Rights for Indian Women, of which Two-Axe Earley was the eastern vice-president, was established in Edmonton.[88] Overall, its membership refuted the idea that a woman could renounce her "Indianness" through intermarriage, an idea that pervaded its messaging. In the organization's early years, president Cecilia Philips Doré, originally from Kahnawà:ke but at the time living in Lasalle, a Montreal borough about 6 kilometres from the community, wrote a letter to Jean Chrétien, the minister of Indian affairs and northern development from 1968 to 1974 and a future prime minister. Referring to the Canadian Citizenship Act of 1947, Philips Doré applied the same logic to First Nations' nationality, writing that "at birth she was registered as such, and is it legal for the Indian Act to erase her name from the Band Roll, leaving her without an identity like a person who has never been born at all? Is it morally right for an Act, a Department, a Law, or a Minister, to 'steal' one's birthright?" Pointing to the irony of the situation, the rejected woman was frequently called upon to look after her aging parents. "As long as the grasses grow, the mountains stand, and the rivers flow," as Philips Doré put it, echoing treaty language, "we are Indians and most desperately want the Government and Canadians to recognize us as such." The members of Equal Rights for Indian Women were fighting not only for their rights but also for those of their children. "We and our children," as Philips Doré wrote, "have a contribution to offer our people, thus saving the Indian people from having to search for outside help."[89] In short, for nonstatus women, reclaiming membership and self-determination went hand in hand.

National Steering Committee of Native Women

In the early 1970s, sixty-five representatives from regional women's organizations – including from Kahnawà:ke – came together under the auspices of the National Steering Committee of Native Women to discuss shared issues affecting women and their communities.[90] In 1971, the Voice of Alberta Native Women's Society (VANWS) initiated the call to plan a national conference for Indigenous women. With financial assistance from the Citizenship Branch of the Department of the Secretary of State, the organization successfully brought together women from all over the country. The organizing committee was already experienced in conference planning. Alberta women had been meeting yearly at least since 1968 to initiate conversations on poverty, education, housing, migration to urban centres, infant mortality, sexism in the workplace, and domestic abuse.[91] So when participants of the First National Native Women's Conference arrived in Edmonton in March, they were welcomed by well-connected, conference-savvy organizers who were experts in bringing together women from diverse Indigenous communities. The executive of the VANWS, for example, honoured the guests with a "give-away" dance, where each guest was given a necklace and a small tree branch with one dollar attached. The necklace symbolized a longstanding tradition of presenting visiting nations with gifts of clothing, blankets, or beaded buskin outfits, and the tree branch represented a horse – one of the greatest gifts one could bestow on an esteemed visitor.[92] Attendees were able to meet like-minded women in 1971, participate in politics on a larger scale than in the past, and get an even stronger taste of multinational organizing.[93]

The First National Native Women's Conference was a mostly female space, yet it was open to men. A platform was given to George Manuel, who was then president of the National Indian Brotherhood, co-author of *The Fourth World* (1974), and founder and president of the World Council of Indigenous Peoples (1975–81). Manuel gave a speech at the gathering, for which he received a standing ovation: "They say, 'behind every great man is a woman.' I am glad that the women have decided to come from behind us 'great' men and become 'great' themselves, because I think that the native women in Canada, whether they are Métis or Indian or Eskimo, have been exposed to the hardships of life to a greater degree than any other people in Canada, including our men."[94] There was a sense that Indigenous women had to catch up to their male counterparts, or in the words of conference attendee Flora Mike from Saskatchewan, "We, too, must be organized provincially and nationally so that we too will enjoy the same recognition." Even though women took part in NIB gatherings, for example, a women's organization would enable women to create a partnership, with the goal, as Mike said, "to take one step forward and walk beside our men."[95] As participant Rose Yellowfeet put it, "The way I see it, for years Indian Affairs were our Great White Fathers. They did all the planning; they did everything for us ... We were never given the privilege of doing things for ourselves."[96] By organizing autonomously, Indigenous women were able to negotiate with a lot of different people on many different fronts. Although these conferences did not preclude relations with men, grassroots organizers created spaces where women could ponder their own, albeit diverse, concerns.

The First National Native Women's Conference was in part funded by federal monies, the majority of which just barely covered transportation costs. Several participants came at their own expense, and a small group of young people even hitchhiked from Vancouver. Quebec, for its part, was allocated two delegates, but they received the cheques for their train fare only on the Friday immediately preceding the conference, which was too late. Due to the lack of time, the second delegate could not travel from Montreal to Edmonton by rail. However, the first delegate, Eileen Marquis of Kahnawà:ke, was able to make alternate arrangements since she was attending a meeting of the National Indian Princess Pageant Committee on 21 March in Edmonton at the same time. An editor for *Kahnawake News* and always involved in community projects, Marquis had lots of conference and travel experience, from coast to coast and down to the United States. Other delegates to the Edmonton conference had comparable experience with political meetings and community organizing, frequently holding membership in one, if not two, political groups. One participant was a member of the Ontario Indian Homemakers' Club and the Union of Ontario Indians. The BC Homemakers' Club, the BC Native Women's Society, the Manitoba Indian Brotherhood, the Manitoba Métis Federation, the Lethbridge Friendship Centre, the Union of Nova Scotia Indians, and of course the Voice of Alberta Native Women's Society, among others, were also represented at the gathering. The president of the BC Homemakers' Club, for example, came with four other members of her club by car from Vancouver to Edmonton in order to pick up additional delegates on the way and to save money. They had some "hair-raising" experiences en route through the mountains, later claiming that it was an "exciting but tiring trip."[97] The participants' enthusiasm was certainly palpable and likely infectious.

The Voice of Alberta Native Women's Society mobilized already-existing networks to put the conference together. Their initial contacts were made through well-known Indigenous women of other western provinces, some of whom had attended previous meetings of the VANWS and the Indian Homemakers' Clubs.[98] With deep roots in Indigenous communities across the country, including in Kahnawà:ke, the Indian Homemakers' Clubs were at the forefront of women's social activism from the late 1930s through the 1960s.[99] Still, there was a novelty to the 1971 gathering. The First National Native Women's Conference created, to an unprecedented degree, affective ties among Indigenous women from all the provinces and territories. As stated by Alice Steinhauer, co-founder of the VANWS, at the beginning of the conference, "It really makes me feel wonderful to see so many women from all different parts of Canada. I never thought this would ever come true ... but ideas like this do become realities."[100]

One of the items on the agenda was the potential establishment of a pan-Canadian organization. Quebec's delegate, Eileen Marquis, was very much in favour of an umbrella group, "as it would be a stronger voice in solving the native people's problems across the country." She referred to Equal Rights for Indian Women, remarking that "they would be very interested" in forming a special committee to address the issue nationally. At this time, the group numbered 140 members, all dealing with the negative consequences of exogamy.[101] Marquis also reported that her counterparts were concerned with the discrimination faced by children in the school system and troubled by economic development, including the accompanying fear of "white intruders" on their land.[102] Echoing a common fear related to Kahnawà:ke's demographics, she commented on the increasing presence of white women in the community.[103] In the same breath, Marquis mentioned that "the Indians in the northern part of Quebec speak French and we cannot communicate with each other."[104] For the Kahnawà:ke participant, the language barrier among Indigenous communities in Quebec and the over-representation of white women in Kahnawà:ke would be recurring themes throughout her time on the Steering Committee.

In the days following the conference, an anonymous participant-observer wrote a report outlining delegates' experiences. The diversity of participants' mother tongues, geographical origin, educational level, and age shone through. At the intergenerational gathering, young people learned from their elders. Marquis believed that her experience at the conference would help with her efforts to organize the women in Kahnawà:ke and hopefully throughout Quebec. She was impressed by the ways that "western tribes seem to be able to work well together and maintain so many of their traditions and customs." Several participants, for instance, commented on the pleasure of hearing other Indigenous languages and dialects. One fluent Cree speaker found it "fascinating" to meet women from different nations, and other attendees were able to meet fellow nationals from other communities. At their first out-of-province conference, two women from Poundmaker Cree Nation, located in Saskatchewan, relished the chance to converse with Cree-speaking women from northern Alberta. Both members of their nation's Homemakers' Club – the younger one also actively involved on the education committee – the pair stated that they would certainly advise their counterparts to travel to other conferences.

Overall, the conference was deemed a success by the participants. The only complaint, one that was repeatedly brought up in the post-conference report, concerned the presence of camera and news people, whether men or women. Non-Indigenous people filmed the panel presentations, angering participants and giving them the impression that they were being "studied again." For example, as stated in the report, the secretary of the Saskatchewan Women's Group and a board member of the Prince Albert

Friendship Centre lamented, "Indian people should not allow themselves to be on public view at all times, surely we can be allowed to do things our own way for a change without being on record for someone else to comment or criticize, much less government officials – we are getting very tired of this kind of approach to our people." Another woman similarly remarked, "Is this the way they (non-Indians) always do things? Do they have to take pictures all the time?" According to the post-conference report, the idea of the film crew had been imposed on the Steering Committee and reflected the drawbacks of having to accept federal funding. As the participant-observer wrote, "Often times when a group of Indian people receive government grants, they are made to feel that they must comply to certain conditions. One wonders if this would be done to any other ethnic group – new immigrants, for example." She proposed that the money that had gone toward the video could have instead been used for travel.[105] Indigenous women's organizations had to fight tooth and nail for governmental funding in order to cover basic operating costs.[106] Although accepted by organizers, as shown here, federal monies were used strategically and not without critique.

Despite the obvious interest in a pan-Canadian Indigenous women's organization, there was a reticence in some quarters, especially in relation to section12(1)(b) of the Indian Act. Grassroots organizers proceeded with caution, establishing the Native Women's Association of Canada only in 1974. Previously, in 1970, Jeanette Lavell, an Anishinaabe-kwe of the Wiikwemkoong Unceded Indian Reserve in Ontario, had decided to contest section 12(1)(b) in the courts on the grounds that it discriminated against women on the basis of race and sex and thus contravened the Canadian Bill of Rights.[107] In 1973, the *Lavell* case became associated with the related *Bédard* case,[108] which was also about a woman – Yvonne Bédard of the Six Nations – who had lost her Indian status. The case was eventually brought before the Supreme Court of Canada. Although the push to eliminate section 12(1)(b) was always conceived as a battle against the federal government and not in opposition to other First Nations groups, the turn to legislative recourse on the part of some women still resulted in a rupture among Indigenous political leaders. Organizations such as the National Indian Brotherhood and the Indians of Quebec Association, fearful of the case's legal implications in the wake of the White Paper, challenged the two women.

The Indian Act, even if paternalistic, at least recognized the special status of First Nations peoples within the Canadian colonial framework. For Harold Cardinal, if the Canadian Bill of Rights was to reign supreme over the Indian Act, "that decision would wipe out the Indian Act and remove whatever legal basis we had for our treaties." This position was not taken lightly. Cardinal called the emotional fallout, internal debate, and external critique "one hell of a mess to get into," one that "the government was extremely happy to see unfold."[109] In 1973, the Supreme Court ruled against the two nonstatus women in a five to four decision, thereby upholding the patriarchal criterion for determining Indian status under section 12(1)(b).[110]

Meanwhile, Mary Two-Axe Earley and several other women from Kahnawà:ke travelled to Mexico City in 1975 in order to attend the inaugural United Nations World Conference on Women. Two-Axe Earley spoke independently there, carrying on a Haudenosaunee tradition of using international forums to enact self-determination.[111] Held in Mexico City (1975), Copenhagen (1980), and Nairobi (1985), the conferences of the UN Decade for Women (1975–85) entailed in fact two concurrent events. The first was a formal and official meeting, attended by national governments, whereas the second, the Tribune, sometimes called the Forum, was a cacophony of grassroots activists. Indigenous women were either absent or tokenized at the first, official conference, where they were excluded from the official Canadian delegation, as were women of colour. At Forum '75, in contrast, Indigenous women from North American territories cultivated ties and built political knowledge alongside other women with whom they shared a similar social location. For example, they participated in a panel on racism where the leaders of South African, Zimbabwean, Namibian, Chicano, and Australian Aboriginal liberation movements "all identified the main problem of each native group as colonization by one or another European power." Madonna Thunder Hawk of the Yankton Sioux Reservation in South Dakota was in attendance. The prominent American Indian Movement leader was known for her participation in the 1970 Occupation of Alcatraz and in the 1973 Wounded Knee Occupation as well as for her role in Women of All Red Nations, founded in 1978 to defend Indigenous families, communities, and culture by articulating an early version of reproductive justice.[112] The UN gathering thus offered an essential platform – one that was in fact part of a much larger strategy to promote "solidarity among all native peoples in this hemisphere" in order to gain "recognition by the rest of the world" and "the right to lands on which to live as sovereign peoples."[113] In the words of Madonna Thunder Hawk, "We're fighting as a people for survival."[114]

When in Mexico City, Two-Axe Earley learned that the Kahnawà:ke band council had decided to expel her and two other women. Taking advantage of her platform, she exposed the Indian Act's gender-based discrimination on the global stage, gaining the attention of women from around the world, many of whom were from newly independent countries. Delegates adopted a resolution, showing their support for nonstatus women facing expulsion. The order was eventually withdrawn but only after Two-Axe Earley had succeeded in attracting national and international attention to these women's plight.[115] This episode prompted action on the part of feminist organizations in Montreal. In March 1976, the Fédération des femmes du Québec, the Voix des femmes/Voice of Women, and the Comité des femmes immigrantes issued a press statement in support of the elimination of section 12(1)(b). By then, the three women had taken their case to the Cour supérieure du Québec. However, the provincial court had ruled that Indian status was an exclusively federal issue. The Quebec government demonstrated its sympathy toward nonstatus women by supporting their pleas vis-à-vis Ottawa. The coalition consequently encouraged other women to come out in support of nonstatus women: "We call on women all across Canada to appeal to provincial governments and the federal government on behalf of their Indigenous sisters, to amend the Indian Act to include equal rights for women."[116]

Although in theory simple, this claim was far more complex when viewed from the ground. On the doorstep of Montreal, Kahnawà:ke's seemingly ever-shrinking land base was consistently encroached upon by outsiders, causing increased housing shortages and racial tensions. In 1973, for example, the Quebec police – the Sûreté du Québec – and the newly founded Warrior Society, along with its supporters in the American Indian Movement, had a serious altercation over a white family's refusal to leave the community, resulting in the arrest of Kanien'kehá:ka people on their own territory. Members of the household were behaving in ways inappropriate to the setting and were asked to leave for that reason. Racial tensions increased as a result of the incident.[117] Caught between a rock and a hard place, nonstatus women bore the brunt of this stressful situation. Criticized for invoking their right to belong, they endured a citizenship of "grief" when it was not granted.[118]

Quebec Native Women's Association

In 1974, Indigenous women came together to form the Association des femmes autochtones du Québec/Quebec Native Women's Association at a meeting held at Loyola College, an anglophone Jesuit college merged that same year with Sir George Williams University in the Notre-Dame-de-Grâce neighbourhood.[119] However, only in 1980 did the QNWA receive anything resembling substantial funding from the provincial and federal governments, which finally made it possible for the association to implement a permanent secretariat and, at times, to pay staff salaries.[120] The QNWA was an autonomous organization open only to Indigenous women because, according to one of its reports, "the needs considered essential by men and by women are very different."[121] Its membership consisted of activists both with and without status and from all Indigenous communities in Quebec.[122] To maximize participation, the association coordinated regular elections, ensuring that its echelons were representative of the population. In this regard, if the president was a status Indian, the vice-president would be someone without status, or if the president identified as Haudenosaunee, the vice-president might be someone who identified as Inuit. If the president favoured English, the vice-president would be someone who preferred French.[123] In some cases, one woman would speak English, one French, and one an Indigenous language when travelling to communities across Quebec.[124] The diversity within its ranks, its multilingualism, and the political experience of its leadership contributed to the QNWA's effectiveness. Members used the association to fight for full citizenship, primarily within their own nations but also within Quebec and Canadian society.

For many women in the QNWA, citizenship and belonging entailed Indian status.[125] In 1976, the association spearheaded a study entitled *Réveille-toi femme autochtone/Wake Up Native Woman!* to inform communities of the Indian Act's consequences for out-married women. Respondents articulated their discontent, as well as their confusion about the legislation.[126] That same year, the QNWA declared its support of Cecilia Charles of Kahnawà:ke, facing eviction as a nonstatus woman. The association once again teamed up with the FFQ, trying to halt her forced removal.[127] As the largest women's organization in Quebec and with relatively close ties to the state, the federation provided nonstatus women with a powerful political network, fostering a basis for strategic linkages. Adept at navigating these spaces, the QNWA found ways to make use of what were mostly white feminist organizations.

In an interview, Évelyn O'Bomsawin, born in Odanak and the QNWA's president from 1977 to 1983, recounted how the FFQ's president, Sheila Finestone of Montreal, made a series of phone calls to successfully halt the forced eviction of another nonstatus woman from Pointe-Bleue (Mashteuiatsh), an Innu community 6 kilometres from Roberval in the Lac Saint-Jean region.[128] In 1978, the QNWA officially became affiliated with the FFQ for this reason.[129] In a letter to the federation, Marthe Gil-Dufour of Pointe-Bleue remarked that she was "touched" by the welcome she had received at the 1980 General Assembly, thanking the FFQ for its support. Signing off, "Indigenously yours," Gil-Dufour nonetheless indicated the intended stance of her letter, as well as her refusal to assimilate. She hoped to see an Indigenous woman preside over the federation: "I firmly believe that the Native woman must also have a place in the sun."[130] In the early 1980s, Gill-Dufour was on the lists of the FFQ's administrative council.[131]

For the most part, however, the QNWA organized independently, focused on the well-being of Indigenous peoples. The association compiled an incredible amount of data during the 1970s and 1980s, using research and report writing as tools for social change. By documenting socio-economic disparities, members were able to make sense of their own lives. The QNWA tackled disparities related to social services, health, economic development, and education. These public-facing reports hint at a path to full equality for Indigenous women vis-à-vis their own nations and settler society. More specifically, the QNWA – not unlike the Congress of Black Women of Canada, as we will see in the next chapter – exhibited extreme mistrust toward social services. In 1977, the association conducted a study on out-adoption, submitting a report to the Quebec government two years later that described how Indigenous children were placed among white families in very large numbers and with little consideration for their cultural identity.[132] The periodical *Akwesasne Notes*, for this reason, referred to adoption services as "social genocide."[133] Provincial bodies regulated the placement of children for foster care and adoption. In one case, a woman signed away custody of her sick child, although she could read neither English nor French.[134] The QNWA recommended that the money otherwise given to foster families be given to birth mothers. The association also proposed that all efforts be geared toward finding Indigenous adoptive families.[135] In the case of customary adoption, for example, a child was usually given to relatives or members of the extended family. Contact with the family of origin could be maintained, with no termination of parental rights or secrecy regarding the identity of the biological parents.[136]

In 1980, the QNWA conducted a study on health care matters in partnership with Equal Rights for Indian Women. Although disparities in medical care between Indigenous and non-Indigenous Quebecers were most pronounced in the northern part of the province, the QNWA also noted incidents of poor service and racism on the periphery of Montreal. In one instance, a nurse refused to assist an allophone patient, claiming a language barrier. After waiting eight hours, the woman's husband finally approached the hospital staffer, only to get the response, "How can we treat her, we don't even know what she has!" Indeed, the lack of medical personnel on the reserves and the serious communication problems stemming from cultural and linguistic differences were criticized on many occasions. Near Quebec City, an elderly woman even lost her sight. She thought the medication that she was given was for her eyes instead of her ears.[137] The QNWA also emphasized the immediate need to abolish involuntary sterilization.[138] Indigenous communities criticized coerced sterilization, as well as surgical interventions where patients were kept in the dark regarding the consequences. There were times when doctors convinced a new mother to undergo sterilization for financial reasons, although one must question what this choice meant in contexts of economic marginalization. The association did not have the exact numbers regarding sterilization rates; indeed, some women may have refused to divulge the information.[139] There was the impression, however, that some women chose sterilization as a form of contraception, short of other options.[140]

In 1983, the QNWA published a report on the socio-economic challenges facing Indigenous communities across Quebec, again in conjunction with Equal Rights for Indian Women. In January 1979, the QNWA had put together a committee of six women to work on the report, most of whom had been selected from the Montreal area to cut down on transportation costs: Mary Two-Axe Earley, Gail Stacey-Moore, Josie Cohen, and Pearl Jacobs, all of Kahnawà:ke; Nicole O'Bomsawin of Odanak; and Évelyn O'Bomsawin, at the time living in Boucherville for employment purposes.[141] The team chose forty-five women, ranging from twenty-one to seventy years old, to collect and analyze the necessary data on a volunteer basis. The only qualification was that the women had to be able to speak the appropriate local language; they did not necessarily have to belong to one of the two organizations. The turnout was impressive. A total of 1,451 people filled out the questionnaire, 683 of whom were nonstatus. But the results were worrisome, indicating the extent to which Indigenous peoples registered a significantly lower living standard than other Quebecers. In the Cree and Innu communities, for example, the housing crisis was striking, with eighteen people living under one roof not an unusual occurrence. In 1974, the National Indian Brotherhood declared the management and quality of housing on reserves "an unwarranted national disgrace."[142] The statistics did not lie. First Nations communities across the country needed at least 15,000 new homes. Among the existing lodgings, 31 per cent had running water, 24 per cent had indoor toilets, and 25 per cent had telephones. This situation contrasted with Euro-Canada, where 98 per cent of houses had electricity, 97.4 per cent had running water, 96.1 percent had indoor toilets, 93.3 per cent had indoor baths, and 94.3 per cent had telephones.[143] Precisely because of the poor conditions and lack of job opportunities, a growing number of people decided to leave their homes to settle in bigger cities, namely Montreal and Quebec City. The issue of Indigenous people living off the reserve had become only more pressing by the 1980s, changing the focuses of women's activism.[144] Since its incorporation in 1987, the Native Women's Shelter of Montreal, for example, has offered frontline services to Indigenous women and children. Although both status and nonstatus women moved to urban centres, the latter left in larger numbers.[145]

The reasons behind out-migration were complex and linked to broader socio-economic problems.[146] In the 1982 report, the QNWA and Equal Rights for Indian Women described the alienation that women experienced in urban centres. Although nonstatus women were excluded from band activities, they frequently returned to visit relatives and friends. Among the people surveyed by the two organizations, the vast majority listed family and cultural reasons for why they wanted to return home. Considering "the future of the Indian nation," the QNWA emphasized the essential role of mothers in ensuring national vitality and continuity by helping children to grow up in a culturally appropriate manner. Thus, for the association, the fact that some women were forced to leave their home communities increased the odds of cultural loss. Whereas in the past non-Indian women had been assimilated into Indigenous cultures when they married into the community, these days, with intermarriage on the rise, the children born into these unions had very little chance of being raised "the Indian way." The surveyed women agreed, with 66 per cent indicating that mothers were primarily responsible for cultural transmission. Most respondents also underlined the importance of the father in teaching young people, especially activities such as hunting and fishing. Whatever one's perspective, "culture" in many cases was nonstatus women's strongest link to their nations.[147]

The QNWA stressed the need for community control over education, continuing its focus on the next generation. In several briefs, the association outlined how Indigenous youth were ill-served by the French and English school sectors: students were torn between their communities' values and the educational material presented in the francophone or anglophone Québécois education system. Textbooks made scant mention of Indigenous issues, or they promoted racist stereotypes, hence subtly or in some cases explicitly encouraging assimilation.[148] Schools serving communities in rural areas, moreover, were often located far from the child's primary residence, forcing young people to board with white families for long stretches of time. After returning home, youngsters demonstrated difficulty speaking their mother tongues, reinforcing cultural alienation and the accompanying generational gap.[149] For these reasons, the QNWA was a strong proponent of language learning, a decolonized education system, and increased local control over schooling.[150] With these goals in mind, a predominantly female team established the Kahnawà:ke Survival School in 1978.[151] The Mohawk language was taught, and the student council was based on the principles of the Longhouse and the Haudenosaunee Confederacy.[152] Today, there are five schools in Kahnawà:ke, from daycare to secondary.[153] These initiatives, as we will see in subsequent chapters, were reminiscent of initiatives taken by Black communities in Montreal to educate their young people. The similarities between these two groups occasionally brought them together. In the early 1980s, Congress of Black Women member Dorothy Wills led workshops with Indigenous and Black youth across Canada and in Kahnawà:ke.[154]

The QNWA also paid close attention to the relationship between colonization, mental health, and conjugal violence.[155] To overcome these challenges, the association proposed two interrelated solutions. First, the concept of "community healing" was developed and discussed by Indigenous women across the country. This internally oriented approach was based on raising awareness, putting into place education programs, and establishing an open dialogue concerning conjugal violence and the abuse suffered by children, now adults, in residential schools.[156] In the late 1980s, for example, the QNWA organized workshops in Indigenous communities to open a dialogue. Grassroots organizers plastered posters in five languages and put out messages on the radio where an elder, a politician, and a child addressed the community in its mother tongue. For Michèle Rouleau, the president at the time, born to an Ojibway mother and a Québécois father in Senneterre, Abitibi, the overarching goal was the cessation of violence rather than removing women or men from the household or the community.[157] Second, the women's organization stressed self-determination, viewing it as essential to "the promotion of self-esteem and Indigenous identity necessary to regain social peace and family harmony."[158] The relative lack of influence wielded by Indigenous women within their own communities was understood as operating within the colonial context.

The QNWA entered discussions with the Quebec government on this basis. In 1983, the association invoked the power that women had held in pre-colonial societies, emphasizing that it was only with colonization that Indigenous women had lost political sway within their own communities. After the church and the state "imposed its conceptions of male superiority," women were doubly undermined. Or as the QNWA eloquently put it, referring to the women's movement, "Now that the rest of the world has come to see the world from the perspective of the eighteenth-century Indian, it is sadly ironic to note that Indigenous people today seem to cling to the absurd system that was imposed on them."[159] The QNWA tailored its message to a francophone Québécois audience, stating in the National Assembly,

It is with the same respect that we have for you, French-speaking non-Indians who defend your own culture with so much skill, energy, and determination, that we intend to defend ours with the same open-mindedness that you have shown toward minority groups in this part of our lands.

We know you are capable, even if our languages keep us apart ... Our goals bring us together. In defence of our respective cultures and with the respect shown by groups around us, even the majority, we do not intend, any more than you do, to be assimilated, to let our cultures be diminished, or to be forced to abandon both our languages and our customs.[160]

The QNWA gratefully acknowledged Premier René Lévesque's decision in October 1980 to recognize nonstatus women as Indians, but it still offered a critical view of state structures within the province and the rest of the country. Recognition by the Parti Québécois, although important, was more symbolic than practical.[161] The association recommended that both the provincial and federal governments offer funds to help nonstatus women transition back to reserve life and, of course, that Ottawa amend the Indian Act.[162] Indigenous women persisted in reaching out to the provincial government, demonstrating the depths of their political strategizing. When the first ministers at a 1983 constitutional conference refused Mary Two-Axe Earley's request to speak, Lévesque gave her his chair at the table, forcing the other political leaders to listen to her pleas for justice for First Nations women. She told them, "Please search your hearts and minds, follow the dictates of your conscience. Set my sisters free."[163]

In 1985, 127,000 people saw their status restored due to a combination of grassroots organizing, legal challenges, and an adept use of international forums.[164] In 1981, Sandra Lovelace of the Wolastoqiyik (Maliseet) Nation in New Brunswick went to the United Nations to argue that section 12(1)(b) was in violation of article 27 of the International Covenant on Civil and Political Rights, which "protects the rights of minority groups to enjoy their culture, practice their traditions, and use their language in community with others from their group." The UN ruled against Canada and in favour of Lovelace, thereby forcing the federal government to change the Indian Act. To bring the legislation in line with the Charter of Rights and Freedoms,

Ottawa enacted Bill C-31, or the Bill to Amend the Indian Act.[165] After many years of frustration, Two-Axe Earley was the first woman to regain her Indian status.[166] But Bill C-31 did not wholly equalize matters. Although it was an important victory, these developments ushered in decades of divisive debates within First Nations communities over identity, belonging, and already limited resources.[167] Further, the Indian Act continued to impose tighter restrictions on the rights of exogamous women to pass their Indian status to their children and grandchildren as compared with men, thus re-emphasizing the patrilineal method of descent.[168] The amendments also separated Indian status from band membership.[169] With Bill C-31, many First Nations communities, women especially, were forced to continue to make unattractive adaptations to the "colonial scene."[170]

In Kahnawà:ke, the incorporation of changes under Bill C-31 was read by many residents of the community in terms of concerns about a diminishing land base, housing shortages, and an attack on sovereignty. Some community members argued that they should be able to determine their own citizenship policy, or in the words of Audra Simpson, "The collective will of Kahnawa'kehró:non will decide which people in the future will have a right to live on the land and partake of the history that flows from it."[171] In contrast, the amendments did nothing to undo colonial forms of thinking or governance. Power relations were still asymmetrical under the modified Indian Act, and its racializing and patriarchal logic was as strong as ever.[172] For these reasons, the painful conversations surrounding membership continued into the 1980s when the community anticipated the 1985 amendment, consenting to the Moratorium on Mixed Marriage in 1981 and to the Mohawk Law on Membership in 1984. Reinstatement to the band list "was far from automatic" due to these pre-emptive measures, which were largely based on blood quantum. New members descended from nonstatus women had to have at least 50 per cent Mohawk blood to be welcomed back into the community.[173] Historically, however, notions of "race" or "blood purity" had no place in concepts of belonging or identity in Kahnawà:ke.[174] No one was completely happy with these new measures, but everyone agreed that "something had to be done," as Simpson argues. Kahnawà:ke's "struggles with and against a membership policy, their own regime of recognition, is a symptom of the continued colonial requirement that they disappear and a symptom, I would say, of colonialism's ongoing life and simultaneous failure."[175]

The QNWA focused its critique of Bill C-31 on competing claims of what or who could guarantee cultural continuity. In a presentation to the National Association of Women and the Law in 1988, Gail Stacey-Moore, at the time the director of the Native Women's Shelter of Montreal, stressed that the "Indian Act continues to discriminate against us and our children," reminding her audience that "in countless speeches, representations, policy statements and court cases, Aboriginal people have emphasized that their rights, be they legal, political, social, economic, cultural, or other, must be recognized and maintained not only for themselves, but also for their children and their children's children." Since recently reinstated women had more difficulty passing on band membership to their children or ensuring their inheritance, they argued that the membership and well-being of future generations were at risk. In contrast, "our brothers," as Stacey-Moore explained, "who married non-Indian women before the coming into force of Bill C-31, are able to transmit band membership to their children." This sort of gender-based, legal discrimination contravened both section 15 of the Canadian Charter of Rights and Freedoms and the Universal Declaration of Human Rights, especially articles 2 and 7. Nevertheless, Stacey-Moore, a nonstatus woman of Kahnawà:ke, acknowledged some bands' fear of a "takeover," proposing that "the right[s] of non-Native spouses be limited to residency with his family only" and that they "not include the right to vote on any matter or the right to possess land." In her mind, with these provisions, the possibility of a "takeover" would be "virtually nonexistent." Once again, the QNWA called upon the federal government to rectify a historical injustice. Or in the words of Stacey-Moore, "The imposition of a narrow definition for the determination of Indian status (and the Federal responsibility which goes with it) is nothing more than a continuation of the old policy of 'termination' by which the simple solution for getting rid of the 'Indian problem' was to redefine the 'Indian' out of existence. This is unacceptable."[176] Women thus continued to argue that their full membership in the national community was necessary in order to resist colonial encroachment.

The Resistance at Kanehsatà:ke

During the resistance at Kanehsatà:ke (11 July to 26 September 1990), a community fifty-three kilometres west of Montreal with close ties to Kahnawà:ke, women were once again at the forefront of the struggle.[177] What started as a conflict over a golf course in Oka became a full-blown conflict between the Sûreté du Québec, the Canadian military, and land defenders. To the confusion of the Sûreté du Québec, women were the ones who greeted the officers on 11 July. When asked by an officer, "Where's your leader? We want to speak to your leader," Denise David-Tolley was the first to answer. "There is no leader here," she said. "You are looking at the leaders. Everyone's the leader. The people are the leaders."[178] To affirm their responsibilities, they cited wampum 44 – "Women shall be considered the progenitors of the Nation. They shall own the land and the soil"[179] – thus reminding other community members and outsiders of these systems of governance while fortifying their own position within them.[180] For example, Ellen Gabriel, a future QNWA president, served as spokesperson for the land defenders, demanding nation-to-nation talks with the prime minister of Canada and explaining their demands to a francophone Quebec public.[181] Building on longstanding forms of diplomacy, and anticipating more violence, Kahnawà:ke and Kanehsatà:ke women purposely cultivated ties with international human rights organizations and pressured Quebec and Canada to stop acts of aggression, most likely saving lives.[182] A traumatic event with continuing consequences for the people who lived through the summer of 1990, the resistance movement highlighted the living legacy of the Great Law of Peace.[183]

The Oka Crisis prompted several solidarity movements. The QNWA set up a food depot in Montreal, and it was swamped with donations.[184] From the beginning of the resistance movement, pan-Indigenous political ties were reactivated, bolstering local actions through moral support and reigniting grassroots politics. Journeying across the country, the Grandmothers Walk in Solidarity with the Mohawk Clan Mothers made it clear to the federal and provincial governments in a communiqué that "A NATION IS NOT BROKEN UNTIL ITS WOMEN ARE DOWN."[185] The Regroupement de solidarité avec les autochtones was born at a protest in Montreal on 11 July, following the Sûreté du Québec's invasion of Kanehsatà:ke. Bringing together people from various walks of life, the network organized a series of events and actions. For example, its members launched a campaign in the aftermath of the crisis to raise money for the Mohawk legal defence fund, as those who awaited trial had enormous legal costs to cover.[186] On the first anniversary of the resistance, the Regroupement de solidarité reported on a trip to Montreal undertaken by a delegation of South African anti-apartheid activists. Sitting alongside Kahentinetha Horn, Smangaliso Mkhatshwa declared his solidarity with the Kahnawà'-kehró:non twenty-seven days before the end of apartheid in South Africa. Horn had returned to her community from Ottawa to participate in the events of 1990. She was eventually fired from her position at Indian Affairs due to this decision.[187] Marie-Célie Agnant, a Haitian writer based in Montreal, also declared her support for the movement. These examples of Black-Indigenous solidarity demonstrate some of the alternative political imaginaries in Montreal and Kahnawà:ke.[188]

In short, women's contributions to the resistance at Kanehsatà:ke – a still unresolved conflict, as the federal government has yet to transfer the land back to the community – were unquestionable. As Bill C-31 continued to anger members of the community, as well as leaving others out, women involved in the protest showed the nation what belonging should be.[189] "Regardless of blood quantum, clan, or reserve," they were once again willing to defend their people and their territory.[190]

Conclusion

To assert their own view of citizenship and belonging, women waged a battle on several fronts. At times, they made strategic linkages with Euro-Québécois or Euro-Canadian feminists. When interviewed by journalist Judy Rebick, however, Gail Stacey-Moore underlined that a deep and genuine relationship was difficult not only because of the significant differences in life experiences among activists but also because of white women's racism.[191] Whether trying to reclaim status or taking on leadership roles in Red Power actions, Indigenous women were, in fact, acting according to their birthright. Their role in land defence, from the St Lawrence Seaway debacle to the resistance at Kanehsatà:ke, highlighted the importance of territory to their political work and thus their ongoing relationship and responsibilities to the nation. Kanien'kehá:ka women formed meaningful pan-Indigenous ties at several levels, from the Haudenosaunee Confederacy to the United Nations to the QNWA. Certainly, more research needs to be done on Indigenous women's organizing in Quebec, including on the presence of the QNWA in other parts of the province as well as on the histories of the Indian Homemakers' Clubs and the Friendship Centres. Energizing community organizers' local actions, pan-Indigenous and international experiences translated into an increased sense of collective power. In Mexico City, for example, Mary Two-Axe Earley and her counterparts met other women who, like them, combined national and women's liberation, fighting two battles at once. Although opinions within Kahnawà:ke regarding section 12(1)(b) were diverse, those seeking to take part in political life used women's historical role in the community to assert their place within the contemporary collective. These principles provided a basis for women to calm the waters with other community members who were opposed to their views. For many organizers, the unconditional acceptance of Indigenous women, either as leaders or as mothers, was needed in order to guarantee cultural continuity and vitality. Combining women's and communal concerns provided a powerful basis for community rejuvenation.[192]

In this regard, Kanien'kehá:ka women resembled members of the Congress of Black Women of Canada, the focus of the next chapter. With deep roots in Montreal, Black nationalism and pan-Africanism closely paralleled their Haudenosaunee counterparts: both political movements combined local, community-based action with transnational linkages and ideas. Connected to locales and movements elsewhere, Black Montrealers were dedicated to undoing racial biases in the education system, critiquing social services, and creating parallel structures for self-determination. They too attended international conferences to create new ways of conceiving politics and grassroots organizing.

2

Searching for Zion
Diasporic Feminism in English-Speaking Black Montreal

In 1968, the Congress of Black Writers was held at McGill University. Bringing together some of the major Black thinkers and activists of the period, the event portrayed the rising global Black Power movement for all of Montreal to witness. Stokely Carmichael, Walter Rodney, Alvin Poussaint, C.L.R. James, Rocky Jones, and so many others descended on the city from 11 to 14 October. None of the presenters were women, and there was a dearth of speakers from the African continent, Latin America, and the non-anglophone Caribbean, but "Josephine" remembered the event fondly.[1] Interviewed by Samah Affan in 2011, she stated in reference to the Congress of Black Writers,

> It was such a large assembly of progressive, politically progressive black people from all over the world. It was just exhilarating. For me it, in some ways it was like going to a rock concert ... For me it was an eye opener. You know, because it wasn't – well it was all political. But then there were a lot of artists; all kinds of artists, painters, musicians. Poetry was definitely the word of the day, I mean everybody became a poet, you know reading and writing liberation poetry. But there were all of those people; it was very exciting, exhilarating. Um, it was a party; it was a learning experience; it was fun. I can't think of anything positive that it wasn't. And I can't think of anything negative that it was. Except maybe it could've gone on longer and that everybody went back to where they came from for the occasion (laughs).[2]

The Congress of Black Writers was part of the long Black Power movement, whose origins can be traced to, among other political and economic
developments, slave resistance, Garveyism, pan-Africanism, and the birth
of the civil rights movement in the 1950s. Its goal was to build a sense of
collective power, with African-descended peoples defining their own priorities, leading their own institutions, and fully participating in the decision-
making processes that impacted their lives.[3] In Montreal, Black women's
politics were particularly attuned to the realities of African-descended
women across the city as well as the diaspora. Not only did Black Power
politics play a generative role in activating Black feminism, as we will see,
but women also continued to enact Black Power principles after 1975 and
the waning of prominent organizations.[4] Due to its distinct intellectual and
political genealogies, Haitian women's community organizing will be the
subject of another chapter.

Although their organizing confronted the common struggles of African-
descended peoples across the continent, even the world, Black women's actions came directly out of the Montreal context, where the community's
heterogeneous makeup, as well as the discrimination that Black Montrealers
faced in the housing, taxi, employment, and educational sectors, informed
their commitment to social justice. As historian David Austin points out,
Canada had its own version of Black Power, which, "like so many social
movements around the world in the 1960s and 1970s, drew inspiration from
African American struggles against economic and racial oppression, but
nonetheless native to Canada."[5] African-descended women have deep roots
in Quebec and an equally longstanding reputation for resistance to economic
inequality and racial oppression.[6] For instance, the Portuguese-born Marie-
Joseph Angélique was a rebellious enslaved woman, vocal in her hostility to
servitude. Later, she was tortured and hanged after being accused of setting
fire to Montreal in 1734 when her owner, Thérèse de Couagne de Poulin de
Francheville, denied her freedom.[7] Modern Black Montreal was equally diverse, with its roots in Canada, including the Maritimes, the United States,
and abroad. Over the twentieth century, the community was repeatedly bolstered by recent arrivals from the Caribbean, whose contributions to the
Black left in North America and to the global pan-African movement were
undeniable.[8] With multiple origins, multiple histories, and multiple political
perspectives, Montreal's historically English-speaking Black community

came together under a syncretic Black nationalism – that is, "the political view that people of African descent constitute a separate group or nation on the basis of their distinct culture, shared history, and experiences."[9] Within this framework, women carved out a role for themselves, working for their own emancipation as well as that of the rest of the community.

Most Black women worked for wages in Montreal, hinting at their integral role in community building as well as their heightened social and political awareness. From the earliest days of the Universal Negro Improvement Association to the Black Power movement, women engaged in grassroots organizing to better the collective fate of Black Montrealers, even if much of the early scholarship on Black freedom struggles and feminism erased women's agency and empowerment in these spaces.[10] By taking on leadership positions within various political movements, they refused to view their contribution to the Black struggle solely in terms of revolutionary motherhood or as subordinates to men. Starting off within the Caribbean Conference Committee and the Negro Citizenship Association respectively, Anne Cools and Dorothy Wills, for example, also became involved in the Congress of Black Women, a mostly English-speaking yet bilingual organization that reached out to Haitian Montrealers. Reporting in *Habari Kijiji* (*Village News*), Wills described the galvanizing effects that the 1974 Montreal meeting had on Black women: "What can we say, except that we seem to be becoming more self-sufficient each day as we acquire the necessary skills to run our own show. Maybe one day we will run our own community and it will be a glorious day."[11] Well into the 1970s, Wills played an integral role within the National Black Coalition of Canada and at the Sixth Pan-African Congress, held in Dar es Salaam, Tanzania. In fact, politically active Black women were present in multiple political contexts during this period, including Black women's organizations, male-dominated Black groups, and multiracial, women-only settings.[12] This multifaceted approach to community organizing largely defined their gender politics.

Laying the Foundation

According to the historian Dorothy Williams, "To understand black women and their history we cannot only compare them to other women – they must be placed in the context of their families, their black sisterhood and especially their communities."[13] Historians and geographers have portrayed Montreal as a centre for Black radical thought and community organizing, arguing that this more contemporary form of politics can be traced to past forms of resistance,[14] which were both intertwined with and distinct from Indigenous history. Settler colonial projects in North America, as other scholars have argued, tried to alienate Indigenous peoples from their land and African-descended peoples from their labour.[15] Even if the history of enslavement in this part of North America can be traced to pre-contact geopolitics, slavery was legalized and expanded upon under French rule in the early 1600s through the *code noir* and remained on the books until 1834 under the British.[16] Once the economy transitioned from resource extraction to settlement, colonial administrators lobbied the French Crown to allow them to import African workers. From 1681 to 1818, there were approximately 4,100 enslaved women and men in French Canada. Although the majority were Indigenous, called Panis, Black people made up about a quarter of the unfree population, or just over 1,000 souls. Most enslaved women performed domestic labour, making the homes of wealthy colonial families Black spaces.[17] "Quebec," as geographer Délice Mugabo argues, "has its own memories of slavery that, together with other histories of slavery in the Atlantic world, merge to constitute part of the global history of anti-black violence and resistance."[18] Later generations built on their foremothers' political work in order to claim their place in the social and political landscape.

By the end of the nineteenth century, Black Montrealers had set up a distinct institutional network, working, socializing, and creating vibrant neighbourhood cultures. Montreal's emergence as a railway hub led to the migration of hundreds of Black workers from the United States, the Caribbean, and the Maritimes. This early internal diversity has continued until today, making heterogeneity a defining feature of community life. These porters and their families settled in the St Antoine district, close to the Windsor and Bonaventure train stations. In the beginning, the heart of the community was concentrated east of Guy Street and west of Peel Street. The expanding downtown commercial district and the subsequent loss of residential housing prompted a shift westward into what is now known as Little Burgundy, located in the Southwest Borough between Saint-Henri and Griffintown.[19] Well-educated and worldly, many of the porters were graduates of historically Black colleges in the American South, giving them a keen awareness of the problems facing African-descended peoples on both sides of the border. They consequently developed, in the words of historian Sarah-Jane Mathieu, "a powerful diasporic consciousness,"[20] becoming "the vanguard of local, national and international organizations dedicated to the interests of blacks in Canada."[21] Their notion of social mobility was collective, and thus they were held in the highest esteem by the growing community.

Porters and their wives founded "virtually every major community institution before the 1960s."[22] As the largest metropolis in Canada, Montreal had its share of unemployment, poor housing conditions, and social divisions in the first half of the twentieth century. Entering this mosaic, Black Montrealers organized accordingly, making the "City Below the Hill" as liveable as possible.[23] Since its inception in 1902, the Coloured Women's Club of Montreal (cwc) had been dedicated to the well-being of Montreal's Black collectivity "in every possible way." The cwc would later host a pan-Canadian gathering of Black women in Montreal in 1974, paving the way for the city's branch of the Congress of Black Women.[24] Black women's dedication to their community prompted its founders to establish the club. They were also largely ignored by suffragist groups. The women's organization offered scholarships to students, gave warm clothing to recent arrivals from the Caribbean, and lobbied the government for just immigration laws.[25] During the flu epidemic of 1918, the club not only maintained, as it did for many years afterward, a bed in the Grace Dart Hospital, but it also sent its members to look after the homes and children of hospitalized parents and provided a plot of land in the Mount Royal Cemetery for the interment of members of the community whose relatives could not afford burial. Throughout the Great Depression, the cwc operated soup kitchens for the unemployed. It also addressed unsanitary conditions in the Little Burgundy neighbourhood. More broadly, the club afforded moral guidance, emotional support, and a sense of belonging to the city's longstanding residents as well as new arrivals from the West Indies.[26] The cwc's focus on the socio-economic issues facing the entire community also created the framework for women's political experience and social involvement.[27]

The cwc's membership was frequently involved in more than one organization, extending its energies to the Union United Church and to the Negro Community Centre (ncc), founded in 1907 and 1927 respectively.[28]

The cwc worked closely with the Union United Church on Delisle Street, drawing on its own resources to provide the church with furniture, a christening font, and linen.[29] Since men were frequently out of town for work, women deaconesses ensured the operation of the religious services.[30] Open to Black Montrealers of all denominations, many of whom had been refused by other churches, the institution's very existence countered the prejudice in the city, becoming a centre for advocacy and belonging. The Reverend Dr Charles Humphrey Este, for instance, waged a ten-year battle starting in the late 1930s for Black women to be trained and admitted as nurses and teachers in Montreal institutions.[31] From its beginnings to its closure in 1991, the NCC, located at 2035 Coursol Street, embodied a similar ethos. Serving the city's Black residents, regardless of place of birth or origin, the centre ensured "cradle-to-grave" services, offering arts and educational programming, sports camps and school lunch services, and an affirming and empowering space for children.[32] The Coloured Women's Club established an Afrocentric library at the NCC shaping the minds of the rising generation.[33] In a time when broader society told Black youth that they could be only porters or domestics, community-based female educators ran grassroots educational initiatives such as Sunday schools to bolster self-esteem and to complement the day-school curriculum.[34]

Women were also well-represented within the ranks of the Universal Negro Improvement Association (UNIA), a Black nationalist organization founded in Kingston, Jamaica, by Marcus Garvey in 1914.[35] Established by porters in 1919, the Montreal branch of the UNIA was originally housed in a Canadian Pacific Railway building on Saint Antoine Street.[36] One of 1,200 organizations worldwide, Montreal's UNIA was a vibrant community hub. As community leader and educator Leo Bertley explains, in the first half of the twentieth century, the city was a key site for Garveyism, an internationalist ideology that promoted Black self-determination, African repatriation, and separate Black political and cultural institutions.[37] Quickly becoming a stronghold, Montreal welcomed Garvey for the first time in 1917, just weeks after he founded a UNIA in Harlem.[38] The families at these sorts of events were usually working-class West Indian migrants, "too often," in the words of Mathieu, "excluded from other social venues."[39] The year 1917 coincided with an influx of West Indian migrants, and by 1929 the community numbered 5,000.[40] Although they were a highly diverse group of people, certain commonalities emerge, namely higher than average levels of formal education, circulatory patterns of labour migration, experience in trade unions, and a strong pan-African consciousness.[41] With the involvement of both men and women, the UNIA "married political activism and entertainment," aiming to educate the community in the history of African-descended peoples, promote global Black unity, and nurture the next generation.[42]

Women were the "backbone" of the Montreal branch of the UNIA, playing key roles at the executive and organizational levels.[43] Proving to be loyal Garveyites, they launched every possible auxiliary, from the Ladies Division to the Black Cross Nurses.[44] Thus women helped the city to become a hub of Black nationalist politics. Ideas and networks connected activist locales and generations, which women were able to expand on in later decades.[45] For example, Louise Little (née Langdon), the mother of the pre-eminent civil rights activist Malcolm X, joined the UNIA in Montreal as soon as she arrived from La Digue, Grenada, in 1917. Like many others, she worked as a domestic, and indeed, as historian Ashley Farmer points out, "Many Black Power foremothers started the backbreaking work of cleaning white women's homes at the same time as the UNIA began its ascent."[46] Amy Jacques Garvey, who was Garvey's second wife, passed through the city as well.[47] A passionate pan-Africanist and journalist, Jacques Garvey stressed the emancipatory potential of Black nationalist organizing for women in her UNIA column, "Our Women and What They Think."[48] According to US scholar Ula Taylor, Jacques Garvey was a "community feminist," which allowed her to "balance her commitment to Garveysim and Pan-African ideas, and her commitment to her own personal development and feminist interests."[49] Jacques Garvey was on the organizing committee of the Fifth and Sixth Pan-African Congresses in 1945 and 1974, the second of which was attended by Montrealers like Dorothy Wills and Brenda Paris. Ultimately, the UNIA served as a "political incubator" for activist women, wherein they took up far more room, and acquired more autonomy, than Garvey could ever have envisioned. By enabling women to transcend prevailing gender norms and to develop their leadership skills, the UNIA paved the way for the Black Power and pan-Africanist women of the 1960s and 1970s.[50]

Women and the Civil Rights Movement

Continuing the tradition of "community feminism," politically minded
women were unwavering in their dedication to their community. Born in
Dominica on 13 March 1933, Dorothy Wills, for example, immigrated to
Canada in the early 1950s to attend Mount Saint Vincent University in Halifax, Nova Scotia. She then made her way to McGill University, where she
completed a degree in social work and a doctorate in education, making a
career as a teacher and eventually becoming a dean of Vanier College in
Montreal.[51] Heavily involved in the global pan-African and anti-apartheid
movements – even adopting the name Abike after a visit to Africa in 1971[52]
– Wills held key leadership positions in both the National Black Coalition
of Canada and the Congress of Black Women of Canada. Her initial political involvement, however, can be traced to the Negro Citizenship Association, a civil rights organization that promoted integration and anti-
discrimination legislation. Founded in 1952, the group consisted of 400
members, born in Canada, the United States, the West Indies, and Africa.
The organization's motto, "Dedicated to the Principles of Good Citizenship," was interpreted as pushing Montreal society to uphold at home the
objectives that the association supported on the world stage, as outlined,
for example, in the Universal Declaration of Human Rights.[53] Two prominent battles waged by its members were the integration of the taxi industry
in 1960 and an amendment to the Hotels Act in 1963, making it illegal to
refuse service to customers because of their race.[54] As for Wills, her gender
did not seem to impede her involvement. Taking on a public role, she was
vice-president and chair of the board. In reference to a sit-in demonstration
in response to segregation within the Diamond and LaSalle Taxi companies,
Wills described a run-in with law enforcement: "I was quite visibly pregnant
at the time, and when a policeman said to me 'Lady, in your condition you
ought to be home,' my immediate and spontaneous reply to him was 'If I
cannot help create a better world in which to deposit what I am carrying,
I may as well not have it, so I don't care what you think, say or do.'"[55]

The Negro Citizenship Association served as a bastion of moral support
for Montreal's Black community. It was a place where, in the words of Wills,
one could "seek relief from some of the frustrations of this society, due to
discrimination, by learning more about our past grandeur."[56] Montreal in

the 1950s and 1960s was a cold place for Black residents; segregation hindered people's movements, opportunities, and access to resources such as education and housing. During this period, the community was once again bolstered by energetic new arrivals from the Caribbean. Rosemary Brown (née Wedderburn), for example, arrived at McGill University from Kingston, Jamaica, in 1950. She was from a politicized, middle-class family, her grandmother being the "first – and most political person" she had "ever known." In a memoir, she remembered getting a single room at Royal Victoria College because no other resident would bunk with her, and she told of the rejection she experienced at the hands of white landladies.[57] When describing how she dealt with prejudice, Brown stated, "Unlike Black Americans and Black Canadians, I did not become a member of a racial minority group until I was an adult with a formed sense of myself. By then, it was too late to imprint on me the term 'inferior.' I knew that all the things that we were told Blacks could not do, all the jobs that were closed to us in this country, were in fact being done ably, competently and sometimes in a superior way by Blacks at home and in other parts of the world."[58]

Brown's self-concept served her well. In 1972, she became the first Black woman elected to the Legislative Assembly of British Columbia. She came second to Ed Broadbent when she ran for the leadership of the New Democratic Party in 1975. That same year, Rosemary Brown travelled to Canberra, Australia, as part of a contingent of "overseas guests" at the "Women and Politics" conference organized by Australian feminist Elizabeth Reid. Designed to mimic Mexico City's Tribune at the 1975 United Nations World Conference on Women, the gathering hosted a star-studded list of prominent women, including the iconic Flo Kennedy.[59] Like their Garveyite predecessors, Caribbean newcomers – among them Rosemary Brown – reinvigorated Black political life in Montreal. Arriving in the city with memories of the burgeoning nationalist and anti-colonial movements from their respective homes, they too seemed to be overrepresented within the ranks of the community's postwar institutions.[60]

Montreal's Black leadership was increasingly frustrated by the mid-1960s, especially with regard to the Quebec government's failure to implement a "full programme of Human Rights Legislation."[61] Although Quebec would inaugurate its progressive Charter of Human Rights and Freedoms in 1975,[62] in the mid-1960s, the Negro Citizenship Association equated the absence of legislation with the "humiliating situation as existed in the United States," Canada's foil in matters of race, "prior to the passage of the 1964 Civil Rights Bill."[63] During the years leading up to Expo 67, a member of the association commented on how visitors would receive better treatment than some of the city's hosts, namely those who, "because of their racial origin[,] will be denied the right to rent apartments of their choice, while many of their guests will have no problem in renting the same apartments."[64] Due to these everyday displays of segregation, there was the belief that discrimination toward Black Montrealers was not taken seriously or portrayed as "insignificant." The organization's newsletter, *Expression*, raised the question of the government's role in protecting its citizens, or more specifically, extending protection to those overlooked by the law in its current form.[65] In light of the federal and provincial authorities' apathetic response to the community's push for legal equality, as well as the atmosphere of Expo 67, it would have been unsurprising when the Negro Citizenship Association became a member of the National Black Coalition, an umbrella organization that was, as will be discussed, more assertive and pan-Africanist in outlook.[66]

Another contributor to the political shift among some Black Montrealers could be the demographic changes occasioned by immigration patterns. Although racial restrictions were eased in the 1950s to allow for domestic servants, many of whom were from the Caribbean, Canadian immigration law did not fully liberalize until 1967, opening the door to those from countries outside of Europe if they met the selection criteria. The population estimates for the city vary between 7,000 Black residents in 1961 and 50,000 in 1968, although the latter may be an overestimation.[67] Significant numbers of students came to Montreal from the Caribbean during this period, many of whom were highly politicized. According to historian Sean Mills, West Indian youth came to the city to pursue university studies, often returning home to take up political careers. They "introduced anti-colonial ideas into Black Montreal, at first upsetting many established members of the community, but ultimately changing the way in which the community conceived of itself and understood its relation to the rest of Quebec society and the world at large." Signalling the renewal of the community's leadership, a group called the Caribbean Conference Committee on West Indian Affairs was convened in the mid-1960s.[68] The Caribbean-based New World Group, one of the most important pan-Caribbean (largely anglophone) intellectual organizations after the Second World War, found a home in Montreal. Working alongside the conference committee, the group, which included the economists Lloyd Best and Kari Polanyi Levitt, published the *New Work Quarterly*, a renowned economic, social, and cultural journal.[69] The anti-colonial ideologies espoused by these two groups further laid the intellectual groundwork for resistance to racial domination in Montreal throughout the late 1960s and 1970s, when Montreal's Black community was permeated with a renewed assertiveness that by no means passed over women.

The Caribbean Conference Committee invited a range of speakers to the city, including the historian and anti-colonial thinker C.L.R. James, author of *The Black Jacobins: Toussaint L'Ouverture and the San Domingo Revolution* (1938). Leading study sessions and giving a series of public lectures in 1966, the Trinidadian Marxist had a remarkable impact on young men and women like Tim Hector, Robert Hill, Franklyn Roberts, Anne Cools, Gloria Simmons, Bridget Joseph, Jean Depradine, and Alfie Roberts. James would return to Montreal for the Congress of Black Writers in 1968, another galvanizing event for Quebec's Black community.[70] By then, however, a political shift had taken place. As David Austin outlines, more Canadian-born men and women had taken the helm of the community leadership, and many members were in Montreal to stay, looking away from Caribbean politics to focus on the well-being of African-descended peoples in Canada. Black Montrealers increasingly felt the influence of the American Black Power movement as well. In addition to C.L.R. James and Walter Rodney, notable figures of the US struggle attended the conference, officially entitled "The Congress of Black Writers: Toward the Second Emancipation, the Dynamics of Black Liberation." The star-studded lineup included the charismatic Stokely Carmichael, whose electrifying speech on the Black Power movement was the highlight of the conference for many attendees. Women were among the hundreds of people who crowded into the ballrooms and classrooms of McGill to hear these prominent intellectuals and grassroots activists, yet they were excluded from the list of panellists.[71] The speakers at the congress consistently addressed the mixed audience as "brothers," and the iconic Miriam Makeba, the wife of Carmichael at the time, never spoke.[72] Women were reportedly ignored, then, despite their integral role on the organizing committee.[73] Toward the end of the congress, the participants passed a resolution to emphasize the role of Black women in Black struggles, perhaps a belated recognition of this oversight.[74]

The atmosphere at the Congress of Black Writers set the tone for the subsequent events. When a professor at Sir George Williams University (now Concordia University) was accused of systematically marking down Black students, younger community members took a stand. For two weeks in February 1969, a multiracial group of approximately 200 students, including thirty women, occupied the university's Computer Centre in the heart of downtown Montreal. Later known as the Sir George Williams Affair, the arrests that followed a mysterious and damaging fire attracted national and international attention, exposing the racism entrenched in Montreal society. The trial of the students in question, which led to the imprisonment of Rosie Douglas and Anne Cools, for eighteen and four months respectively, was biased from the beginning.[75] Not only had Montrealers been bombarded with media coverage for weeks focused nearly exclusively on the forty-eight Black protesters, but the jury also consisted entirely of white men, as women of any racial identity could not serve on juries until 1971. Juanita Westmoreland-Traoré, the Sorbonne-educated lawyer and former French-language liaison for the Negro Citizenship Association,[76] denounced the all-white panel as inconsistent with one of the cornerstones of the criminal justice system, namely trial by one's peers. This racial bias was explained by Westmoreland-Traoré in *UHURU* (Swahili for freedom),[77] a recently founded community newspaper: "Only persons who have a common experience can fully understand and appreciate the issues in a particular situation. This principle has been tested and has endured throughout the ages. No one can say that the fact that all of the 10 accused are Black is a coincidence. We maintain that they cannot have a fair trial unless there are also Black people on the panel from which their jury will be chosen."[78]

The Sir George Williams Affair represented something much larger, going beyond one incident of prejudice to encompass anti-Black racism in key Canadian institutions. In an editorial published in *Expression*, the authors drew parallels between Sir George Williams University and Canada. Referring to the country's role in the "underground railroad" and to the university's reputation for welcoming migrant students, the authors wrote, "Both enjoy the reputation for fair-play and humanity in their relationships with all groups; both are respected as successful models of a multiracial society." But hidden underneath the surface had been "the covert and often unconscious acts of racism of which Canadians are guilty," from jurors to university administrators. Worse was the mythology surrounding the benevolence of race relations, maintained "with traditional Canadian self-righteousness."[79] As the authors concluded, the country was "riddled with paradoxes and contradictions," for it claimed to be "the champion of equality for all races" internationally and rhetorically but overlooked "in silence the unequal treatment of its non-white peoples" at home, namely the Japanese, Indigenous, and Black communities. Further, the domestic scheme was a "modern variant of the slave-master relationship" in terms of both geopolitics and immigration policy "since very few blacks would be able to reach these shores otherwise."[80] These types of articles multiplied after the Sir George Williams Affair.[81]

There were numerous divisions between African-descended Montrealers, yet similar experiences with racial prejudice served as a basis for civic engagement. So did pan-Africanism, an anti-colonial ideology fitting for this era of decolonization and ongoing discrimination in North America. The concept of "internal colonialism" was implicit in pan-African thought, considered the "highest form of Black Power" by Stokeley Carmichael.[82] But as discussed by Sean Mills in his nuanced study, the notion of empire was complex in Montreal, and Black Montrealers were aware of the distinctions among Canadians. Although the journalists of *UHURU* maintained that the community was the object of discrimination at the hands of both the English and the French, they recognized the similar forces operating against francophone Quebecers. French Canadians, for example, had trouble getting hired by Anglo-controlled businesses, as did African Canadians.[83] Feelings of solidarity went both ways. Throughout the Sir George Williams Affair, many French-speaking leftists came out in support of the students, including the Union générale des étudiants du Québec.[84]

In the pages of *UHURU*, there was also favourable mention of the Red Power movement – additional proof of Canada's failure to work toward a "Just Society."[85] For Rosie Douglas, Canada's record regarding the oppression of Indigenous and Black populations was put into the larger perspective of British imperialism. In the same article, Douglas examined the role of Canadian businesses in the twentieth-century Caribbean, painting their

workings as neo-colonial. Canadian banks, the bauxite industry, and insur-
ance companies were dominant parts of the region's economy.[86] As we will
see in chapter 4, Haitian Montrealers put forth a strikingly similar critique.
Douglas commented on the presence of Canadian troops in Jamaica, sta-
tioned there supposedly to "acclimatize themselves to tropical conditions
for the United Nations." The revolt against racial discrimination at Sir
George Williams University, a bourgeois institution with links to the military
and corporate elite, thereby took on multiple meanings. Douglas was eventually deported to Dominica in 1976 but not before visiting several centres
of Indigenous activism, namely Thunder Bay, Grassy Meadows, Winnipeg,
Regina, and Vancouver.[87]

Although internationalist, the collectivity's discourses on gender equality,
belonging, and citizenship were grounded in its everyday experiences in
Montreal. In a 1968 episode of the television show *Tirez au clair*, Jacques
Keable hosted a roundtable with members of Montreal's growing and diverse Black community. During the discussion, participants, who included
the Haitian-born Vivian Barbot, a future Fédération des femmes du Québec
president, expressed a wide-range of opinions. As anglophones and francophones, native-born and recent arrivals, men and women, Black Montrealers experienced 1960s and 1970s Montreal in a multitude of ways.
There was, however, a noticeable consensus regarding the presence of discrimination in the housing sector, the workforce, and immigration law,
where Italians with low levels of formal schooling were chosen over well-
educated Caribbean migrants. Likewise, both French and English speakers
voiced their anger at being refused service in downtown restaurants. Speaking to the racialized nature of gender relations, one Haitian-born man expressed his exasperation regarding the suspicious looks that white women
directed toward him on the subway, later drawing parallels between Amer-
ican-style segregation and its Canadian counterpart. Black men reportedly
could not frequent cafes without Black women, as owners and clients
feared they would interact with white women.[88] The same person believed that the Québécois expression "travailler comme un nègre"[89] should
be banished.[90] The word was a product of a time when slavery was syn-
onymous with a Black person's skin.[91] The past, then, weighed heavily on
the present for the Black as well as the Indigenous descendants of enslaved
peoples. Indeed, as Austin argues, "Contemporary Canada has inherited

the racial codes and attitudes that slavery engendered, and certainly the fact of slavery in Canada cannot be taken for granted."[92]

Similar sentiments were echoed in the writing of Anne Cools, the Barbados-born member of the Caribbean Conference Committee and one of the two political prisoners in the Sir George Williams Affair. In an essay, Cools denounced the sexism and racism embedded in the economic and political systems, without denying the oppression experienced by her male counterparts. She wrote, "Black women, the slaves of the slaves, can have no peace, no rest until they have evolved new social structures within which men can be Men, women can be Women, and their children, freethinking creative human beings." Cools continued to work in the Black community as well as in multiracial settings.[93] On behalf of the Montreal International Collective, Anne Cools, Marlene Dixon, an American professor at McGill University who will come up again in the next chapter, and others submitted a brief to the Indochinese Women's Conference, where they lauded Montreal as the most important site of revolutionary struggle in North America and asserted Black people's right to self-determination.[94] The young women also participated in the Wages for Housework Campaign with Selma James, the wife of C.L.R. James. At the Montreal Feminist Symposium in 1973, Cools not only spearheaded the conference but also successfully presented the final resolution on salaries for homemakers. Indicative of the pervasive whiteness within this women's movement, however, Cools was the only, or one of the few, Black women in attendance at the event.[95] Francophone Québécois feminists were also absent, as the McGill-hosted gathering was unilingual.[96] In 1974, Cools moved to Toronto, co-founding Women in Transition, a shelter for survivors of domestic violence. She also attended Congress of Black Women events, the focus of a subsequent section.

By then, Black Montrealers were fighting new battles. Like so many other Black neighbourhoods in North America, the St Antoine district was targeted for demolition under the guise of urban renewal in the 1960s.[97] The English-speaking Black community was subsequently dispersed to neighbourhoods such as Côte-des-Neiges and Notre-Dame-de-Grâce, hurting Black-owned businesses and weakening the longstanding NCC.[98] "The far-reaching efforts of Mayor Jean Drapeau to modernize Montreal were undertaken in the name of [Québécois] national uplift." But as historian Steven High explains, "The routing of the highway through the heart of the Black city below the hill and Chinatown further to the east, the city's two historic racialized neighbourhoods, could hardly be just coincidence."[99] At the same time, Black Montrealers – women especially – also situated their domestic organizing within a global, explicitly pan-African, context.[100] At the Congress of Black Writers, African American activists were "blown away" by C.L.R. James's effortless combining of pan-African sentiments with Marxist-Leninist theory.[101] The seeds of the idea for the Sixth Pan-African Congress (PAC) came out of this encounter, germinating in Black Power circles for a few years before a small cadre of US and Caribbean organizations travelled abroad to meet heads of African states and liberation leaders in 1971.[102] After preparations began in earnest, women became the primary congress organizers. Inspired by her mentor, James, Geri Augusto of Dayton, Ohio, even wrote the call to the PAC, proclaiming this era "the Century of Black Power," as defined by a "unified conception of peoples who have been colonized" and by the "unparalleled degeneration of white power."[103]

Black Women's Diasporic Activism

By the early 1970s, women were at the forefront of this period of renewed pan-African organizing, "forging diaspora," to use the words of historian Keisha Blain, by "vigorously pursuing relationships with activists in other parts of the globe and creating spaces and mediums through which to engage in global political dialogue and collective political action."[104] At the African Liberation Day rally in 1972, Dorothy Wills, going by her adopted name, Abike, called on her "brothers and sisters" to help Africa to become "truly free and independent, because in so doing we are helping ourselves." She outlined the difficulties faced by the new African countries subjected to the Western-controlled market and spoke of the challenges of being African-descended in Canada. Global Black unity was one answer to overcoming this dehumanization, or in the words of Wills, a means to reclaim a sense of self by doing "what needs to be done in order to realize my full potential and be a real person." For Wills, like the other pan-Africanists of her time, the presence of the white power structure at home, and ongoing economic domination abroad, contributed to a far-reaching notion of "our brother's keeper."[105] For this community leader, pan-Africanism was the key to first-class citizenship: "Do you have any idea of the psychological implications for you and I if we were to live to see the liberation of Afrika? Can you imagine what dual Citizenship would mean to you and I and all Black people? It would mean that we would have an alternative available to us – that we would no longer be doomed to a life sentence of white domination – but we would have the choice of going back home where we originated – indeed where human life originated."[106]

Black Power icons such as Angela Davis and Betty Shabazz, the widow of Malcolm X, played an integral role in the establishment of African Liberation Day, a series of rallies and marches held in honor of African liberation movements and global Black unity.[107] Both Dorothy Wills and Brenda Paris were selected by the largely women-led organizing committee as delegates to Tanzania, the sought-after location for the Sixth Pan-African Congress because of its Ujamaa socialism, commitment to self-reliance, and role as the primary base for liberation movements engaged in armed struggle in southern Africa and the Portuguese colonies.[108] Pan-Africanist politics easily gained traction in Montreal, a city with a longstanding tradition of Black internationalism.

The Sixth Pan-African Congress followed a long history of PACs, which began in 1900 under the leadership and direction of Trinidadian barrister Henry Sylvester Williams. W.E.B. Du Bois, the renowned African American intellectual and activist, organized succeeding conferences in Europe and the United States. The Fifth Pan-African Congress, held in Manchester, England, in 1945, was primarily focused on "how and when African societies would achieve political independence from European powers."[109] Convened just months after the Second World War, the Fifth PAC was arguably the most significant. With the Haitian, Ethiopian, and Liberian flags literally hanging over the proceedings – the only free Black countries at the time – its aspirations were concrete and represented a "changing of the guard in global Black leadership." No longer dominated by middle-class Americans and Brits, the PAC welcomed West Indian and African delegates for the first time, including the likes of Kwame Nkrumah and Jomo Kenyatta.[110] Du Bois requested that Amy Jacques Garvey serve as co-convener. Although Jacques Garvey was unable to attend the gathering due to a lack of finances, she was delighted to be finally included among the vanguard after years of struggling to have her voice heard by men.[111] The Sixth PAC conversely, as historian Fanon Che Wilkins explains, "turned inward and set the task of examining the shortcomings of decolonization and the newly independent nation-states of Africa and the Caribbean."[112] Even if flag independence had been achieved for many countries, the economic domination of these newly established states persisted, leading to new patterns of colonialism, or neo-colonialism. According to political scientist Robert Williams II, the "inherent ills" of global capitalism and racialism, which were negatively impacting African-descended peoples around the world, served to join the North American and "Third World" struggles together. The Sixth PAC "marked the beginning of revolutionary Pan-Africanism," a movement with strong echoes in Montreal for both women and men.[113]

Held at the University of Dar es Salaam from 19 to 27 June 1974, the Sixth PAC attracted more than 600 participants from the Black world. The North American contingent was by far the largest, with approximately 200 delegates. Participants travelled to the Tanzanian capital to discuss material support for liberation movements, African youth and economic development, and science and technology.[114] For North Americans, the debates were intense, specifically the discussion of race versus class, and spilled over to the halls, bathrooms, and plenary sessions.[115] For the first time, moreover, delegates resolved "to give [their] total support to the political struggles for equality undertaken by Black women" and to "tackle the problems of the oppression of women thoroughly and profoundly."[116] According to Ashley Farmer, women participants "transformed the Sixth PAC into an event in which delegates from across the globe acknowledged their equality to men and indispensability to Pan-African liberation."[117] The Grenadian delegation, for example, emphasized women's vital role in its country's independence struggle and applauded women freedom fighters in African liberation movements. Sierra Leone insisted that because "the world is a patriarchal society," liberation struggles overall were hindered. The North American participants, for their part, argued "that the 'freedom' of women is dependent upon men, children, and women casting aside the mindsets and lifestyles which perpetuate the practice that women are caretakers, sex objects, and clerics only." They maintained that "existing ideas about black manhood and gender hierarchies crippled the larger pan-African liberation project." In a position paper, the authors reiterated their support for their male counterparts yet rejected men's dominance of political and intellectual leadership. They also rebuffed the idea that the path to an emancipated

Africa was through a restored Black manhood. In this time of movement building, women therefore sought to extend the discussion of race versus class to include gender hierarchies within pan-African organizing.[118]

Women at the Sixth PAC insisted on their centrality to Black liberation, using these years to construct an identity based on their tangible solidarity with African-descended peoples. By positioning themselves as part of the activist vanguard, they – however subtly or explicitly – challenged men's positions as the exclusive leaders of the global liberation struggle in its multiple ideological iterations.[119] In 1974, Dorothy Wills authored a series of articles in *Contrast* entitled "The Status of the Black Woman Today." Exemplifying the political leanings of their author at the time, these articles were infused with anti-colonial language.[120] As Wills editorialized, "The role of the Black woman in the liberation struggle cannot be underestimated and this is the way it ought to be. We have a role to play wherever we are." When in Tanzania, Black women brought medical supplies to freedom fighters and donated blood; in Canada, they had an integral role to play in the family, raising children to embody Black values.[121] (The North American delegation brought 300 pounds of medicine to the Sixth PAC and donated blood to freedom fighters in East Africa.)[122] As indicated by her travels to the United States and Africa, Wills was not an advocate of a passive, subordinate role for women. For this leader, revolutionary motherhood was instead a means to counteract the hegemonic whiteness faced by African-descended Montrealers when, for example, children were racially slighted at school and came home in tears, seeking comfort. By transmitting racial pride to children, the reasoning went, they would grow up ready to contribute to the struggle. Mothers were therefore playing the all-important role of dictating "the shaping of tomorrow and the building of the Black nation." Through their empowerment in the home, Black women contributed to the well-being of their families and, by extension, of the entire community because "a nation is comprised of units."[123]

The Sixth PAC "served as a bridge connecting late 1960s Black Power militancy to 1980s struggles against apartheid,"[124] which, as we will see in the next section, was one of the priorities of the Congress of Black Women of Canada. Montreal-based Brenda Paris, the secretary of the African Liberation Support Committee, was at the Sixth PAC. The committee was formally established after the 1972 African Liberation Day demonstrations and did a tremendous job of mobilizing Black North Americans from all walks of life, whether workers, students, or middle-class professionals.[125] The committee aimed to provide concrete material support to African liberation movements, collecting funds to help them purchase military equipment such as walkie-talkies.[126] In 1973, Paris, who would later attend Congress of Black Women meetings,[127] was part of a delegation that delivered the money, over $300,000, and the supplies to southern African leaders in Tanzania.[128] Involved in the anti-apartheid movement as well, Wills used her time in Dar es Salaam strategically, speaking "with as many representatives of the liberation groups as possible in an attempt to discover how we, on the North American continent, could assist in the struggle for the liberation of Africa … without being on the African continent." In the East African country, this activist discovered that printing costs were very high, so since coming back to Canada, she had printed and resent 2,000 copies of the propaganda booklet used by PAC Azania, a South African liberationist group.[129] As illustrated by the letters that she received in return, her contribution to the South African liberation movement was greatly appreciated. She was described as "a great soul, real daughter of Mother Afrika," by the author of one letter, Elias L. Ntloedibe of Dar es Salaam.[130] Also writing from Tanzania, Okdt Bernard R. Seme's letter in 1975 echoed a similar sentiment: "I am taking this opportunity to say thank you very much for all you did to us and the kindness you showed us while we were in [Montreal] … The feeling I had while I was there is of the kind that makes someone less lonely and more at home than ever. We have mothers, fathers, sisters and brothers in Canada."[131] These were the sorts of affective ties that defined diasporas.

Delegates to the Sixth PAC shared their experiences when they returned to Montreal, thereby increasing the impact of the event.[132] Dorothy Wills, for one, commented extremely positively on her experience in Dar es Salaam, where as guests of the Tanzanian government, African Canadians "were extended the hand of brotherhood, and treated like long lost relatives."[133] In August of the same year, during a speech that Wills gave in Nova Scotia and later republished in *Contrast*, she reported, "It was beyond description to see, assembled in Nkrumah Hall, Blacks from around the world seeking a solution to problems which we all face."[134] Worldly, with enviable political experience and connections, Wills was undoubtedly respected by her community. Reporting on the foundation of the National Black Coalition of Canada in *Contrast*, President John Harewood wrote, "You didn't hear so much about women's lib at that time, but the men who knew of her abilities had no doubt that she would lead the [coalition] before long," which she eventually did in 1972. Her position in the organization was never called into question because "you felt she had the talent, experience and charisma to make it work."[135] When honoured at the Black Awards Banquet in 1976, Wills described the motivating force behind her far-reaching community involvement: "It is a tremendous feeling of reciprocal love by the Black Community." Within this mutual singing of praises, Wills was hailed by at least one of her male counterparts as "a brilliant example of a Black woman's contribution to the Black man's struggle for liberation."[136] This semantic emphasis of the Black "man's" experience, however offhand or colloquial, offers an example of the lack of extensive gender-based analyses in male-dominated spaces.[137] Even if they never left mixed or male-dominated groups, Black Montrealers founded a women's organization in the early 1970s, deciding to ponder gender issues more fully among themselves.

The Congress of Black Women of Canada

In 1973, the Canadian Negro Women's Association organized the first Congress of Black Women of Canada, attended by 500 women. Meetings held across the country, from Montreal to Halifax to Edmonton, followed these initial conventions.[138] The Congress promoted togetherness among members of all ages and national provenances, and as a result, women born in Canada, the United States, the Caribbean, including Haiti, and Africa were involved from its inception. The Congress was a multigenerational space, or as stated in the 1973 proceedings, "There was enthusiastic participation by the delegates in expressing their various viewpoints, from the seemingly impatient sentiments of the youth to the more tempered outlook of the senior citizen." In political contexts across North America, historians have indeed found evidence of "positive intergenerational exchanges between veteran black nationalist women and a younger generation of activists during the Civil Rights–Black Power era."[139] Although culturally and ideologically heterogeneous, Congress members were bound together by a common mission. Setting the tone for later meetings, conference attendees resolved in 1973 that this "cooperation, joint action and community work must be based on informed mutual respect, reciprocal information, and a conscious political analysis of the international, economic and military system."[140] The Congress aimed not only to tackle systemic racism but also to "love, honor, and nurture" Black women. Writing in 2008, members Shirley Small and Esmeralda Thornhill maintained that the organization "embraces every Black woman regardless of whether she is a paid-up member" and irrespective of her "linguistic affiliation, ethnic, social, marital, or financial status, or sexual preference."[141] Directed by women to serve women, the Congress adhered to Black nationalist and internationalist principles in a manner that reflected its membership's unique concerns.

The opening remarks of Rosemary Brown during the First National Congress of Black Women of Canada, held in Toronto on 7 April 1973, outlined these principles. As Brown stated in the opening remarks of the 1973 conference, "Because we are Black and because we are female, this conference has given us the opportunity to explore the two liberation struggles which we are sitting astride at this moment." She went on explain the difficulty of walking this tightrope, recounting the surprise that many people expressed when they realized that she was an active participant in the women's movement, which in her view was because they expected her to be exclusively concerned with Black liberation. This amazement came from men and women alike, whereas, in her words, "to not participate in the Women's Liberation movement would be to deny my womanhood."[142] Brown added, "I made the choice for liberation because I believe in our men – I believe that they are strong enough to accept me as an equal – and to join with me and stand with me in my struggle to be myself even as I stand and will always stand with them in theirs, and I know that we must work in and draw strength from both of these liberation struggles if we are to hasten the day when the dream of those early pioneers is realized – and we all live as truly equal human beings in this country."[143] The two social movements ultimately fed off each other. As Brown took the pains of explaining, women's liberation did not "drain her energies," taking away valuable time from the Black struggle. On the contrary, the women's movement was "strengthening" her, as she had greater faith in her own abilities, bringing to the broader community a greater confidence and ultimately contributing to the liberation of both Black men and women.[144] By this logic, suppressing the contribution of Black women would hinder freedom struggles more broadly.[145] Brown was neither "concerned nor surprised" by the racism that she knew existed within the women's movement. For this activist, the imperative was placed on mobilizing other women.[146]

The Congress of Black Women of Canada was active on several fronts, tackling issues relevant to the entire community as well as women specifically. The Congress was gravely concerned with Canadian immigration law practices, appointing an Immigration Committee, which included Juanita Westmoreland-Traoré, to deal with 1973 changes to immigration law, which prevented people on tourist visas from applying for landed immigrant status from inside the country.[147] The law proved to be "more discriminatory towards Black and Third World peoples."[148] Race and gender went hand in hand, producing, as discussed by the Congress, a "marked imbalance in the male/female ratio of immigrants in the black community."[149] The plight of domestic servants, although independent agents with their own agendas and migration strategies, was on the minds of Congress attendees, who were concerned with the widespread reports of abuse under the auspices of the 1955 West Indian Domestic Scheme.[150] Employment in domestic service (i.e., working directly under wealthy white women) was one of the few ways that Black women could immigrate to Canada prior to 1962, and women already in the country still struggled to find a foothold in the nondomestic labour force.[151] After the Second World War, the federal government turned to the West Indies in order to satisfy its demand for this form of cheap female labour. With business interests in the Caribbean, Ottawa was forced to comply with the efforts of these countries to ease population pressure and unemployment. This strategy came about, however, only after European women refused to take on this role. In the early 1950s, Italians and Greeks promptly abandoned domestic service – the most reviled of professions, where sexual harassment, among other indignities, was a constant threat – almost immediately upon arrival.[152]

Delegates also discussed issues of a more personal nature. Addressing the issue of birth control at the 1973 National Congress of Black Women (attended by Anne Cools), attendees were prepared for serious discussion on the matter, but the conversation was deemed inappropriate "once the subject of 'Genocide' was raised from the floor."[153] Scholar-activist Angela Davis notes that the "cries of genocide" on the part of Black women, if seemingly "an exaggerated – even paranoiac – reaction," stemmed from the birth control movement's historical advocacy of involuntary sterilization, "a racist form of mass 'birth control.'"[154] However, as Rosemary Brown stated at the same conference, "I cannot accept the theory that the most valuable contribution that I have to make to the Black struggle is that of giving birth to additional Black male children."[155] Indeed, a number of male activists within the Black Power movement insisted that a Black woman's greatest contribution to Black liberation was "having babies for the revolution."[156] Caught between pro-natalist male nationalists and a Eurocentric birth control agenda that considered "Third World" birth rates to be a threat to global well-being, Black women and women of colour in several contexts walked a tightrope.[157] In the early 1970s, the Congress of Black Women of Canada was mainly concerned with "Conception Control as it pertains to the birth of children into a society where there is no 'home' situation for them." Referring to out-adoption, the 1973 conference proceedings indicated "that black women, in particular single migrant women, were sexually exploited by black men and by white men."[158] Some had children out of wedlock and were forced, out of circumstance, to put their children up for adoption.[159] Numerous sides of this issue were addressed at the 1973 conference, from the pitiful assistance available to single mothers and the racial biases in the social service sector to the community's attitudes toward young mothers and intracommunal adoption.[160]

The Congress engaged in anti-racist education initiatives – not unlike the Quebec Native Women's Association, as we saw in the previous chapter, and not unlike Haitian organizations, as we will see in chapter 4. Although the teaching profession offered social mobility for Black women, the educational system was riddled with racist stereotypes, such that "belonging," as historian Funké Aladejebi explains, "was drastically limited for black Canadians who remained completely invisible until they became 'problems' that needed to be addressed."[161] Starting in 1973, participants in the workshop session on education, where Gwen Lord, Joan Lawrence, Marjorie Griffiths, and Marion de Jean represented Montreal, made four recommendations. First, they sought the creation of community-planned daycare and nursing centres outside "the aegis of the public school system and staffed by people experienced with living in the black community." Second, they advised that school curricula should give "proper recognition to our ethnic contributions, past and present." Third, they advocated on behalf of immigrant students, suggesting that these newcomers "be given courses to orient them to their new academic environment." Finally, they demanded that teacher-training colleges, in response to an increasingly multiracial Canada, help teachers to "free themselves from those stereotypes which can prejudice their relationships with children."[162] Both formally and informally trained, these educators sought to create culturally affirming spaces for Black children.[163] The Congress also took on an advocacy role vis-à-vis the Quebec government. In 1982, for example, Congress members met with the minister of education to demand the retraction of two texts from a reader, *La lecture sous toutes ses formes* (1974), one containing a story about a Black boy awarded blue eyes for good behaviour and the other recounting a confrontation between white children and Black cannibals in Africa.[164] A constant in the history of Montreal, community members expended a great deal of energy mobilizing against anti-Black racism in the education system.

In 1974, the Coloured Women's Club of Montreal offered to host the Second National Congress of Black Women of Canada, due to the overwhelming success of the first meeting.[165] During the November conference, participants could attend workshops on economics and immigration, education, health and social welfare, and the "triple repression of Black women." The aims of the conference were, among others, to develop the "positions of Black women on issues pertaining to the Black community" and to "reinforce relations between French- and English-speaking Black women."[166] The Congress of Black Women of Canada also expressed "its solidarity with Indigenous peoples and communicated with the Quebec Native Women's [Association] to explore ways and means of collaboration in the struggle for justice."[167] Shared notions of community control and social locations, then, led to cross-cultural solidarities; because Indigenous peoples, like African Canadians, lived in "enclaves" within an already established, colonial nation-state, independence could not be achieved in the traditional sense by pushing out the colonizers or taking control of the territory's most important institutions. In the periodical *Akwesasne Notes*, journalists frequently claimed that "Black and Indigenous peoples shared a common history of exploitation in North America," pointing to a shared social location.[168] Abenaki Évelyn O'Bomsawin, a future president of the

Quebec Native Women's Association, similarly recalled leaving Odanak to
work in a factory near Montreal during the Second World War. Speaking
about her experiences with discrimination, she mentioned the support networks to which she belonged alongside other racialized women, especially
Black women who were in a comparable position.[169] Therefore, Indigenous
and Black nationalist definitions of self-determination – if not identical –
shared similar ideological underpinnings, especially in the 1970s.

Congress women critiqued official multiculturalism, instead arguing in
favor of structural and institutional change.[170] In 1978, Esmeralda Thornhill
and Nancy Warner presented a brief to the Canadian Consultative Council
on Multiculturalism on behalf of the Congress. In the document, the authors questioned aspects of the federal policy:

> The National Congress of Black Women of Canada feels that for too
> long Black Canadians have been treated as "invisible Canadians" and
> second-class citizens … The recent proliferation of the jargon of
> multiculturalism – "pluralistic society, multiethnic studies," "cultural
> identity" etc. [–] has permeated our environment. However, what is
> multiculturalism? How does it translate into concrete action for a
> more equitable society? To date, talk of multiculturalism has been just
> talk. Regular international folkloric festivals with weekend multiethnic
> conferences punctuated here and there by an international buffet by
> themselves cannot create a harmonious pluralistic Canadian society.
> The real problems are shoved aside, ignored amid the folkdances,
> ethnic costumes and exotic dishes.[171]

Rather than embracing tokenistic celebrations of cultural diversity,
Thornhill and Warner broached topics of pressing concern to the Black
community. "Folk-dancing and amateur theatre are quite meaningless,"
the authors wrote, "if peoples are excluded from participation in the mainstream of Canadian society." Their proposals centred on four themes: employment, media, education, and immigration. The institutions representing
these areas conveyed the idea that "Canadian" was still tacitly understood
and defined as "white." As Thornhill and Warner explained, "This image is
so ingrained in the psyches of whites living in Canada that old line Black
Canadians are greeted with incredulously raised eyebrows and inquisitorial

cross-questioning on their genealogical past." From discriminatory hiring practices to history textbooks that made scant mention of Black Canadians, the omissions and erasures practised by public servants carried concrete consequences, notably in terms of refusing asylum, or in the words of the authors, "the ruthless deportations of Black political refugees."[172] Referring to Haitian migrants – whose experiences with deportation will be explained more fully in chapter 4 – Congress members, suffice it to say, sought policies much more profound than those offered by official multiculturalism. They put forth an alternative interpretation of citizenship, relying on ideas of Black internationalism to promote social justice and global solidarity among African-descended peoples.

In 1980, the Congress participated in the conference "Women under Apartheid," organized by the Ligue des femmes du Québec and held in Montreal from 9 to 11 May. The Quebec Native Women's Association participated in the gathering as well.[173] The hemispheric conference brought together over 200 delegates and observers from Africa, South America, North America, and the Caribbean. The organizers sought to determine what could and should be the role of women's organizations outside of the continent in mobilizing support for Black women in liberation struggles in South Africa, Namibia, and Zimbabwe. The seminar adopted a declaration to be submitted to the United Nations secretary general, the Special Committee against Apartheid, the International Seminar on Women in Helsinki, and the 1980 UN World Conference on Women in Copenhagen. The declaration called for economic sanctions against South Africa, support for divestment campaigns, the release of political prisoners, and more efforts to disseminate information on women in southern African liberation movements.[174] Since they committed the world community to imposing economic sanctions against the southern African regimes, the question of apartheid was a contentious issue during the UN Decade for Women (1975–85). In Mexico City, Copenhagen, and Nairobi, the official Canadian delegation shied away from these conversations. In 1985, in Kenya, the country again abstained on on four controversial paragraphs related to apartheid, as well as the failure of the international community to establish a new international economic order and the plight of Palestinian women and children.[175] In short, the federal government was tepid in approving sanctions against Pretoria. Canada, for its part, continued to ship arms to South Africa and refused to break trade relations until the late 1980s.[176] Perhaps the vibrant grassroots anti-apartheid movement contributed to a shift in policy under Prime Minister Brian Mulroney.[177]

Shortly after the conference, the Congress of Black Women held a solidarity rally at Notre-Dame-de-Grâce Park. The recent seminar resolved to request that the United Nations officially declare 9 August South African Woman's Day in order to focus world attention on the significant and active role that Black women played in the anti-apartheid movement. Later that day, the Congress hosted a documentary screening at the NCC. The goal of these events was to show solidarity "with the Black Women of Quebec in the liberation struggle for all those who are victims of discrimination in all of its forms."[178] Invoking the UN Decade for Women and the Decade for Action to Combat Racism and Racial Discrimination (1973–83), the Public Relations Committee issued a statement a few days before the rally. Not only did the statement reflect the reasons behind the Congress's prioritizing of anti-apartheid activism, but it also demonstrated the evolution of its members' thinking:

> The very fact that we are Black Women and the very essence of the goals of the National Congress of Black Women decree our close identification with the Black Women of South Africa. Being members of the African Diaspora, we are products of the institution of slavery and we have inherited a legacy of genocide, racism, oppression, and exploitation ... Just as our Black South African sisters must overcome "the three-pronged obstacles of sex, race and class," we too are victims of a triple oppression even though it might be subtle, hidden and underhanded.
>
> Along with our South African sisters we understand the universal truth articulated by Kwame N'Krumah that no African can be free until all Africa is free. And in the words of Betty Riley, a Black Québécoise at the First Conference of the National Congress of Black Women of Canada, "There can be no Black Women's Rights until there are Black People's Rights."[179]

In 1983, the Congress organized another solidarity conference, "End Apartheid in Our Lifetime," hosting two guest speakers, renowned South

African activists Caroline Mogadime and Motlalepula Chabaku.[180] Chabaku was one of the organizers behind the 1956 Women's March of 20,000 to the Union buildings in Pretoria in order to protest apartheid-era pass laws. By the 1980s, the goals of the Montreal branch of the Congress of Black Women were therefore clear. Its members sought to create a forum where they could tackle Black women's issues "within a feminist context *and* within the context of a white-dominated society." In addition to "demystifying feminism" and "improving the equality of the present discourse on feminism," the Congress wanted to enrich the "on-going debate within the feminist movement by bringing in the perspective of the BLACK EXPERIENCE" and to "initiate a lucid and rigorous debate on RACISM by using feminism as a catalyst."[181] Over time, the two liberation struggles came together, making them one and the same.

In contexts where women predominated, then, Black Montrealers maintained an internationalist mindset. So when the members of the Congress of Black Women resolved to intervene in favour of including domestic servants under the Minimum Wage Act, insisting that these workers benefit from social security measures, or when they attended the trial of Haitian exiles facing deportation defended by Congress member Juanita Westmoreland-Traoré, or when they wrote letters to Prime Minister Pierre Trudeau demanding economic sanctions against apartheid South Africa, they were not strictly acting within the national sphere but as members of a global diaspora.[182] Montreal's women activists continued to exercise a form of "dissident transnational citizenship," to borrow the terminology of sociologist Daiva Stasiulis and political scientist Abigail Bakan, by attempting to protect the rights of community members who bore the brunt of the international political economy's negative consequences, which extended beyond the borders of the country where they resided yet were intrinsically related to it.[183]

Despite these far-reaching focuses, one criticism levelled at the Congress of Black Women was the relatively homogeneous socio-professional makeup of its participants. In a 1977 editorial in *Contrast*, a journalist asked, "In a congress intended to address itself to the problems of the average black woman, where was the domestic, the factory worker? One would hardly expect to find her in the carpeted corridors of the Holiday Inn." The author nevertheless acknowledged the necessity of this get-together: "It is

this group of people that will lay the foundations of a nation-wide black
women's organization."[184] Moreover, the Congress was open to all Black
women, regardless of whether they paid the membership fees or whether,
if immigrants, they were documented.[185] In 1980, moreover, the Congress
applied for a $17,860 grant to pay for travel funds and received $12,550 from
the Multiculturalism Directorate, demonstrating a concerted attempt on
the part of the organization to make its gatherings accessible.[186] Like so
many other grassroots organizations, however, the Congress appeared to
be between a rock and a hard place when it came to money. Its members
both wanted and needed the financial resources yet wanted to maintain its
autonomy vis-à-vis governmental forces and funding bodies.[187]

Conclusion

Tracing the roots of Black feminism in Montreal to the early twentieth century in order to subsequently draw a common thread between the Garvey
movement, 1970s pan-Africanism, and the anti-apartheid activism of the
1980s, the chapter reveals the deep roots of Black community organizing in
Montreal. Taking on leadership roles in key community organizations and
events, from the Coloured Women's Club of Montreal to the National Black
Coalition of Canada, women played an integral role in making Montreal a
central node of Black politics. Their networks extended across the city to
develop ties with French-speaking Haitian women under the umbrella of
the Congress of Black Women of Canada. Its members were well represented
within the Quebec Board of Black Educators, pushing for institutional
change, especially within educational milieus. Congress member Esmeralda
Thornhill, for example, taught the first Canadian university-accredited
course in Black women's studies, "Black Women: The Missing Pages from
Canadian Women's Studies," at Concordia University's Simone de Beauvoir
Institute in 1983.[188] In 1987, the Congress made the strategic decision to nom-
inate Thornhill for a position on the Conseil du statut de la femme (CSF),
a well-funded government body.[189] As the first Black woman to be appointed
to the CSF, however, the lawyer and human rights advocate expressed difficulty making the experiences of women of colour understood to the CSF.
Nevertheless, she points to the ways that Congress members mobilized and
maintained an oppositional consciousness.[190] By the 1980s, members were

more explicit in their use of the term "feminism," tying it, again, to their understanding of racism. The two political movements went hand in hand for many grassroots organizers.

Since Quebec and Canadian institutions failed to fully take into consideration the needs of these citizens, the community turned to ideologies of worldwide Black nationhood as a framework to facilitate links with other Black diasporas. Black Montrealers embraced pan-Africanism precisely because it allowed them to inscribe their fight for equality at home within a more powerful activism of global proportions. Activists and thinkers moved in and out of the city. Bringing together the major players of the day, the Congress of Black Writers planted the seed for the Sixth Pan-African Congress. In Dar es Salaam, Tanzania, delegates resolved, for the first time in the history of the congresses, to tackle the oppression of Black women and support them in their struggles. Women attendees stressed their indispensability to pan-African liberation. They also reinforced their commitment to anti-apartheid activism, bringing this steadfastness back to Montreal. The Congress of Black Women similarly relied on the same ideology and methods as other community organizations – that is, Black consciousness, local organizing, and internationalist perspectives. The Congress teamed up with the Ligue des femmes du Québec, joining the "Women under Apartheid" conference in 1980. For the most part, however, these organizations operated separately while highlighting their shared destiny with Black women everywhere, who were working to overcome the legacies of colonialism, enslavement, and exploitation. Thus Black Montrealers ultimately promoted a strand of women's activism inseparable from various forms of Black nationalism. Given the emphasis on human liberation within some manifestations of pan-Africanist thought, this brand of activism extended pan-Africanism rather than breaking from it.[191]

In the late 1960s, when more and more white women began adhering to women's liberationist principles, they needed to find images of revolutionary women in order to contest patriarchal structures. In search of empowering figures, Québécois women looked to the American Black Power movement and to "Third World" anti-colonial movements. Applying these ideas to their own lives, not entirely unproblematically, francophone Quebecers gained much-needed inspiration from Black, North American First Nations, and other Indigenous women.

3

Québécoises deboutte!
Feminism, Nationalism, Language, and the Front de libération des femmes du Québec

On 28 November 1969, after marching onto Saint Laurent Boulevard in chains, 200 women sat down and waited to be arrested. This action was in response to Regulation 3936, a law enacted by the municipal administration to ban public protests in the aftermath of a demonstration demanding the freedom of two political prisoners, Front de libération du Québec (FLQ) members Pierre Vallières and Charles Gagnon. Bringing together a group of young people dedicated to the demise of colonialism and capitalism, the FLQ considered itself the armed wing of the Quebec liberation movement. Although many members of the left condemned the legislation and tried to bring people together to oppose it, these women were the first to act and, within one hour, 165 of them were behind bars. Two members of the FLF, Lise Landry and Suzanne Plamondon, served three years in prison for refusing on principle to pay the $25 fine.[1] In the lead-up to the protest, members of the Montreal Women's Liberation Network had joined forces with French speakers associated with a range of leftist groups to establish the anti-hierarchical Front commun des Québécoises. Shortly thereafter, French- and English-speaking activists had come together to found the FLF.[2] The action received extensive coverage in the media, where protesters made sure that journalists understood that they had, to quote one woman, "neither a president, nor a leader, nor an official feminist movement that supported us."[3] This chapter focuses on the Montreal Women's Liberation Network, the Front de libération des femmes, and the Centre des femmes to portray leftist feminisms in Montreal and their evolving rapport with the Quebec liberation movement. The Centre des femmes was founded by two former FLF members. Fearful that autonomous feminist organizing could drain resources from the liberation struggle, Québécois women initially trod lightly. In the words of Véronique O'Leary and Louise Toupin, "Here, neo-feminism had to pass through nationalism."[4]

Well into the 1960s, women were largely absent from neo-nationalist debates. According to historian Micheline Dumont, women's issues were rendered invisible by major political circles, where the understanding of the collective "us" was inherently male, thus erasing women's voices and concerns.[5] For some, Catholicism was combined with nationalism. Although churches were emptying around the province, several prominent thinkers endorsed the papacy's statement condemning contraception, *Humanae Vitae*, proclaimed in 1968 by Pope Paul VI. Marking the triumph of the conservative wing of the Catholic Church, the encyclical reaffirmed the *Casti Connubii* (1930) and once again condemned contraceptives.[6] The editor of *Le Devoir*, Claude Ryan, was vehemently opposed to improving access to abortion services within the first trimester, arguing in the most respected newspaper in Quebec that it could only be "detrimental to the French-Canadian people."[7] The focus of this chapter, the left was no better. Rather than being taken as serious political subjects, women were used as symbols to express Québécois men's subordination. The left dismissed women's concerns and took advantage of their political labour, and women struggled to control their sexuality. Whereas there was a dynamic rapport between nationalist radicalism and feminist radicalism, as historian Stéphanie Lanthier argues, the influence went only in one direction: women were inspired by their male counterparts, yet the reverse never materialized. For Lanthier, this outcome was due to radical nationalism's inherent dependency on sexist and reductionist views of women.[8] By relying on a feminist nationalism, however, feminists on the left were able to make a tremendous amount of progress in a relatively short period of time. They used this same language to explain Québécois women's experiences with anglophone domination, capitalism, and patriarchy.

Adopting a transnational and cross-cultural analysis, this chapter explores the specificity of feminist radicalism in Montreal. The FLF's slogan – "No liberation of women without the liberation of Quebec! No liberation

of Quebec without the liberation of women!" – exemplified feminists' dual
allegiance. The chapter also explores the contradictions of this form of feminism. The Québécois left never fully reckoned with its own nation's history
of colonization and settlement, thus erasing Indigenous nations' sovereignties and politics in the process.[9] "With the goal of indigenizing settlers to
Indigenous lands," as anthropologist Theresa McCarthy explains, "settler
colonialism draws upon an array of strategies to make the Indigenous inhabitants of the land disappear."[10] Leftists' "moves to innocence,"[11] however
unconscious, were accompanied by a heightened interest in "Third World"
struggles. Stressing their colonization at the hands of the English, Québécois
feminists turned to anti-colonial movements for inspiration, looking for
new role models to combat their own oppression. More specifically, the FLF
owed a heavy intellectual debt to Indigenous political movements in many
locales, as well as to the Black Power movement. Showing that the roots of
leftist Québécois feminism can, in part, be traced to these ideologies, the
chapter builds on the previous two chapters' analyses of the Red and Black
Power movements.

Marxism influenced Québécois feminists on the left as well, remaining
in the backs of their minds throughout the period.[12] Feminist radicals were
inspired by Friedrich Engels's *The Origin of the Family, Private Property and
the State* (1884), specifically his socialist and feminist analysis of the family
at a time when women struggled to control their reproduction.[13] Interestingly, Engels's hypotheses drew on the research of Lewis Henry Morgan, an
amateur American anthropologist who studied the collectivist organization
and matrilineal structure of Haudenosaunee societies.[14] Québécois workers
– women included – were involved in several labour struggles in the postwar
period. Activists such as Madeleine Parent and Léa Roback rose to prominence, becoming key figures of the union movement. Respectively francophone Catholic and anglophone Jewish, both Parent and Roback are
remembered as activists who built bridges between women from diverse
backgrounds. Parent will come up again in chapter 5, as will Roback briefly
in this chapter, but their political work is mostly outside the scope of this
study.[15] Although the relative weight of neo-nationalism, as opposed to
Marxism, changed over time, the FLF and its successors consistently wanted
francophones of all social classes to be able to thrive. Far from considering
gender the only category of analysis, the FLF and its successors combined

several ideologies to demand much more from their society. However, they focused on their own idea of the people rather than on the multitude of nations and communities in their midst.[16]

The Montreal Women's Liberation Network

In the fall of 1969, mere months before the protest, English-speaking white women approached their francophone counterparts, attempting to convince them of the necessity for a women's liberation movement in Montreal.[17] At the time, French-speaking activists did not see the need to organize along gendered lines. The historical context behind this choice is important. Many of these women were coming to feminism for the first time. As they were getting their feet wet, they were simultaneously deciding on strategies and priorities. Unambiguously feminist groups had to justify their existence to a public unfamiliar with their new ideas and frequently hostile to women's concerns, the latter threatening to divide an already fragile national minority. After several conversations, this group of approximately ten women came to the full realization that they were often relegated to secondary, "feminine" tasks within these leftist formations. They were expected to remain locked in traditional gender roles rather than actively participating in decision-making processes, and men refused to discuss women's liberation.[18] In the United States, historian Sara Evans explains, the path of white radical feminists followed a somewhat similar trajectory as they "gain[ed] experience in organizing and collective action,"[19] found "a language to name and describe oppression," and began to espouse "a belief in freedom and equality" within the New Left and civil rights movements.[20] Since they were excluded from leadership positions within these same groups, these women went on to organize autonomously, relying on social networks to create, in the words of Evans, a "growing sense of collective power."[21] Political and friendship ties played a key role in the resurgence of feminist activism, with the result that, in some cases, word of mouth determined group membership.

Within forty-eight hours of the city's administration imposing its draconian law, English- and French-speaking leftist women assembled 200 women in the streets of the city.[22] The friendship between Naomi Brickman, a McGill University student, and Nicole Thérien, an employee of the Confédération des syndicats nationaux, served as the initial impetus behind this action. After meeting as members of the Milton-Park Citizen's Committee, the two created an informal group consisting of women from their respective milieus.[23] In the summer of 1969, Thérien travelled to Cuba, a country that symbolized the possibility of "Third World" revolution throughout the 1960s. There, she realized that socialism had not liberated women. Ensconced in the feminist radicalism sweeping anglophone campuses at the time, Brickman spoke enthusiastically to Thérien about the possibility of creating an autonomous women's group. Thus several anglophone students, along with militant employees of the Confédération des syndicats nationaux, started to meet at its Centre de documentation. The same group of women would later organize the protest.[24]

Initially, however, several English-speaking leftist women found a political home in the Montreal Women's Liberation Network (MWLN), founded by university students in October 1969.[25] The MWLN's headquarters were in the downtown area near McGill. Its members first met at the University Settlement on Saint Urbain Street. They then moved to Saint Laurent Boulevard before eventually gathering on Sainte Famille Street. Occasionally, members would host other women in their own homes, especially for consciousness raising or study groups. Neither a hierarchy nor an official leadership characterized these meetings, which attracted women by the dozens.[26] Influencing these young women, Marlene Dixon, a prominent American feminist, joined the Department of Sociology at McGill in the fall of that same year.[27] Covering topics as diverse as women in labour movements, women and colonization, the family, and the education system, Dixon's classes exemplified the reach of left feminism, where gender was not the only category of analysis.[28]

There were multiple intellectual currents behind young leftists' politics. In the first place, the MWLN's members, many of whom were from the United States and had come to Montreal with male draft dodgers, were "deeply shaped by American feminist theory."[29] It was these women who would familiarize the FLF with key Anglo-American writings, such as Kate Millett's *Sexual Politics* (1970), Juliet Mitchell's *The Longest Revolution* (1966), and Germaine Greer's *The Female Eunuch* (1970).[30] Black Power and anti-colonial ideologies were evident in the MWLN's newsletter as well.[31] In the opening article, denouncing marriage "as a minute system of imperialism," the author wrote, "Not only does the husband own and control the family property; not only has he legal power over his wife and children; not only does he direct the labour of his domestic slave, his wife, for his own benefit, but he also engages in a psychological stance as 'lord and master.'"[32] The difficulty that women faced within the family was reminiscent of the status of Black people in North America. Black feminists eventually attacked these sorts of analogies.[33] Still, radical white women utilized an already available discourse to advance their cause, one that was very powerful. To free themselves from detrimental social constraints, these feminists advocated sexual liberation as part of a larger quest for individual and collective self-sufficiency. As argued by Mary Porter of the Women's Liberation Study Group, "It is very important that women be sexually independent for the same reasons that they must learn to be psychologically and economically independent. Women need to learn to be free autonomous human beings." Quoting an eminent Black Power leader, Porter explained that women did not look for "dominance over men. But as Stokely Carmichael has said, 'We want them to get off our backs.'" Women sought, as it was referred to in the MWLN's newsletter, "self-determination."[34]

Autonomy for a lot of women meant having control over their bodies.[35] In 1968, Donna Cherniak and Allan Feingold published *The Birth Control Handbook*. For the two McGill students, the implications of effective birth control measures were enormous, leading to the redefinition of society writ large because, "if bearing children becomes an option, certainly the role of socializing children can be seen as a matter of choice as well."[36] *The Handbook* also criticized racist notions of population control, global inequality, and American interventionism in the "Third World." Cherniak and Feingold reproached male doctors who denied reproductive choice to middle-class white women but "offered" poor and especially Black women abortions, "with the stipulation that they must accept sterilization as well." They called this tactic "merely a cover for racist genocide," a position that was taken, as we have seen, by Indigenous and Black women.[37] They linked domestic policies to global geopolitics, arguing that the "population control movement" was a "weapon of imperialism," referring specifically to the Vietnam War and the accompanying indiscriminate killing of civilians. The medical establishment's efforts to limit the "natural increase" of "black, brown, and yellow peoples of the world" exposed, in the view of the authors, the tenuous hold that the United States had on its neo-colonies, at the time rife with liberation movements calling for a more equitable distribution of wealth between nations and peoples.[38] *The Handbook* became so well known that it was not only distributed by the Montreal Women's Liberation Network but also shipped to the United States and positively referred to in *Our Bodies, Our Selves* (1970), published by the Boston Women's Health Book Collective.[39]

White feminists have frequently been described as inattentive to the specific needs of racialized women.[40] Why, then, were Cherniak and Feingold different? On this point, we can only speculate; however, perhaps the authors' Jewish backgrounds offer key insights. Feingold was born in Israel to Holocaust survivors, who then immigrated to Montreal. He spent his youth surrounded by the city's vibrant, left-leaning Jewish community on the margins of the "two solitudes," French and English, due to anti-Semitism. A towering figure in progressive circles, Léa Roback, for example, was born in Montreal to Polish Jewish parents who were embedded in this Yiddish-speaking world of poetry and radical thought.[41] In 1937, Roback led a successful strike of 5,000 mostly Jewish, Italian, and French Canadian garment workers as an organizer for the International Ladies' Garment Workers' Union. A multilingual suffragist, pacifist, and one-time member of the Communist Party of Canada, Roback exemplified Montreal's cosmopolitan Old Left.[42] For her part, Cherniak was raised in Windsor, Ontario, where her father ran as a candidate for the federal Co-operative Commonwealth Federation, the forerunner to the New Democratic Party.[43] Historians have found that many "red-diaper babies" such as Cherniak and Feingold turned to 1960s social movements, applying "'their parents' own 'original values'" to the New Left, especially in Montreal,[44] "one of 'the four important centers' of North American Jewish student activism."[45]

In addition to sharing a family background that lent itself to leftist and feminist politics, Jewish Montrealers identified as part of a minority group. Even though the community was undergoing a "whitening" process, with religious affiliation decreasing in importance during this period, Jewish Montrealers were not entirely mainstream Canadians or Quebecers.[46] In 1961, a full 40 per cent of Jews in Canada were foreign-born, and Yiddish was widely spoken. In fact, Yiddish was the third most spoken language in

Montreal until that year, when it was surpassed by Italian. Institutionalized anti-Semitism, such as quotas at McGill University, had only just disappeared, and Anglo-oriented conformity was still the means to social mobility.[47] It is therefore significant, and perhaps applicable to Canada, that American Jewish women, along with lesbian women, were among the first to articulate a feminism that accounted for racial difference and, in particular, as sociologist Becky Thompson explains, "a politic that accounted for white women's position as both oppressed and oppressor – as both women and white."[48] Speaking to the possibility of alliances across group lines, Cherniak and Feingold wrote, "From the understanding of one's own oppression as a woman comes a better understanding of the oppression of others also enchained in master-slave relationships."[49] In other words, women's alternative subjectivity *as women* created the affective possibility of cross-group political linkages. For Jewish women and men, the intellectual leap toward a dual positionality was even shorter.

Donna Cherniak and Allan Feingold paid close attention to local politics, writing "Montréal" and "Québec" in French, and three years later, they translated *The Handbook* into French with the help of native speakers. The rise of neo-nationalism, the Quiet Revolution, and Opération McGill français made the authors see the relevance of a francophone *Birth Control Handbook*, one that was not a direct translation. By no means the majority, English-speaking students were nevertheless a key contingent of Opération McGill français. Pushing for the university to become a French-speaking institution and closer to the working classes, over 10,000 people from various walks of life flooded the streets on 28 March 1969.[50] Both English and French speakers worked together to produce the culturally appropriate handbook *Pour un contrôle de naissances*, first published in February 1970, with the second edition coming out a year later. Here, the authors asserted, in what historian Christabelle Sethna calls "a high wire balancing act," women's right to control their bodies in a minority national context.[51] They critiqued the Church's historic role in regulating sexuality, where "only the 'duty' to carry on the race, French and Catholic, could make the sin of the flesh acceptable," instead emphasizing that women's access to contraceptive measures was "the first step toward controlling one's own existence and that of the entire collective." Birth control's benefits would accrue not only to women but also to the Québécois nation, or the "we" that the authors invoked in the text. Since capital was frequently in the hands of English speakers, neo-nationalists argued that francophones constituted an exploited ethnic class. For these women, reproductive rights served a nationalist purpose: "Quebec women will no longer have the function of ensuring the perpetuation of 'cheap labour'; the children they will choose to have will join the ranks of those who are currently fighting for a way of life that is more fair, in a Quebec that is free."[52] By 1971, 200,000 copies of the French-language edition had already been distributed.[53]

Language and Feminism

The Front de libération des femmes du Québec was one of the groups that distributed the booklet as part of its dedication to reproductive choice, specifically for francophone Quebecers.[54] By then, the FLF was at a crossroads. In 1970, it decided to exclude English speakers from its ranks, many of whom were responsible for the group's very origins. Anglophones were overrepresented in the ranks of the FLF, comprising nearly half of its membership.[55] This decision, which created much internal strife, was due to what was considered ideological domination. Since English speakers had access to Anglo-American writings, they were perceived to be pushing the group in a direction that, in the words of O'Leary and Toupin, had "little regard for the specific realities of Quebec."[56] Apart from works by Simone de Beauvoir and French translations of Betty Friedan and Friedrich Engels, unilingual francophone women had little access to feminist tracts in the early years, putting them at a distinct disadvantage. Many English-speaking members, however, were deeply hurt by this decision, with a few forever distancing themselves from the movement. In solidarity with the anglophone members, one francophone woman left the group, considering the expulsion intolerant.[57]

Writing in 2007, former FLF member Marjolaine Péloquin explains the emotions behind this decision more fully: "We loved our English-speaking friends, who had been formidable partners of radical feminist consciousness. Despite the bonds of complicity with these comrades, we feel the urgency to assert ourselves, to find our own path and our own voice." She added, "For my part, I have the feeling that our comrades understood, at least those who have been most closely linked to some of us. This does not prevent them from suffering cruelly and, like us, from being deeply saddened." Péloquin addressed the class differences among the two groups of women as well. Whereas the English speakers, according to her, were oftentimes Montrealers from more comfortable backgrounds, the French speakers were more likely to be from more modest, working-class origins and were originally from outside the city.[58] They were trying to decolonize themselves, to engage with radical feminist and anti-capitalistic ideas, and to organize politically all at the same time. This situation led to difficult decisions concerning membership.

Since its beginnings in 1969, the FLF had sought to reconcile three kinds of struggles: the feminist one, the *indépendantiste* one, and the socialist one. Although they, too, wanted to free Quebec from Anglo-Canadian colonialism and American imperialism, these women did not trust other sovereigntists to liberate women, nor did they want to have to rely on other socialist groups to analyze their specific condition.[59] Their critique of the left in this regard was biting. FLF members expressed their frustration at being undervalued in mixed settings, where men's sexism was compounded by women's inability to speak up due to a gendered socialization process that conditioned women to be the meeker, quieter sex. With lower levels of self-confidence, women became, and were expected to perform, the "cheap labour" of the left, making coffee, taking care of secretarial tasks, or answering the phone. Men frequently ignored women's concerns since their emancipation was not considered a priority, focusing instead on the liberation of Quebec or the working class.[60] For this reason, supposedly progressive men refused to invest the time or energy needed to critically examine their own patriarchal behaviour, such as forcing their wives to stay home and watch the children while they attended political meetings, and women who invoked issues surrounding gender equality spoke from a position of defensiveness, needing to justify the little attention brought to what were seen as secondary or frivolous complaints.[61] Perhaps for this reason, the FLF dedicated extensive time to analyzing the social function of unpaid labour in the home.[62] Reading Friedrich Engels's *The Origin of the Family, Private Property and the State* (1884), these feminists linked female subordination to capitalist production and the family, namely the latter's role in isolating women and in exploiting their labour by rendering them dependent as well as its function as a site of both production and consumption in perpetuating capitalism.[63] Danièle, an active member of the Centre des femmes, recalled more than subtle sexism pervading mixed groups. The Comité ouvrier de St-Henri, to which she belonged before joining the FLF, proposed that women dance as go-go girls to fund their activities. When American and French feminist texts became available in Montreal, the young woman breathed a sigh of relief.[64]

The novelty of autonomous women's organizing, for these women, was apparent in the sources, or as FLF member Martine Éloy reminisced, "It's hard to imagine how nothing was a given."[65] In the FLF bulletin, the group's members determined its raison d'être, stressing the importance of creating affective ties among women. To reach as many people as possible, the FLF and later the Centre des femmes issued newsletters, the *Bulletin de liaison FLFQ* and *Québécoises deboutte!* respectively. By publishing radical, feminist journals, the editors responded to the lack of information in the mainstream press, specifically the subpar, intellectually bereft "women's pages" relegated to the back of popular magazines.[66] The publications portrayed the difficulties faced by women and exposed the oppression that they dealt with on a daily basis.[67] In addition to promoting feminist politics, the *Bulletin de liaison FLFQ* and *Québécoises deboutte!* were written in joual, exemplifying the leftist, neo-nationalist leanings of their authors. Like the journal *Parti pris*, these newsletters were published in the urban slang of Montreal East to portray the harsh reality of poverty and cultural degradation in the province and to build a literature of struggle.[68] Their authors wrote informally as a means to declare their solidarity with, and remain close to, the working class, as there were very real differences between francophones of Outremont and St Henri.[69] For the FLF, in particular, its bulletin served as an organizational tool that linked together its nonhierarchical and disparate "cells," each one responsible for a specific undertaking, such as free daycare, contraception, or direct action.[70] The bulletin also served to unify an unstable, constantly growing membership, based increasingly in Montreal East. In the fall of 1971, the FLF moved to a new and nicer site on Mentana Street. By relocating its headquarters to the more French-speaking part of the city, organizers felt, to quote the newsletter, "more at home."[71]

The FLF's mixed membership included artists, writers, nurses, teachers, students, a handful of housewives, and employees of the Confédération des syndicats nationaux. Ages ranged from eighteen to forty, and most members were associated with one of the many social movements flourishing in Montreal at the time.[72] FLF members were "relatively privileged," as they were better educated than the average Québécoise and benefited from greater access to contraception.[73] Although they experienced a degree of material comfort, these feminists aimed to ally themselves with working-class women, specifically housewives, factory workers, and the unemployed. They wanted to learn more about their problems in order to help them organize, stay informed, and mount an action plan.[74] Like other leftists in Montreal, feminists sought to build grassroots democracy. Starting in the 1960s, for example, the Conseil des oeuvres de Montréal began to hire "social animators" in order to mobilize residents of poor neighbourhoods around issues that affected their daily lives. Indeed, community groups and citizens' committees burgeoned during these years. In these settings, women were frequently the majority, gaining the skills to assert themselves as workers and as women.[75] Since they were concerned about the "missionary" aspect of their mobilization efforts, the FLF approached the awkwardness of reaching out to marginalized women with self-awareness. For example, during a strike at Daoust-Lalonde, a skate-making factory on Hochelaga Street, the group posed the question, "Who are we to *help* them?"[76] Feminists invoked the same line of questioning regarding housewives, trying to reach out, with limited success, to women in the working-class Papineau neighbourhood. The FLF was thus trying to cultivate relations with working-class francophone women in Montreal.[77]

The FLF adopted a new way of political organizing, distinct from male-dominated groups. Nonhierarchical organizing was one of its most important principles. The latter was as important as creating women-only political spaces. At every meeting, members did their best to ensure that a different person ran the meeting and that an array of women got a chance to voice their opinions. They wanted everyone, regardless of their previous experience, to learn how to speak to a crowd. Each member was supposed to be listened to in an equally attentive manner. In their view, this approach to doing politics was essential to women's liberation, as it was the only way that women could learn to analyze, could start to express their opinions, and could develop self-confidence.[78] Rather than falling into "male intellectualism," these feminists wanted to create "their own language," a way of

analyzing oppression unique to them. Even though they insisted on the necessity of an autonomous women's movement, the FLF never conceived of
women's liberation outside of questions surrounding national oppression
or economic exploitation, where the feminist struggle was linked to, and
expected to remain alongside, that of male workers.[79] Therefore, the FLF
advocated links with other political formations whose mandate did not con-
tradict its feminist principals, such as the elimination of the sexual division
of labour. Since working-class men and women were subjected to similarly
oppressive conditions, they had to engage in a shared struggle to transform
capitalistic social structures. The same logic was extended to the status of
francophone Quebecers, described as "the men and women living in a country dominated by a wealthy minority" that had to fade away, regardless of
whether this minority was Québécois, English Canadian, or American. For
the FLF, women comprised a category that was not unified but sharply divided between those women who profited from the capitalist system and
those who were exploited by it. Only the former, save rare exceptions, could
engage in a true struggle for women's liberation.[80]

Of course, francophone women who could read English engaged with
Anglo-American works, citing Kate Millett, Betty Friedan, and Germaine
Greer, as well as Anne Koedt's *The Myth of the Vaginal Orgasm* (1970).[81]
However, after a women's group in France translated major feminist texts
from a range of countries into French, all members of the FLF rushed to
read this literature. *Libération des femmes, année zéro* – edited by Les Partisanes, first published by Les Éditions Maspero in 1970, and made available
in Quebec in 1971 – maintained a permanent position on the group's coffee
table and was often referred to during meetings. One woman, formerly a
member of the Comité ouvrier de St-Henri, called it a "revelation."[82] In fact,
women of the group considered one of the book's texts – entitled "L'ennemi
principal," which consisted of a Marxist-feminist analysis of the family – to
be one of the founding documents of the women's movement in Montreal.[83]
"Cell I" met to collectively discuss select texts from the book. Those present
remarked afterward that the conversations were valuable. Some women
thought that it was necessary to acquire theoretical training before acting,
whereas others wanted to engage in concrete efforts immediately.[84] Before
the translation of major feminist works, Québécois feminists also looked

to Simone de Beauvoir's *The Second Sex*. Whereas this book went virtually unnoticed in Quebec when it was first published in 1949, mainly due to the "lethargy" of the Quebec women's movement in the wake of the 1940 suffrage victory,[85] by the 1960s, as political scientist Chantal Maillé explains, it had become "the encyclopaedia on the condition of womanhood for many Quebec women."[86]

Although France and Marxism remained key reference points for feminist radicals, some of whom spent time in France before joining the FLF,[87] they were perhaps most inspired by Quebec's own Pierre Vallières.[88] In 1968, Vallières wrote a semi-autobiography in prison after he and Charles Gagnon were arrested for disturbing the peace in front of the United Nations building in New York City, where they had hoped to garner support for the cause of Quebec independence. In his now infamous book, Vallières described the cultural alienation experienced by working-class French Quebecers, especially in Montreal.[89] As he explained, "The author of this book is a Québécois, a French Canadian, a proletarian, a colonized man and a baptized son of the Church. Hence, an extremely frustrated individual for whom 'freedom' is not a metaphysical question but a very concrete problem."[90] From his own humble origins and his student days to his Paris trip and encounter with the French Communist Party, Vallières outlined his own coming to radical politics and his study of revolutionary thinkers such as Che Guevara and Rosa Luxemburg alongside the history of Quebec.[91] Speaking of all that ailed his homeland, Vallières sought a remedy that was not independence for the sake of independence but rather a complete transformation of social relations and the overthrow of imperialism.[92] Since both "the English-speaking and French-speaking petty bourgeoisie" were tied "to imperialism and profit from the sale of Quebec to foreigners," Vallières believed that exchanging one dominant class for another would accomplish very little. To achieve "the revolution that Quebec needs," nothing short of the "disappearance of capitalism itself" was necessary. The path to true freedom was tied to global anti-capitalism and anti-imperialism.[93] Pierre Vallières was widely read by those on the left; for example, his condemnation of religion and capitalism was one of the lead quotes in the handbook *Pour un contrôle de naissances*, second only to a citation on free love and contraception by the anarchist Emma Goldman.[94]

Some were skeptical about Quebecers' claim to colonized status, even in the late 1960s when French speakers were near the bottom the socio-economic ladder.[95] Indeed, Indigenous peoples were almost completely absent from the early writings on Quebec decolonization. Vallières, for example, made scant reference to Indigenous history, divorcing this reality from his own time, and Raoul Roy, a prominent nationalist and socialist, felt that francophone Quebecers were a legitimately indigenous people because of the *métissage* in the colony's past.[96] Although Albert Memmi, an advocate for North African independence, did not discount French Canadians' experiences of oppression – even if the North American colonized benefited from better living conditions than African peoples – he stressed, "All domination is relative. All domination is specific."[97] Memmi addressed the devaluation of the French language in Quebec, which was rarely, if ever, spoken in the hallways of Montreal businesses run by English Canadians or Americans and hence had become a source of shame for the native speaker.[98] "Colonial bilingualism," or the forced knowledge of two languages and cultures, rendered the colonized "a foreigner in his own country."[99] However, as David Austin explains, Albert Memmi "opted for the term 'domination' rather than 'colonization.'" As Austin hypothesizes, "Perhaps his familiarity with colonialism in North Africa ... and his consciousness of the dire situation of Indigenous people across Canada, including those in Quebec, did not permit him to give an unqualified nod to the notion of French Quebecers as colonized."[100] The conflation of African Americans with the Québécois working class in Vallières's thinking certainly was stark. For Vallières, "the only difference between them [was] the colour of their skin and the continent they came from. After three centuries their condition remains the same. They still constitute a reservoir of cheap labour whom the capitalists are completely free to put to work or reduce to unemployment, as it suits their financial interests."[101] By Vallières's own admission, he meant the English n-word in his book's title, despite originally publishing the book in French. He also claimed that there was "no black problem" in Quebec, a statement rife with problems.[102]

The FLF drew inspiration from ideologies inspired by the Black Power movement as well. Calling themselves "the slaves of the slaves," FLF members claimed their place alongside other "Third World" women, an identity that encompassed racial minorities in North America.[103] Like English-speaking women, they instrumentalized the historical experiences of African Americans to express the concept of women's subordination, but they also, significantly, appropriated Black people's understanding of racial oppression to energize their feminism.[104] In 1970, for example, in a press release issued after a pro-choice protest in Parc Lafontaine, the FLF stated, "Our movement is part of the struggle for the freedom of the Quebec people. We belong to a hierarchical society. We define ourselves as 'the slaves of the slaves.' We believe that women can become free only within a process of global liberation of all of society. This liberation will come about only with the full participation, at all levels, of women, who make up half of Quebec's population."[105]

The FLF saw parallels between gender and national oppression. As stated in the same text, "We know that not all women will achieve total freedom the way things are, just as we do not believe that any French Canadian can become rich and powerful given the current state of Quebec society."[106] Certainly, anti-colonial ideas helped francophone Quebecers to understand their own social location in Quebec and Canada relative to other, English-speaking Euro-Canadians. However, they disregarded the lived reality and histories of racialized and Indigenous peoples. Their proponents minimalized, as anthropologist Émilie Nicolas writes, the violence of slavery and territorial dispossession in Quebec and in other parts of the world.[107] By centring their own experiences, they excluded Black and Indigenous communities from the national narrative and thus from conversations on national liberation and social justice. Although Vallières later reckoned with the contradictions in his work, explicitly stating his solidarity with Indigenous peoples during the Oka Crisis of 1990, these ambiguities hung over political discussions in Montreal and throughout Quebec.[108] In this moment of possibility, then, many Québécois feminists overlooked the marginalized women in their midst.

Scholars have pointed to the transformative and subversive potential of feminist nationalism as an ideology that is inherently paired with, but also critical of, other liberation movements.[109] In Montreal, one can note both sides of the coin. Québécois feminists' experiences with anglophone domination shaped their politics, but their "structured ignorance" of colonization and slavery reiterated an incomplete interpretation of Quebec and North American life.[110] These sorts of metaphors were by no means uncommon for white feminists at the time. In 1967, for example, both Laura

Sabia of the Royal Commission on the Status of Women and the Fédération des femmes du Québec compared "women" to African Americans and Black Rhodesians respectively.[111] Despite upholding many of their own society's biases, a reality further explored in subsequent chapters, francophone Quebecers were nevertheless successful in nuancing elements of the Quebec struggle. Regardless of how dedicated they were to the *indépendantiste* cause, Québécois feminists maintained a degree of distance vis-à-vis neo-nationalism, fearful of a return to its patriarchal pro-natalism.[112] "Is one first a woman or a Quebecer?" was a question repeatedly posed within the Front de libération des femmes. The 1970 elections served as a catalyst to this discussion, provoking heated debate. A faction of the FLF wanted the group to join forces with the Parti Québécois (PQ), becoming the "feminist wing" of the party. Others were vehemently opposed, whether because the PQ was not leftist enough or because they wanted the FLF to maintain its status as an autonomous women's group. In the end, women were encouraged to vote according to their "conscience … as women or Quebecers." Some FLF members voted for the PQ, whereas others decided to push candidates from all parties on women's issues during electoral assemblies. Due to these discussions, activists who felt more "Québécoise" decided to leave the FLF to work within the PQ. This dossier, however, was far from closed.[113]

An Alternative Feminist Narrative

The intersection of gender and nation played out in other arenas of feminist activism. The Abortion Caravan was perhaps the most striking example of how national divisions influenced feminist politics, this time at the pan-Canadian level. In 1970, the Vancouver Women's Caucus organized a march to Ottawa, travelling across the country and stopping at various locations along the way to demand the complete legalization of abortion. Time was of the essence. From 1960 until 1966, 150 Canadian women lost their life to a failed abortion. In the mid-1960s, botched procedures were the principal reason behind women's hospitalizations. In 1968 alone, 43,491 women wound up in the hospital, yet a lack of regulations meant that few abortion practitioners faced any consequences.[114] Concerned about Trotskyist activity, the Royal Canadian Mounted Police (RCMP) followed the protesters from Vancouver to the capital, even though the Vancouver Women's Caucus and its associates did not advocate for the overthrowing of the Canadian state.[115] Instead, they fought for women's ability to control their bodies as well as the social support to raise children in an egalitarian society. The Abortion Caravan conceived of contraception holistically, seeking low-cost housing, child are facilities, maternity leave, and good-quality pre-natal and post-natal care. They also criticized the "population control" movement, where women of colour as well as poor and "Third World" women were readily offered means to limit or terminate pregnancies, in contrast to their white, middle-class counterparts. The Abortion Caravan noted Canada's hypocrisy in this regard, as Maurice Strong, the president of the Canadian International Development Agency, was in the process of considering a $15 million project for birth control in the Global South, whereas the federal government had no equivalent domestic policy.[116]

The Abortion Caravan made two demands: that the government "remove all mention of abortion from the Criminal Code" and that it pardon "all persons charged under sections 209, 237, and 238."[117] With the Omnibus Bill of 1969, Prime Minister Pierre Trudeau decriminalized abortion, as well as homosexuality, "in accordance with the more secular mood of the country."[118] The battle was far from over, however, as an abortion, which had to be performed in a hospital and required the permission of three doctors, was allowed only when the mother's life or health was in danger.[119] In a symbolic action, the Abortion Caravan marched onto Parliament Hill, where participants watched guerrilla theatre, sang, listened to speeches, and waited for a government spokesman to meet with them. When one never came, the Vancouver Women's Caucus suggested that the protesters go to Trudeau's residence. The Montreal Women's Liberation Network, whose members had travelled to Ottawa to join the Abortion Caravan, recounted the event in the pages of its newsletter, describing the RCMP's confusion at their presence and how, after Trudeau failed to make an appearance, they left a coffin and the dangerous tools of "butcher" abortionists on his doorstep.[120]

The FLF was invited to participate in the Abortion Caravan, yet because its members "did not recognize the legitimacy of the Government of Canada," the group refused to travel to Ottawa. In a press release, given to the MWLN to pass on to the rest of the participants, the FLF nevertheless "proclaimed its solidarity with Canadian women" because, "as women, we are subjected to the same oppression."[121] Women in Quebec were victims of botched operations as well. Further, francophone Catholic hospitals were less likely to have a therapeutic committee than their anglophone counterparts, even in Montreal, where 80 per cent of abortions took place at the Montreal General Hospital.[122] In 1970, for example, there were 11,200 therapeutic abortions across Canada but only 5 took place at francophone hospitals in Quebec.[123] Making similar appeals as the Abortion Caravan, the FLF organized a parallel event in Parc Lafontaine for the next day.[124] The MWLN was also in attendance to take part in the activities and to answer questions about the events in Ottawa.[125]

Before activists could confront these issues, however, they had to contend with the War Measures Act. Precipitated by the murder of Pierre Laporte, the minister of labour, and the kidnapping of James Cross, the British trade commissioner, by the Front de libération du Québec, the 1970 October Crisis had deep reverberations within feminist activism. Founded in 1963, the FLQ evoked the Cuban and Algerian revolutions and thus a world outside of Quebec. With its slogan "We Will Prevail," the FLQ inspired the Front de libération des femmes's name. Rather than using "movement," the group adopted "front," demonstrating its solidarity with the Quebec liberation movement.[126] Transforming the politics of the FLQ to suit its purposes, the FLF wanted to ensure that a future independent Quebec offered a place for women such as themselves.

After the federal government enacted the War Measures Act, suspending civil liberties, and Canadian army tanks rolled into Montreal, the FLF held an emergency meeting to debate its position. The FLF momentarily considered officially supporting the FLQ until one member reminded the rest of the room that there was "nothing on women" in its manifesto. In the view of this woman, feminists were once again let down by male-dominated nationalist groups.[127] After a year and a half of reflection, the FLF's members were looking for a way to make a meaningful, direct political intervention.[128] Seizing the opportunity, the group came to the defence of Lise Balcer, one of the witnesses in the trial of *félquiste* Paul Rose, after she approached the FLF for help.[129] Balcer was part of a group of thirty-six young people associated with Rose who were accused of sedition with the intent to overthrow the Canadian government. Since women were not allowed to sit as jurors in Quebec, Balcer refused to testify as a witness and was consequently found in contempt of court. After protracted discussions and many late-night meetings, the FLF decided on its strategy. Arriving at the courthouse separately and disappearing into the crowd, "Cellule X Action-Choc" bided its time. As Balcer explained in her testimony, "I don't understand why they talk about contempt of court, when I am simply defending my rights and those of all women. How can I, as a woman, testify at a trial where women are deliberately excluded from the jury? It only took two hours to pass the War Measures Act; why should it take forever to pass a measure that would benefit half the population of Quebec?"[130]

On cue, the women ran to the front of the courtroom, yelling "discrimination" and "justice is shit!"[131] The slogan summarized the FLF's view of the judicial system, specifically its biased nature. In a vivid, detailed manuscript, Marjolaine Péloquin described their reasoning: "We want to open the door to other values, other definitions, other images of women in the future … And these definitions, these images, these new values must be created by us."[132] They were determined to stand up and express their outrage, for which they were eventually imprisoned for several weeks in a women's prison north of Montreal, the Maison Tanguay. The impact of the action lasted more than the months in question. During this time, the FLF came up with its memorable slogan – Québécoises deboutte! (Quebec Woman Standing!) – which was soon plastered all over Montreal, and as of 18 June 1971, women could serve as jurors in Quebec.[133] Their tactics resulted in concrete gains for women, illustrating the energizing character of feminist nationalism.

This alternative nationalist narrative played out on the global stage, demonstrating the far-reaching consequences of internal divisions. In the early 1970s, activists opposing the Vietnam War organized the Indochinese Women's Conferences. The gatherings were held in Canada because its status as an officially neutral country enabled face-to-face contact between North American and Vietnamese women. Initially, the conferences were set to take place in three cities, Toronto for East Coasters, Vancouver for West Coasters, and Montreal for Midwesterners. In a letter addressed to the Interim Work Committee, the Montreal International Collective, which consisted of Anne Cools, Marlene Dixon, Estelle Dorais, Susan Dubrofsky, Vickie Tabachnik, and Eileen Nixon, outlined why Montreal would be an ideal setting "as the centre of revolutionary activity in Canada." By hosting an Indochinese Women's Conference, Montreal "would focus *world attention* and *world support* on the liberation movement of the Québécois people." Moreover, the city had "been instrumental in exposing Canadian Imperialism and Militarism in the Third World areas of the Americas, in particular the Caribbean territories." Thanks to a highly active Black community, Quebec's major metropolis was intimately connected, the authors maintained, to both the North American and the Caribbean liberation movements. The activism of the Barbados-born Anne Cools, for example, exemplified the centrality of Montreal to these struggles. An Indochinese Women's Conference held in Montreal "could easily pull together the entire revolutionary movements of the New World" and Southeast Asia, "thereby fostering revolutionary internationalism" based on genuine "solidarity and comradeship."[134]

The FLF was initially enthusiastic. A few of its members accompanied Marlene Dixon to New York City in order to discuss the possibility of hosting an Indochinese Women's Conference, taking the opportunity to attend a demonstration for the release of African American political prisoners.[135] In the end, however, the FLF rescinded its support. In an open letter addressed to American feminists, the women's group expressed its concern about the security of the Vietnamese delegates in the wake of the War Measures Act. The authors explained how the October Crisis had reoriented its priorities, making it "urgent to work first and foremost with Québécoises." The group reiterated its claim to colonized status, stating that it would interpret the taking place of a meeting organized primarily by English Canadians and Americans on Quebec soil as "another gesture of colonization," one no more excusable than the kind that francophone Quebecers were "subjected to on a daily basis." Despite ten years in Montreal, Dixon never learned enough French to communicate directly with the Front de libération des femmes, nor was the American feminist a member of the Montreal Women's Liberation Network. For the FLF, the best way for francophone Quebecers to struggle with the women of the world was to dedicate their energies to the Quebec women's liberation movement.[136] Interestingly, Dixon was willing to promote the Quebec cause internationally, but to a degree, she was rejected by the FLF because she did not abide by local, linguistic norms. The MWLN had a similar discussion, remarking in the pages of its newsletter that the Indochinese Women's Conference would be "a great opportunity to try to bring together women from as many cities and countries as possible." In 1970, the network was in the process of contacting women's groups across Canada to see whether they could garner the necessary interest. However, the MWLN questioned its own ability to organize the gathering because its members, to quote an unsigned article, had "not truly involved ourselves in the reality of the Quebec revolutionary struggle."[137] Thus the tensions between Montreal-based feminists with regard to the Indochinese Women's Conferences were reflective of the larger impact of national questions.

Although the Montreal conference was cancelled, the Toronto and Vancouver meetings took place as planned a year later in 1971. According to historian Judy Tzu-Chun Wu, the gatherings brought together four groups of people: "old friends," usually older women relying on a maternalist-feminist discourse to justify their involvement in the political sphere while working within, for example, the Voix des femmes/Voice of Women; "new friends," or liberal, radical, socialist, and lesbian "second-wave" feminists, who looked to anti-colonial women for inspiration in their search for new political roles and identities; "Third World" women, a category that encompassed activists from marginalized groups in North America who had become active during the late 1960s in liberation movements; and, finally, delegates from Southeast Asia.[138] Rather than solidifying links among activists, however, the Indochinese Women's Conferences exasperated existing tensions. Diverging sexual, racial, and national identities came to the fore, making genuine partnerships difficult – at least among the North Americans.

For Canadians, the delegates' very different understandings of colonization, both between themselves and vis-à-vis the Americans, were the main source of dissension. Much to the irritation of English-speaking Canadian participants, women from south of the border dominated the Vancouver conference, both in numbers and in attitude. In response to American chauvinism, Canadian organizers distributed a forty-page alternative women's history, *She Named It Canada: Because That's What It Was Called* (1971). Written by Vancouver's Corrective Collective, the comic book was heavily indebted to feminist, Marxist, and anti-imperialist writing.[139] But Indigenous attendees rejected English Canadians' claim to colonized status in Vancouver, and as we saw in chapter 2, the Caribbean Conference Committee, of which Anne Cools was a member, was highly critical of Canada's role in the Caribbean.[140] Although we know neither the exact number of women of colour from Canada who participated in the Indochinese Women's Conferences nor the details of their contributions, the criticisms voiced by Los Angeles's Third World Women's Caucus provide key insights into the conferences' shortcomings: "White women appear to be eager to meet with the Indochinese women and sympathize with their struggle while at the same time ignoring the struggle of Third World people in North America." The latter were "tokenized" and not included "on an equal level" within the ranks of the conference's organizing committee.[141]

Two additional points are worth noting. First, Vietnamese women, as Wu explains, "cultivated the widest possible range of allies," as they were "literally engaged in a struggle for life and death." Global sisterhood, then, originated in the "East" as well as a "West," complicating traditional understandings of this usually Eurocentric phenomenon, a concept further explored in chapter 4.[142] Second, Québécois feminists – as Péloquin's words, quoted above, regarding the jury action so eloquently illustrate – were among those women looking for new role models and new ways of imagining gender roles. Like revolutionary youth from other parts of North America and the world, francophone Quebecers travelled to China in the 1970s to bear witness to the cultural revolution. Sparked by the publication of Maria-Antonietta Macchiocchi's De la Chine (1971),[143] leftists from the Global North romanticized China during these years, making political pilgrimages to the country.[144] Women who gravitated to the FLF and the Centre des femmes also looked to the country for inspiration, impressed by what appeared to be the significant progress that women had made there in a very short period. As the authors of a Québécoises deboutte! article wrote, "What is remarkable in the struggle for women's liberation in China is that this liberation is not imposed from above: it is really the women who have taken charge of their liberation."[145] Québécoises deboutte! analyzed the Algerian revolution as well, explaining how, after massive participation, women were forced to return to their traditional roles of mother and wife.[146] Indeed, women's experience in postcolonial Algeria became emblematic of the ways that women's interests could be subverted, if not completely submerged, following independence.[147] In another article, an unnamed author linked the subjugation of Indigenous women to European colonization, critiquing the Jesuits' so-called civilizing mission and its effects on social relations, namely the erosion of women's power and the usurpation of First Nations' sovereignty.[148]

In publications that were so concerned with the Quebec liberation movement, articles on women who were not francophone Quebecers were a rarity. Focused on Chinese, Algerian, and Haudenosaunee women, those exceptions were nevertheless telling and can be read alongside the FLF's Black Power rhetoric. Revolutionary women figured prominently in these movements as fighters who were willing to take up arms to defend their countries and themselves. Desperate for alternative ideas of womanhood, Québécois feminists turned to Indigenous and Black women, knowing, at this point, that women's pivotal role on the battlefield, however real or imagined, did not necessarily translate into full equality when the revolution was over.[149] "Third World" iconography was thus a powerful tool of resistance for Québécois feminists.[150]

The Legacy of the FLF

The Front de libération des femmes du Québec was dissolved in December 1971, coinciding with the beginning of the Marxist-Leninist shift in leftist Montreal politics and an upswing of anti-poverty activism.[151] In the 1970s, thousands of young people joined En lutte! or the Parti communiste ouvrier, formally the Ligue communiste (marxiste-léniniste) du Canada. These formations attracted people of all walks of life, from teachers and students to trade unionists and community workers. Disillusioned by the repression that followed the October Crisis and inspired by the Chinese cultural revolution and the rise of labour struggles in Quebec, they moved politics further to the left in order to engage in "ideological struggle" as the precursor to the creation of a mass proletarian party.[152] A faction of the FLF indeed abandoned the group for En lutte! because they believed that autonomous women's groups diluted radical forces, that patriarchy was an ideology versus a material reality, and that feminists were nearly always of "petit-bourgeois" origin.[153]

Only one month after the death of the FLF, however, two former members of this group, Martine Éloy and Véronique O'Leary, co-founded the Centre des femmes in January 1972 with two activists of the Comité ouvrier de St-Henri, Danièle Lamoureux and Denise Fortier. Gradually, other women joined the ranks of the Centre des femmes, oftentimes from the social services sector. The average age was quite young, at twenty-five. In contrast to the FLF, the Centre des femmes limited its membership to approximately fifteen people. With a different modus operandi, it sought a degree of isolation to create a core of revolutionary feminists and encourage the implantation of similar nuclei in other milieus. The Centre des femmes analyzed women's oppression in Quebec within the framework of its overarching goal: the elimination of both capitalism and patriarchy.[154] Continuing the FLF's referral service, it also joined forces with other prochoice groups in Quebec, playing an integral role in defending abortion doctor Henry Morgentaler.

The Centre des femmes was in the former FLF headquarters at 3908 Mentana Street. Doctors allied with the centre paid the rent and the salaries of two workers.[155] The centre used the abortion question to spark mass mobilization and to unleash a "propaganda offensive" especially relevant during the Morgentaler Affair.[156] Dr Henry Morgentaler was arrested and tried for carrying out illegal abortions several times in the 1970s. A Holocaust survivor and son of Jewish socialists, Morgentaler graduated from the Université de Montréal in medicine in 1953 and began a general practice in 1955 after acquiring Canadian citizenship. In 1967, on behalf of the Association humaniste de Montréal, the doctor presented a *mémoire* in Ottawa advocating for abortion on demand. Afterward, he received several panicked phone calls from women wishing to terminate unwanted pregnancies. A year later, he started performing illegal abortions at his private clinic, located on Beaugrand Street in a predominantly francophone, Catholic, working-class neighbourhood in Montreal East.[157] Police raided this clinic, arresting Morgentaler for the first time in 1970.[158] If feminists rallied behind the doctor, it was because he never refused a patient, regardless of means, and he always practised under safe conditions.[159]

The commitment of the Centre des femmes to abortion referral was only strengthened after it was subjected to a police raid itself. At eleven in the morning on a February day in 1973, four police officers from the Sûreté du Québec arrived at the centre, staying for an hour and half. They were reportedly looking for instruments or drugs used to carry out abortions, claiming that someone had issued a complaint. Since they did not find what they were looking for, the officers appeared to "forget" their mandate and proceeded to requisition all the materials that they managed to get their hands on. They even interrogated activists and women in the waiting room, asking them point blank, "Are you pregnant?"[160] The first time that the police raided the organization, they confiscated the list of *Québécoises deboutte!* subscribers, but when they did the same thing again in December 1974, the centre's workers had already made copies. Seven people were arrested this time, a group that included women seeking abortions. The six women and one man were interrogated for six hours at the police station and denied the right to a lawyer.[161] With several doctors in Montreal under arrest and others too nervous to perform abortions, the centre encouraged women seeking abortions to travel to New York, mentioning a gynaecologist who charged only $100 yet never refused anyone with less.[162]

Shortly after Morgentaler was put on trial for the first time, the Centre des femmes formed the Comité de lutte pour l'avortement et la contraception libres et gratuits in the spring of 1974. Although it interacted with the Comité de défense du Dr Morgentaler, the Comité de lutte wanted to move beyond strictly judicial issues and focus on an all-encompassing approach to the pro-choice movement.[163] On the occasion of International Women's Year in 1975, for example, the Centre des femmes signed the first manifesto in favour of free abortion and contraception on demand. The *Manifeste des femmes du Québec pour l'avortement libre et gratuit* called for "free abortion on demand, in their community, in their language, under proper medical conditions, without discrimination based on class, nationality, race or age."[164] Significantly, Quebec juries acquitted Morgentaler on three separate occasions from 1973 to 1976. The decision was later overturned by the Quebec Court of Appeal, an outcome upheld by the Supreme Court of Canada, resulting in Morgentaler's eighteen-month imprisonment, but these decisions suggest that public opinion on abortion was more lenient than the law. Elected for the first time in 1976, René Lévesque's Parti Québécois subsequently granted immunity from prosecution to all doctors qualified to perform abortions, demonstrating the importance of jurisdictional context in determining women's experiences with abortion. The 1969 omnibus bill would remain in effect until 1988, when the Supreme Court of Canada struck down the law on the grounds that it contravened women's rights under the Charter of Rights and Freedoms.[165] As political scientist Diane

Lamoureux argues, the pro-choice movement allowed feminists to enter the discussions on the "national question" on their own terms. Since the criminal code was under federal jurisdiction and health care was in the provincial domain, the abortion question ensured their place at the table during the post-independence era, avoiding the convenient forgetting of women's concerns once or if sovereignty was achieved.[166]

When the worst of the repression was over, the Comité de lutte changed focus, deciding to lobby the recently elected Parti Québécois provincial government for reproductive rights.[167] Feminists' relationship with the PQ remained complicated throughout the 1970s. In a *Québécoises deboutte!* article titled "The PQ: Hope or Illusion?" an unsigned author commented on its 1973 program, calling the appointment of two women to the party executive and the adoption of women-friendly policies a "deceptive mask." The author accused the party of using the rhetoric of "national unity" to hide its desire to "see a Québécois bourgeoisie allied with American imperialism develop and take control." In the interim, the PQ needed to rally middle- and working-class men and women, "whose objective interests diverged and opposed each other." The author hinted at the central conundrum behind women and national liberation movements. For some women, "Already, the day after the convention, in the PQ's official publication (March 1973), an article signed 'housewife' stated 'that we must first work at putting the PQ in power because it is the only party (to date) with a program that will take care of us!'" Critical of the class backgrounds and political interests of the PQ leadership, the author continued, "Clearly, the PQ has the same policy toward women as it does toward workers in general: first, give them crumbs to rally them around 'national unity,' and then we'll see." For this reason, the author accused the political party of "demagogy" and "electorialism" and encouraged readers "to look closer," specifically noting that the PQ never called into question the "capitalist order" or took measures to legalize abortion (before 1976). Women went from "Christian mothers to national mothers."[168] As the author explained, "For women, as well as for the people in general, self-determination is a right, and constitutes progress, as long as it is done by them and for them."[169] Indeed, in a variety of contexts, women have typically been viewed as the biological, cultural, and symbolic reproducers of the nation.[170] In contrast, the Front de libération des femmes du Québec and the Centre des femmes centred the reproductive rights and anti-capitalist movements in their version of self-determination. This approach had its effects.

Due to local efforts in Montreal, the PQ "feminized" over the years. Rank-and-file militants pushed the male-dominated executive to "modernize" its policies.[171] Without women, as Jacques Parizeau, finance minister and future premier, pointed out at the time, "the Parti Québécois could not hold together." Women accomplished the most humble of daily tasks, those that kept the party afloat. Despite this contribution, women had little formal power within the PQ.[172] In 1974, a Centre des femmes member and Andrée Lavigne, a PQ militant, submitted a brief, "The Status of the Quebec Woman," to the PQ's Fifth National Congress, the same event at which Camille Laurin announced the establishment of a committee dedicated to women's issues. Nevertheless, Lavigne, a long-time member of the PQ and its predecessor, Mouvement souveraineté-association, never recovered her enthusiasm for the party, especially after Lévesque vetoed a proposal in favour of abortion. The activist then resigned in order to co-found the Regroupement des femmes québécoises (RFQ) in 1976 with her sister, Denise, and with Andrée Yanacopoulo, married to Hubert Acquin, a renowned novelist.[173] A former member of the Rassemblement pour l'indépendance nationale, Acquin was one of most distinguished and anguished literary figures of the 1960s and 1970s. Until his death by suicide in 1977, he was an impassioned advocate for Quebec's independence.[174]

Many, although not all, of the RFQ's members were former PQ adherents, demonstrating the ongoing tension between the party and the many feminist groups that flourished in the years following the FLF's dissolution.[175] In the lead-up to the PQ's Sixth National Congress in 1977, held a year after the party came to power, the RFQ wrote an open letter to delegates explaining its stance: "We want independence, but we want it to be achieved with us and for us, too. In other words, women should stop sticking stamps for the PQ *before* independence if they don't want to be sent back to their pots and pans *after* independence."[176] These types of interventions had positive effects. In 1979, Lise Payette was appointed minister of state for the status of women and given the mandate to put into practice the recommendations of the Conseil du statut de la femme, as outlined in its publication *Pour les*

Québécoises: Égalité et indépendance (1978). In the lead-up to the referendum, the PQ actively recruited women's votes, authorizing publicly funded day-care, laws on labour standards, and civil code reform.

There were some changes at the grassroots level as well. After International Women's Year, the women's movement in Quebec entered a phase of expansion and decentralization. Joining large, longstanding women's organizations, such as the Fédération des femmes du Québec, feminist groups of all kinds multiplied in Montreal. Many of these autonomous women's groups focused on service provision "for and by women." Funded by the provincial or federal government, their purpose varied, encompassing shelters for women fleeing domestic violence, women's centres or women's health centres, and women's committees within unions and universities.[177] Queer women gained visibility in the women's movement as the 1970s wore on, becoming the majority on the Comité de lutte and in the journal *Les têtes de pioche* as well as founding some of the longest-lasting and most important feminist organizations and institutions in Quebec, such as the publisher Éditions du remue-ménage, the Centre d'aide aux victimes de viol de Montréal, which was the first rape crisis centre in Montreal, and Théâtre ESPACE GO. Despite significant participation in autonomous women's groups, lesbians remained invisible until the late 1970s. Established in 1976, Coop femmes asserted the queer presence within the feminist movement on the francophone side of the city, building off the Front de libération des femmes du Québec and the Centre des femmes to contest heterosexuality as an institution.[178] Relations among francophone and anglophone queer women were uneasy but existent. Becoming the first autonomous lesbian-feminist organization in the city in 1973, Montreal Gay Women, for example, attracted about fifty women to its weekly meetings and began publishing Canada's first lesbian magazine, *A Long Time Coming*. There were some francophones in the group, yet its journal, published only in English, was more widely read outside of the city than within it.[179]

There were moments of coming together, as well as times of tension. In August 1973, Montreal Gay Women were part of a press conference for Dr Henry Morgentaler, showing their support at a crucial moment. In January 1974, the same organization held the first lesbian conference in the city. Attracting roughly 200 people from cities all over Canada and the northeastern United States, the gathering allowed attendees an opportunity to explore their budding sexual identities. With workshops on lesbian mothers, lesbians at work, feminism, women's centres, and gay liberation, the conference was an intense experience. Out-of-towners bunked up with Montrealers, making for a highly social few days. Montreal Gay Women organized another conference the following year, this time more attuned to the francophone reality of the metropolis with bilingual and separate French-language workshops. Before losing interest in the mid-1980s, anglophone organizers of lesbian conferences across Canada used the charged language of "binationalism" to refer to the divide between Quebec and the rest of the country. They also publicly supported the idea of sovereignty for Quebec and used government grants to supply bilingual conference materials and simultaneous-translation services.[180] Although the two scenes were largely separate in Montreal, especially as francophones developed their own lesbian spaces in the late 1970s and early 1980s, queer women came together on several occasions to organize against homophobia and sexism. The 1974 boycott of the Chez Madame Arthur Bar, for example, brought together lesbians fighting against voyeurism and harassment from men, using the analytical and political tools that they had gained in the women's movement to counteract lesbian repression in the city.[181]

Regardless of their political leanings, feminists continued to engage with neo-nationalism. After the PQ came to power in 1976, the party called a referendum on sovereignty association in 1980, asking Quebecers to vote on the future of the province within the Canadian federation. Conversations within activist circles were intense. For Nicole Lacelle of Éditions du remue-ménage, "The Parti Québécois has no social project. It serves white, petit-bourgeois men, little kids playing politics." However, Lacelle was still going to vote "yes." As she explained, "It's very important for us not to say No, insofar as it seems to me that No is very clearly to the right; we want to say Yes to change. What the Parti Québécois is proposing is very little, but without a Yes, it is very difficult to imagine it." When asked by journalist Colette Beauchamp whether she was prioritizing national liberation over women's liberation, Lacelle responded unequivocally, "Oh my God, no! No, no, women's liberation is the most important thing. But we didn't choose to have a referendum on May 20, not a single woman in Quebec chose to have a referendum on May 20, but there is one."[182] By participating in the national debate, feminists ensured that women's concerns were on the agenda. In the words of Andrée Yanacopoulo, "What we want is independence, but not just any kind of independence."[183] This appeared to be the stance of many feminists in Montreal. After an emotional campaign, the "yes" side lost to the "no" side by a margin of 40 per cent to 60 per cent. Whereas older activists remained suspicious of overtly nationalist discourses, fearing a return to Duplessis-era policies, younger women rallied to the "yes" side.[184] Presumably, this decision was not taken lightly. Québécois feminists and union women remained critical of neo-nationalism, endorsing a "critical yes" in 1980.[185] (In contrast, the Regroupement des femmes québécoises suggested at one of its meetings that women write "woman" on their ballot rather than "yes" or "no." The proposition was then rejected by other PQ and activist women.)[186] In engaging these questions, feminists succeeded in using the national question to change the terms of political discussion.

This shift occurred at multiple levels, from the labour movement, to grassroots social movements, to the state. When Michèle Gauthier, a member of the Front de libération des femmes du Québec, died of an asthma attack after the police charged the crowd during a protest in defence of locked-out workers at the newspaper La Presse, major union figures served as her pallbearers along with an FLF representative. The far left also contended with feminist critique. After attacking the women's movement in the 1970s, arguing that feminism was a bourgeois ideology that sought to put women in positions of power without revolutionizing the class structure, Marxist-Leninists tempered their views in the early 1980s, seeing "petit-bourgeois" feminism as a potential ally in a wider struggle. For their part, women within En lutte! disapproved of its hierarchical structure and gendered division of labour; indeed, the rise of new social movements such as feminism and queer liberation contributed to the group's demise a few years later.[187] Moreover, after Morgentaler's arrest and another failed conviction attempt, the PQ decided not to enforce a law that appeared to be unenforceable, even if access was still severely restricted at the hospital level.[188] After much hemming and hawing, the Parti Québécois established the Office des services de garde à l'enfance in 1979. Far from perfect, the new policy administered by this office nonetheless explicitly recognized both the necessity of quality services for young children and women's right to work.[189] By reproaching the patriarchy, then, the women's movement changed political life. Once feminist radicals saw power imbalances in the world around them, there was no going back.

Conclusion

Thanks to feminist radicalism, in short, women in Quebec made real progress in a relatively short period of time. Combining socialist, sovereigntist, and feminist ideologies, grassroots organizers forced mixed political groups to contend with questions related to women and gender. Once feminism was combined with nationalism, activists were able to put a mirror in front of their male counterparts, using the same language of self-determination to contest the sexism within the left. They advocated for independence but not just any independence. Rather, they supported a sovereign Quebec where women would be full citizens and maintain complete control over their reproduction while francophones of all social classes flourished. They refused to be mothers of the nation or vessels for cheap labour. By the mid-1970s, the women's movement had become increasingly diffuse, with grassroots organizers establishing a true panoply of feminist groups that frequently provided services to other women with the help of government funding. Emboldened by English-speaking Montrealers and heartened by American, French, and Marxist writings, francophone Quebecers were also inspired by Third World struggles, broadly defined. They used the same iconography of resistance to advocate for an inclusion of women's concerns in the Quebec liberation struggle.

The anti-colonial and "slaves of the slaves" rhetoric, while jarring at the hands of white women, reveals a significant intellectual debt to the Black Power and global decolonization movements. The margins were thus at the centre of feminist radicalism for Québécois women, even as the Front de libération des femmes du Québec showed little awareness of the Black or Indigenous women in their midst. As we saw in the previous chapters, women were an integral part of Red and Black Power politics. They backed these social movements on behalf of themselves as well as their broader communities and nations. When francophone Quebecers similarly combined feminism with anti-colonial nationalism, however fraught or contradictory their approach, they brought Quebec's national question to the forefront at the local, pan-Canadian, and international levels. Neo-nationalism therefore succeeded in shaping feminism in Montreal, Quebec, and Canada. As we will see in chapters 4 and 5, grassroots organizers, regardless of cultural background, place of birth, or mother tongue, focused their attention on the Québécois, rather than the English-Canadian, women's movement.

Anti-colonial ideas appeared to circulate *into* the metropolis (as opposed to already being there) for francophone Quebecers, whereas the politics of the Global South were front and centre for Haitian Montrealers, the focus of the next chapter, who maintained ties with their homeland while cultivating new ones in Montreal and beyond. For example, Haitian women were well represented at events hosted by the Congress of Black Women of Canada, overcoming the language barrier to further complexify Black diasporic politics in the city. By masterfully navigating their new setting, they contributed to feminist politics in Montreal, set the tone among immigrant women, rejuvenated community organizing writ large, and provided a much-needed perspective on struggles for democracy at international women's conferences. Women's organizing continued apace after International Women's Year in 1975, further mainstreaming feminist demands.

4

Remaking Home
Montreal's Transnational Haitian Feminism

By the mid-1970s, feminist activism was picking up steam, not only in Montreal but also around the world. The United Nations World Conference on Women in Mexico City, as we have seen, kicked off the UN Decade for Women (1975–85) and thus intensified transnational feminism. Haitian-born economist and teacher Mireille Neptune-Anglade argues that women of the Global South gained confidence as the Decade for Women progressed. Their voices got louder, and their emphasis on genuine equality, going far beyond equality before the law, was only amplified.[1] Haitian Montrealers consistently attended international conferences, the Third UN World Conference on Women, held in Nairobi, Kenya, in 1985, being no exception. Building on a longstanding tradition, partly explored in this chapter, they used the gathering to combine gender politics with a larger project of social transformation and coalition building. Part of an ad hoc committee with New York activists, they hinted at this approach to grassroots organizing in their submission to the conference's Tribune: "Of course, as Haitian women we must deal with our own particular problems, but as Black women, we share with many others the same harsh destiny. We all agree that we must recognize that the situation of Haitian women is part of a greater, global problem that includes both American and Haitian societies; therefore, the solutions to these problems are political, and it is up to us, women, to take up the fight."[2]

A defining component of their activism, with deep roots in Haitian history, transnational connections lent momentum to their local initiatives. According to sociologist Carolle Charles, three elements shaped Haitian women's activism in the diaspora: opposition to the dictatorship of François Duvalier (1957–71) and Jean-Claude Duvalier (1971–86), anti-racist struggles, and exposure to the ideas of North American feminists.[3] In Montreal, their political trajectories closely mirrored, and occasionally intersected with, those of their English-speaking, African-descended counterparts, even if they resided in different parts of the city since Haitian immigrants overwhelming settled in the predominantly French-speaking East End.[4] Although there was a panoply of Haitian women's groups in Montreal, in the interest of coherence and brevity, this chapter focuses on the activities and membership of two groups active in the 1970s: Nègès vanyan (Strong Vibrant Women), established in 1973, which is sometimes referred to as the Rassemblement des femmes haïtiennes (RAFA); and the Point de ralliement des femmes d'origine haïtienne, established in 1971. RAFA consisted primarily of women associated the Maison d'Haïti, an organization founded in 1972 to help new arrivals adjust to Quebec society, whereas the Point de ralliement was based on the personal networks of mostly middle-class professionals, especially nurses. Both groups responded to the socio-economic marginality faced by the Montreal community at large. They continued in their struggle for the restoration of democracy in Haiti, even – or especially – while exiled abroad.

Scholars trace the beginnings of organized feminism in Haiti to the Ligue féminine d'action sociale (LFAS), a middle- and upper-class women's group established in Port-au-Prince during the final months of the 1915–34 US occupation, and virtually every publication authored by diaspora women in Montreal referenced the LFAS, paying homage to the organization.[5] There were connections between the two feminist traditions despite temporal and physical distance. Many Haitian Montrealers were in fact related to the LFAS's original members.[6] For example, renowned author and community activist Ghislaine Charlier, granddaughter of LFAS co-founder Alice Garoute, remembered attending women-only gatherings at Garoute's house. It was in Garoute's library that Charlier first encountered leftist thought.[7] As we will see, 1970s-era women's groups built on the LFAS's emphasis on international feminism, fostering affective and political ties between women across national and community lines. They too maintained close relations with their male counterparts by avoiding a language of gender separateness.

A history with leftist political parties in Haiti, experiences abroad, and the global resurgence of feminist and anti-colonial activism, however, made diasporic women more conscious of class issues. This class consciousness built on a leftist feminist tradition in Haiti as well as on Haitian Marxism.[8] Women leaders eased their community's transition to Montreal, demanding more genuine forms of belonging in their adopted city and working to ensure that they and their counterparts benefited from its relative prosperity.[9] By the mid-1970s, more immigrants were arriving in Quebec from Haiti than from any other country, making community organizers' work vitally important.[10]

This chapter examines the important ways that Haitian women's social justice project was aided by the Maison d'Haïti, by the World Congress for International Women's Year, held in East Berlin in 1975, and by the Congress of Black Women of Canda. Using a transnational lens, the chapter stresses diasporic women's role in building social movements across borders. "Global" feminism has been rightfully criticized due to its flattening of differences among women and indeed due to its profound disregard for history, context, power, and intranational heterogeneity. The grassroots reality, however, paints an altogether different picture. As pointed out by Peggy Antrobus, a Caribbean scholar, public servant, and attendee of the UN Decade for Women, speaking of the international women's movement, "I am amazed to find that its image remains one of a movement associated with white, middle-class women from North America and Europe."[11] Thanks to the political work of women of colour in North America and especially of women in the Global South, women's (and men's) experiences of development in neo-colonial contexts and the macro-economic policies that reflected this colonial relationship came to the fore in the 1970s, changing "the terms of debate on women's issues worldwide."[12] By grounding the unequal international political economy as a key component of their feminism, Haitian activists in Montreal exposed Canadian and Quebec economies and societies to a global anti-colonial analysis, showing not only their extractivist principles but also their complicity in propping up the Duvalier regime. When some Haitian Montrealers returned to Haiti after the overthrow of Jean-Claude Duvalier in 1986, they brought their experiences with them, contributing to Haiti's political rebirth. Others remained in Montreal, continuing to serve as the vanguard in Haitian and other local organizations. For all these reasons, it is unsurprising that the Montreal Haitian feminist narrative started in Haiti.

The Intellectual Origins of Haitian Diaspora Feminism

The Haitian Revolution of 1804 captured the imagination of African-descended peoples. The first Black Republic, Haiti became a beacon of hope. From 1791 to 1804, armies of enslaved women and men managed to defeat the French, Spanish, and English militaries, the most sophisticated armies of the day. Marking its place in history, Haiti became "the second New World colony to achieve political independence from its European master and the first slave society to achieve the permanent destruction of the slave system."[13] As historian Michael O. West writes, Black nationalists the world over have an "abiding interest in the Haitian Revolution, the most thoroughgoing and glorious assertion of self-emancipation by enslaved Africans in the Americas – indeed by enslaved people anywhere in the world – in any historical epoch."[14] Haitian women's movements reflected the pride of this history, fortifying the resolve of activists through crushing disappointments and political repression. In the face of foreign occupation, neo-colonialism, and a brutal dictatorship, they argued that the status of women was intrinsically linked to the state of Haiti as whole, such that one could not be improved without the other.[15] Although all citizens worked together to combat American encroachment, the *désoccupation* of 1934, proclaimed to be Haiti's "second independence" by newly elected president Sténio Vincent, left women out of the reconstruction process. They were denied full enfranchisement despite their contribution to the anti-colonial movement.[16] Pursuing the franchise, legal recognition in the penal code, and improved access to education, prominent women such as Madeleine Sylvain-Bouchereau, Alice Garoute, Alice Mathon, and others, many of whom were the country's first female lawyers, doctors, and social workers, founded the Ligue féminine d'action sociale in 1950.[17] Early Haitian feminists were therefore coming out of a period of mass mobilization, one that saw "a reinvigoration of national discourse."[18]

Having failed to reap the full rewards of Haiti's "second independence," these leaders founded an autonomous women's organization. Relying on a powerful feminist nationalism, prominent women's activists made sure that they too could take part in reconstruction. The LFAS grounded its claims in Haiti's glorious past, invoking the role that women such as Suzanne L'Ouverture, the wife of General Toussaint L'Ouverture, had played in fighting for national liberation: "We like to find, at the dawn of our national life, this model of mother and Christian wife, loving, charitable and hard-working, symbol of the Haitian woman, already carrying within her all the virtues found in our ancestors and our mothers." For the LFAS, women always fought alongside their fathers and brothers, equally dedicated to true freedom and independence.[19] They gained male allies. Using anti-colonial nationalism as a rhetorical gateway to full political citizenship for women, historian Dantès Bellegarde argued in the preface of an LFAS publication that "Haiti's independence was achieved under unique conditions in the history of peoples. We abolished slavery by ourselves, without anyone's help. We forced men of all races to recognize us as equals, with the same rights and dignity. Haitians who protest today against the legitimate claims of Haitian women are putting themselves in exactly the same position as colonists who, denying the equality of human races, wanted to keep Black people in servitude because of their innate inferiority. I do not believe that Haitian women are inferior."[20]

This view of Haitian history translated into a certain type of women's politics. For instance, Madeleine Sylvain-Bouchereau, Haiti's first woman lawyer and a graduate of Bryn Mawr College, considered fellow LFAS member Alice Garoute's brand of "feminism to be but a form of patriotism."[21] In 1950, Garoute reiterated these ideas during a speech to the constitutive assembly: "Give the Haitian woman the right and dignity to participate in rescuing the Homeland, overthrow barriers that made her a minor in life, and set out together, with hearts and hands united, for the growth of our beloved homeland once and for all."[22] Similar language was used during the First National Congress of Haitian Women, a landmark event held from 10 to 15 April that same year. The proceedings of the conference, *Le féminisme en marche* (1951), offer a vivid recollection of the gathering. Welcoming delegates, Sylvain-Bouchereau purposely invoked Haiti's national slogan, "Union fait la force," to describe the conference's overarching goal, namely the coordination of women's efforts. "In the days that follow," she explained, "we will try to envision the 'feminine problem' in its entirely." Participants were there to discuss the situation of the family and childhood, education, work, and finally, "the fundamental question of civil and political rights that will allow women to take their rightful place in the national community."[23] Although heavily impregnated with an upper-class bias, Haiti's first lady, Lucienne Estimé, gave an opening address indicative of this new era of women's organizing, which was finally moving, according to Estimé, from the "social" to the "political sphere."[24]

If the number of speeches was any indication of the event's significance, the First National Congress of Haitian Women in 1950 was truly momentous. Not only did the wife of President Dumarais Estimé share her remarks with the crowd, but India's Lakshmi Menon, head of the Status of Women Section of the United Nations, also addressed the audience. There was a diversity of attendees at the conference, from other associations and the unions as well as, significantly, from abroad. The LFAS's Jacqueline Scott called upon delegates to reflect on the notion of "foreigner" immediately before Menon's speech, proclaiming that there were "no foreigners here" but rather "fervent hearts" working in unison toward a common goal.[25] Although the UN representative paid homage to British and American feminists, who won the battle "not only for themselves" but also "for women the world over," Menon drew parallels between Haiti and India: "It has long been understood that no state or people can be partially enslaved and partially free. This is especially true of countries like ours, that is, yours and mine, which, after a long period of political turmoil, are still on the path of greater cooperative freedom with tendencies toward constructive ends. Needless to say, women, as both human beings and citizens, have a big responsibility that should not be ignored."[26] In addition to Menon, several other non-Haitian women made the trip to Port-au-Prince, representing Puerto Rico, Cuba, Jamaica, and the National Council of Negro Women, based in the United States.[27] The ability to network across borders would prove to be one of Haitian feminists' greatest strengths.

Anti-colonial and focused on women's concerns, the Ligue féminine d'action sociale appears to have been a mostly middle-class or bourgeois organization. Even if there is some scholarly debate over the degree to which the organization occulted the concerns of working-class women, the LFAS did advocate for the expansion and democratization of the education system, pay equity, and the closing of brothels.[28] And it was not alone in its concern with such issues. In 1926, women associated with the Union patriotique established a local branch of the Women's International League for Peace and Freedom in response to cases of sexual assault committed by United States marines against women and girls in Haiti.[29] In the months following the First National Congress of Haitian Women in 1950, the LFAS staged a dramatic protest for women's suffrage during a meeting to adopt a constitution in historic Gonaïves, the city where revolutionaries proclaimed Haiti's independence in 1804. Women from all corners of the country descended on the town that late November, holding signs and chanting slogans directly outside the diocese where constitutional discussions were taking place. The marchers' signs bore slogans such as "The peasant votes, the lawyer does not – Seduction must be punished – Women want rights."[30] In the end, women achieved a partial victory, as the Constitutional Assembly ratified the Eighth Amendment, granting women twenty-one years and older the right to vote in all elections. However, once President Estimé, an LFAS sympathizer, was ousted from power shortly after the First National Congress of Haitian Women, Paul Magloire was slow to enact the legislation.[31] Ironically, the first presidential election that women could vote in was in 1957, the year François Duvalier came to office with a "noiriste platform." In his attempt to eliminate dissent, Duvalier unleashed a reign of terror, targeting the educated elite and the organized opposition.[32] Not only was the LFAS reduced to virtual powerlessness, as its membership disappeared, emigrated, or aged, but pro-democracy advocates across the country were also subjected to violent state repression. Politically engaged women joined the struggle against Duvalier, picking up where the LFAS had left off, oftentimes in the diaspora.[33]

Regardless of their ties to the Ligue féminine d'action sociale, the leaders of Montreal's Haitian women's organizations acquired extensive political experience in the Caribbean. Before co-founding the Point de ralliement des femmes d'origine haïtienne and the Bureau de la communauté chrétienne des Haïtiens de Montréal, Josette Jean-Pierre Rousseau, for example, volunteered with the Jeunesse étudiante catholique in Port-au-Prince's marginalized neighbourhoods. In 1961, Rousseau left for Quebec shortly after the violent repression of the student strike at the École normale supérieure de Port-au-Prince.[34] Established in 1946–47, the school was founded during an era of national development, when President Estimé actively sought to create a new, young leadership.[35] The impact that its rigorous training and social purpose had on the transnational Haitian nation was undoubtedly considerable, especially since an estimated one-fifth of its graduates eventually settled in Montreal.[36]

Many women were involved in the organized resistance. Adeline Chancy, one of the founders of the Maison d'Haïti and the Rassemblement des femmes haïtiennes, was a member of Femme patriote, a committee of women from different leftist parties and anti-Duvalier groups active in the early 1960s. The organization's reason for being was reflected in its newsletter: "Struggling for the establishment of a democratic society, struggling for the betterment of the Haitian woman, these are the objectives of Femme patriote. The two struggles are inseparable." The women's group was associated with HAÏTI-DEMAIN, a clandestine anti-regime movement that published a widely distributed French- and Creole-language newsletter.[37] In an otherwise self-effacing memoir, Chancy hints at the life that she led, one dedicated to politics, when she quotes Gérard Pierre Charles, a one-time member of the Haitian Unified Communist Party, who commented that her "courage never swayed for a moment during this long path of struggle."[38] Due to these and other leftist activities, Adeline and her husband, Max, had to flee the country in 1965. Family and friends risked their lives helping the couple and their three children to seek refuge in the Chilean embassy and then Montreal.[39] When Haitians arrived in the city, they brought their previously acquired political baggage with them into the new context, which sometimes included their studies in Europe, oftentimes in Paris, where Haiti's petite bourgeoisie deepened its knowledge of Marxism.[40] Building on these experiences, they were able to put forth a critical analysis of Haiti and also of Quebec, where their sphere of political activity only expanded.

Women and Political Life in the Diaspora

Settling in Quebec as its state apparatus was undergoing a massive expansion, the French-speaking Haitian middle class bolstered the French-speaking population and received a warm welcome from sovereigntists at a time when Montreal was asserting its francophone character. Since French speakers were needed to fulfill important public service jobs, Haitian exiles were hired in the educational and health care sectors with relative ease, even if they were at times hired below their qualifications.[41] Starting in the 1960s, the Quebec health and education systems were revamped in order to promote equality and collective well-being. Many Haitians newcomers, for example, were teachers back home, having experienced a brutal regime where educational institutions were among the most harshly attacked and repressed. Upon their arrival in Montreal, they were hired at universities, colleges, and high schools, bringing well-developed notions of collective empowerment and transformative pedagogies into these spaces. With significant cultural capital and political savvy, the *exilés* injected a new dynamism into Quebec institutions and the Montreal left.[42] Like their English-speaking counterparts, they too had a long history of dedication to informal educational initiatives. At times, these worlds merged. Adeline Chancy, for example, taught French at the NCC and attended the Congress of Black Writers, reinforcing her focus on Marxism and learner-centred ways of teaching in the process, and there was at least one Haitian woman, a Miss J. Pierre-Louis, on the organizing committee of the Congress of Black Writers in 1968.[43] Exile only "furthered their political convictions," in the words of scholar Désirée Rochat, as their activism provided a way to "struggle against exile itself."[44]

The Haitian Diaspora became increasingly heterogeneous as time passed, influencing women's activism. In 1969, another wave of repression caused a new exodus, solidifying the diaspora centres. Anti-Duvalier activists found their way to Canada, the United States, Mexico, France, and Cuba, among other places. When François Duvalier died in 1971, with his nineteen-year-old son, Jean-Claude, taking over his presidency, the dictatorial regime continued, birthing another era of economic and political hardship, as well as new waves of emigration.[45] Whereas the average Haitian woman in Montreal had acquired more years of schooling than her typical Quebec-born counterpart, from 1972 onward, recent arrivals, oftentimes women who started the process of "chain migration" for their families, came with fewer years of schooling and a shakier knowledge of French.[46] In the 1970s, 95 per cent of Haitian citizens spoke Creole as their mother tongue, the language in which they lived, worked, and spoke to each other. In Haiti, at most, only about 20 per cent of the population had some knowledge of the French language. For a host of reasons, from religious to political, the Creole culture of the majority was systematically devalued in the country until recently, whereas French and European notions of civilization were revered. Marginalized at home, Creole speakers were also alienated in Montreal.[47] From 1976 to 1980, 60 per cent of women immigrants who came to the city had not completed primary school. The statistics were not much better for men, or only slightly so. For these reasons, new arrivals, women specifically, were segregated in the manufacturing, textile, and domestic service sectors, areas with poor pay, long hours, and weak unions.[48] The reality of low levels of formal education and female-headed households aggravated the problems inherent in migration, such as ensuring an adequate family wage. The issues that the Haitian community faced, one could argue, were in fact women's issues, although at times they took on other forms.

Max and Adeline Chancy founded the Maison d'Haïti in 1972–73, along with other political exiles and students. The latter were becoming frustrated with older adults' focus on overthrowing Duvalier, an aim that downplayed, however unintentionally, the importance of other political questions.[49] Initially located in the YMCA on Parc Avenue before moving to Saint-Michel Boulevard in 1983, the Maison d'Haïti became a reference point for the community, financing its work solely through donations until 1978. Although the organization was government-funded from this point onward, providing salaries for two full-time employees and paying for select programs, grassroots participation remained the driving impetus behind its initiatives. Young, progressive students such as Yolène Jumelle, who would later preside over the Congress of Black Women of Canada as well as found the Maison des jeunes de L'Ouverture, and mature adults with a history of political engagement worked together in this cultural and political space with, significantly, a predominantly female clientele.[50] The organization played an advocacy role, fighting for the rights of immigrants in the workplace, housing sector, and vis-à-vis immigration authorities. In the *Bulletin Maison d'Haïti*, for example, the editors printed an article entitled "Slavery in Montreal" (1975) "that highlighted the dire conditions facing domestic servants in both Haiti and Montreal" in the 1970s.[51] According to the article, "This form of slavery is possible because of the complicity of Canadian immigration authorities. In fact, the rules in effect since 1972 favour work visas rather than granting permanent residency."[52] Focused on the adaption, rather than the assimilation, of Haitian Montrealers, the Maison d'Haïti helped first- and second-generation community members to maintain their culture as well as adapt to the receiving society. Its workers were continually adapting to their evolving needs.[53]

In line with its mandate for collective advancement, popular education was an integral component of the Maison d'Haïti's mission. Since its inception, the Maison d'Haïti had hosted French-language classes to assist Creole-speaking newcomers. By 1978, the objective of these courses had shifted, with the organization deciding to focus more extensively on combatting illiteracy, particularly prevalent among women.[54] In one of many articles in *Collectif paroles: Revue culturelle et politique haïtienne* that addressed the issue, Adeline Chancy, a high school teacher in Haiti and later in Montreal, argued that weak literacy and numeracy skills were a problem embedded as much in the sending as in the receiving society, as the inability to read only exacerbated the challenges related to the adaption process. Poorly educated newcomers from the Global South were segregated in low-paying "subaltern" occupations. Since they possessed a precarious legal status, Haitian workers were oftentimes unwilling to contest their poor treatment in the workplace, and their children, subjected to social, economic, and racial discrimination, risked high dropout rates.[55]

Young people who started their education in Haiti also faced difficulties. Whereas the congregational schools were top-notch, comparable to the most academically rigorous schools in Montreal, the state-run or private system suffered from poorly trained and poorly paid personnel – many of the country's best teachers left for Montreal or the Congo – a lack of libraries, and a dearth of pedagogical equipment. After students from these schools emigrated, many had difficulty adapting to the Quebec public school system. Since the school boards were unresponsive to their needs, community organizations picked up the slack, dedicating resources to homework clubs, cultural programming, and advocacy work.[56] The Maison d'Haïti, for example, worked in conjunction with the Quebec Board of Black Educators to guarantee the success of Haitian youth in the school system.[57] However, as Chancy made clear, the social disenfranchisement of these migrants and their offspring served a purpose, as their presence fuelled "the cogs of the economic machine." She wrote, "They work very well indeed, from the point of view of the system that uses them."[58]

Although not labelled a women's-only or a feminist activity per se, literacy work enabled community organizers to reach out to women. Reflecting their interest in Paolo Freire's *Pedagogy of the Oppressed* (1968), teachers implemented an active learning style and made the curriculum relevant to students' lives, such as by incorporating storytelling. Illiteracy rates on the part of men from rural areas were also quite high – 85 per cent in certain cases – yet women were more likely to attend adult education classes. The difficulties that less educated immigrants faced in Montreal were many. Whereas in Haiti they were familiar with their surroundings and spoke the language of the majority, the same was not true in their adopted city. These relative newcomers, faced with difficulty navigating the subway system, resorted to counting stops or memorizing the first few letters of each station. Their relatives would help them to find work in the manufacturing sector, but they had to bring home any necessary paperwork for other members of their household to read and fill out. If an announcement was posted on the factory floor, they would wait until the other workers had read the document, listening to their comments in order to get an idea of the notice's content. Some women were hesitant to change jobs, fearing the discovery of their illiteracy in a new setting. These were not women with a lot of time, as they worked day and night to provide for their families. Still, they enrolled in community-run courses, advertised through word of mouth or via bilingual (Creole and French) radio programs such as *La voix d'Haïti*. Students professed, among other things, a profound motivation to learn French as well as to learn to write so that they could communicate with relatives in Haiti or in other diaspora centres. Those who could not rely on the written word instead sent tapes with recorded messages on them to far-flung family and friends. Since the classes offered by the Centre d'orientation et de formation des immigrants were poorly equipped to teach French to people who struggled to read and write in their mother tongue, community organizers took on this task.[59]

Women's progress toward full literacy suffered due to overwork, making the undertaking a difficult mission. Writing in the early 1980s, Adeline

Chancy remarked on the tenacity of these students: "The Haitian immigrant woman overcomes many of these obstacles through determination and endurance, but at great cost to herself. Opportunities for recreation, culture and personal growth are virtually impossible for her." In courses organized by the community, working students frequently complained of back pain and irritated eyes, such was their fatigue.[60] As the pillars of the economy and of the family, Haitian women, especially those from the working classes, had been socialized, from their earliest years, to be self-sacrificing and resourceful, to take on a lot of responsibility, and to do their best to materially support their families, migrating if necessary. Women worked endlessly once abroad in order to remit as much money as possible.[61] As part of this push for improved adult education, community organizers stressed the need for increased awareness, specifically the idea that education should be considered a right for immigrants who struggled to read and write.[62] In 1980, the Maison d'Haïti submitted a brief to the Commission d'étude sur la formation des adultes. The paper made three recommendations, echoing, in part, UNESCO policy on adult education. First, its authors demanded improved funding for grassroots organizations such as the Maison d'Haïti to guarantee their autonomy and help them to fulfill their purpose. Second, the brief proposed that governments and businesses facilitate immigrant workers' access to additional training either by offering language classes during the workday and without a salary deduction or by providing subsidized education leaves. The brief urged that "adult education should include proper training on international solidarity, the effects of transnational corporations, the causes and consequences of immigration, and the deep roots of racism."[63] Ultimately, Haitian community leaders wanted to give adult learners the tools for them to take charge of their own education as well as feel pride in their Creole-speaking heritage.[64]

Although they never left mixed groups, women eventually felt the need to meet separately. For Marlène Rateau, a founding member of the Point de ralliement des femmes d'origine haïtienne, Haitian Montrealers relished the opportunity to establish voluntary organizations after settling in Quebec, as they were coming from a country under dictatorial rule. Women, according to Rateau, were denied the right to express themselves freely within anti-Duvalier associations, ignored by men who insisted on setting the agenda.[65] In response to feelings of exclusion, the Point de ralliement was officially established in 1971 and remains active to this day.[66] Its community involvement was far-reaching. In the 1980s, for example, the organization took a leading role in providing assistance to Haitian families afflicted by the AIDS crisis, simultaneously combatting racist stereotypes, misinformation, and an unresponsive medical establishment.[67] The Point de ralliement, however, initially focused on consciousness-raising efforts, trying to get women to overcome prevalent gender norms that constructed them as the meeker, more submissive sex. This "state of affairs" made some women uneasy, especially given the resurgence of feminist activism in Quebec. To do away with internalized sexism, a group of middle-class women, many of whom were nurses, decided to get together on a regular basis in the early 1970s. In these early years, they read and discussed feminist texts.[68] These meetings, led by women who had previously loitered in the kitchen while their male partners engaged in heated political debates, were empowering and exciting, even if at first the participants, not used to discussing their opinions, felt awkward and hesitant. With time, they grew more confident, acquiring an increased sense of self-esteem and the ability to speak in public.[69]

In an interview with *Collectif paroles*, Rateau described the various influences shaping the Point de ralliement, noting that this group of women had developed a heightened feminist consciousness after noticing the "malaise" within the community caused by gender roles and after coming into contact with francophone Quebecers in the workforce who shared, "all things considered," similar problems. These women started to attend FLF meetings held on Sainte-Famille Street, the link between the two groups stemming from a personal connection between a Point de ralliement member and the FLF,[70] which undertook to provide "material support" to the Haitian women's group. When asked how men perceived the group, Rateau responded sarcastically, describing the stereotypes frequently levelled at Point de ralliement members, who were accused of being "troublemakers" or "sexually frustrated." They were suspected of being "Québécois women who bring 'the revolution to their beds.'"[71] The Point de ralliement pushed the broader community to consider women's issues.[72] Although autonomous, the Point de ralliement was not a separatist organization. Its members never left mixed groups, and they maintained close ties with Haitian-based associations. For Rateau, "feminism" was another word for "humanism," a philosophy that could be mobilized to benefit the entire community – men, women, and children.[73]

Affiliated with the Maison d'Haïti, the Rassemblement des femmes haïtiennes took a similar approach. When asked by *Collectif paroles* whether Nègès vanyan – founded after RAFA's dissolution in 1979, with an overlapping membership – was a "feminist organization," the group's unnamed spokeswoman answered, "We define ourselves as a group of women concerned with all the questions pertaining to women."[74] Other prominent leaders similarly referred to women's activism as "the feminist movement (and/or the women's movement)," hinting at the ambiguity surrounding this terminology.[75] RAFA and Nègès vanyan organized a series of information and discussion sessions on women's concerns, including at the Maison d'Haïti, and Nègès vanyan made a point of training less experienced activists to take the meeting minutes, showing the ways that they brought other women into politics.[76] In these cases, then, the vocabulary was not as important as the claims to a politics based on helping women as well as the broader community.

Nègès vanyan and RAFA members grounded their activism in their own first-hand experience. They not only witnessed, but also lived through, "the problems that came with being a Black immigrant woman." Coming from a range of professional and class backgrounds, group members shared a dedication to the overall well-being of Haitian Montrealers. Although some had met in Haiti as members of the Union des femmes haïtiennes, an organization close to the Haitian Communist Party, others had met through their community involvement in Montreal. When asked by *Collectif paroles* whether she adhered to a separatist philosophy, Nègès vanyan's representative responded that the group's members were not concerned with adhering to a specific feminist line, preferring to focus on Haitian women's problems in an all-encompassing manner. They were the ones, as she specified, most suited to do so. Although members maintained that their lives would not improve unless Haiti's "national question" was resolved, the organization refuted the notion that they had to remain "silent" on women's issues even if they had come from an undemocratic country. Resistance to tyranny could, and should, be undertaken in a manner sensitive to women's concerns.[77] For this reason, they reached out to Caribbean and Latin American women and considered themselves active participants in the international feminist movement, not unlike the Point de ralliement, which also professed its allegiance.[78] Personal and political networks played the most decisive role in determining group membership in the 1970s.[79]

East Berlin '75

Based in Montreal, RAFA took its activism to the international stage, sending delegates to meetings in Cuba, Panama, and Moscow. The group also submitted a brief to the World Congress for International Women's Year, held in East Berlin in 1975. Whereas Mary Two-Axe Earley and Madonna Thunderhawk went to Mexico City, North America's leftist or radical feminist groups tended to favour the East German gathering, as it was supposed to internationalize a "socialist" vision of women's rights."[80] Notably, Black Power icon Angela Davis and Hortensia Bussi de Allende, the widow of Salvador Allende, the socialist president of Chile from 1970 to 1973, were in attendance, as were the Women's International League for Peace and Freedom, the Afro-Asian People's Solidarity Organization, the All Arab Women's Organization, and so many others. Reflecting the demographics, conversations were dominated by concerns with racism, imperialism, and poverty.[81] The conference was organized by communist governments and international nongovernmental organizations, including the Women's International Democratic Federation. Founded in Paris in 1945, the federation relocated to East Berlin as the Cold War intensified. Although it played an integral role in getting the UN Decade for Women off the ground, the organization has largely been written out of international feminist histories, which, as historian Francisca de Haan argues, "is part of a larger process of constructing white, Western, liberal feminism as hegemonic."[82] The historiography on feminism in Haiti has biases as well, with the result that the role of the LFAS has been amplified to the detriment of other organizations, including unions, for example, among tobacco workers, at Bata shoe factories, or in the manufacturing sector. Attached to the socialist movement, these women-dominated spaces have been largely left out of historical accounts.[83] In other words, there remain several currents of domestic and international Haitian feminism, only one of which is presented here.

In the lead-up to the International Women's Year conference, RAFA attended a meeting with the other Montreal groups bound for East Berlin. The Ligue des femmes du Québec, the Parti communiste du Québec, the Conseil québécois de la paix, and the FFQ (as an observer), among others, met to discuss the international gathering as well as women's issues more generally. The meeting's minutes indicate the primary themes evoked by each organization. For the Haitian group, "the immigrant woman and discrimination" were the most important concerns.[84] By 1975, immigrant women were increasingly on the radar of mostly Quebec-born feminist organizations. In preparation for Mexico, the Conseil du statut de la femme and the federal Department of the Secretary of State organized Carrefour '75, a province-wide consultation on women's issues. Already, the tenuousness of the category "immigrant women" was obvious during the round table on the topic since they faced different barriers depending on their social location. Nevertheless, the thirty or so participants explained the conditions that immigrant women faced in the labour and housing markets, as well as vis-à-vis social services, the health care system, and the education sectors. The Ligue des femmes du Québec, moreover, presented its pilot project for International Women's Year, mounted with the goal of strengthening ties among immigrant and Québécois women in Montreal.[85] For its part, in 1975, the FFQ founded both the Comité des affaires internationales at the encouragement of Simonne Monet-Chartrand, a well-known labour activist and pacifist, and the Ligue des femmes du Québec.[86] The committee had the dual mandate of seeking to better understand women's lives around the world in order to prepare for International Women's Year and, as explained in the *Bulletin de la* FFQ, "to inform Québécois women about the thinking of women of different ethnic origins so that they can integrate immigrant women more easily into the Québécois milieu."[87] Without the resources, however, the committee was unable to penetrate immigrant communities' political spheres.[88] Although not entirely separate, women's movements in Montreal appeared to run mostly in parallel to one another, including on the world stage.

Haitian Montrealers used transnational networks to amplify their voices and to champion their causes. In East Berlin, surrounded by women who faced similar challenges, they found a receptive audience. Numerous reports mentioned Haiti alongside countries such as Chile, Brazil, Guatemala,

Nicaragua, the Dominican Republic, and South Africa, stressing the dire necessity of "freedom, national independence, democratic rights, social progress, democracy and peace." Professing support for "all peoples who are fighting for their independence," delegates demanded "freedom for all political prisoners and respect for the most elementary human rights."[89] The text that RAFA submitted to the conference quickly became a reference point as a "pioneering study of the condition of women in Haiti in the context of the struggle for democracy." More specifically, it provided a summary of the history of Haitian women and their activism, as well as a critical synthesis of their challenges. *Femmes haïtiennes* (1980), written with the help of Haitian women working in various professional sectors, was widely distributed throughout progressive circles in Haiti and abroad.[90] The publication rendered homage to the Ligue féminine d'action sociale, yet at the same time, its authors demarcated themselves from the, by then, practically defunct women's group. Relying on the proceedings of the First National Congress of Haitian Women, *Le féminisme en marche* (1951), RAFA outlined the LFAS's accomplishments as well as its shortcomings, namely its "elitism" and "class biases." The authors maintained that "its interventions in the social field were dominated by the spirit of charity, which explains the limited outcomes of its social actions."[91] Despite the LFAS's imperfections, *Femmes haïtiennes* contained a historical account of its push for the vote, written by Ghislaine Charlier, Alice Garoute's granddaughter.[92] However, these activists focused more extensively on contemporary battles, namely the devastation that came with violent state repression. Whether in Haiti or elsewhere, as RAFA emphasized, women like its members sought concrete political action and community engagement.[93]

The World Congress for International Women's Year provided an ideal setting for activists to speak out against the Duvalier dictatorship. As Jolanda Ferrer, a member of the National Secretariat of the Cuban Women's Federation, explained in her report on women and development, "In many contributions to the discussion, it was emphasized that there still exist bloody, pro-imperialist regimes of oppression in Latin America, who are preventing their peoples from breaking the fetters of neo-colonialism." Listing Haiti, Chile, Nicaragua, and other countries as examples, Ferrer stressed that "many women there are fighting under difficult conditions, in many cases in illegality, and torture and massacres are carried out."[94] At the conference, Anita Blanchard, a self-identified "peasant woman," recounted her experiences in prison, recalling how the Tontons had come to her village in search of her brother, accused of being a communist. Rather than finding and arresting him, the Duvalier militia captured Blanchard, torturing the young woman to get her to divulge the names of her sibling's companions. After five years, Anita was released during a series of negotiations following the kidnapping of the American ambassador in Mexico. A political group demanded the release of political prisoners, and as a result Blanchard was sent to Mexico, the culmination of a strange series of events that ultimately saved her life. Now in East Berlin, the Haitian woman asked the international community to stand in solidary with the citizens of Haiti, especially the men and women who chose to speak out against the regime. She drew attention to the case of Laurette Badette, who, like many others, had been imprisoned without trial since 1971, the whereabouts of her children unknown.[95] By relying on a global network, then, Haitian feminists based outside the country were able to foster international support for both democratic and women's rights. Badette's liberation in 1977 was thus considered a major victory for the pro-democracy movement, especially, as *Femmes haïtiennes* makes clear, for women in the diaspora, who were heavily invested in this national project even while abroad.[96]

Haitian activists' presence in East Berlin was part of a broader – and, in effect, longstanding – practice of engaging with the international women's movement. Speaking in Panama at the Women's International Democratic Federation's 1977 regional meeting, Lisette Romulus recounted the events leading up to her husband's disappearance in 1974. After completing his university studies in Montreal, Marc Romulus had returned to Haiti without his wife and son, intending to send for them soon afterward. The Romulus family's plans for reunification were interrupted, however, when Marc was arrested on the street and then taken to the police for questioning. Since that day, his relatives had received no news of his whereabouts. During her speech, Romulus, in the name "of thousands of wives and mothers, of daughters and sisters," drew attention to the plight of political prisoners' families, who, in addition to the emotional pain that came with the imprisonment of a loved one, had to contend with the reality that they, and especially their children, frequently lived an impoverished, precarious existence. For Lisette Romulus, addressing an audience of Latin American and Caribbean "sisters" – women who, in many cases, were living through horrors similar to those endured by their Haitian counterparts – freedom of expression and freedom of association were essential for "development" as well as "for the recovery of our natural resources and for national sovereignty."[97] The fate of women and their families, in other words, was intrinsically tied to that of their countries. The Congress of Black Women of Canada, as we will see in the next section, took up the cause of Haitian political prisoners.

RAFA tied immigrant women's socio-economic conditions to unequal global power relations. *Femmes haïtiennes*, for instance, attributed Haiti's underdevelopment to the country's neo-colonial relationship with many industrialized countries, including Canada – one of the foreign powers propping up the regime by supplying aid in exchange for important concessions to businesses.[98] The Caribbean country, as RAFA argued, was in a state of economic catastrophe due to Duvalier and the imperial penetration of its economy, and the two, significantly, were related. Not only was the country mired in dependency and underdevelopment, but this fundamentally unequal rapport had also led to the exodus of thousands to the Global North. There, both political exiles and economic migrants faced exploitation, the fear of deportation, and racism daily.[99] The former were often, not coincidentally, young, dynamic, and in the prime of their lives, as Canada (and the United States) sought to attract highly educated immigrants after racial quotas were eliminated in the 1960s. However, these immigrants entered the labour market as an underpaid, exploited workforce, ultimately serving the interests of global capitalism.[100] This sort of analysis was part of a broader community discussion of the connections between neo-colonialism – starting with missionaries to Haiti, some of whom were francophone women and men from Quebec, and the businesses that followed them – political repression, emigration, and racial oppression in North America. Max Chancy published a landmark article in *Ovo Magazine* in 1977 entitled "The Chain Must Be Broken," addressing this very subject.[101] *Nouvelle optique*, a journal published in Montreal from 1971 to 1973 and disseminated throughout the diaspora, also contained a number of articles on Canada and Quebec's role in the neo-colonial penetration of Haitian society.[102] Only one *Nouvelle optique* article, however, was authored by a woman. But even Suzy Castor's "L'occupation américaine en

Haïti" (1971) elided gender-based analyses to instead concentrate solely on the legacy of American occupation, linking actions by the United States in the early twentieth century to problems in the 1970s.[103]

Femmes haïtiennes also stressed the gendered nature of emigration because for many women, "their position as primary financial supporters of the family forced them to migrate in order to fill this role," as well as the integral part that women played in the Haitian economy. For example, multinational corporations, including those run by Quebecers and Canadians, took advantage of Haiti's large reserve of cheap labour and lax legislation. Approximately 70 per cent of workers in these industries were women, making baseballs or television and radio parts for residents of the Global North. The presence of these companies only reinforced Haiti's economic dependence and further delayed development, which, in part, led to emigration.[104] As we saw in chapter 3, similar patterns emerged in the English-speaking Caribbean. In this case, then, Canadians' immigration patterns resembled those of their American counterparts, whose migrant trajectories in the 1960s, historian Donna Gabaccia argues, "mirrored the geography and history of American empire-building in Latin America, the Caribbean, and Asia." Gabaccia states, "It was no accident that the immigrants Americans deemed least desirable by century's end came from those places in the world … where investors, merchants, missionaries, and diplomats worked to expand American influence."[105]

In response to this unequal rapport, grassroots activists in Montreal organized a conference in September 1983, the Third Conference of Latin American and Caribbean Women. Attended by a host of organizations, including the Comité démocratique haïtien, the Comité de défense des droits de la femme chilienne, the Ligue des femmes du Québec, and the Union des travailleurs immigrants du Québec, this forum portrayed the living conditions of women in these parts of the world and their struggles for peace, freedom, and a return from exile, if so desired. Significantly, delegates called on the Canadian government to cease all diplomatic relations with Latin American and Caribbean dictatorial regimes. They also suggested that Indigenous organizations in Quebec and Canada send representatives to Guatemala in order to foster ties with Indigenous nations of Central and South America.[106] Euro-Canadian colonialism can therefore be understood as extending past the country's borders by going beyond, as well as complicating, the Indigenous-settler dynamic. Indeed, Paul Dejean, community leader and priest, referred to recent arrivals as the new "wretched of the earth" in his well-regarded book on the Montreal diaspora, an explicit reference to anti-colonial thinker Frantz Fanon.[107]

Movement women echoed these views. Amanthe Bathalien, social worker and founder of a French-speaking chapter of the Congress of Black Women, pointed to the feelings of solidarity that she felt with white francophones in terms of defending the French language. Shortly after she arrived in Montreal in 1970, moreover, the federal government enacted the War Measures Act. As she stated in *Sisters in Struggle* (1991), a documentary on Black feminism in Quebec and Canada, the October Crisis made quite the "impression," causing her to "relive what she left behind." Bathalien also underlined the exclusionary, racializing attitudes that Haitians experienced: "We have a lot in common with Quebecers. We were colonized by the same French colonizers ... but I believe Québécois society is uneasy with the Haitian community because we're Third World people, because we're Black. They consider us immigrants who can't be integrated."[108] In an interview, Bathalien described her short-lived involvement with the Fédération des femmes du Québec in a later period. Brought into the FFQ by Madeleine Parent, the social worker was eventually turned off, distancing herself from the group due to the maternalistic attitudes that she encountered.[109] Likewise, Marlène Rateau, a founder of the Point de ralliement des femmes d'origine haïtienne, underlined her community's specific, neglected needs.[110] As part of the larger FFQ network, Rateau felt that she, being a "minority" woman, always had to remind the "majority" that she and others like her "existed."[111] Rateau and her colleagues never considered themselves outside the broader women's movement. Rather, they fought for their place within it, standing side by side with feminists of other backgrounds, especially on key issues such as equal pay and maternity leave. To this end, the Point de ralliement had participated in almost all the major feminist demonstrations since the 1970s.[112] Whereas the category of immigrant woman proved to be an important basis for mobilization, the way that this terminology was used by mostly white, Montreal-born organizations pointed to some feminists' reinforcement of second-class citizenship categories, including the notion that immigrant women needed to be "saved."[113]

Multiple Activist Homes

Although exposed to the discourses of the Québécois women's movement, and in select cases to members of predominantly white organizations, women from the Maison d'Haïti appeared to work primarily within the Haitian community or within the broader Black community. Regardless of mother tongue or neighbourhood, Black Montrealers put forth a similar anti-racist critique, challenging discrimination in the judicial, housing, and employment sectors.[114] In the context of women's organizing, grassroots activists formed connections with one another in order to create a common front. Most notably, Haitian Montrealers had attended numerous events organized by the Congress of Black Women of Canada since its inception in the early 1970s.[115] Even if they lived on opposite ends of the city, Haitian women travelled to the NCC to attend Congress meetings.[116] English- and French-speaking women took a public stand together in 1974, during the traumatic deportation crisis of that autumn, when approximately 1,500 Haitian migrants faced expulsion. Congress members attended the trial of Haitians facing removal, defended by lawyer Juanita Westmoreland-Traoré, and advocated on their behalf. The trial occurred at the same time as the Second National Congress of Black Women, held in Montreal.[117] The Chancys even put their own status on the line, as they had yet to acquire permanent residency.[118] After a broad-based mobilization, the federal government finally relented, making some concessions. Roughly 55 per cent of this group managed to stay in the country, and many eventually acquired permanent residency. The remainder were deported, went underground, or tried their luck elsewhere.[119] The Congress of Black Women thus served as a site of encounter for African-descended women, enabling them to advance, at times, a shared agenda.[120]

This cross-cultural rapport among women was cultivated over time. The sources hint at mutual recognition among Black Montrealers, as well as a concerted effort to cultivate relationships and contribute to the community's longstanding institutions and organizations in the city. At the 1977 conference, Constance Beaufils spoke of the "need for strengthening the bonds of sisterhood between black Canadian women and the women of Haiti." Françoise Ulysse was in attendance as well, giving a speech that would have resonated broadly. "To be a woman in North America is already

difficult," she began, "but to be a woman and a Black immigrant can become a nightmare … As a woman she must face the social and economic
discriminations that exist against the women in our society." As she explained, "What is more, she undergoes a cultural shock resulting from the
migration process." Part of this adjustment included living with "constant
fear," as women were kept unaware of their rights and thus "haunted by the
specter of expulsion," making them "vulnerable to the exploitation of employers." Their problems were compounded by dependency on male partners since, according to Ulysse, "the fear of being abandoned and obliged
to take care of herself and her children alone constitutes one of her worst
nightmares." For Haitian women, the situation was even more complicated,
as "their husbands are often refugees or political exiles." Ulysse's husband,
Edner, had been detained for thirteen years in Haiti, and as his wife reminded the audience, "it is the same for thousands of others." What she
proposed was "a new political thought" that would "permit the Black
woman to assume, in a positive way, the differences of culture and way of
living in North America."[121]

Part of this new political thought entailed an even deeper engagement
with ideas of Black internationalism. Authoring two resolutions at the same
conference, Adeline Chancy brought attention to the specificities of life
under Duvalier and to the importance of transnational political engagement. In the first, the Fourth National Congress of Black Women expressed
its "solidarity with the struggles of people of Namibia, Zimbabwe, and South
Africa for their liberation against colonialism and from apartheid" and demanded that "the Canadian government stop any form of aid to the racist
government of Ian Smith and B.J. Vorster." In the second, the Congress not
only vowed to support "the struggle of Haitian people for democracy," demanding that "the democratic rights of political prisoners be respected;
namely those of Laurette Badette and Denise Prophète, imprisoned since
1971 and 1973 without judgment," but also stated its aim to push "the Canadian government to take a stand against the violations of human rights in
Haiti." The Congress insisted that the Canadian government intervene on
behalf of the husbands of two Haitian women living in Montreal, Françoise
Ulysse and Lisette Romulus.[122] Perhaps, Haitian women became better acquainted with the Black anglosphere through Congress events. In 1987, for
example, the Congress of Black Women, the Ralliement des infirmières et

infirmières auxiliaires haïtiennes, and the Point de ralliement des femmes haïtiennes invited bell hooks, the renowned author of, among other books, *Ain't I a Woman? Black Women and Feminism* (1981) and *Feminist Theory: From Margin to Center* (1984), to come to the city in order to give a lecture, "Forward Together beyond Sex and Color."[123] Thus Haitian women's networks reinforced, and broadened, the Congress's transnational reach.

Anglophones' and francophones' critiques of official forms of pluralism were strikingly similar as well, even if their respective focuses hinted at differing imaginaries. As readers will remember from chapter 2, Esmeralda Thornhill and Nancy Warner demonstrated a guardedness toward federal multiculturalism, pushing for genuine, not tokenistic, forms of inclusion. Shortly after the end of her term with the Comité d'implantation du plan d'action à l'intention des communautés culturelles, Adeline Chancy expressed her dissatisfaction with the results. In a policy brief written on behalf of the Maison d'Haïti in 1984, Chancy criticized, in her case, the provincial government's action plan in matters of integration, as it relied on a "neutral," "asceptized" terminology that referred to "ethnic groups" as "cultural communities, erasing all racial connotation." More specifically, the provincial government's publication *Autant de façons d'être Québécois* (1981) made no overt reference to racial prejudice, avoiding the word "racism" or even "Black." For Chancy, this choice was not "innocent." Rather, it reflected "a minimizing if not a negation of problems stemming from interracial relations." The challenges related to integration, or lack thereof, were identified as being the result of "language barriers or cultural barriers." Never once, as Chancy specified, was racial discrimination mentioned, a reality that affected Indigenous populations and "the so-called visible minority communities, especially the Black populations." Black women, according to Chancy, were subjected to a "specific form of discrimination." The publication's elision of racism consequently raised the ire of the Montreal Regional Committee of the Congress of Black Women, whose president, as Chancy wrote in the same report, denounced the complete absence of anglophone Black Quebecers and their struggles. Adeline Chancy therefore stressed the importance of "naming racism" in the same brief.[124] Black people were also "scripted as late arrivals," to use the words of sociologist Sherene Razack, in intercultural as well as multicultural policy.[125] Or as Adeline Chancy wrote in her 1984 brief, "So much so, that an uninformed reader would be correct in imagining that there is no Black population in Quebec. The references to Haitians, a recent immigrant population, are not enough to explain the complex reality of Black communities in Quebec and Canada."[126]

The Congress of Black Women provided a space where its members could discuss issues in a manner that pertained directly to them, allowing Black women to further explore the complexity of their lives. As we saw in chapter 3, the committee addressing birth control at the 1973 National Congress was prepared for serious discussion on the matter of birth control; however, the conversation was deemed inappropriate, according to the report, "once the subject of 'Genocide' was raised from the floor."[127] Congress attendees were responding to a Westernized birth control agenda that regarded "Third World" birth rates as a threat to global well-being.[128] Although presented in another forum, in *Collectif paroles*, Adeline Chancy put forth a similar argument regarding the role of nongovernmental organizations in Haiti. Chancy criticized a UNESCO study where it was suggested that the source of the Caribbean country's infant mortality could largely be explained by overpopulation due to "the moral laxity regarding sexual matters of the working classes."[129] In addition to evoking racist stereotypes about Black sexuality, this hypothesis failed to capture the structural reasons behind high birth and death rates, such as poverty in an agricultural society.[130] Chancy feared that the author's solution – that is, concerted family planning initiatives targeting the poor working and peasant classes, essentially solving a problem through elimination – could be taken to its extreme and result in forced sterilization, "as was the case in Bolivia, Puerto Rico, in poor black neighbourhoods in the United States, and for Haitian women in the Dominican Republic." For Chancy, only equitable development policies, in conjunction with access to contraception, would ensure healthy population levels. "These are, in my opinion, basic human rights," she explained, referring to contraception – "that is, the right to a freely consented maternity that any democratic society must guarantee."[131] In other words, women's control over their own bodies deserved the same safeguarding as Haiti's sovereignty, and the two were related.

Although as a pan-Canadian organization the Congress of Black Women was bilingual from its inception, French-speaking Black women in Montreal still founded their own chapter in 1987, as differing linguistic preferences among activists interrupted the flow of meetings. According to Amanthe Bathalien, president of the organization, Haitian women found communication with other Black and immigrant communities difficult. Even after the francophone chapter's establishment, for example, the group had warm and friendly relations with Filipina women, yet because these women favoured English, the relationship was short-lived. In response to the language barrier, French-speaking Black women from various ethnic and class backgrounds came together under their own section, the Ville-Marie chapter of the Congress of Black Women. Even if mostly Haitian and middle-class, the group managed to attract people from manufacturing sectors as well as from other countries. Creating a multigenerational space, women brought their children to the meetings.[132]

Despite a preference for French, Maison d'Haïti founder Yolène Jumelle, who was Bathalien's colleague and had introduced her to the pan-Canadian organization, assumed the presidency of the Congress in 1988–89 and was vice-president from 1984 to 1988. Arriving in Montreal in 1971, at the age of twenty-seven, Jumelle was at the epicentre of the first wave of highly politicized Haitian emigrants.[133] In 1979, she spoke out at a feminist conference in Quebec, critiquing the whiteness of the space and the majority vantage point of the audience members. Her feelings of marginalization in mostly white feminist settings continued into the 1990s.[134] Perhaps unsurprisingly, Jumelle argued in favour of other forms of belonging, including the multigenerational family, as providing the most "authentic" and "satisfying" social structure. In both its "heterosexual" and "homosexual forms," the family served as a bulwark against "a dehumanizing modernity," especially in highly "individualistic" industrialized countries. In order to avoid alienation, as Jumelle specified, immigrant families attempted to maintain their culture of origin, resisting the social norms emanating from the state and the school system.[135] For Black and immigrant women, then, the family frequently meant something different from what it meant for some white feminists.[136]

Haitian women relished the opportunity to take part in the events of the un Decade for Women, continuing the momentum that had defined their feminism from its earliest days. More specifically, the Congress of Black Women and other Haitian women in the diaspora enthusiastically attended the Third un World Conference on Women, held in Nairobi, Kenya, in 1985.

Attending the conference's Tribune, Le comité ad hoc des femmes haïtiennes was one of the grassroots organizations that travelled to Nairobi from Montreal and New York City. Not unlike Montreal, New York, specifically Brooklyn, had a dynamic, highly organized Haitian community dedicated to the restoration of democracy in Haiti as well as to anti-racist local politics.[137] Reporting on the experience, the committee stated, "We thought that Nairobi was a favourable place to present our problems, our struggles as well as the resistance and mistrust we faced on the international stage. For us, it was a matter of bringing the word of Haitian women to the public arena."[138] The group's members went to as many workshops as possible. For example, they attended a meeting on African American women, where they discussed the barriers faced by Black immigrant workers in the United States. They also witnessed a discussion by Chilean and Guatemalan refugees, praising these activists' astute understanding of international relations, critique of American interventionism, and level of political organization. On 16 July, the committee gave its own presentation. Consisting of delegates from Latin America, Canada, France, Saint Lucia, and Africa, the audience learned about the tough realities faced by many Haitian women. As the committee's members explained, "We insisted on the need to support the cause of Haitian women and to denounce the political repression, the economic misery, and the discrimination suffered by our people, 51 per cent of whom are women." Overall, their experiences in Nairobi were positive, even if they did comment on the arrogance and ethnocentrism exhibited by a good number of feminists who prioritized East-West relations over the struggles of Palestinian refugees and Black South African women living under apartheid. The committee hoped to repeat the experience in the future, representing Haiti rather than the diaspora.[139]

It was also in the 1980s that the Duvalier dictatorship began to crumble. After democracy was restored to Haiti in 1986, many members of the Montreal community returned to their country of birth in order to contribute to the rebuilding process. The reasons for this choice were undoubtedly complex. As we can glean from Adeline's biography on Max, the Chancys decided to return to their country of birth out of a sense of duty. Their eldest son, for example, returned a few years before the fall of the dictatorship because of the "education" that he had received from his parents. Despite their concern for his well-being, he decided that his engineering degree would be put to better use in Haiti.[140] Myriam Merlet, chief of staff of Haiti's Ministère à la condition féminine et aux droits des femmes from 2006 to 2008 and the country's representative to the Association caraïbéenne pour la recherche et l'action féministe, painted a slightly different picture: "I got my degree in economics from Canada and studied women's issues, political sociology, and feminist theory. But while I was abroad I felt the need to find out who I was and where my soul was. I chose to be a Haitian woman. I couldn't see myself being forever a nigger in the United States, an immigrant in Canada, or a stranger in Europe. I felt the need to be part of something. This couldn't be the black cause in the United States or the immigration cause in Canada. It could only be the cause of the Haitian people. Thus, I decided to return to Haiti."[141]

For some, then, Quebec society did not provide a sense of belonging or purpose. After arriving in Montreal in 1974, Merlet studied economics, sociology, and feminist studies, later working for L'union des travailleurs immigrants et québécois on Parc Avenue. Upon her return to Haiti, Merlet founded ENFOFANM in 1987, a feminist organization that collected information on Haitian women and defended women's rights. ENFOFANM also produced the only Creole-language newspaper, *Ayiti fanm*, as well as radio and television shows.[142] Whereas women participated in the overthrow of Duvalier as Haitians, they mobilized shortly afterwards as women, staging a 30,000 strong protest in Port-au-Prince on 3 April 1986 to demand jobs, political rights, and the elimination of prostitution and all forms of gender discrimination. At least fifteen women's organizations participated in the march, adhering to a range of political perspectives and representing citizens from all walks of life.[143]

With this rebirth came a resurgence of women's activism. According to sociologist Carolle Charles, "The presence and rate of participation of diaspora women in most of the new Haiti-based groups was striking."[144] Nearly two-thirds of the founding members of new groups like Solidarité fanm ayisyen (Haitian Women's Solidarity) and Kay fanm (Women's House) had returned from outside Haiti.[145] Pointing to activist continuities across borders, Adeline Chancy, a leader in literacy work in Montreal, assumed the position of director of the Office national pour la participation et l'éducation populaire in Port-au-Prince. She served as secretary of state for literacy from 1996 to 1997 and headed the Ministère à la condition féminine et aux

droits des femmes from 2004 to 2006. In Haiti, Chancy remained committed
to women-centred political spaces, running a workshop on "the rights and
role of women in Haitian development." For Chancy, overcoming gendered
norms in the formal and informal education of women was integral to
Haiti's future, as "the democratic battle requires the wide participation of
women. But sexist ideology is one of the obstacles to this participation."[146]
Highlighting an intellectual shift, Suzy Castor, author of the *Nouvelle optique*
article "L'occupation américaine en Haïti" (1971), put forth an anti-colonial
Marxist-feminist analysis, promoting the establishment of autonomous
women's organizations in order to "struggle WITH rather than AGAINST
men."[147] Part of a larger push on the part of Haitian feminists to assert the
integral role that women played in national development and reconstruction, this seminar was, significantly, funded in part by the Conseil du statut
de la femme du Québec and the Canadian International Development
Agency.[148] In this moment of reclaiming basic civil rights and liberties,
women's rights activists opened up conversations on the patriarchy and domestic violence that remain on the table to this day. Haitian feminists asserted the weight of patriarchy and domestic violence, alongside capitalism
and neo-liberalism, in shaping the life of the country's citizens. In response
to this analysis, they were criticized for bringing "foreign" ideas into the
country, for being lesbians, or for being exclusively of the bourgeoisie, ac-
cusations never levelled at socialists, despite some similarities between the
two traditions. In the post-dictatorship era, activists were from a range of
class backgrounds: the middle classes (probably the majority), the urban
working class, and rural women. Unlike at the turn of the twentieth century,
rarely did feminists belong to the elite.[149]

Attending the seminar organized by Chancy in Port-au-Prince, Suzanne
Fontaine, a representative from the Conseil du statut de la femme, spoke
from a starting point of respectful solidarity. Fontaine opened her speech
on Quebec's feminist movement with the following words: "Essentially, in
this seminar, I bring you a message of friendship and solidarity from the
women of Quebec, who, in the last few years, have taken important steps
toward the acquisition of their rights. However, I am not here to suggest
what or how to do it in your particular context. Only you know what to do,
and how to do it, to improve the situation of women in your country. Believe
me, we have known many 'Good Samaritans' in Quebec, who 'show up' and

claim to know our problems and especially the solutions."[150] Fontaine evoked an alternative national identity, pointing to how outsiders' paternalistic misunderstanding of Quebec society influenced her own feminist identity. These ideas were present in mixed spaces as well, demonstrating an openness to decolonize North-South relations on the part of francophone Quebecers. In the early 1970s, in an article published in *Relations*, Franklyn Midy had encouraged progressive Quebecers to call into question their neo-colonial role in Haiti,[151] and in the same journal, nearly a decade later, the opening editorial – entitled "Jouons-nous les impérialistes?" ("Are We Playing at Being Imperialists?") – likewise interrogated the development narrative criticized by Midy.[152] Written with the help of Georges Anglade, a geography professor at Université du Québec à Montréal, the editorial's contents demonstrated the product of a fruitful, and self-critical, intellectual exchange.[153] Similarly, Mireille Neptune-Anglade was on the board of *Recherches féministes*, illustrating an incipient diversity within Quebec's intellectual circles.[154] Fontaine, however, made no reference to racial exclusions within predominantly white women's groups at home.

Haitian women's transnational activism continued even after 1986. Although still based in Montreal, Marlène Rateau was a regular contributor to Haitian political discussions in the post-Duvalier era. Because of her presence in the press, according to Rateau, "people were surprised that she had not returned to Haiti."[155] For example, she put her background in nursing to good use, writing an article on the links between gendered violence and AIDS published by the Port-au-Prince women's organization ENFOFANM.[156] Likewise, the Point de ralliement fought for its place on community radio in the early 1990s, hosting *Pawòl fanm*, a Creole-language show geared toward Haitian women of all classes that continues to this day. With a popular education mandate, *Pawòl fanm* addresses a range of pressing issues, from health to education, reaching out to women who sometimes possess weak French skills or do not have time to attend meetings held by women's groups. Moreover, the Radio Centre-Ville show in part attempts to rectify the ethnocentrism present in the Quebec media, where racial and ethnic minorities are severely underrepresented or, if present, are of European provenance.[157] The show is so popular that Rateau regularly meets people who "recognize her voice." By pushing for their rightful place within the community, moreover, women have gained in leadership positions. For

example, Rateau headed the Bureau de la communauté haïtienne de Montréal in the 2000s.[158] Similarly, even though she returned to her country of
birth, Adeline Chancy left behind a rich legacy. More specifically, Marjorie
Villefranche, heading the Maison d'Haïti, attributes her success to Chancy,
as the older woman, twenty years her senior, had mentored Villefranche
since she was sixteen.[159]

Conclusion

Through their political work, women organizers exemplified "diasporic
homemaking," in the words of Désirée Rochat. Their ability to recreate
and refigure politics, meaning and purpose, and affective ties in a new setting enabled them and their families to adjust to Quebec society. Like the
Universal Negro Improvement Association and the Negro Community
Centre, the Maison d'Haïti and other Haitian institutions provided welcoming and stimulating environments, complementing, for example, the
formal education system. The women within the ranks of these organizations were at the forefront of cultural transmission, ensuring that the next
generation had a strong sense of themselves and thus the ability to confront messages of unbelonging. Over the years, community organizations
worked together, fostering coalitions. For instance, various Haitian
women's groups hosted the Colloque des femmes haïtiennes in 1983 and
1984, and several Haitian women were part of the Congress of Black
Women of Canada from its inception until Yolène Jumelle's leadership in
the 1990s, as well as part of other Black institutions in the city, such as the
Coalition des associations de la communauté noire de Montréal, founded
to denounce racial profiling and police violence against Black youth. From
East Berlin to Nairobi, Haitian women were a steady presence at international gatherings, tying neo-colonialism to the fate of the country and its
citizens. In 1988, members of Nègès vanyan travelled to the Third Conti-
nental Women's Meeting in Cuba, demonstrating the ongoing importance
of Haitian Marxism to women's movements.[160] The list surely goes on. In
short, Haitian Montrealers' presence in Quebec's dynamic community sector, grassroots social movements, and international women's movement
was undeniable. Given the politicized nature of the community, future

studies are needed to paint an even richer picture of diasporic and Haitian gender politics, perhaps using Creole-language sources in particular.

Women's activism tied a heterogeneous community together, forming an integral part of multiple political traditions. As we have seen, Adeline Chancy published a brief on behalf of the Maison d'Haiti in 1984 detailing her disappointment with aspects of Quebec's official policy in matters of integration, namely its inability to recognize the existence of anti-Black racism. Before that, however, Chancy and other grassroots organizers had attended the "Femmes immigrées, à nous la parole!" conference in 1982. Organized by the Table de concertation des femmes immigrées and funded with state monies, the conference gave grassroots organizers a broader audience. Haitian Montrealers' "popular multiculturalism" was yoked to an engagement with official or state forms of pluralism, as hinted at in this chapter and the next.[161] Haitian Montrealers were also involved in multiracial grassroots organizations, forming coalitions and alliances with women from other backgrounds. They were well represented, for example, in the ranks of the Collectif des femmes immigrantes du Québec. Formed in 1983, the collective brought together women working within various immigrant organizations. As will be explored in the next chapter, it promoted critical conversations regarding systemic discrimination both within and beyond the women's movement. Immigrant women's organizations indeed proliferated in the late 1970s and 1980s. For example, the Centro Donne Italiane di Montreal, the focus of chapter 5, first opened its doors in 1978, coinciding with the rapid increase in women's centres across Quebec. These frontline organizations aimed to reach all women, including those who had not been previously politicized. In the Centro Donne's case, its founders provided much-needed feminist-inspired services in Italian, fulfilling a niche in the women's movement.

Refuting Stereotypes
From the Centro Donne Italiane di Montreal
to the Payette Controversy

By the late 1970s, feminists had claimed their place in the public sphere. The Quebec Charter of Human Rights and Freedoms (1975) had improved access to maternity leave, the Office des services de garde à l'enfance (1979) had been created, and women's increasing involvement in the labour movement symbolized its impressive gains.[1] Feminism's success was such that mainstream news outlets proclaimed the ideology redundant. Compounded by the rise of neo-liberalism in the early 1980s, leftist politics more generally appeared to be losing steam.[2] Despite the turn toward austerity, however, grassroots organizers kept the momentum going.

In the later 1970s and 1980s, women's centres multiplied, popping up all over Montreal and elsewhere in Quebec. In only a decade, feminists created over seventy women's centres in the province. Even if they did not necessarily share a common vision of society or of feminism, their proponents agreed that they represented the "base" of the women's movement, its "multiplier agents."[3] According to one representative attending a conference that led to the establishment of L'R des centres de femmes du Québec in 1985, "We may not have the words to say how things are changing. But we see it. The women's movement has entered homes, kitchens."[4] In general, women's centres aimed to encourage women's autonomy and equality, to foster social ties among women, and to promote their individual and collective empowerment. They did so in a difficult economic context, especially as the 1980s were a time of economic downturn, high unemployment, and budget cuts for women's organizations.[5] Supporting feminist principles and providing concrete services, they were able to reach women in need in every corner of the city, from Hochelaga-Maisonneuve to Montreal North. In order to explore the workings and ethos of these feminist organizations, this chapter will focus on one women's centre, the Centro Donne Italiane di Montreal. Founded in 1978, this Italian women's centre was initially in the municipality of Saint-Michel and later in the borough of Ahuntsic. Both neighbourhoods hosted large proportions of Italian immigrants.

Women's centres took on an added importance in allophone communities, as the Italian case study will illustrate. With ties to other progressive Italian-speaking groups in the city, including the Movimento Progressista Italo-Quebecchese and the Associazione di Cultura Popolare Italo-Quebecchese, the Centro Donne provided a gamut of much-needed Italian-language services to immigrant women, many of whom were locked in some of the worst-paying jobs in the city. Due to long hours on the factory floor and onerous household responsibilities, first-generation Italian Montrealers rarely got the chance to improve their language skills, which only reinforced their relative marginalization. Whereas the outside world saw a poorly integrated, traditionalist Catholic community, younger women, many of whom had come to Montreal as children, grasped at a chance to make a difference. Inspired by what was happening around them, the founders of the Centro Donne worked hard to ensure that more women in the Italian community would benefit from the resurgence of feminist activism.[6] Using their newly acquired cultural capital and multilingualism, they took advantage of the funding opportunities available to fledgling women's centres. Successful, these women spent the next forty years bringing feminism to Montrealers who otherwise may not have become acquainted with the women's movement. The Centro Donne also fostered connections with other feminists in the city, playing a role, for example, in organizing the "Femmes immigrées, à nous la parole!" conference in 1982 and in founding the Collectif des femmes immigrantes du Québec in 1983. French appeared to be a lingua franca in both these settings. However, the challenges faced by Italian women were mostly generational, as younger Italian Montrealers developed a more egalitarian rapport with Quebec and Canadian institutions over the course of their lifetimes. As women of European provenance, Italian immigrants and their children benefited from favourable immigration policies and the structural advantages that came with a hold on whiteness.[7] Perhaps Italian Montrealers were favoured over women from other backgrounds by funding bodies, which would explain, in part, the existence of the Centro Donne. With an emphasis on progressive Italian immigrants after the Second World War, this chapter will shed light on, as historians Donna Gabaccia and Franca Iacovetta explain, "perhaps the least understood aspects of Italian women's diasporic lives," namely "their role as resisters, protesters, and activists."[8] Indeed, historians of Italian immigrant women in North America have long pointed to the "invisible" or "lost" history of their activism.[9]

Starting with the background behind the establishment of the Centro Donne, before moving to its workings, the "Femmes immigrées, à nous la parole!" conference, and L'R des centres de femmes du Québec, the chapter stresses the importance of languages other than English or French to politics in Montreal. For some first-generation, working-class immigrants, comfort in a language other than their own was a luxury. Young people often eased the transition, taking on the burden of helping their elders to adapt. Grassroots organizers therefore served as go-betweens, connecting allophone women to feminist services or the welfare state. Although Italian and Italian-language sources are the focus here, the chapter implicitly argues for a more robust use of all third languages in Quebec and Canadian historical research. Not only could newcomers interact with other people like themselves in nonjudgmental, warm, and welcoming environments, but they could better engage with the receiving society through these spaces as well. In addition, the chapter highlights the importance of local, rather than transnational, political ties to the Centro Donne, in contrast to works of other scholars who have studied Italian immigrant women's activism in the early decades of the twentieth century.[10] Despite some ties with social movements in Italy, Italian Montrealers, for the most part, focused their energies on seeking pluralistic forms of belonging to Quebec society, as evidenced by their participation in initiatives led by immigrant women in the 1980s and 1990s and by the Italian-language feminist services that they provided. In contrast to their Caribbean counterparts, they did not propose radically different forms of citizenship.

Lastly, this chapter addresses the controversy over journalist and politician Lise Payette's documentary *Disparaître* (1989), pointing to the tensions within the ranks of the women's movement surrounding its release. The former minister of state for the status of women under René Lévesque's government, Payette implied that the Québécois nation was at risk of extinction due to insufficient measures to integrate newcomers. The immigrants in question, for Payette, were people of colour. Since Payette was chosen as the figurehead for a celebration of the fiftieth anniversary of women's suffrage in Quebec, the Collectif des femmes immigrantes du Québec boycotted the event. In part a response to the controversy, the 1992 conference "Un Québec féminin pluriel" tried to mend relations among grassroots organizers, with mixed results. Finally, the chapter hints at a new era of feminist activism, coinciding with the intensification of neo-liberal policies. As some women moved up the socio-economic ladder, taking advantage of expanding opportunities for women, others remained vulnerable to external forces.

Background

A group of young women with hybrid identities and experiences spear-headed the Centro Donne Italiane di Montreal. As explained by Assunta Sauro, one of the original founders, who had arrived in Montreal at the age of seven, the Centro Donne was the result of a merging of two groups.[11] The first, Il Collettivo, a student-run group that consisted of young Italian Mon-trealers starting to reflect on women's issues, was associated with the Asso-ciazione di Cultura Popolare Italo-Quebecchese, located on Fenelon Street in Saint-Michel, a mixed, leftist group that aimed to address the "essential" issues facing Italians "at work, in school, in the neighbourhood, and within the family."[12] The second, the Associazione Femminile di St-Michel, was made up of older women who gathered in a church basement. Isa Iasenza served as the connection between Il Collettivo and the Associazione Fem-minile di St-Michel. At the time, Iasenza worked for the St-Michel Centre des services sociaux du Montréal métropolitain. She was hired with the spe-cific mandate to develop services for the Italian community.[13] Chaired by Giuseppina Barbusci, the Associazione Femminile di St-Michel was more representative of the Italian-born generation than was Il Collettivo. Its mem-bership tended to be older workers. Barbusci, for example, came to Montreal in 1957 from southern Italy as an adult. Immediately upon arrival, she was hired by a men's suit factory, where she worked long hours and never fully learned English or French.[14]

It was women like these whom Sauro had in mind when she explained the Centro Donne's genesis: "We must consider that during the 1970s in

Quebec something was beginning to happen … People gathered and wanted to form groups with a specific purpose. And then various women's centres came into being. These centres fought for gender equality – equality at work, in politics, in the family, and in society. We saw francophones concerned with all these themes that affect women's lives, and we asked ourselves: 'And our women, where will they go, who will take care of them?' We decided to mobilize and do something as well."[15] Although the Centro Donne's foundation can in part be attributed to the heady atmosphere of the 1970s, its leaders aimed to provide services specific to first-generation immigrant women: "To overcome our destiny as 'new immigrants,' 'new wives and mothers,' and 'second-class citizens,' we felt the need to establish an autonomous women's centre where we could confront our needs, our anxieties, and our life experiences with other women who lived with the same social and family pressures."[16] Italian Montrealers sought to spearhead their own women's group as a means to, in the words of Sauro, more effectively "contribute to the lives of our people."[17]

After the Second World War, immigrants to Montreal built on a long-standing tradition of emigration that was closely tied to the history of the fledgling Italian nation-state. Unification (1861–70), the beginnings of mass migration (1870s), and colonialism (formally 1882) all started at around the same time in Italy, prompting scholars to underline the transnational character of the young country and its citizens.[18] From 1876 to 1976, more than 26 million Italians left the country, moving either temporarily or permanently to locales all over the world. Between the end of the war and 1976, more specifically, 7 million Italians followed in the footsteps of their predecessors. Hundreds of thousands of people left for the United States, Latin America (especially Argentina, Venezuela, and Brazil), and Australia. After a slow start, Canada became one of the most important receivers of Italian immigrants.[19] Although emigrants have come from every corner of the peninsula, the immigrant flows have been dominated mostly by peasants from the southernmost regions. Pulled by the logic of chain migration and the promise of a better life, these new arrivals were escaping *la miseria* of economic depression, overcrowding and difficult living conditions, and a pervasive sense of hopelessness, especially prevalent in the South. They left their country of origin and came to North America as members of extended families and networks of co-villagers. Initially, "many men preceded their families to Canada," as Franca Iacovetta explains, "but as wives and children joined them they sparked off the largest movement of sponsored families the country has ever witnessed." Upon arrival in Montreal and other urban centres, they began their transition "from being peasants in an underdeveloped rural economy to becoming proletarians in an urban industrial economy."[20] With its roots in the first half of the twentieth century, Montreal's Italian community ballooned in the postwar era, making Italians and their descendants the largest ethnic minority group in the greater Montreal area and Italian the third most widely spoken language in the city from 1961 until the early years of the twenty-first century.[21]

Most of the founders of the Centro Donne came to Montreal as children, thus going through the Quebec school system and acquiring English and French language skills. Their adaption to the city was eased, at least somewhat, by their youth. Their political engagement, however, was informed by their parents' difficulty in establishing a foothold in Montreal, or as one person explained, these young people sought to "revenge" their parents.[22] The city's Italian-language newspapers were rife with descriptions of the hardships faced by newcomers, regularly reporting on fatal workplace accidents and showing pictures of the wives and children left behind.[23] Whereas *Il Cittadino Canadese*, a newspaper with a more conservative outlook, rarely evoked women's concerns – one woman wrote the editor to ask, "Do we not exist?" – leftist men seemed somewhat more aware.[24] In the words of labour activist Francesco di Feo, Italian women in the garment industry endured "exploitation at its maximum," typically working long and gruelling hours with "no job-security, no days off, no holidays, no hygiene, lots of dust, 300 machines crammed one beside the other, no space to breathe, and the boss up there always watching women work."[25] For the Movimento Progressista Italo-Quebecchese, writing in 1971, "Our women are the ones who do the heaviest and most essential jobs for society, but unfortunately we also know that wages are not proportionate to the importance of this role."[26] Not only were they poorly paid and seldom unionized, but southern Europeans rarely learned much English or French, which further accentuated their marginalization. Segregation in the workforce was one reason. Giuseppina Barbusci, involved in the Centro Donne since its early days, described her time working at a men's suit factory: "I learned Campobassano, Calabrese, Sicilian, Abruzzese – all types of Italian. I learned a word from each, except English or French."[27] Until approximately the early 1970s, Italian women constituted the largest contingent of garment industry workers, and they were frequently nonunionized since employers systematically subjected them to intimidation in order to keep it that way.[28] Left-leaning newspapers put forth a critical narrative of the immigration experience in the workplace by refuting the "bourgeois ideals of integration" propagated by the more established Italian leadership and instead promoting "the unity of the exploited," namely Montreal's working class.[29]

These publications also brought to light the experiences of the children of Italian immigrants. According to the Movimento Progressista Italo-Quebecchese and the Associazione di Cultura Popolare Italo-Quebecchese, students of Italian origin faced the same challenges in the school system as their parents did in the workplace.[30] In an article entitled "School and the Children of Emigrants," the unnamed author outlined the ethnic and class biases omnipresent in the classroom, noting that "school was where young people became conscious of their second-class status." Yet rarely did a "political dimension" accompany this realization. They did not learn "the causes behind the existence of ghettos and first- and second-class citizens." As a result, Italian youth were made to feel ashamed of their background, leading to deep-seated confusion and insecurity.[31] Their experiences in Montreal mirrored southern Italians' tenuous place in their home country as well, where their cultures, darker complexions, and dialects were objects of disdain at the hands of northern elites. Standard Italian was slow to catch on in Italy, making regional dialects the mother tongue of most emigrants. They then passed these languages onto their children, who inherited an emigrant version of Italy's language question.[32] Due to a hostile work environment, long hours on the job, and poor language skills, Italian parents, moreover, tended to perceive the school system, and the receiving society in general, with wariness, as it could take their children away from them.[33] This insularity only exacerbated the generational conflict inevitably present within the immigrant family.[34] Since the values present in the schools contradicted those in the home, as explained by Isa Iasenza, another Centro Donne founder, young people were caught between two worlds. They either did not want to shed their roots out of an emotional attachment or could not do so in good conscience, as they were aware of the sacrifices made in their name. Meanwhile, their parents were fearful that their decision to emigrate would inadvertently tear the family apart.[35] Thus Italians and their children were in a double bind. By the 1970s and 1980s, however, young people had started to find their voice.

The ideological underpinnings of the Movimento Progressista Italo-Quebecchese and the Associazione di Cultura Popolare Italo-Quebecchese merit an aside because of the scant attention that they have received from historians, the personal connections between the two groups, as well as the latter's link to the early years of the Centro Donne. Overall, progressive Italian-speaking associations adhered to socialist ideologies, promoted the unity of workers across linguistic lines, and demonstrated openness to Quebec neo-nationalism. They also maintained that immigrants faced a unique form of marginalization.[36] For instance, the Movimento Progressista took a more divergent stance on language legislation than did the Fédération des associations italiennes du Québec or the Consiglio Educativo Italo-Canadese, arguing that the mobilization for a French Quebec was a "just demand" and an "integral part of the Québécois people's struggle for liberation."[37] A faction of the Italian community opposed language legislation once neo-nationalists started to focus on the children of immigrants and their presence in the English-language sector, maintaining their preference for free choice and bilingual or trilingual schools. The rising petite bourgeoisie formed several associations during this period to mobilize against the push for French-language education for all children of immigrants and francophone Quebecers. Their logic was principally economic, as they believed that an English-language education would guarantee their children a better future. In contrast, progressive Italian Montrealers focused their concern elsewhere, seeing no choice but to unify with the Québécois working class: "We must recognize the struggle of the people of Quebec against US imperialism and Anglo-Canadian colonialism as legitimate and take part in it because the struggle of the people of Quebec and our struggle against the exploiters are the same struggle. We can change the present state of things only if we are united as a common front against our enemy."[38]

Due to their similar socio-economic situation, then, the Movimento Progressista Italo-Quebecchese understood working-class francophone Quebecers and Italians as "class brothers."[39] Since the world of Italian immigrants (both women and men) who were active in unions – such as the Confédération des syndicats nationaux, the Amalgamated Clothing and Textile Workers

Union, and the Italian-language locals of the International Ladies' Garment Workers' Union – remains largely unknown, it is difficult to paint a full picture of this rapport.[40] But some of the children of immigrants more fully expressed this affinity. Part of several progressive Italian-speaking groups and a public supporter of language legislation throughout the 1970s, Marco Micone immigrated to Montreal from Italy in 1958 at the age of thirteen. Rejected by the French-language school in his neighbourhood, he enrolled at an English Catholic institution in Montreal East, attended overwhelmingly by other Italian immigrants. Before Bill 101, some French-language schools in Montreal refused children of immigrants, including Italians. Although not necessarily a policy, this practice of exclusion did occur.[41] In the English-language sector, however, Micone felt a "double marginalization," never truly mastering English nor integrating into an English-Canadian milieu. He was also isolated from his French-speaking neighbours.[42] This distance would disappear after he read Gabrielle Roy's *Bonheur d'occasion* (1945), a haunting portrait of Saint-Henri during the Great Depression. Ending his alienation from his adopted society, Micone finally realized that there were non-Italians who "shared his deepest concerns."[43]

These perspectives were echoed by the Movimento Progressista in its periodical *Il Lavoratore: Organo del movimento progressista italo-quebecchese*, which levelled scathing remarks at all factions of the "ruling class" and disparaged the *Montreal Gazette* for constantly invoking Italians' demographic weight, as if they could single-handedly determine the language spoken in Montreal.[44] The Parti Québécois, largely "animated by the francophone bourgeoisie," was accused of "instrumentalizing the language question to divide workers," substituting socialism for a single-minded nationalism.[45] Referring to the nascent class cleavage within the community, the Movimento Progressista derided the Italian-language media for, in its defence of the notion of "social peace," insinuating that immigrants should remain deferent simply because they were offered a job.[46] Progressive members of the younger generation were thus much more critical and assertive than many of their elders or even their peers. They were also willing to align their fate with that of francophones.

Whereas some members of their community associated English with social mobility, for these young people, there was a sense that an English-language education was not necessarily a ticket to success. Since more white-collar jobs demanded high levels of education, ambitious youngsters would not only have to speak English but also need to obtain a university degree. Once on campus, "surrounded by people who spoke a better-quality English and were of a higher social standing," they found themselves in a minority position. The "possibilities of integration" for Italians at elitist institutions such as McGill University "were practically nonexistent." According to *Il Lavoratore*, Italian Montrealers tended to associate only with other alienated peoples, namely francophone Quebecers, other children of immigrants, and African Canadians, as they were constantly reminded of their difference and thus experienced the same "mortification" at McGill as their parents did at work.[47] This marginality was relative and should not be exaggerated, as the university and indeed the entire Quebec school system, as we have seen, privileged Eurocentric curricula and European peoples. It is difficult to tell, moreover, whether Black, Indigenous, or other students of colour recognized Italian Montrealers as existing on the margins of the institution. Probably not, as Italians existed in the same "structured ignorance" as other Euro-Quebecers.[48] However, young Italian Montrealers did have unique, if at times incomplete, language skills, the latter reflecting their allophone working-class origins.[49] Like many children of Italian immigrants, Isa Iasenza spent her childhood in Saint-Michel and Montreal North after arriving in Montreal at age five, speaking English at school, French on the streets, and Italian at home. When interviewed regarding her parents' choice of an English-language education, Isa Iasenza responded, "It was automatic … It was a time when it was like that." After studying at McGill, she became a social worker with the Centre des services sociaux du Montréal métropolitain.[50] With high levels of multilingualism and increasing levels of social capital, these young people were able to serve as advocates for themselves and for their community.

Women had trouble carving out an equal place within the larger Italian community. There appeared to be very little room for discussion on gender inequalities in the Italian-language press. *Il Cittadino Canadese*, for instance, published several articles ridiculing the women's movement both in Canada and in Italy.[51] As journalist Michele Pirone wrote, "The feminist movement is in many ways 'a youthful fever.'" Referring to women's protests in Rome, he continued, "After a while, women will leave the streets to find a job … and a husband."[52] In another article, Claudio Antonelli maintained that francophone Quebecers were exaggerating the challenges that women faced in Quebec. Compared to other societies, the journalist argued, North Americans had relatively little work to do, and more importantly, women elsewhere did their duties "without complaining."[53] Although far less hostile, the Associazione di Cultura Popolare Italo-Quebecchese similarly elided women's concerns, prompting the founding of Il Collettivo. The approximately ten women involved, after hearing about the possibility of a government grant, got together in the basement of one woman's home to pitch the idea of starting a women's centre. Il Collettivo, even if partly "in agreement" with what it referred to as the more "traditional" aspects of the community, still felt the "need for change." Wanting the Italian community to benefit from the larger push for gender equality, it intended for the centre to "give back" and to help immigrant women acquire "emotional," "social," and "economic" autonomy. With the know-how, these women were successful, founding the Centro Donne Italiane di Montreal in 1978 with funding from Centraide. By merging two groups, Il Collettivo and the Associazione Femminile di St-Michel, the Centro Donne managed to join younger and older women from the beginning.[54] Since then, the Centro Donne has consisted of an intergenerational activist project. Although the ethos of the centre came from younger women, who had spent most of their lives in Montreal, their focus was on the women who needed the greatest support: their mothers' generation.

Writing in a special issue of *Des luttes et des rires de femmes* focused on immigrant women in 1978, the Centro Donne's founders laid out their feminist politics. By doing so, they pushed the Movimento Progressista Italo-Quebecchese's and the Associazione di Cultura Popolare Italo-Quebecchese's critique of emigration, the dynamics of receiving societies, and the Italian community even further:[55] "We are a group of women of Italian origin who are trying to escape the control of community structures set up by the notables. Throughout our lives, we have been controlled by the state through a father, a boss, a priest, a notable, who decided for us, who controlled our life, our body, who denied our autonomy as women. We were made to understand that it was up to us, as it was up to our mothers, to perpetuate the role of the immigrant by producing and reproducing cheap labour."[56] Thus women gave birth to children who were destined to leave their hometowns in order to work in the factories of another locale. This cycle of underdevelopment, reproduction, and emigration resulted in strong notions of social control, with women living under the thumb of male honour and remaining locked in patriarchal families. After arriving in Montreal, they experienced only more restraints as their male relatives struggled to adapt to a new reality. Notables ran the community's charitable organizations, using them to "control the life of the Italian community and reinforce the reactionary and sexist ideology against women."[57] The long hours that women spent doing domestic labour, combined with their relative isolation from the receiving society, made them ripe for exploitation. The Centro Donne's founders agreed, however, that no one could do the work of creating a social space for them; they would have to do it on their own, for themselves, and for the community. "We try to do this despite the difficulties," they wrote. "There is no telling whether we will survive or be defeated. But, in any case, maybe some of the ghetto walls will come down." In this vein, the Centro Donne sought links with other immigrant women to see what they could accomplish together. They also wanted Québécois feminists to overcome their stereotypes regarding immigrant women, to strengthen the women's movement, and to analyze the woman question in all its complexity.[58]

Over time, the Centro Donne accomplished these goals, although coalition politics among immigrant women in Montreal should not be overstated. Foreign-born women occupied diverse social locations, impacting dynamics within the women's movement.[59] When compared to other immigrant-led organizations, moreover, the Centro Donne's founders directed most of its energies toward the Italian-born generation in Montreal. This form of "communal" or feminist consciousness, when juxtaposed with that of Caribbean women, illustrates the differing political stakes for immigrant or diasporic women: some women aimed for pluralism and services for newcomers, whereas others needed complete social change for all generations. Immigrant women were thus a heterogeneous group of people, with more differences than similarities among them in many cases. Nevertheless, at times, they worked together, joining forces based on this shared identity. From the 1980s onward, members of the Centro Donne were well represented in the ranks of the Collectif des femmes immigrantes du Québec.[60] They were also among the organizers of the landmark 1982 conference "Femmes immigrées, à nous la parole!" In the early 1990s, the Centro Donne joined L'R des centres de femmes du Québec, formally making connections with other women's centres in Montreal and Quebec. They engaged in all these initiatives while serving their community, bringing the women's movement to its doorstep.

Centro Donne Italiane di Montreal

At first, the Centro Donne was in Montreal's East End on St-Michel Boulevard and then on Christophe Colomb Avenue, later moving to Fleury Street in Ahuntsic in the 1990s. At the time of its opening, the centre had two full-time employees and a budget to cover the rent and its activities. The Centro Donne's location in Italian neighbourhoods allowed for its success, attracting the women who lived nearby. Speaking about the need for a women's-only space, the founders stressed the long hours on the job, the "double duty," and the lack of social outlets for women. For the younger women, however, founding the centre came with certain sacrifices. These women, students or recent graduates, renounced their social lives to give their "heart and soul" to the project. They needed to incorporate the Centro Donne, establish an administrative council, and most importantly, define its objective. The latter was the hardest, as each founder had her own vision. The group was divided between women who saw the Centro Donne as a basis for radical feminism and others who wanted to focus on providing services to newcomers. Meetings were long and heated. Some women even left the fledgling centre.[61] Assunta Sauro recalled the "passion" and the "idealism," as well as the "enormous amount of work, dedication, enthusiasm and love for the feminist cause."[62] In the end, the Centro Donne aimed to increase Italian immigrant women's "participation in the social and political life of Quebec." With culturally specific programming, the founders promoted the "emancipation" and "autonomy" of Italian women, furthering their "adjustment" to Quebec society. In service of the community, the Centro Donne's mandate was to create a meeting space in order "break the isolation" and "loneliness" experienced by immigrant women. They also sought to promote "consciousness raising" and links with women of other backgrounds.[63] Organized as a collective, the Centro Donne was "autonomous" and "autogestito" (i.e., under worker management).[64]

From 1978 to 1985, the Centro Donne developed its expertise in the provision of assistance for Italian-speaking women. Numerous information and educational sessions were held, addressing everything from literacy, unions, and legal issues[65] to menopause and family planning.[66] It held a series of public events as well, including two conferences, "Ruolo e problemi delle donne immigrate nella nostra società" ("The Role and Problems of Immigrant Women in Our Society") in 1978 and "Violenza fatta alle donne" ("Violence against Women") in 1981.[67] The Centro Donne, in short, addressed issues of common concern for immigrant Italian women, becoming a public face for feminism. Like other women's centres in Montreal, the Centro Donne's approach to empowering women was, at least in part, quasi-therapeutic. Feminist scholars have pointed to the depoliticizing effects of a therapeutic logic, where instead of using a political analysis of a patriarchal socio-economic system, grassroots organizations begin to focus on finding solutions for individual women.[68] Over time, the therapeutic element behind this work may have stalled a deeper structural critique, but even in the 1980s, women's centres were aware of the potential shortcomings behind this tactic, recognizing the possibility of passivity and dependence. Still, there was something unique about these settings, especially in these early years. For allophone communities, the sense of possibility was even greater, namely the supportive environment, collectivist ethos, and overt feminist messaging. Further, the Centro Donne, at times, could not refer women to social services because of the language barrier and thus had to take matters into its own hands.[69]

Seen as a pathway to social citizenship, language courses for first-generation immigrant women were one of the mainstays of the Centro Donne Italiane di Montreal. In the centre's early days, these courses were funded and taught by representatives from Quebec's Ministère des communautés culturelles et de l'immigration. Under its "custom-made courses" programing, the ministry, with the help of grassroots organizers, was able to reach women who were ineligible for French-language courses through the Centre d'orientation et de formation des immigrants. In the late 1970s, Italian, Haitian, and Spanish-speaking women were able to benefit from this initiative. From 1978 to 1980, the Centro Donne, the Federazione Italiana Lavoratori Emigrati e Famiglie, the Centre local de services communautaires (CLSC) Rivière-des-Prairies, the Notre-Dame du Mont-Carmel Church, and even a woman who lent out her basement in the borough of Saint-Leonard hosted French-language courses. At the Centro Donne, a total of forty-five students took twelve sessions of French classes. According to their teachers, the average age was approximately forty years old. These were women who had been in Quebec for quite some time, ten years at least. Whereas they knew very little French at the beginning of the class, they had made quite a bit of progress by the end. Moreover, they got the chance to experience additional formal schooling, appreciating the opportunity to sit in the classroom. As the instructors attested afterward, "The graduation ceremony at the end of the year is a real celebration because they receive their 'first diploma.'"[70] Indeed, very few southern Italian women had the luxury of staying in school past the third or fifth grade. In 1951, for example, one-quarter of the population over six years of age was illiterate, compared with one-sixteenth in the North. In some areas, such as parts of Sicily and Basilicata, illiteracy surpassed 40 per cent.[71] For the community organizers and the teachers, these French courses were more than simply a certificate. Rather, they were a chance for allophone women to acquire self-confidence as well as familiarity with the francophone community.[72]

In the 1980s, the Centro Donne got its first newsletter off the ground. Published from 1983 to 1988, *Il Bollettino Centro Donne Montreal* contained Italian-language articles, with the occasional piece in English or French. According to its first issue, "We need to reflect more on ourselves, on the place that we occupy in our community and in the world that surrounds us. In this context, our newsletter can become a tool, a means to communicate in writing what we live, feel, and desire to all the other women who read it."[73] It was in the pages of *Il Bollettino* that Italian-speaking women were exposed to the ideologies embraced by the Centro Donne's founders, as well as to subversive analyses of the community to which they belonged. Sometimes going no further, the monthly newsletter simply wrote in black and white what most women surely felt. In an article entitled "The Italian Canadian Woman," one woman wrote that in her view, "according to the Italian family, women were important only for procreation, only to be a wife and mother." Upon marriage, a woman was supposed to "lose her own identity, ignore her own thoughts and emotions." Speaking to the difficult process behind emancipation, the unnamed author referred to the "modern woman, who today is in search of herself and leaves home, freeing herself above all from the chains of an abstract ideology. It seems easy, but in reality the experience is traumatic. Courage seems to be the only way to continue down the chosen path because the psychological struggle is the hardest battle." She continued, "The victim of her own altruism, the Italian woman loses a sense of her own importance for the benefit of others. Sometimes she feels like she is a prisoner of her own thoughts." The author stressed the importance of treating daughters and sons equally as the role of women in society evolved, pointing out the necessity of opening her eyes to a "complex world."[74] *Il Bollettino* put forth an internal critique without, however, a judgmental or condescending attitude.[75] The author acknowledged that the "domineering" attitudes of Italian fathers stemmed from their "low status" in broader Montreal society, noting the "dangers" that this domination posed to the physical and mental health of women.[76]

Il Bollettino contested the male-centric image of the community presented by other community publications, putting forth another view of emigrant life in Montreal. Several articles addressed Italian women's emotional well-being, openly talking about depression and isolation. In one article, for example, an anonymous author posed the question, "How many of us have mornings when we wake up and ask ourselves, 'Is this it?' Soon afterward, we feel guilty, full of rage and anxiety, accompanied by the following question: 'What's happening to me?'" As this author wrote, "In general, women close in on themselves. They don't talk to anyone about their difficulty because they feel embarrassed and because they think that they are alone in feeling dissatisfied."[77] In another article, entitled "Women and Health: Solitude," the author asserted that loneliness, whether "occasional," "chronic," or "existential," can lead to depression or daydreaming, characterized by fantasies about satisfactory relationships.[78] According to *Il Bollettino*, women had difficulty forming healthy relationships with one another because, after they returned from work, they were "exhausted" and "taciturn." They then had to cook, clean, and get ready for the next day. There was always something waiting for them, "either in the kitchen or the bedroom."[79] Since the Centro Donne was involved in the International Wages for Housework Campaign, a movement with northern Italian origins, several articles by Mariangela di Domenico and Antonella Perzia denounced housework within the larger framework of capitalism, where women's free labour in the home served as the uncompensated base for the industrial economy. The authors also encouraged women to "stop feeling guilty" and stressed the need for an equitable division of household labour, deemed a "woman's right."[80]

In 1984, Il Bollettino published several articles on Catholicism as Pope John Paul II was set to come to Montreal. This visit, as stated in the opening editorial of the October issue, "did not leave the Centro Donne indifferent"; rather, its members "denounced the negative influence that the Catholic Church had on women."[81] The centre supported women's right to free contraception and abortion on demand, publishing its official position in the same issue. The newsletter stated that these matters should remain in the hands of women rather than the state, the church, or the medical establishment. The Centro Donne sought the greater diffusion of information to avoid unwanted pregnancies, free access to birth control, the abolishment of articles 251 and 252 of the penal code, and increased medical access for immigrant women on temporary work visas.[82] On the next page, Antonella Perzia authored an article asking whether procreation was the only reason for sexual relations, arguing against the notion that sex was "dirty." She maintained that denying women the use of contraception would be equivalent to banning medicine, pointing to the nuanced discourse around these issues for ostensibly Catholic women.[83] Aware that the majority of the community's women were practising Catholics, at least to a degree, they chose to work within this framework.[84] In another article, Perzia argued that it was in fact possible to reconcile "feminism" and "faith." In this view, sexism within Catholicism reflected male chauvinism in a patriarchal society, not vice versa. According to Perzia, some Centro Donne members, then, went against the prevailing notion that "the majority of self-identified feminists weren't believers and [that] the believers weren't feminist."[85]

Breaking the code of silence surrounding abuse, Il Bollettino tried to convince the community's women to do the same. The newsletter provided advice to battered women, telling them to go to the doctor and seek legal advice.[86] In one article, "Family Violence," the author provided basic information, explaining that domestic violence cut across ethnic, religious, and socio-economic lines. Pointing to the informational role played by the Centro Donne, Il Bollettino informed its readership that spousal abuse was a criminal act, rather than the fault of the victim, and that denouncing the aggressor to the police did not necessarily result in incarceration. In the same article, the author encouraged women to talk about what happened behind closed doors and stated that, if needed, the centre could help find temporary refuge or legal assistance.[87] Centro Donne intervention workers accompanied Italian-speaking women to court or to the doctor, sometimes serving as translators for battered women in these settings. They frequently dealt with the aftermath suffered by women who signed forms that they did not understand. To this day, a trilingual lawyer comes to the Centro Donne once a week to provide free legal advice.[88] More than providing victims with advice or a ready ear, the centre engaged in prevention work with the broader Italian community. In 1997, for example, it initiated a roundtable on domestic violence, televised on Tele-Italia. Afterward, the Centro Donne received several phone calls asking for more information. *Il Corriere Italiano*, an Italian-language newspaper, published several articles on the issue at the insistence of the Centro Donne.[89] Regardless of the problem, the administration strove to foster a culture where seeking assistance was no longer viewed as shameful.[90]

Generational tension was openly acknowledged in *Il Bollettino* and steps were taken to rectify the situation. The Centro Donne organized activities for young girls, stressing the importance of good relationships with parents and friends, as well as the value of self-esteem and education.[91] With the aim of promoting dialogue, the centre geared its programming in this area toward older women. Giuseppina Barbusci, for instance, organized a discussion session to explicitly address mother-daughter relationships.[92] In conjunction with another Italian community organization, the Centro Donne held a workshop to discuss a range of issues, namely family, work, and childrearing. Parents were encouraged to embrace the tactics of "communication" and "comprehension" rather than authoritarian approaches. These strategies were thought to be a means to ease the cultural differences among mothers and daughters.[93] Indeed, young people fought with their parents, including their mothers, over the ability to leave the house. For girls especially, their parents' mentality prohibited the North American style of dating and socializing.[94] The Centro Donne aimed to provide avenues for young women to seek advice because most "had no one to talk to."[95] In the view of member Maria Morabito, writing in the 1990s, Italian women in Montreal were placed under significant family pressure regarding marriage, lifestyle, and tradition. With divorce, for example, came stigmatization and alienation. They were raised by stricter than average parents, whose parenting techniques were out of step with those of the broader society.[96] The effects of immigration therefore played out at even the most intimate levels of family life, with women often the ones adversely affected.[97] Since the Centro Donne was multigenerational, its membership was able to at least try to productively work through these differences.

From the beginning until now, the Centro Donne has demonstrated a commitment to broader feminist principles. The centre joined L'R des centres de femmes du Québec in 1992 and participated in the anti-poverty march Du pain et des roses in 1995.[98] Over the years, the Centro Donne mobilized in favour of poverty-reducing measures across Canada, attending rallies in Quebec City and Ottawa.[99] Similarly, Centro Donne members denounced the sexism that they saw in the Italian community. Antonella Perzia, for example, wrote a letter to the editor of *Il Cittadino Canadese* in the 1980s after the newspaper published a questionable article.[100] The transformations engendered by the Centro Donne were also personal. Its programming effectively broke immigrant women's isolation, providing a women's-only space that made participants feel comfortable and motivated them to attend. Domenica Casola, for her part, "found comfort, kindness, and lots of encouragement" at the "remarkable" Centro Donne, whose staff assisted her in "learning to love herself" and acquiring "self-confidence."[101] Both the participants and the founders gained valuable lessons in self-empowerment. Writing in the 1980s, Isa Iasenza editorialized, "The opening and organization of Centro Donne Italiane was for me – like for many others – the realization of a dream, a desire, a will to create something for myself and the Italian women of Montreal." According to this co-founder, her involvement led to vital "personal growth," "knowledge of the Italian community," "political experience with regard to organizing, planning, contact with the public, etc.," "a feeling of belonging to something outside her family and her job," and "so many other things impossible to put into words."[102] Feminism, then, was a deeply affective experience.

The Centro Donne was loosely defined as a place to "belong," receive "advice," "increase personal autonomy," "overcome difficulties," and "discuss freely among women."[103] Participants considered the centre a "big family"[104] and described their time there as like being at "home."[105] These ideologies of home and belonging are reminiscent of Donna Gabaccia's notion of an

Italian diasporic culture, where "home" has been regarded as a "face-to-face community – not the idea of a people rooted to a place, but the place itself."[106] There has been a scholarly discussion regarding whether Italian emigrants constituted a diaspora as circulatory migrations connected villages of origins with workplaces worldwide.[107] Although family and cultural ties linked Centro Donne members to their place of birth, sources do not indicate a sustained sense of transnational feminism on the part of this organization comparable to that of Caribbean women. Quite simply, the stakes were not the same. Moreover, Italy's postwar status as a democratic country may have reinforced the importance of local, rather than transnational, political ties.[108] Even if there was the occasional article in *Il Bollettino* on happenings in Italy, such as when a women's political party was formed in the country,[109] Italian feminist theory was seemingly never referred to, perhaps due to its inapplicability to the lives of emigrants. According to gender studies scholar Vincenza Perilli, much of feminist theory in Italy held up an essentialist definition of womanhood, making differences among women difficult to conceptualize.[110]

Nevertheless, the Centro Donne was affiliated with the Federazione Italiana Lavoratori Emigrati e Famiglie, an international labour organization founded in Rome in 1967 by Carlo Levi. Members of Montreal's multigenerational branch of the organization, consisting of both students and workers, read *l'Unità*, the organ of the Italian Communist Party, demonstrating the internationalizing of these ideas and their influence on some Italian immigrants.[111] In the 1980s, some of the Centre Donne's founders, including Margherita Morsella, Tiziana Carafa, Roberta Giorgetti, Assunta Sauro, and Marie Antoinette Simoncini, established a women's committee within the Federazione Italiana Lavoratori Emigrati e Famiglie to reach out to workers in the garment industry and to second-generation Italian Montrealers. In 1988, for example, they participated in the Seconda Conferenza Nazionale dell'Emigrazione.[112] In Rome, delegates argued that emigration policies as well as the successes and challenges of Italian communities abroad should constitute national issues. Special mention was given to emigrant women, specifically their right to equality in the workforce, to professional training, and to social integration. Participants also called on the Italian government to organize a national conference on immigration because, by then, Italy had become a receiving as well as a sending society.[113]

"Femmes immigrées, à nous la parole!"

The Centro Donne prioritized making links with other immigrant women. Although influenced by political ideas with Italian origins, as evidenced by the centre's participation in the International Wages for Housework Campaign – indeed, Mariarosa Dalla Costa published an article on the links between reproduction and emigration[114] – Italian Montrealers tended to mobilize around the identity of immigrant women, even if the centre's workers were limited in this respect by their heavy workload.[115] Starting in 1981, the Centro Donne became a member of the Table de concertation des femmes immigrées, working alongside the Conseil du statut de la femme, the Centre d'information et de référence pour femmes, the Ligue des femmes, the Centre social d'aide aux immigrants, the Association personnel domestique, and the FFQ. The umbrella group organized a conference – "Femmes immigrées, à nous la parole!" – to "create common solutions to specific problems." Funded by the Ministère des communautés culturelles et de l'immigration, its members sought concrete policy changes in response to recent developments.[116] That same year, the provincial government formulized its approach regarding diversity and immigration, publishing *Autant de façons d'être québécois*. The document asserted Quebec's role as a receiving society, emphasizing the French language as a marker of belonging. The publication enacted several important anti-racist measures, promoting, for example, anti-discriminatory hiring practices in the civil service.[117] According to the Table de concertation, there was still much work to be done in matters of socio-economic equality. Their timing was right, as the Comité d'implantation du Plan d'action à l'intention des communautés culturelles, announced by the provincial government a few months before, aimed to increase the participation of immigrant communities in all sectors of Quebec society, from health care to social services.[118]

Throughout the summer of 1981, the Centro Donne Italiane di Montreal took part in a series of meetings to plan the conference, hammering out the details alongside other women's groups. During these meetings, participants raised questions, such as "How to overcome the language barrier? How to ensure proper representation from all communities?"[119] A working document outlined the procedure for the conference, explaining, for example, that workshop leaders were expected to verify the French-language ability of each attendee and, if needed, to ensure assistance with translation from another participant. Similarly, animators were told to "respect language difficulties," accommodate "the rhythm of the participant," "slow down the conversation if necessary," "summarize regularly to ensure comprehension," and "foster the participation of all people present."[120] When Adeline Chancy attended one of the meetings, representing the Comité d'implantation, the Maison d'Haïti founder was also unhappy to see the lack of funding available for simultaneous translation. Nevertheless, Chancy agreed with the Table de concertation regarding the necessity of limiting the languages of the gathering to French and English.[121] About a month before the conference, the Table de concertation had an extended conversation about panel chairs, debating whether a representative of the FFQ should co-preside to demonstrate collaboration between immigrant and Québécois women. After a long conversation, attendees decided on the original format, as they believed that immigrant women might feel more comfortable if they led the conference.[122] Thus increased state funding arguably enabled immigrant women to encounter each other in a more sustained fashion. The activities that they planned were focused on building a genuinely pluralistic democracy.

The conference, held from 4 to 6 June 1982, was a novel gathering. The Table de concertation sent out invitations to any association claiming to assist immigrant women, including the Association of Muslim Women at the University of Montreal and the Congress of Black Women of Canada, as well as multi-ethnic associations such as the Mouvement québécois pour combattre le racisme and immigrant organizations like the Maison d'Haïti and the Greek Workers' Association. (The history of many of these organizations still begs to be written.) According to the conference proceedings, 198 women attended, representing thirty-two "nationalities" and fifty-two nongovernmental organizations. Whereas 14 of these women declared Québécois as their nationality and many different organizations were represented, the largest pluralities went to women claiming an Italian or Haitian background. Attendees discussed the place of immigrant women in the family, in the workforce, and in Quebec society. At the end of the three days, participants made 110 recommendations to the Ministère des communautés culturelles et de l'immigration, proposing improved French-language training, protection in the workforce, reinforcement of laws on minimum wage, recognition of foreign diplomas and qualifications, and more rigid anti-discrimination measures. The conference proceedings, written entirely in French, provide a wealth of information on the gathering. Still, "no written document," as explained in the publication, "could translate the joyous atmosphere and the intense work conducted over three days by the participants and the organizers."[123]

These sorts of state-directed initiatives provided community-based activists with a wider audience. Danae Savides, a member of the Table de concertation and the CSF, gave the welcoming address. Born in Egypt to Greek parents, Savides had come to Montreal at the age of eleven. After protesting the Vietnam War in high school, Savides was launched into activism when a right-wing military junta took power in Greece in 1967. Since her family was outside of Greece, she could oppose the regime without fear of reprisals. Her anti-junta activism led to her involvement with the Greek Workers' Association, and within this organization, she formed a women's committee, as she decided that the best way to help her compatriots would be to get involved in social justice work in Montreal.[124] Savides then frequented the Communist Party, even though she considered herself more of an anarchist, and eventually became a member of the Ligue des femmes, a Marxist women's group. Shortly afterward, Savides was appointed to the CSF and began travelling between Montreal and Quebec City.[125] In her opening remarks, she reminded audience members of the stereotypes that women like her confronted: "The stereotype of the immigrant woman is that of a hard-working but shy woman who does not take initiative and is sometimes completely submissive to her husband. Those we come across who do not reflect this image are seen as exceptions."[126] Although she felt the need to bring together foreign-born women under one organization, Savides recognized the particularity of each community's needs at the 1982 conference, specifying that the problems faced by southern Europeans were much different from those confronted by Vietnamese or Latin American women. She also signalled Black immigrant women's triple jeopardy, demonstrating at least an awareness of her racial privilege.[127] By the early 1970s, demographics in Montreal had indeed changed, with increasing numbers of women arriving from the Caribbean (especially Haiti), East Asia (such as Vietnam and Cambodia), South America, and North Africa.[128] Perhaps the presence of southern Europeans in spaces like the csf indicated that they were favoured over women of other backgrounds.

The conference was divided into four workshops: immigrant women in the family, in the workplace, in the community, and in Quebec society. In the first session, participants highlighted the difficulty that allophone women faced in accessing information on family services, women's "double duty," and the marital problems that arose from starting over in a different cultural setting. These women pointed to the increased possibility of domestic violence, on the one hand, and to the isolation that came with divorce in an adopted country, on the other. Drawing on their experience in community settings, attendees proposed that the Ministre des affaires sociales et de la justice find a way to maintain family unity.[129] Immigrant women, then, walked a tightrope, and the conference's recommendations provide ample indications of why the tightrope was so thin. For example, participants advocated family planning and free abortion on demand; however, they suggested that employees meet with men and women separately and in their mother tongue. Attendees appealed to the feminist movement, asking women's organizations to increase the presence of immigrant women within their ranks. They hoped to see the Table de concertation expand to include more associations.[130] Many of the same themes carried over to the workshop on the workplace. Participants emphasized the lack of resources available to allophones, the majority of whom were women, pointing to the barriers faced by those who spoke neither French nor English. They also demanded that employers recognize foreign qualifications, practise affirmative action, and improve conditions in the garment industry.[131] Similarly, they hoped that the government would put in place the means to ensure adequate working conditions for domestic workers, hire women from the appropriate communities to serve as liaisons, and work to diffuse information on worker's rights in a wide range of languages.[132]

These questions crystallized in the last two workshops on immigrant women vis-à-vis broader society, where participants made sure to stress that they were speaking on behalf of themselves, not their entire communities. Members of the audience believed that they were perceived in negative terms by their Montreal-born counterparts and received a cold welcome. Feelings of isolation were compounded by the role that they

played within their own families and communities as "cultural guardians."
In charge of passing down language and tradition, fighting negative forms
of assimilation in a frequently hostile context, these women were under a
lot of pressure to ensure the well-being of the next generation. Attendees
said that the mainstream media underestimated the presence and contribution of immigrants, and they criticized the "ethnic media" outlets for
perpetuating traditionalist views on gender roles and for making it all the
more difficult for women to participate in community organizations.[133] Participants recommended, among other measures, state-sponsored, subtitled
television programs to educate the general public on immigrant women
from various countries, curriculum reform to eliminate racial stereotypes,
and a popular education program to explain immigration in its historical
context.[134] Throughout the conference, delegates were also able to discuss
issues of a more personal, subjective nature. Some women, for example,
shared that although born in Montreal, they still felt like immigrants, as
they were constantly reminded of their presumed foreignness. Notions such
as "freedom of speech" were highly relative because when immigrants explained their "real problems," they were treated as "ungrateful." In sum,
there was the general impression that foreign-born women had to be "twice
as good as Québécois women" and "four times as good as Québécois men"
in order to do well in the workforce.[135]

Women were able to speak on their own behalf about the problems that
they faced in their adopted country, thus finding the conference liberating.
As reported in *Le Devoir* by Renée Rowan, well known for writing on feminism in Quebec, some attendees felt like first-class citizens for the first time
since arriving in Montreal.[136] As the two groups rarely had the opportunity
to interact and discuss their common problems, participants hoped to see
another conference – this time, one conceived to build bridges between
immigrant and Québécois women.[137] In anticipation of such a gathering, a
number of attendees joined the FFQ. As president Huguette Lapointe-Roy
wrote, "We wish to extend a special welcome to them because they are an
asset to the Quebec community." As she explained, "Some 'hot' issues at the
FFQ have become even more pressing for our compatriots of other origins."[138] *La vie en rose* and *Communiqu'elles* covered "Femmes immigrées,
à nous la parole!" as well, describing the numerous barriers faced by immi-

grant women.[139] During the conference, participants suggested that the Conseil du statut de la femme's *Gazette des femmes* publish articles reflecting the diversity of women in Quebec.[140] In the months following the conference, feminists wondered what happened to resolutions after they were passed to politicians, especially in the 1980s, an era of budget cuts and austerity, when immigrants were once again perceived as "job stealers."[141] By the 1980s, then, immigrant and racialized women had started to make their needs known to broader society, as well as to quarters of the women's movement where francophone Quebecers predominated.[142] In comparison to the previous two decades, the voices and concerns of non-Québécois feminists were present in a wider range of activist settings and publications.

As for Italian Montrealers, their circumstances were changing, even if they safeguarded certain linguistic and cultural specificities.[143] In 1982, *Quaderni culturali: Pubblicazione dell'associazione di cultura popolare italo-quebecchese* interviewed Italian women who had lost their jobs during a recent wave of textile factory closings. Although they were affected by the economic downturn, they were mothers of adult children who could work, or already did, in the tertiary sector. Their Haitian and Vietnamese colleagues, in contrast, were much more likely to have school-age children, such that every factory closure meant that someone in the community was living an even more precarious existence.[144] Moreover, Italian and Portuguese garment workers were known to prefer hiring women from their own communities and to favour them in the allocation of work, pointing to the relative advantages acquired with a longer stay in the country.[145] In this evolving context, some Italian community leaders deplored their counterparts' apparent lack of concern for the more marginalized.[146] As an indication of the role that the community played in the maintenance of white power and privilege in the metropolis, Italian and Greek landlords in Montreal East, for instance, had been known to discriminate against Haitian families and other people of colour.[147] Through the Centro Donne, first-generation Montrealers continued to reach out to other immigrant women, more often than not those who were southern European. In the 1990s, for example, the centre hosted a conference on family violence with the Greek and Portuguese organizations Bouclier d'Athéna and Centre d'aide à la famille portugaise.[148] Mainly for funding purposes, furthermore, the Centro

Donne Italiane di Montreal changed its name in 2014 to Centro donne sol-
idali e impegnate/Centre des femmes solidaires et engagées. The Centro
Donne is still trilingual and Italian, but it is no longer attached to Italian
Montrealers in name.

Un "rendez-vous manqué"

By the 1980s and 1990s, Québécois feminists had started to reflect on competing understandings and definitions of feminism. Historian Micheline
Dumont hypothesizes that the third United Nations World Conference on
Women, held in Nairobi in 1985, constituted a major turning point for francophone Quebecers, who returned from their trip completely changed by
what they had learned. As a result of this experience, they became more
attuned to the power dynamics within the women's movement at home.[149]
This shift was apparent within L'R des centres de femmes du Québec. The
network never overtly excluded racialized, immigrant, or Indigenous
women.[150] In fact, it recognized these groups' right to organize according
to their specificities. However, as explained by Françoise David, the president of the organization at the time, a former En lutte! member, and the
future FFQ president, "The discussions surrounding this exception ... indicate that we need to deepen our understanding of the situation of women
from minority communities."[151] Indicative of the social distance among
women's groups, David's comments speak to a potential "rendez-vous
manqué," or missed opportunity, among feminists in Montreal,[152] where
francophone Quebecers' position as a minority within the Canadian federation did not necessarily translate into closer political relations with feminists outside of this category.

Feminists were forced to face inequalities within the women's movement
head-on in the 1990s, especially after the debacle surrounding Lise Payette's
documentary *Disparaître* (1989). The documentary's central premise was that
the Québécois (or French Canadian) nation was losing ground due to the
low Québécois birth rate and insufficient measures on the part of authorities
to ensure that immigrants learned French. Although couched in terms of
language, the documentary relied heavily on racist messaging directed
against people of colour. Shortly thereafter, the controversial Payette was

chosen as the figurehead for the "50 heures du féminisme" conference, planned to celebrate the fiftieth anniversary of suffrage legislation. Criticizing the choice of Payette as the conference's host, the Collectif des femmes immigrantes du Québec threated to boycott the event. The decision was not reversed, pushing these women to refuse to participate.[153]

The Collectif des femmes immigrantes was established in August 1983 by seventy-five women working within various immigrant organizations, including the Maison d'Haïti and the Centro Donne. Unfortunately, we do not know a lot about the collective's internal workings or whether there were tensions among this diverse group of women. Founders attended a general assembly to officially form the organization, dedicated to the building of a "new and francophone" society. As stated in the opening lines of its founding document, "There is little mention of immigrant women, whether within the Women's Movement or elsewhere. We formed a collective because, as immigrants ourselves, we felt the need to come together to take action." Despite actively contributing to social and economic life in Quebec, immigrant women remained "unknown, almost invisible."[154] In November of the same year, the Collectif des femmes immigrantes opened its doors at 6865 Christophe Colomb Avenue in the Petite-Patrie neighbourhood. From the beginning, in addition to creating ties with francophone Quebecers, the collective had three objectives: to foster solidarity between immigrant women, to improve their living conditions, and to raise awareness of the specific problems facing this demographic.[155] More specifically, the organization sought to combat racism and sexism while informing the receiving society of the immigrant reality. Its members made a series of recommendations, such as improving access to French-language training (including for sponsored immigrants), making courses in intercultural relations a mandatory part of the curriculum for future teachers, allocating resources for community organizations in order to better prepare parents to become involved in the education system, and accurately representing people of colour in the media.[156] Rather than background, then, members were united by common cause. The Collectif des femmes immigrantes organized several conferences and workshops, such as "À la recherche de l'équité raciale" and "Liens entre femmes immigrantes et femmes québécoises," in the aftermath of the Payette debacle.[157]

Some francophone Quebecers publicly condemned *Disparaître*. Véronique O'Leary, for example, wrote an open letter to Payette, republished in feminist newsletters. One of the founding members of the Front de libération des femmes du Québec, O'Leary was also involved in the Centre des femmes and the Théâtre des cuisines. Writing to *Le Devoir*, O'Leary made her discomfort known. As she explained, "I have a bad taste and an aching heart after your documentary *Disparaître*. It started with: 'The Tremblays who have been here forever!' This is what we mean by 'old stock.' So, there was no one when they arrived here?" Debunking Payette's belief in the perennity of the Tremblays and critiquing this erasure of history, O'Leary wrote, "Our colonizing great-grandparents, the Tremblays and others, willing or unwilling participants, came here to rob the Indigenous nations of their land, their cultures, their languages, and to exterminate them, with a sword in one hand and a cross in the other." She was uneasy with Payette's painting of immigrants as threatening, even though she recognized that the French-speaking character of Montreal had not always been a given. She went even further, pointing out, "Another fundamental reality omitted in your program is that if France and England pay their colonial debts, we pay our debt to be North American, and our growth is at the expense of the South, which is always in debt." In contrast to Payette, O'Leary argued for a broad-based solidarity, both between the Global South and North and between migrants and their working-class Quebec-born counterparts. The nation's elite had its own role to the play in betraying the "economic" and "cultural" interests of most of the population.[158] Écho des femmes de la Petite Patrie and Centre des femmes d'ici et d'ailleurs issued a similar critique, commenting on Payette's vicious stereotyping of immigrant men of colour.[159] Thanks to the political and intellectual work of Indigenous and racialized activists, Québécois feminists now had a language that enabled them to understand and critique their own society.

Madeleine Parent also came out in support of immigrant and racialized women following the *Disparaître* controversy. Born into a middle-class family in Montreal in 1918, the prominent labour organizer and feminist belied simplistic stereotypes regarding identity and political allegiances. In the late 1960s, Parent made her way to Ontario, where she worked for, among others, the National Action Committee on the Status of Women, founded in 1971 in order to lobby the federal government to implement the recommendations of the Royal Commission on the Status on Women. Through the committee, Parent became a dear friend of Mary Two-Axe Earley. "Very few non-Native women have shown so much solidarity with the cause of Native Women," wrote Michèle Rouleau, a one-time president of the Quebec Native Women's Association. "It is with great sincerity and respect that Madeleine has lent us her help. She doesn't act out of political correctness, and contrary to others, her support consists of more than just words. She works side by side with us."[160] Parent was granted honorary membership in the association for her steadfast commitment to the cause.[161] After returning to Montreal in 1983, Parent got involved in the FFQ to fight neo-liberalism. A few years later, she refused an invitation to the fiftieth anniversary celebrations of women's suffrage, citing the mean-spiritedness and racism of Payette's documentary. Shree Mulay of the South Asian Women's Centre explained, "Madeleine's perspective made us feel that we, women from immigrant communities, had an ally" among francophone Quebecers. Parent then facilitated meetings between immigrant and Indigenous women's organizations and the FFQ, the latter organizing a conference to rectify the damage done by Payette.[162] The president of the FFQ at the time, Françoise David, later claimed that she was indebted to Parent for facilitating the rapprochement among various women's organizations.[163]

In 1992, the FFQ organized "Un Québec féminin pluriel," a conference that drew over 1,200 women to Montreal.[164] The forum aimed to address power dynamics that favoured francophone Quebecers and other white women within the women's movement, an imbalance that deprived larger feminist organizations "of the potential and solidarity of women from minority communities."[165] Participants could attend workshops on "Feminism and Pluralism in the Women's Movement" and "Pluralism and Diversity of Families," moderated by the leaders of several organizations of women of colour and Indigenous women.[166] The forum adopted a vocabulary of tolerance and openness, speaking of "respect for differences," "equality and solidarity among all members of society," and the "double oppression" of Indigenous women.[167] Never before had such a large and diverse group of grassroots organizers been in the same room together.[168] Shortly after the conference, referring to Indigenous women in particular, an author wrote in the FFQ's newsletter, "We know that this implies raising awareness and 'cleansing' within our own ranks. We are not so naïve as to believe that racism and discrimination do not exist around our own actions and mindsets."[169] The early 1990s were therefore a moment of reckoning and self-reflection.

After the resistance at Kanehsatà:ke, non-Indigenous women considered, more than in the past, what it meant to be a settler in Quebec.[170] As literary scholar Isabelle St-Amand explains, "During the Oka Crisis, the Quebec and Canadian societies saw their troubled relationship with Indigenous peoples exposed; they appeared as the heirs to the less than brilliant colonial history and the settler colonial present, and were therefore seen in an unflattering and even alarming light."[171] In an article entitled "Crisis of Indifference," Anne Kettenbeil of the Centre de femmes d'ici et d'ailleurs recounted her disenchantment with the broader societal response to the confrontation. The solidarity movement was tireless, making phone calls, attending meetings, organizing demonstrations, and delivering food to Kahnawà:ke. The problem, Kettenbeil wrote, was not with the people involved in these actions but rather with the limited number of people who took on the work. She asked, "Why were we so few?" After a few months had passed, she was as fatigued as she was disappointed: "We refuse to recognize as a nation the original inhabitants of the territory of Quebec, a territory which we hope will one day become a country for another people, which is also oppressed." Even though international observers critiqued the actions of the Quebec and Canadian governments, her counterparts, she explained, "choose not to hear them, not to believe them." Denial, combined with a complex of cultural superiority, made for blindness. "All the Mohawk people want is to be recognized as a Nation, which is what they have always been … with their own territory, of course!"[172] The lesbian-separatist quarterly *Amazones d'hier, lesbiennes d'aujourd'hui* made a similar comparison, reflecting more deeply on racism, settler colonialism, and neo-nationalism.[173] In other words, parts of the women's movement were more critical of the effects of colonialism in Quebec.

We have seen in previous chapters the wide array of strategies adopted by feminists in Montreal. Travelling to every corner of the world, leading grassroots organizations, and attending feminist gatherings in Montreal, they were far from passive. They were, however, largely overlooked by mostly white or Québécois women's organizations until the 1980s or even the 1990s. As noted by L'R des centres de femmes du Québec in 1993 at its "Femmes différentes et semblables" conference, "In recent years, the feminist movement in Quebec was strongly challenged by immigrant, visible minority, and Indigenous women for not taking their realities and perspectives into account. Although women of all origins have come together around the struggle for equality between women and men, the fact remains that equality among women has not yet been achieved."[174] For some Québécois organizers, this shift toward a more overt pluralism created possibilities for regeneration. At its 1993 gathering, the organization also noted, "The daily lives of women from First Nations and minority communities are affected as much by racism, xenophobia, sexism, and poverty. Integrating such concerns into the feminist vision and practice is quite a challenge, but so promising for their renewal!"[175] After more than two decades of intensified activism on the part of Indigenous and diasporic women, Québécois feminists, and hopefully other Euro-Québécois feminists as well, were forced to reconsider their own understanding of feminism.[176]

This renewal did not come to be. According to political scientist Diane Lamoureux, writing about the 1992 "Un Québec féminin pluriel" conference, "These kinds of ideas opened up a new chapter in the development of Quebec feminism, although they did not heal all wounds."[177] Only a few months later, the Meech Lake Accord was rejected by some of the Canadian provinces, straining relations among feminists in Quebec and the rest of Canada, as well as among feminists in Quebec. During the 1995 sovereignty referendum campaign, tensions among feminists arose once again after the FFQ decided to support the "yes" side despite Lucien Bouchard's "embarrassing" comment that francophone Quebecers constituted "one of the white races" in the world that was "producing the fewest numbers of children."[178] Bouchard was the leader of the federal Bloc Québécois, a sovereigntist party. He later tried to explain his statement as a purely demographic observation, to the satisfaction of the FFQ president, who appeared with him two days later.[179] "Even greater damage was done," as Lamoureux explains, "on the evening of the referendum," when Parti Québécois leader and premier Jacques Parizeau made a speech blaming the "yes" side's narrow defeat on "'money and the ethnic vote.'"[180] Although opinions at the grassroots level were diverse, Parizeau's comments were a hard pill to swallow.

The women's movement was therefore not immune to the unease in Montreal and Quebec society.

In addition to power dynamics within the women's movement, feminists were reacting to the austerity measures and budget cuts of these decades.[181] Historians trace the end of the Quiet Revolution to the beginning of the 1980s, when the social consensus surrounding the role of the state started to break down. No longer seen as the vector for collective emancipation, the relatively large Quebec state was increasingly seen, by some, as an impediment to economic and social development.[182] Many feminists were, consequently, on the defensive. Neo-liberalism placed them in the unlikely position of engaging in direct action through service provision, on the one hand, while condoning the subordinate integration of women's concerns into public policy initiatives, on the other.[183] On the ground, the rigamarole around securing funding, especially for women's centres, remained an exhausting and seemingly never-ending exercise, taking time away from grassroots mobilization and service provision. The latter, as Diane Lamoureux points out, "served as smokescreens for public-sector inaction, allowing the government to buy social services at a discount." For Lamoureux, "This type of transaction was the epitome of neo-liberal logic: the state had ensured that civil society would shoulder the burden of social solidarity." For instance, the low salaries paid to the employees of women's centres raises the question of whether they became a cheaper version of the welfare state. Regardless of the political party in power, successive government administrations were committed to cost-cutting measures.[184] In 1995, feminists of all stripes protested the erosion of the welfare state at the successful antipoverty march Du pain et des roses. But even then, the Quebec government refused to add "zero poverty" to its "zero deficit" policy.[185] Thus a new era of feminist activism seems to have begun in the 1980s and 1990s.

Conclusion

As we have seen, immigrant women's organizations proliferated in the late 1970s and 1980s. These organizations and grassroots organizers occasionally came together in order to strengthen their position. Shortly after the Payette Affair, Juanita Westmoreland-Traoré, who readers will remember from chapter 2, was the keynote speaker at an event organized by the Collectif des femmes immigrantes du Québec. Speaking as the president of the Conseil des communautés culturelles et de l'immigration, the experienced human rights lawyer stressed the importance of mutual understanding. She invoked her friendship with Madeleine Parent, described as one of her "spiritual guides" and someone she frequently phoned for advice. Westmoreland-Traoré then broached the topic of tension within the women's movement: "As women from minority communities, we cannot always distinguish between our affiliation as women and as members of ethnic, cultural, and religious groups. In fact, deep down, we have multiple identities and simultaneously a simple identity." With the goal of forwarding social justice, Westmoreland-Traoré hoped that participants would be able to share their diverse experiences.[186] At this point, political spaces dominated by white women appeared to be increasingly receptive to anti-racist or other critical analyses.[187] After decades of political labour on the part of Indigenous and racialized activists, the women's movement as a whole was forced to listen to their critiques of predominantly white feminist organizations.

Despite a turn toward official pluralism at both the federal and provincial levels, true belonging was still a struggle for some women active in social movements in Montreal.[188] Scholars have indeed criticized the shortcomings of official multiculturalism, a policy put into place during a period marked by the rapid influx of immigrants from the Global South and by a growing rivalry between the French and the English. The policy, they argue, served as a muting device for francophone national aspirations, sidelined the claims of Indigenous nations, deflected attention from a racializing political economy, and represented the polity in cultural terms. "An element of whiteness quietly enters into cultural definitions," as sociologist Himani Bannerji explains, "marking the difference between a core cultural group and other groups who are represented as cultural fragments."[189] Although ostensibly developed in opposition to its federal counterpart, Quebec's interculturalism similarly ignored the implications of its colonial history and present. As we have seen in previous chapters, grassroots organizers were guarded in their reactions to these policies from their beginnings and proposed other mechanisms to guarantee genuine equality for their communities. Meanwhile, the Centro Donne's community-based feminism focused on changing the state and Quebec society rather than transforming them, demonstrating the role that whiteness can play in immigrant women's politics.

Future historians will contemplate new questions, yet it appears that some social movements remained oppositional in the 1980s and 1990s, despite an overall turn to more conservative thinking. More specifically, grassroots organizers remained consistent in trying to force the state's hand during a time of budget cuts. Racialized women continued their fight for social justice both within and beyond the women's movement, and Indigenous women defended their land as well as their quest for legal rights and belonging in their own nations and beyond.[190]

Conclusion

Despite the momentum that women activists continued to generate at the grassroots, or perhaps because of it, the 1980s and 1990s were a time of reactionary gender politics. In Quebec, the repercussions were wretched. From 17 July to 8 August 1989, headlines were monopolized by a court battle between Chantal Daigle and Jean-Guy Tremblay over the fate of a fetus and the right of a young woman to determine whether she could terminate her pregnancy. Tremblay applied for an interlocutory injunction from the Quebec Superior Court to prevent Daigle from receiving an abortion. The future father was known to be violent, and his order to stop the abortion came after Daigle had fled their shared household. The trial judge ruled that the fetus was a "human being" within the meaning of Quebec's Charter of Rights and Freedoms and had a right to life under section 1. The Quebec Court of Appeal upheld the decision. Daigle then appealed to the Supreme Court of Canada. In Montreal, the Coalition québécoise pour le droit à l'avortement libre et gratuite organized a rally that brought together 10,000 people asserting their right to abortion on demand. Meanwhile, Chantal Daigle, who was running out of time, covertly travelled to Boston to acquire an abortion with the help of the Centre de santé des femmes. The court set aside the injunction, finding that the rights alleged – those of a fetus or a potential father – did not exist.[1]

Things only got worse. On 6 December 1989, Marc Lépine walked into Université de Montréal's Polytechnique with a semi-automatic rifle, shooting fourteen young women and wounding thirteen others before committing suicide. After ordering the men to leave the room, he made his intentions obvious: "I am here to fight against feminism, that is why I am here."[2] In his suicide note, he blamed feminists for ruining his life. The note contained a list of fifteen prominent women whom he claimed to have wanted to kill as well. Although his motivations were painfully obvious, the media and the authorities found it difficult to admit that the attack represented a real case of misogyny. Feminists were even accused of appropriating the tragic massacre for their own political ends.[3] The authorities eventually declared 6 December an official day of commemoration for women victims of male violence, and the Supreme Court of Canada supported Daigle's right to an abortion, but these two incidents show the need for vigilance, exposing the stubborn nature of patriarchal and misogynist thinking.[4]

The Daigle versus Tremblay Affair and the Montreal Massacre call to mind the words of American writer Susan Faludi: "The antifeminist backlash has been set off not by women's achievement of full equality but by the increased possibility that they might win it. It is a pre-emptive strike that stops women long before they reach the finish line."[5] Writing in 1991, Faludi argues that backlash is nothing new in the history of feminism; rather, it returns every time women make headway toward equality. In the decades following the Second World War, especially from the 1970s onward, some women made substantial advances before the patriarchal counterattack. But millions of others did not make the same gains, forced to contest their marginalization from an already tenuous position.[6] *Countercurrents* ends here, with the intensification of neo-liberalism and the specter of backlash in the late 1980s and 1990s. Since then, progressive forces have turned to fighting the erosion of social gains, doing what historian Lana Dee Povitz calls the "politics of damage control," and scholars are already thinking about the intersections between neo-liberalism and grassroots social movements in Quebec.[7]

Still, the women's movement succeeded in mainstreaming feminist analysis, giving the next generation something to build on. In Montreal and Kahnawà:ke, the tenor of these conversations was unique. Conceptions of feminist nationalism varied cross-culturally, but all historical actors, on balance, drew strength from their culture of origin. It is significant that Kanien'kehá:ka and other Indigenous women viewed their ancestors as strong, powerful, and equal to men. Drawing heavily on pan-African ideas or the legacy of the Haitian Revolution, Black Montrealers similarly referred to the past in empowering terms as they launched their political project into the future. Grassroots organizers in the orbit of the Quebec Native Women's Association (QNWA), the Congress of Black Women of Canada, the Maison d'Haïti, the Point de ralliement des femmes haïtiennes, the FLF, the Centro Donne Italiane di Montreal, and the Collectif des femmes immigrantes du Québec also remained affiliated, to varying degrees, with other political movements in Montreal and beyond. For example, members of the Congress of Black Women and the Maison d'Haïti organized locally against anti-Black racism, joined the global struggle against apartheid in South Africa, and continued their fight to restore democracy in Haiti. By seeing their emancipation as tied to their respective imagined communities, the women in this study combined national and women's liberation struggles, making these two goals one and the same. Taking on leadership roles, founding autonomous women's organizations, and in some cases, explicitly critiquing their male counterparts, none of the book's protagonists waited for national liberation to demand equality.

Just as they refused injustice closer to home, so too did Indigenous and Black organizers reject second-class citizenship vis-à-vis the broader women's movement. At their height in the late 1960s and early 1970s, coinciding with the emergence of the FLF, the Black Power and anti-colonial movements resonated strongly in Montreal, serving as a forceful undercurrent that energized autonomous women's organizing writ large. FLF members relied heavily on a "Third World" iconography of resistance, using these movements to understand their own oppression as francophone Quebecers.[8] With women leaders encountering one another more frequently as the years wore on, Québécois feminists were compelled to reconceptualize their politics, becoming more attentive to the shortcomings of their society and the women's movement. Despite fractious internal debates, feminist collectives, women's centres, and a vibrant, dynamic, and diverse community sector carried grassroots politics forward. Meanwhile, the QNWA, the Congress of Black Women, the Point de ralliement, and the Maison d'Haïti continued to navigate the political waters, carrying on their own longstanding traditions of grassroots organizing on multiple fronts at once.

During the period under study, Indigenous and Black political actors proposed genuinely new and different visions of citizenship. Their priorities were twofold: they contested the inequalities of their surroundings while also fashioning their own forms of belonging. Pursuing highly local goals and building coalitions, they ultimately bypassed the nation-state. For instance, Mary Two-Axe Earley first met with her neighbours and friends in Kahnawà:ke to discuss their predicament concerning band membership. In their minds, as women, they were vital for future iterations of the collectivity. From Kahnawà:ke, not only did Two-Axe Earley and her counterparts foster ties with Indigenous women from all over Quebec and Canada, but they also deftly navigated the United Nations system, engaging in diplomatic relations that continue to this day. At the 1985 Nairobi conference, Indigenous women from the Americas, Australia and New Zealand, and Sápmi (straddling Sweden, Norway, Finland, and Russia) rejected the status of "minority." Instead, they put forth a precedent-setting resolution asserting that Indigenous women and their families have unique fundamental rights and interests flowing from their original use of resources and their occupancy of the land.[9] Through these actions, they asserted their rights and exercised their responsibilities to their nations, thinking not only of themselves but also of future generations. What made their politics distinct was their focus on territorial integrity.

African-descended organizers, for their part, adopted diasporic definitions of citizenship, insisting that women's needs were always on the agenda in the process. With deep roots in Montreal, the heterogeneous English-speaking Black community came together under a syncretic form of nationalism. When Haitian newcomers arrived in the metropolis, the two communities made their way together, albeit sometimes at a distance. The Negro Community Centre, the Congress of Black Writers, and the Congress of Black Women may have been predominantly English-speaking spaces, but French speakers were never entirely absent. Women appeared to be the ones making these connections through their community work, with organizers overcoming the language barrier to establish coalitions. These community leaders were master networkers, maintaining links to their homelands and cultivating new political ties, such as at pan-African conferences, at international conferences on democracy and human rights, at Congress of Black Women events, or at the conferences of the UN Decade for Women (1975–85). Black internationalism was alive and well in the metropolis, as was community and institution building for the benefit of all generations. Black Montrealers' politics were nourished by both the anglophone and francophone intellectual worlds, making the city's communities a unique political space for the diaspora.

Montreal's history of double colonization by the French and the English, perhaps ironically, allowed women who fell outside of these settler groups to go up the middle, carving out a bigger space for themselves than they would have otherwise. For the QNWA, as readers may remember from Ellen Gabriel's comments in the Introduction, this reality impacted diasporic women as well. For example, the Collectif des femmes immigrantes du Québec brought together a highly heterogeneous group of grassroots organizers with more differences than similarities. Their choice to come together was strategic, and they used the homogenizing views on "immigrant women" present in broader society to their advantage.[10] The collective asked predominantly Quebec-born organizations to respect its members' different political priorities and ways of organizing.[11] Although not all of the collective's members were well versed in the history of colonial dispossession, it forced other feminist organizations to listen to its critiques of the women's movement and the receiving society. Members of the Collectif des femmes immigrantes talked openly about systemic racism and the structural barriers impeding allophone women from learning French.[12] After language laws came into effect in the 1970s, francophone and allophone newcomers had to adjust and thus began dialoguing even more explicitly with francophone Quebecers. The collective's goal of creating a "*new* and francophone society"[13] appealed to Québécois feminists directly but not unconditionally. They spelled out their terms for participation, refusing a minoritized status or obscured position within the women's movement.

The protagonists in this study were more "nationalistic" in a setting where they had to compete with at least one other group, if not more, for power and resources. The French-English rivalry in Montreal and elsewhere in Quebec served only to strengthen grassroots organizers' assertions and identities, from the FLF to the QNWA. Combining nationalism and feminism, the Front de libération des femmes du Québec forced the left to contend with women's concerns and feminist critiques. The heightened political atmosphere created more opportunities for Indigenous and racialized women to express their discontent, such as when Kahentinetha Horn made sure to name French Canadians "the first invading race" at the Commission for Bilingualism and Biculturalism in 1963. The political context also enabled

them to build bridges in a manner rooted in their principles, such as when
the QNWA stated in the Quebec National Assembly in the early 1980s, "It is
with the same respect that we have for you, French-speaking non-Indians
who defend your own culture with so much skill, energy, and determination,
that we intend to defend ours, with the same open-mindedness that you
have shown towards minority groups in this part of *our* lands."[14] They also
proposed new political projects. Writing on Quebec in 2017, Marjorie Villefranche, director of the Maison d'Haïti, self-identified as a "woman, Black,
feminist and free." As she wrote, "Independence for Black feminists or racialized immigrant women or refugees would be advantageous if, and only if,
it allowed new perspectives to develop under their influence that led to a
society where we would not be defined only according to our race, ethnic
origin, or legal status." Attentive to Indigenous nations as well, Villefranche
endeavoured to create a place for everyone in a future, imagined country.[15]

By linking colonialism to territorial dispossession, Indigenous organizers
implicated Québécois feminists, as well as other white settler women, in
colonial dynamics. In an evolving context, one that was accompanied by
the territorialization of the Quebec identity and state, the QNWA drew attention to systemic racism in the health care and social service sectors, combining these issues with a gendered critique of the federal Indian Act. As we
saw in chapter 1, First Nations women seeking to regain Indian status after
out-marriages used strategic linkages to advance their cause. They reached
out to relatively powerful reformist organizations such as the FFQ, which
gladly offered its support, making important phone calls, writing letters,
and lending its moral authority to the cause of nonstatus women. With ties
to the provincial and federal governments, the federation was best positioned to help those seeking to reclaim status. Although the federation's
emphasis on legal change opened up points of contact, its members' understanding of Indigenous women's issues, at least initially, never seemed
to go beyond equality under the law. In the 1990s, QNWA leaders called on
non-Indigenous feminists to support "not only the demands of Indigenous
women that relate to their oppression as women but also those that affect
land rights, self-determination, environmental concerns." After the resistance at Kanehsatà:ke, its leadership encouraged Euro-Quebecers to respect
Indigenous women's political strategies, such as that of including men, and
to make the link between Indigenous women's "feminist struggles and their

national demands," in the words of the QNWA's then president, Michèle Rouleau.[16] While taking part in predominantly white feminist meetings (and not only those organized by the FFQ), Indigenous women consistently tied their demands to territorial integrity and made women's issues like reproduction part of a larger struggle for self-determination.

Francophone and anglophone Black women drew attention to the effects of anti-Black racism, appraising the limitations of the institutions in their midst and thus broadening the definition of women's issues to include community concerns. They contested conditions in domestic service, racist immigration laws and social services, and discrimination in the housing sector. Sometimes, they teamed up with white women to gain access to resources or to increase their bargaining position. Alongside the Ligue des femmes du Québec, for instance, the Congress of Black Women of Canada participated in the 1980 hemispheric conference "Women under Apartheid." By and large, however, they were wedded to their own political traditions. Building on a longstanding tradition of community-based education initiatives, these same protagonists, many of whom were trained as teachers, simultaneously spearheaded an anti-racist challenge to the Quebec curriculum, making education an integral component of their community work at a time when the school system was expanding.[17] Inspired by thinkers such as Paolo Freire, Maison d'Haïti workers, for instance, complemented the formal education system through unique cultural programming, homework clubs, and adult literacy classes. Indigenous and Black women, in short, took on leadership positions in mixed political spaces. They also organized autonomously to make sure that women could discuss their problems among themselves.

Feminists from all backgrounds started to think more carefully about international solidarity after International Women's Year in 1975. The UN World Conferences on Women provided a political forum to promote their respective causes, to connect with like-minded organizers, and to gain new perspectives. As increasing numbers of Quebecers travelled abroad for feminist conferences, their perspectives on gender inequality grew more sophisticated. Indigenous and Black women were part of a numerical majority in these settings, constituents of a global resurgence against white supremacy and an unequal political economy. Most women combined their concerns about gender equality with other issues, from apartheid to neo-colonialism to struggles for democracy. Coinciding with the UN Decade for Women and abundantly explored at the 1985 conference in Nairobi, the ascendancy of conservative governments altered the political and economic terrain, usually for the worse. In Quebec, budgetary restrictions in the female-dominated health and education sectors compromised the salary gains that women had made relative to their male counterparts over the past decade. The increase in part-time, rather than full-time, employment hurt women as well. Many feminists argued that the economic downturn placed women at greater risk for exploitation in the labour market and added pressure to their domestic and family duties.[18] The grassroots were thus considering a new set of questions by the end of the UN Decade for Women, linked to a globalized political economy, austerity measures, and the apparent end of the social consensus supporting a relatively large and active state.

In a shifting political and economic context, the Quebec national question remained on the political agenda. With the insights of racialized and Indigenous activists, some Québécois feminists overcame their initial blind spots, as considered in chapter 3. One of the founding members of the Front de libération des femmes du Québec, Véronique O'Leary, spoke out after Lise Payette's documentary *Disparaître* (1989). The former minister of state for the status of women implied that the Québécois nation was at risk for extinction, suggesting that newcomers were the largest threat to its future. As readers will recall from chapter 5, O'Leary opposed Payette's xenophobia, referring to the violent history of colonialism in Quebec. She also called for North-South solidarities, critiquing the ravages of capitalism everywhere, which impacted both migrant and Quebec-born workers.[19] Bridge builders such as Madeleine Parent were effective in cross-cultural contexts as well, recognized as allies by, for example, the QNWA and the Collectif des femmes immigrantes du Québec. Parent, O'Leary, and others like them demonstrated that the Quebec national project can be reconceptualized in a nonessentialist way, with all citizens or residents having an equivalent claim to emancipation, and that multiple sovereignties can coexist equally. In 2004, for example, the FFQ and the QWNA, with memberships anchored in their respective national contexts, co-signed the *Déclaration solennelle de solidarité entre la Fédération des femmes du Québec et Femmes autochtones du Québec*. This protocol affirms the right to self-determination of both peoples and their commitment to undoing the colonial rapport shaping

Indigenous-Québécois(e) relations. The challenge has been putting this declaration into practice.[20]

However, the combination of feminism and neo-nationalism was also used to promote ethno-nationalism and racialized ideas of the patriarchy in Quebec, as we saw in chapter 5. The women's movement as a whole failed to throw its collective weight behind the resistance at Kanehsatà:ke, even if some women were involved in solidarity actions. Other white feminists, remaining impervious to a shift in some quarters of the women's movement toward ideas of "multiple" or "interlocking" oppressions (again, thanks to Black and Indigenous organizers), weaponized francophone Quebecers' minority status in the Canadian federation to promote exclusionary forms of citizenship. On the eve of the 1995 referendum, the leader of the federal Bloc Québécois, Lucien Bouchard, commented that francophone Quebecers were not having enough children,[21] a view that spoke to older ideas about women as "mothers of the nation."[22] Clearly, racist and patriarchal notions die hard, yet the FFQ president appeared with Bouchard two days later. Feminist nationalism in the hands of white settlers can thus quickly degenerate into a quest for power, going from a project rooted in broad-based political aspirations for national liberation and social justice to one rooted in ethnically based principles.

I have chosen to put these competing, at times intersecting, feminist narratives in the same analytical frame, but not everyone would make this decision. Are histories of women's political organizing best captured outside of studies explicitly focused on "feminism," especially if activist women themselves avoided the term? I will leave it to other historians, scholars, and grassroots organizers to debate this question. My aim has been to give credit where credit is due in order to find a more useable past. The goal of this study is to open new conversations on women's politics and grassroots organizing in Quebec. *Countercurrents* hopes to provoke further studies on related topics. Comparative accounts with multiple case studies are by definition "zoomed out," focused on parallels, divergences, and interconnections rather than on distinct epistemologies or culturally specific questions.[23] The study of queer movements, specifically queer movements of colour and two-spirited movements, could further destabilize exclusionary forms of nationalism and citizenship. In attempting to usurp sovereignties and cultural legacies, for example, French and English colonizers tried to disrupt the kinship structures of Indigenous communities in North America and to impose heteronormative gender norms on these communities. Not only do these histories invite more accounts of sexual and gender diversity, but they also allow us to contest and destabilize the heteropatriarchy and white homonationalisms of the later twentieth century.[24] Recuperative historical projects serve a purpose since erasure is part of settler colonialism.

Indeed, mainstream cultural commentators present Québécois men, and sometimes Québécois women, as the movers and shakers of the Quiet Revolution, to the near exclusion of everyone else.[25] Racialized and Indigenous women have been unfairly characterized as passive, their political and intellectual traditions dismissed or minoritized. Even if ideas of "multiple" or "interlocking" oppressions have been mainstreamed, to a degree, among most North American feminists, the broader women's movement has struggled to put these ideas into practice, making solidarity politics and an equitable division of political labour the burning question of many feminist organizations. In recent decades, moreover, women's movements have struggled to find a footing in an increasingly neo-liberalized, interconnected world.[26]

However, the politicized women of a rejuvenated cohort have come to the fore in recent years in Quebec, especially in Montreal. Combining the most dynamic elements of various social movements – whether Idle No More, Black Lives Matter, anti-capitalist and migrant justice struggles, modern abolitionist movements, or the Accommodate This! Campaign in response to Quebec's "reasonable accommodation" hearings – they are thinking about women, gender, and social justice in new ways.[27] Today, non-Indigenous organizers, especially Black organizers, are more attentive to questions related to Indigenous sovereignties and territories than they were in the period under study.[28] This intergenerational group of activists exemplifies the ways that politics can be practised and theorized anew.

Notes

Unless taken from English sources, all translations of non-English quotations are my own.

INTRODUCTION

1 Quoted in Goodleaf, *Entering the War Zone*, 151.
2 Quoted in ibid., 150.
3 York and Pindera, *People of the Pines*, 192.
4 Gabriel, "Aboriginal Women's Movement," 187.
5 Hill, *Clay We Are Made Of*, 53–76, quote at 53.
6 Cannon, *Men, Masculinity*, 8.
7 Hill, *Clay We Are Made Of*, 53–76.
8 Nickel, "Introduction," 3.
9 Gunn Allen, *Sacred Hoop*, 209–21.
10 Gabriel, "Aboriginal Women's Movement," 183.
11 Nickel, *Assembling Unity*, 24.
12 Green, *Making Space*, 1st ed., 4–5.
13 McCarthy, *In Divided Unity*, 9.
14 Anderson, "Interview with Katsi'tsakwas Ellen Gabriel," 53.
15 Nickel, "Introduction," 1.
16 Ibid., 3.
17 Green, *Making Space*, 1st ed., 4.
18 Austin, "Narratives of Power," 23.
19 The scholarship on the 1960s through the 1980s is still getting off the ground. There is a growing literature on "second-wave" feminism in

Canada. For example, see Agnew, *Resisting Discrimination*; Janovicek, *No Place to Go*; Rebick, *Ten Thousand Roses*; Dumont, *Le féminisme québécois*; Luxton, "Feminism as a Class Act"; and Sangster, "Radical Ruptures."

20 Cott, "What's in a Name?," 827.

21 Chapters 1 and 2 will expand on these ideas.

22 Hill Collins, "Intersectionality's Definitional Dilemmas," 5.

23 Simon, *Translating Montreal*, xviii–21, quote at 11.

24 Rueck, "When Bridges Become Barriers," 229.

25 Hill, *Clay We Are Made Of*, 53.

26 Rück, *Laws and the Land*, 15–16.

27 Yuval-Davis, "Belonging and the Politics."

28 Yuval-Davis, "Women, Citizenship, and Difference," 5.

29 Yuval-Davis, *Gender and Nation*, 3, 9.

30 Herr, "Possibility of Nationalist Feminism," 135–9.

31 Ibid., 139.

32 Ibid., 142.

33 See, among others, de Sève, "Féminisme et nationalisme"; D. Lamoureux, "Nationalisme et féminisme"; D. Lamoreux, *L'amère patrie*; and Stasiulis, "Relational Positionalities."

34 Collectif Clio, *L'histoire des femmes au Québec*, 358.

35 Palmer, *Canada's 1960s*, 314.

36 Baillargeon, *Brief History*, 150; Sangster, *Transforming Labour*, 108–44.

37 Dua, "Exclusion through Inclusion," 448–9; L. Desmarais, *La bataille de l'avortement.*

38 Palmer, *Canada's 1960s*, 319.

39 See also Dumont, "La culture politique," 116.

40 Pâquet and Savard, *Brève histoire*, 135–6.

41 In 1961, Marie-Claire Kirkland became the first woman elected to the National Assembly. A deputy for the Liberal Party, she was the first woman to be accepted as a candidate for a major political party after the death of her father, the politician Dr Charles-Aime Kirkland. Elected in his riding immediately following his passing, Marie-Claire Kirkland was then re-elected in 1962, 1966, and 1970. She oversaw significant reforms. Dumont, "Politique active et féminisme."

42 Ibid.

43 Patry-Buisson, "La FFQ," 3. For a more detailed analysis of the FFQ and marginalized feminists, see Ricci, "Un féminisme inclusif?" 106.

44 Patry-Buisson, "La FFQ." Not unlike the suffragist generation and the communist or socialist left, women made linkages, to a degree, with each other across community lines within the FFQ. Baillargeon, *To Be Equals*, 41–3.

45 Gélinas, *Les autochtones*, 50.

46 Palmer, *Canada's 1960s*, 321.

47 S. Mills, *Empire Within*, 52–3.

48 Ibid., 54.

49 Ibid., 53.

50 Lanthier, "L'impossible réciprocité," 111, 108.

51 O'Neill, "Le soleil de la prospérité," 61.

52 Goodleaf, *Entering the War Zone*, 40–1.

53 O'Neill, "Le soleil de la prospérité," 68.

54 Scott, *De Groulx à Laferrière*, 1.

55 Fanon, *Les damnés de la terre*.

56 For a full-length version of the poem and an account of its initial reading, see S. Mills, *Empire Within*, 81–2.

57 For a critique of francophone anti-colonialists' erasure of Indigenous and Black Quebecers, see Meren, "Crisis of the Nation."

58 There exists a robust literature on these themes, including Nash, "Political Life of Black Motherhood"; and J. Brand and Anderson, "Indigenous Mothering."

59 McKittrick, *Demonic Grounds*, 91–120.

60 Mugabo, "On Haunted Places," 89.

61 Laughlin et al., "Is It Time to Jump Ship?" 77, 82.

62 Ibid., 82.

63 Ibid., 89.

64 Ibid., 85.

65 See, for example, Nadasen, "Expanding the Boundaries"; McDuffie, *Sojourning for Freedom*; and P. Brooks, *Boycotts, Buses, and Passes*.

66 Farmer, *Remaking Black Power*, 71.

67 Spencer, "Engendering the Black Freedom Struggle," 99.

68 Hampton and Rochat, "To Commit and to Lead."

69 Spencer, "Engendering the Black Freedom Struggle," 91.

70 Sandwell, "Travels of Florence Mophosho," 99. For other important interventions see Shohat, "Area Studies"; and Roth, *Separate Roads to Feminism*.

71 Laughlin et al., "Is It Time to Jump Ship?" 98, 101 (quote).

72 Goeman and Denetdale, "Native Feminisms," 10.

73 Spencer, "Engendering the Black Freedom Struggle," 100, quoting Perkins, *Autobiography as Activism*, 114.

74 Mohanty, "'Under Western Eyes' Revisited," 518 (quote), 522, 524.

75 Ibid., 524.

76 See on Quebec, for example, Fahrni, "Reflections on the Place of Quebec."

77 McCallum, "Indigenous Labour and Indigenous History," 534. See also Maltais-Landry, "Un territoire de cent pas de côté," 20, esp. 20n7.

78 Mar, *Brokering Belonging*, 132.

79 McKittrick, *Demonic Grounds*, 92.

80 Ibid., 100.

81 Ibid., 99. McKittrick attributes the phrase "absented presence" to Rinaldo Walcott and Dionne Brand.

82 Sangster, *Demanding Equality*, 301.

83 Podmore and Chamberland, "Entering the Urban Frame," 207.

84 Porter, "Transnational Feminisms," 44.

85 See, for example, Austin, *Fear of a Black Nation*, 4. These ideas will be more fully explored in chapter 2.

86 Germain and Rose, *Montréal*, 231, 232; Baillargeon, *Brief History*, 162.

87 Pâquet and Savard, *Brève histoire*, 95.

88 Laughlin et al., "Is It Time to Jump Ship?"

89 S. Mills, *Place in the Sun*, 7.

90 Baillargeon, *Brief History*, 136–41.

CHAPTER ONE

1 Alfred, *Heeding the Voices*, 78–9.

2 Kahn-Tineta Horn, "Miss Kahn-Tineta Horn Speaking for Herself," *Cornwall Standard Freeholder*, 1 May 1968, in RG 22, vol. 88, file 6-10-3, part 1, Library and Archives Canada (LAC).

3 Goodleaf, *Entering the War Zone*, 6–10.

4 Simpson, *Mohawk Interruptus*, 169.

5 Jamieson, *Indian Women and the Law*, 1. Under the controversial article, a wife was reassigned to her husband's band upon intermarriage, as were their offspring. Fiske, "Political Status," 339.

6 Cannon, *Men, Masculinity*, 3, 39, 40.

7 Simpson, *Mohawk Interruptus*, 48.

8 Goodleaf, *Entering the War Zone*, 11.

9 McCarthy, *In Divided Unity*, 17.
10 Rück, *Laws and the Land*, 28.
11 Alfred, *Heeding the Voices*, 152, 156–8.
12 Rueck, "When Bridges Become Barriers," 230, 233.
13 Cannon, *Men, Masculinity*, 4.
14 Barker, ed., *Critically Sovereign*, 11.
15 Hill, *Clay We Are Made Of*, 56.
16 L. Brooks, *Common Pot*, 2, 3.
17 Alfred, *Heeding the Voices*, 78–9.
18 Hill, *Clay We Are Made Of*, 37.
19 Quoted in Gunn Allen, "Who Is Your Mother?"
20 L. Brooks, *Common Pot*, 13, 245.
21 Child, *Holding Our World Together*, xv. See also L. Brooks, *Common Pot*, 27–8.
22 Child, *Holding Our World Together*, 32, 37.
23 Ibid., 39, 46, 61. Connecting people and goods, Indigenous women were the glue that held this new, hybridic world together.
24 There exists a rich scholarship on the intimate partnerships between European men and Indigenous women. Historians such as Sylvia Van Kirk, Adele Perry, and Laura Ishiguro describe the sting of abandonment and abuse faced by some wives, as well as the genuine love and affection among couples. See Child, *Holding Our World Together*, 45; Van Kirk, *Many Tender Ties*; Perry, *Colonial Relations*; and Ishiguro, *Nothing to Write Home About*.
25 Baillargeon, *Brief History*, 6. Historians also note that that there was significant disagreement within the church hierarchy moving forward, although the unions were never criminalized. As Sylvia Van Kirk argues, Indigenous women would have never been accepted as the "founding mothers" of the colony, as cultural replication was essential to imperial projects. Van Kirk, "Marrying-In to Marrying-Out," 4.
26 Baillargeon, *Brief History*, 5–8.
27 Vien, "Un mélange aussi redouté," 59–63, 67. Within the Catholic hierarchy, there was considerable disagreement over the legitimacy of these unions, although they were never criminalized. Further, sexual relations with Indigenous women outside of marriage were considered sinful, to the same extent as incest, bestiality, sodomy, adultery, and pedophilia. Only the bishop could absolve a person of such behaviours. There was a certain

continuity after the Conquest of 1759. Intercultural unions were nondesirable yet tolerated. The church never officially or overtly opposed intercultural unions, but they were frequently condemned by colonial authorities.

28 Alfred, *Heeding the Voices*, 52.

29 Rueck, "Enclosing the Mohawk Commons," 137, 148–9.

30 Rueck, "When Bridges Become Barriers," 230.

31 Simpson, "Captivating Eunice," 119.

32 Coulthard, *Red Skin, White Masks*, 84.

33 Nickel, *Assembling Unity*, 45; Coulthard, *Red Skin, White Masks*, 85.

34 Simpson, *Mohawk Interruptus*, 48.

35 Rück, *Laws and the Land*, 211.

36 Horn-Miller, "My Mom," 81.

37 S. Mills, *Empire Within*, 138–54.

38 Morton, *Indigenous McGill*, 3, 9.

39 Morton, *Black McGill*, 5–6.

40 Horn-Miller, "Otiyaner," 61; Gzowski, "How Kahn-Tineta Horn."

41 "Summary of an Address by Kahntineta Horn, Caughnawaga, Quebec, at McGill University Redpath Museum on April 21, 1964 at 1.30 pm," in RG 10, vol. 7143, file 1/3-8-2, part 1, Complaints and Petitions Received from Kahn-Tineta Horn, vol. 1, October 1963 to May 1964, LAC.

42 Horn-Miller, "My Mom," 84–6.

43 Kahn-Tineta Horn, "Caughnawaga Mess," *Montreal Gazette*, 21 April 1964, in RG 10, vol. 7143, file 1/3-8-2, part 1, Complaints and Petitions Received from Kahn-Tineta Horn, vol. 1, October 1963 to May 1964, LAC.

44 York and Pindera, *People of the Pines*, 122.

45 Simpson, *Mohawk Interruptus*, 52.

46 Quoted in Palmer, *Canada's 1960s*, 397. See also Simpson, *Mohawk Interruptus*, 52; and Alfred, *Heeding the Voices*, 160.

47 Simpson, *Mohawk Interruptus*, 5; Hauptman, *Iroquois Struggle for Survival*, 123.

48 Alfred, *Heeding the Voices*, 156, 162.

49 Simpson, *Mohawk Interruptus*.

50 Government of Canada, Royal Commission on Bilingualism and Biculturalism, "Submission of Miss Kahn-Tineta Horn."

51 Alfred, *Heeding the Voices*, 17.

52 Papillon, "Aboriginal Peoples and Quebec," 114.

53 Indians of Quebec Association, *Our Land*, 1.

54 "Hydro Québec Accused of a Land Grab," *Montreal Star*, 4 May 1971, reprinted in *Akwesasne Notes*, April 1971, 2.

55 Indians of Quebec Association, *Our Land*, 5. For Red Power proponent George Manuel, describing the lead-up to the White Paper, "The greatest single value that the meetings of the National Indian Advisory Council offered was that the Indian leadership from all across Canada got to know one another, and to discover where our common interest lay," a trend that, as we will see, carried over into women's activism. Manuel and Posluns, *Fourth World*, 165. For more on the IQA, see Roy Drainville, "Nous sommes une nation," 127–56.

56 Gélinas, *Les autochtones*, 137; Y. Turcotte, "L'Association des Indiens," 18; Simpson, *Mohawk Interruptus*, 20.

57 Alfred, *Heeding the Voices*, 58–9.

58 Mitchell, dir., *You Are on Indian Land*.

59 Eleanor Dumas, "Decisions Reserved by Judge in Blockade Trial of Indians," *Watertown Daily Times*, 27 March 1960, reprinted in *Akwesasne Notes*, April 1969, 2; "Indians, English Customs Appear in Blockade Trial," *Akwesasne Notes*, April 1969, 2.

60 Mitchell, dir., *You Are on Indian Land*. For more on the IFC, see Stewart, "Indian Film Crews."

61 Deloria Jr, *God Is Red*, 12.

62 Gzowski, "Portrait of a Beautiful Segregationist"; "Mohawk Blazes Trail," *Globe and Mail*, 20 May 1960, reprinted in *Awesasne Notes*, May 1969, 6; "Militant Indians Seek Red Power in Canada," *Flint Journal*, 16 July 1969, 14, reprinted in *Akwesasne Notes*, June 1969; "'I Believe in Apartheid,' Says Spokeswoman," *Montreal Gazette*, 4 June 1971, reprinted in *Akwesasne Notes*, June 1971, 41. See also Horn-Miller, "Distortion and Healing," 35; and Horn-Miller, "My Mom," 93.

63 Quoted in Gzowski, "Portrait of a Beautiful Segregationist," 172.

64 Quoted in ibid., 173.

65 Kapesh, *Je suis une maudite sauvagesse*, 39.

66 Ibid., 151.

67 Ibid., 50.

68 Ibid., 54.

69 Ibid., 95.

70 Nickel, *Assembling Unity*, 5.

71 Cardinal, *Unjust Society*, 94.

72 Indian Chiefs of Alberta, *Citizens Plus*.

73 Quoted in Nickel, "Reconsidering 1969," 235.

74 Coulthard, *Red Skin, White Masks*, 95.

75 Aks, *Women's Rights*, 73.

76 Baillargeon, *To Be Equals*, 142.

77 Glen, with Green, "Colleen Glen," 234.

78 Montour, dir., *Mary Two-Axe Earley*.

79 Sangster, "Words of Experience/Experiencing Words," 359.

80 Jamieson, "Multiple Jeopardy," 164.

81 Two-Axe Earley, "Brief to the Royal Commission."

82 Ibid.

83 Iacovetta, "'In the case of a woman.'"

84 York and Pinder, *People of the Pines*, 174–5; Alfred, *Heeding the Voices*, 164;
    "Kahn-Tineta Wants Her Sister Evicted," *Globe and Mail*, 31 August 1971,
    reprinted in *Akwesasne Notes*, September 1971, 38.

85 With regard to the 1951 revisions, after a few years of delay, the federal gov-
    ernment amended the Indian Act in 1951. On the one hand, as Kathleen
    Jamieson explains, the revisions were positive, for there was "an easing of
    laws on intoxicants, the prohibition on Indian ceremonies and dances were
    omitted, and Indian women were for the first time given the right to vote in
    band elections." But on the other hand, Aboriginal women faced more bar-
    riers because "the male line of descent was further emphasized as the major
    criterion for inclusion." Moreover, "the sections dealing with estates and in-
    heritance were also amended and adversely affected intermarried women."
    First Nations women now faced involuntary enfranchisement, entirely
    against their will and generally contrary to the wishes of First Nations as
    a whole. Jamieson, *Indian Women and the Law*, 59–60, 63.

86 Mrs Cecilia Philips Doré to Hon. Jean Chrétien, Minister of Indian Affairs
    and Northern Development, 21 September 1971, in RG 6, 1986-87/319, box
    96, file CB-9-390-34, Native Council of Canada, LAC.

87 Coulthard, *Red Skin, White Masks*, 84.

88 Two-Axe Earley, "Indian Rights for Indian Women," 430.

89 Mrs Cecilia Philips Doré to Hon. Jean Chrétien, Minister of Indian Affairs

and Northern Development, 21 September 1971, in RG 6, 1986-87/319, box 96, file CB-9-390-34, Native Council of Canada, LAC.

90 Nickel, *Assembling Unity*, 196.

91 *Report of the First Alberta Native Women's Conference.*

92 "Report of Participant-Observer," in RG 6-F-4, 1986-87, box 96, file CB-9-390-45, National Steering Committee on Native Women, National Native Women's Conference, Edmonton, Alberta, 22–23 March 1971, LAC.

93 Downey, *Creator's Game*, 139. As Allan Downey writes, "Sometimes the nation-building activities in contact zones were those of Indigenous nations rather than the nation-state of Canada."

94 Quoted in *Report of the First National Native Women's Conference*, appendix 3, i.

95 Quoted in ibid., 30.

96 Quoted in ibid., 7.

97 "Report of Participant-Observer," in RG 6-F-4, 1986-87, box 96, file CB-9-390-45, National Steering Committee on Native Women, National Native Women's Conference, Edmonton, Alberta, 22–23 March 1971, LAC.

98 Ibid.

99 Harris and Logan McCallum, "Assaulting the Ears," 225, 237; Nickel, *Assembling Unity*, 34–8. On the role that the Indian Homemakers' Clubs played in supporting male-dominated groups, see Nickel, *Assembling Unity*. For example, as Nickel explains, the British Columbia Indian Homemakers' Association "spearheaded fundraising efforts to hold the all-chief's conference in 1969, was involved in the original call for participants, and supported the UBCIC's [Union of British Columbia Indian Chiefs] mandate for unity through its auxiliary (and marginalized) political position." Ibid., 23–4. The 1969 conference led to the formation of the UBCIC.

100 Quoted in *Report of the First National Native Women's Conference*, 21.

101 Quoted in ibid., 41.

102 Quoted in ibid., 16.

103 Quoted in ibid., 16.

104 Quoted in ibid., 41.

105 "Report of Participant-Observer," in RG 6-F-4, 1986-87, box 96, file CB-9-390-45, National Steering Committee on Native Women, National Native Women's Conference, Edmonton, Alberta, 22–23 March 1971, LAC.

106 For a BC example, see Nickel, *Assembling Unity*, 138.

107 *Canada (AG) v Lavell*, [1974] SCR 1349; Jamieson, "Multiple Jeopardy," 166.

108 *R. v Bédard*, 2017 SCC 4, [2017] 1 SCR 89.

109 Cardinal, "Indian Women and the Indian Act." It is also important to note
     that the National Indian Brotherhood's study team proposed alternative so-
     lutions. As Cardinal outlines, "In a non-Indian-Indian marriage, the couple
     would not be allowed to remain on the reserve while married, but the In-
     dian spouse would be permitted to return to the reserve if the non-Indian
     spouse died, or if they were divorced." In the case of "inter-tribal mar-
     riages," "the new provisions would provide equality and a free choice: both
     the man and the woman would retain their tribal memberships, and the
     children would have the option of choosing which tribe to belong to when
     they reached the age of twenty."

110 Coulthard, *Red Skin, White Masks*, 85; Lawrence and Anderson, "Introduc-
     tion to Indigenous Women," 2. See also Coulthard, *Red Skin, White Masks*, 95.

111 For analysis of the Iroquois Nationals lacrosse team and its decision to
     travel internationally on a Haudenosaunee passport, see Downey, "Engen-
     dering Nationality." For more Indigenous global politics, see Lightfoot,
     "Indigenous Global Politics," 66.

112 Theobald, *Reproduction on the Reservation*, 1.

113 "Native American Women Denied Voice at International Women's Year
     Conference," *Akwesasne Notes*, Early Winter 1975, 33. For more on Thunder
     Hawk, see Castle, "Original Gangster"; Ricci, "Making Global Citizens?"

114 Quoted in "Native American Women Denied Voice at International
     Women's Year Conference," *Akwesasne Notes*, Early Winter 1975, 33.

115 W. Brown, "Mary Two-Axe Earley." In Mexico City, Mary Two-Axe Earley
     was introduced by Ghislaine Patry-Buisson, the president of the FFQ at the
     time. Ghislaine Patry-Buisson, interview with author, Laval, 5 February 2015.

116 Fédération des femmes du Québec, Voix des femmes, and Comité des
     femmes immigrantes, "L'expulsion de trois femmes Mohawk," reprinted in
     Dumont and Toupin, eds, *La pensée féministe au Québec*, 352.

117 St-Amand, *Stories of Oka*, 37; York and Pinder, *People of the Pines*, 174–5;
     Alfred, *Heeding the Voice*, 114, 132, 135.

118 Simpson, "Captivating Eunice," 124–5.

119 AFAQ, *Rapport final de la recherche*.

120 Lévesque, Michel, and Bussières, *Our Vision, Our Mission*, 6.

121 Lagacé, *Historique de l'Association*, 3.
122 Ibid., 2, 10.
123 Ibid., 6.
124 Rebick, *Ten Thousand Roses*, 110.
125 Ibid., 57.
126 Lagacé, *Historique de l'Association*, 56.
127 Ibid., 58. See, for example, Finestone, "Une journée à la Commission."
128 Lacombe, dir., *Artisans de notre histoire: Évelyn O'bomsawin.*
129 "Associations," *Bulletin de la* FFQ, June 1978, 39.
130 "Lettre: Pointe-Bleue, le 15 mai 1980," *Bulletin de la* FFQ, July 1980, 5.
131 "Conseil d'administration," *Bulletin de la* FFQ, July 1980, 3.
132 Cull, "Aboriginal Mothering," 144–6; AFAQ, *Primauté de l'intérêt de l'enfant.*
133 Dubinsky, *Babies without Borders*, 79; "The Latest in the 'Social Genocide' Field: Adoption of Indian Children by White Families," *Akwesasne Notes*, Early Autumn, 1972, 31.
134 Lagacé, *Historique de l'Association*, 87.
135 AFAQ, *Primauté de l'intérêt de l'enfant.*
136 Wuerscher, *Problems with the Legislative Base.*
137 AFAQ, *Mémoire présenté le 20 août 1980*, 1, 5, 10.
138 Lagacé, *Historique de l'Association*, 75.
139 Theobald, *Reproduction on the Reservation*, 96. As historian Brianna Theobald notes, "As activists would discover in the 1970s, Native women who had been sterilized sometimes did not want their own families to know, not to mention their entire tribe."
140 AFAQ, *Rapport final de la recherche.*
141 Lacombe, dir., *Artisans de notre histoire: Évelyn O'bomsawin.*
142 National Indian Brotherhood, *Declaration on Indian Housing*, 8, 1.
143 National Indian Brotherhood, *Statement on the Economic Development*, 4–7.
144 See, for example, Janovicek, "'Assisting Our Own.'"
145 AFAQ, *Rapport final de la recherche.*
146 Ibid.
147 Ibid.
148 National Indian Brotherhood, *Strategy for Socio-economic Development*, 24; Deiter and Currie, *Presentation to Senate Committee*, 11.
149 Lagacé, *Historique de l'Association*, 67.
150 AFAQ, *Rapport final de la recherche.* In this regard, the QNWA was like other

Indigenous organizations across the country. Manuel, *Fourth World*, 249, 251. The National Indian Brotherhood, for example, asked the federal government to "transfer to local Bands the authority and the funds which are allotted for [First Nations schooling]." National Indian Brotherhood, *Indian Control of Indian Education*, 6.

151   Goodleaf, *Entering the War Zone*, 24.

152   York and Pindera, *People of the Pines*, 118. Among the leaders of the school committee were Joe Deom, Lorna Delormier, Lorraine Montour, Nancy Deer, and Shirley Scott.

153   Ryan, "Community Control of Education," 144.

154   "Fantastic Fort-Scenic, Lake Fletcher, Nova Scotia," presentation to Black and Native students of Dalhousie University, 9 October 1978, in Dorothy Wills Fonds, MG 31 H179, vol. 7, file 7-27, LAC; "Kahanawake – Preparation and Delivery of a Special Care Certificate Program for the Mohawks, 1984–1988," in Dorothy Wills Fonds, MG 31 H179, vol. 4, "Memo," LAC.

155   Pelletier, with Laurin, *États des lieux*, 1–2, 23, 35.

156   Fiske, "Spirited Subjects," 102. See also Fiske, "Womb Is to the Nation," 74.

157   D. Desmarais, "Violence familiale."

158   Pelletier, with Laurin, *États des lieux*, 74.

159   Quoted in AFAQ, *Mémoire*.

160   Quoted in ibid.

161   This is my analysis, not the words used by the QNWA. In a formal statement issued on 11 October 1980, the Parti Québécois government stated that it would recognize intermarried Aboriginal women, that it encouraged bands to do the same, and that it had its own policies toward Native communities. However, the statement, if perhaps not representative, made no mention of any other social justice measures. This statement was included as an annex to the 1983 brief. The QNWA outlined the numerous shortcomings present in the social services, health, and education sectors. See AFAQ, *Mémoire*.

162   Ibid.

163   Montour, dir., *Mary Two-Axe Earley*.

164   Cannon, *Men, Masculinity*, 4, 66–9.

165   Aks, *Women's Rights*, 79.

166   Rebick, *Ten Thousand Roses*, 108, 110.

167   Cannon, *Men, Masculinity*, 4.

168   Fiske, "Spirited Subjects," 80–1.

169 Cannon, *Men, Masculinity*, 70.

170 Simpson, "To the Reserve," 227.

171 Simpson, *Mohawk Interruptus*, 62.

172 Cannon, *Men, Masculinity*, 67.

173 Simpson, *Mohawk Interruptus*, 22–4.

174 Horn-Miller, "Distortion and Healing," 33; see also 33n5.

175 Simpson, *Mohawk Interruptus*, 58, 33.

176 Stacey-Moore, *Amendments Proposed*, 6. As Stacey-Moore stated at the beginning of her talk, "The paper I am about to present is part of a brief on the implementation of Bill C-31, an Act to amend the Indian Act." Ibid., 1.

177 Simpson, *Mohawk Interruptus*, 148.

178 Quoted in York and Pindera, *People of the Pines*, 21–4, quote at 24.

179 Ibid., 72.

180 Goodleaf, *Entering the War Zone*, 20.

181 York and Pindera, *People of the Pines*, 192.

182 Goodleaf, *Entering the War Zone*, 58–9.

183 Simpson, *Mohawk Interruptus*, 150.

184 York and Pindera, *People of the Pines*, 209.

185 Quoted in Goodleaf, *Entering the War Zone*, 151.

186 "Regroupement," 1.

187 York and Pindera, *People of the Pines*, 377.

188 Néméh-Nombré, *Seize temps noirs*, 99–101.

189 Simpson, *Mohawk Interruptus*, 171.

190 Ibid., 150.

191 Rebick, *Ten Thousand Roses*, 110–11.

192 During the constitutional debates, it should be noted, the Quebec Native Women's Association consistently submitted briefs stressing the importance of gender equality and self-government. Quebec Native Women's Association, "Statement by the Quebec Native Women's Association."

CHAPTER TWO

1 Austin, *Fear of a Black Nation*, 16.

2 Affan, "Ethical Gestures," 52.

3 Austin, *Fear of a Black Nation*, 4.

4 Farmer, *Remaking Black Power*, 12, 13.

5 Austin, "All Roads Led to Montreal," 516.

6 Dorothy Williams, *Road to Now*, 13–14.

7 Cooper, *Hanging of Angélique*, 7. For an important scholarly debate surrounding Afua Cooper's and Denyse Beaugrand-Champagne's respective interpretations of Angélique, see Kolish, "Note critique."

8 Activists based in North America but born in the Caribbean, from Marcus Garvey to Stokely Carmichael, were still overrepresented in the pan-Africanist movement. Drake, "Black Diaspora."

9 Blain, *Set the World on Fire*, 3.

10 Spencer, "Engendering the Black Freedom Struggle," 91.

11 Dorothy Wills, ed., "Second National Congress of Black Women a Tremendous Success," newsletter, *Village News*, December 1974, in Dorothy Wills Fonds, MG 31 H179, vol. 4, file 4-20, National Coalition of Canada, *Habari Kijiji (Village News)*, LAC.

12 Thompson, "Multiracial Feminism," 40–1.

13 Dorothy Williams, *Road to Now*, 13–14.

14 There is an extensive and growing literature on these themes. For a few examples, see Austin, *Fear of a Black Nation*, 7–8; C. Nelson, *Slavery, Geography, and Empire*; and Zellars, "Dreams of a Black Commons."

15 Simpson, "Captivating Eunice," 115.

16 See, for example, Rushforth, *Bonds of Alliance*.

17 McKittrick, *Demonic Grounds*, 91–120.

18 Mugabo, "On Haunted Places," 89.

19 High, "Little Burgundy," 24; Dorothy Williams, *Road to Now*, 38–40.

20 High, "Little Burgundy," 41; Mathieu, *North of the Colour Line*, 17–18.

21 Mathieu, *North of the Colour Line*, 145–6.

22 High, "Little Burgundy," 27.

23 J. Bertley, "Role of the Black Community," 24–5.

24 Small and Thornhill, "Harambec!" 430.

25 See the Coloured Women's Club of Montreal, http://colouredwomensclub.tripod.com.

26 Este, Sato, and McKenna, "Coloured Women's Club of Montreal."

27 Dorothy Williams, *Road to Now*, 50–2.

28 Mathieu, *North of the Colour Line*, 145–6; Dorothy Williams, *Road to Now*, 50–2.

29 Concordia University Library, Special Collections, series F027/A – Negro Community Centre, box HA04810, RC 5921, file 32, Second National Congress of Black Women, History of the Coloured Women's Club Inc.

30 Este, "Black Church," 12.

31 Ibid., 19; J. Bertley, "Role of the Black Community," 103–4.

32 High, "Little Burgundy," 27–8; J. Bertley, "Role of the Black Community," 3.

33 Concordia University Library, Special Collections, series F027/A – Negro Community Centre, box HA04810, RC 5921, file 32, Second National Congress of Black Women, History of the Coloured Women's Club Inc.

34 J. Bertley, "Role of the Black Community," 32, 37.

35 L. Bertley, "Universal Negro Improvement Association," 5–7. Montreal's branch was one of 15 divisions in Canada and 1,200 worldwide.

36 High, "Little Burgundy," 27.

37 Farmer, *Remaking Black Power*, 20.

38 McDuffie, "Diasporic Journey," 155.

39 Mathieu, *North of the Color Line*, 156.

40 J. Bertley, "Role of the Black Community," 11.

41 Marano, "Rising Strongly and Rapidly," 246.

42 Dorothy Williams, *Road to Now*, 60.

43 Ibid.

44 Marano, "Rising Strongly and Rapidly," 255; Mathieu, *North of the Colour Line*, 158; J. Bertley, "Role of the Black Community," 37.

45 Blain, *Set the World on Fire*, 43.

46 Farmer, *Remaking Black Power*, 22.

47 McDuffie, "Diasporic Journey," 155.

48 Farmer, *Remaking Black Power*, 7.

49 Taylor, *Veiled Garvey*, 2.

50 Blain, *Set the World on Fire*, 12–19, 20 (quote).

51 Dorothy Wills, "Curriculum Vitae," in Dorothy Wills Fonds, MG 31 H179, vol. 1, file 1-1, LAC.

52 Abike (Dorothy Willis), "Dorothy Wills: The Persistent Apostle of Identity, Unity, Liberation," extract of Foreword to National Black Coalition of Canada, "The National Black Awards of Canada," 1976, in Dorothy Wills Fonds, MG 31 H179, vol. 5, file 5-1, LAC.

53 Leslie, "Negro Citizenship Association Inc."

54 Government of Quebec, *Some Missing Pages*, 164. See also Gloria Clarke Baylis's case, *Her Majesty the Queen v Hilton of Canada Ltd*, in Flynn, "Hotel Refuses Negro Nurse." The trial took place in 1965. Scholar Karen Flynn explains, "In the absence of a complete transcript of *Her Majesty v. Hilton*, and with the case never having been published, it has not appeared

in legal jurisprudence despite the newspaper and television publicity."
Ibid., 281.

55 Dorothy Wills, "Response to an Award Given by the National Black Coalition of Canada," 1984, in Dorothy Wills Fonds, MG 31 H179, vol. 5, file 5-2,
LAC.

56 Dorothy Wills, "Tribute to Roy Wellington States," Memorial Service, Union
United Church, Montreal, 14 December 1980, in Dorothy Wills Fonds, MG
31 H179, vol. 8, file 8-2, LAC.

57 R. Brown, *Being Brown*, 11, 25, 30,

58 Ibid., 32.

59 Olcott, *International Women's Year*, 495, 496; Randolph, *Florynce "Flo"
Kennedy*, 218–19.

60 Austin, *Fear of a Black Nation*, 29.

61 R.E.I., "Editorial," *Expression*, January 1966, 3–5.

62 Clément, *Human Rights in Canada*, 103, 105. The Fédération des femmes du
Québec played an important role in human rights legislation. "Mémoires,"
Bulletin de la FFQ, September 1975, 3; Patry-Buisson, "Une journée à la
Commission," 8.

63 Dubinsky, *Babies without Borders*, 79, uses the term "foil" with regard to
Canada's relationship with the United States in matters of race and racism.

64 R.E.I., "Editorial," *Expression*, February 1965, 7–9.

65 "Editorial," *Expression*, July 1967, 3–4.

66 Clarence Bayne and Dorothy Wills, eds, "Organizations Represented in the
National Black Coalition," newsletter, *Umoja: Black Dialogue*, 20 October
1969, 1, in Dorothy Wills Fonds, MG 31 H179, vol. 4, file 4-18, LAC.

67 Austin, "All Roads Led to Montreal," 517.

68 S. Mills, *Empire Within*, 97–8.

69 Austin, "All Roads Led to Montreal," 520; Austin, *Fear of a Black Nation*, 32.

70 Roberts, *View for Freedom*, 71–2.

71 Austin, *Fear of a Black Nation*, 17.

72 Austin, "All Roads Led to Montreal," 521, 523.

73 According to the conference proceedings, eleven out of thirty people on the
organizing committee were women. Congress of Black Writers, *Towards the
Second Emancipation*.

74 Austin, *Fear of a Black Nation*, 121.

75 Martel, "'Riot' at Sir George Williams," 97.

76 Leslie, "Negro Citizenship Association Inc."

77 "Framework," *UHURU*, 8 December 1969, 4. As will be discussed, those involved in defending the students founded *UHURU*, a community newspaper, to espouse Black Power.

78 Quoted in "Canadian Justice in Operation," *UHURU*, 2 February 1970, 1.

79 "Editorial: Canadian Liberalism: Fact or Fiction?" *Expression*, special
conference issue, Winter 1968, 3.

80 Ibid., 4.

81 For an understanding of a Montreal Black collective consciousness, see
Austin, "All Roads Led to Montreal," 535.

82 See, for example, Carmichael and Hamilton, *Black Power*, 2–6.

83 S. Mills, *Empire Within*, 115.

84 Ibid., 107; Martel, "'Riot' at Sir George Williams," 103.

85 Asher, "Red Nationalism on the Rise," *UHURU*, 2 March 1970, 7.

86 See, for example, Hudson, "Imperial Designs."

87 Douglas, "Canadian Racism and Sir George," 4–5; Néméh-Nombré, *Seize
temps noirs*, 99.

88 Austin, *Fear of a Black Nation*, 96.

89 As Austin explains, this expression "is often used to convey how hard one
has worked on a given day." See Austin, "Narratives of Power," 24.

90 "Vivian Barbot et la discrimination raciale."

91 Austin, *Fear of a Black Nation*, 62.

92 Ibid., 7.

93 Quoted in Austin, "Embarrassment of Omissions," 370.

94 Anne Cools, Marlene Dixon, Estelle Dorais, Susan Dubrofsky, Vickie
Tabachnik, and Eileen Nixon, "Memorandum to the Interim Work Com-
mittee," 19 December 1970, in Women's Movement Collection, F-166, file 2,
Indochinese Women's Conference, Montreal International Collective,
Simon Fraser University Archives.

95 "Ann Cools: Close-Up with Charles Harding: 'Jail is torment,'" *The Nation*,
24 March 1974, 8, in Dorothy Wills Fonds, MG 31 H179, vol. 2, file 2-14,
Cools, Anne, Canada's First Black Senator: clippings file 1984, LAC.

96 Austin, "Embarrassment of Omissions," 370. For more on the role that
Anne Cools played in the International Wages for Housework Campaign,
see Toupin, *Le salaire au travail ménager*, 143–5. In the words of Akua
Benjamin, a Trinidadian-Torontonian, "Anne Cools came to one of these

meetings, and she blasted the men. She challenged us women in the room as to why we were not talking. In those days, I just sat quietly in the back of the room. I would sit there and sweat. I was afraid to speak, afraid that I would get shut down. Anne cursed the men out, saying, 'fucking' this and 'fucking' that. We had never heard a woman talk like that. She really empowered me. After that I thought, 'I'm going to raise my voice.'" Quoted in Rebick, *Ten Thousand Roses*, 9–10.

97   Other Black communities in Canada were displaced during this period. On the Halifax example, see Rutland, *Displacing Blackness*; and Loo, "Africville and the Dynamics."

98   A. Mills, Rochat, and High, "Telling Stories," 41–2.

99   High, *Deindustrializing Montreal*, 16.

100 Farmer, *Remaking Black Power*, 127.

101 Wilkins, "Line of Steel," 104.

102 Claude, "Some Personal Reflections"; Farmer, *Remaking Black Power*, 139.

103 Farmer, *Remaking Black Power*, 139.

104 Blain, *Set the World on Fire*, 145.

105 Abike (Dorothy Wills), "Statement to the Rally of the African Liberation Day, 12 May 1972," in Dorothy Wills Fonds, MG 31 H179, vol. 7, file 7-9, LAC. See also Carmichael and Hamilton, *Black Power*, 9.

106 Abike (Dorothy Wills), "Address for African Liberation Day, Halifax, Nova Scotia, Saturday Morning, 26 May 1973," in Dorothy Wills Fonds, MG 31 H179, vol. 7, file 7-9, LAC.

107 Farmer, *Remaking Black Power*, 131.

108 Wilkins, "Line of Steel," 101; Farmer, *Remaking Black Power*, 139.

109 Wilkins, "Line of Steel," 99.

110 Blain, *Set the World on Fire*, 160; Farmer, *Remaking Black Power*, 129.

111 Taylor, *Veiled Garvey*, 165, 170, 171.

112 Wilkins, "Line of Steel," 98. Colonial domination continued in the Portuguese colonies and the settler colonial states of southern Africa.

113 Williams II, "From Anti-colonialism to Anti-apartheid," 69.

114 Wilkins, "Line of Steel," 107.

115 Ibid.

116 Roy-Campbell, "Pan-African Women," 47.

117 Farmer, *Remaking Black Power*, 155.

118 Ibid., 149.

119 Ibid., 16, 142.

120 Hill Collins, "It's All in the Family," 63, 77. See also Higginbotham, "African-American Women," 267–8. To paraphrase sociologist Patricia Hill Collins and historian Evelyn Brooks Higginbotham, the concepts of race and family have been double-edged swords for African Americans because, rather than strictly oppressive and (in the case of the family) a site of gendered inequality, they have been frequently relied upon for oppositional purposes and mobilized as a means to liberation and resistance. We notice traces of these discourses in Montreal.

121 Wills, "Status of the Black Woman Today," 14.

122 Farmer, *Remaking Black Power*, 154.

123 Dorothy Wills, "The Status of the Black Woman in Today's World," workshop paper, n.d., in Dorothy Wills Fonds, MG 31 II179, vol. 7, file 7-23, LAC.

124 Wilkins, "Line of Steel," 99.

125 The 1973 African Liberation Day demonstration mobilized an estimated 80,000 people in thirty-five cities across Africa, the Caribbean, the United States, and Canada.

126 Erhagbe, "African-American Contribution," 36; see also 49n49. As historian Edward O. Erhagbe explains, "Gene Locke of Houston and Brenda Paris of Canada were members of a delegation that went to Africa. It was, however, not possible to establish the exact amount collected and what went to each of the liberation movements, and the ceremonies, if there were any, during which the aid was delivered to the groups." Ibid., 49.

127 Concordia University Library, Special Collections, series F027/A – Negro Community Centre, box HA04173, file 6, Congress of Black Women, Montreal Committee 1986.

128 Erhagbe, "African-American Contribution," 36.

129 Dorothy Wills, letter to the National Black Coalition of Canada, 14 September 1974, in Dorothy Wills Fonds, MG 31 H179, vol. 5, file 5-10, Pan African Congress (Azania) Project Contributions for printing "Policy and Programme of the PAC of Azania," 1974, LAC.

130 Elias L. Ntloedibe to Dorothy Wills, Dar es Salaam, 21 November 1974, in Dorothy Wills Fonds, MG 31 H179, vol. 1, file 1-7, personal correspondence titled "The Struggle and Me," 1971–79, LAC.

131 Okdt Bernard R. Seme to Dorothy Wills, Dar es Salaam, 31 December 1975, in Dorothy Wills Fonds, MG 31 H179, vol. 1, file 1-7, personal correspondence titled "The Struggle and Me," 1971–79, LAC.

132 Farmer, *Remaking Black Power*, 147.

133 Dorothy Wills, ed., "The Sixth Pan African Congress," newsletter, *Village News*, September 1974, in Dorothy Wills Fonds, MG 31 H179, vol. 4, file 4-20, National Coalition of Canada, *Habari Kijiji* (*Village News*), LAC.

134 Dorothy Willis, "Black Cultural Development," keynote address, Halifax, Nova Scotia. August 1974, in Dorothy Wills Fonds, MG 31 H179, vol. 7, file 7-12, LAC.

135 Harewood, "NBCC Leaders," 6–7. For more on the National Black Coalition of Canada, see Walker, "National Black Coalition of Canada."

136 Abike (Dorothy Willis), "Dorothy Wills: The Persistent Apostle of Identity, Unity, Liberation," extract of Foreword to National Black Coalition of Canada, "The National Black Awards of Canada," 1976, in Dorothy Wills Fonds, MG 31 H179, vol. 5, file 5-1, LAC.

137 Austin, "Embarrassment of Omissions," 370.

138 See the Coloured Women's Club of Montreal, http://colouredwomensclub.tripod.com.

139 Blain, *Set the World on Fire*, 172.

140 Canadian Negro Women's Association, "Report of the First National Congress."

141 Small and Thornhill, "Harambec!" 433.

142 Canadian Negro Women's Association, "Report of the First National Congress."

143 Ibid.

144 Ibid.

145 Beal, "Slave of a Slave No More."

146 R. Brown, *Being Brown*, 80–4.

147 Dorothy Williams, *Road to Now*, 174.

148 Canadian Negro Women's Association, "Report of the First National Congress."

149 Ibid.

150 Henry, "West Indian Domestic Scheme."

151 D. Brand, "'We weren't allowed to go,'" 190.

152 See Iacovetta, "Primitive Villagers"; and Mina, "Taming and Training."

153 Canadian Negro Women's Association, "Report of the First National Congress."

154 Davis, "Racism, Birth Control," 354, 363. See also J. Nelson, *Women of Color*, 2–4. As scholar Hazel V. Carby argues, key concepts such as the family,

patriarchy, and reproduction that are "central to feminist theory become problematic in their application to Black women's lives." Carby, "White Women Listen!" 214.

155 Canadian Negro Women's Association, "Report of the First National Congress."

156 Farmer, *Remaking Black Power*, 100.

157 Vergès, *Le ventre des femmes*, 116.

158 Canadian Negro Women's Association, "Report of the First National Congress."

159 Dubinsky, *Babies without Borders*, 72–3.

160 Canadian Negro Women's Association, "Report of the First National Congress."

161 Aladejebi, *Schooling the System*, 67.

162 Canadian Negro Women's Association, "Report of the First National Congress."

163 For an Ontario example, see Aladejebi, "We've Got Our Quota."

164 Kouka-Ganga, "Femmes noires au Canada."

165 Constance Riley, Secretarial Committee of the Congress, to Committee Member, 11 October 1974, in Concordia University Library, Special Collections, series F027/A – Negro Community Centre, box HA04810, RC 5921, file 32, Second National Congress of Black Women, History of the Coloured Women's Club Inc.

166 "Schedule," Second National Congress of Black Women of Canada, 8–10 November 1974, Sheraton Mount Royal Hotel, Montreal, in Concordia University Library, Special Collections, series F027/A – Negro Community Centre, box HA04810, RC 5921, file 32, Second National Congress of Black Women, History of the Coloured Women's Club Inc.

167 J. Mills, "Conferencing as a Site," 429.

168 See, for example, "Indian Rebirth," *The Black Panther Party*, 25 May 1969, reprinted in *Akwesasne Notes*, July 1969, 38.

169 Lacombe, dir., *Artisans de notre histoire: Évelyn O'Bomsawin*; J. Bertley, "Role of the Black Community," 149. Thanks to the tireless work of the Reverend Dr Charles Humphrey Este, some Black women managed to secure clerical positions in offices.

170 For a full and nuanced discussion of "recognition" and its downfalls, see Coulthard, *Red Skin, White Masks*.

171 National Congress of Black Women of Canada, "Brief Presented to the Canadian Consultative Council on Multiculturalism, Montreal, March 1978," in Concordia University Library, Special Collections, series F027/A – Negro Community Centre, box HA04173, file 20, Brief National Congress of Black Women.

172 Ibid.

173 Kouka-Ganga, "Femmes noires au Canada." The Bibliothèque et Archives nationales du Québec possesses few written documents on the Ligue des femmes du Québec. For a very brief report on the conference, see "Rétrospective 1977–1980," *Bulletin/Ligue des femmes du Québec*, January 1981, 5–6.

174 Bevien, "Seminar," 88.

175 "The Nairobi Forward-Looking Strategies for the Advancement of Women, Adopted at the World Conference to Review and Appraise the Achievements of the United Nations Decade for Women: Equality, Development and Peace, Nairobi, Kenya, 15–26 July, 1985," in R-1407, box 47, file 47-12, Status of Women, Nairobi Conference, LAC.

176 McKercher, "Sound and Fury," 181–2.

177 Manulak, "African Representative," 378.

178 Jane Kouga-Ganga, Chairperson of the Public Relations Committee, to "Dear friends," Montreal, 30 July 1980, in Concordia University Library, Special Collections, series F027/A – Negro Community Centre, box HA04173, file 30, Congress of Black Women (2 of 3).

179 Public Relations Committee, Montreal Regional Committee, National Congress of Black Women of Canada, "Declaration," Montreal, 30 July 1980, in Concordia University Library, Special Collections, series F027/A – Negro Community Centre, box HA04173, file 30, Congress of Black Women (2 of 3).

180 Juanita Westmoreland-Traoré to Conseil du statut de la femme, Montreal, 12 July 1983, in Fonds Conseil du statut de la femme, E99 1995-11-003/1, file: Congrès des femmes noires du Canada, Bibliothèque et Archives nationales du Québec (BANQ).

181 "Constitution of the Regional Committee (Montreal) of the National Congress of Black Women," original emphasis, in Concordia University Library, Special Collections, series F027/A – Negro Community Centre, box HA04173, file 29, Congress of Black Women (1 of 3).

182 Ibid.; Dorothy Willis, ed., "Second National Congress of Black Women

Follow-Up," newsletter, *Village News*, January 1975, in Dorothy Wills Fonds, MG 31 H179, vol. 4, file 4-20, National Coalition of Canada, *Habari Kijiji* (*Village News*), LAC; Juanita Westmoreland-Traoré to Conseil du statut de la femme, Montreal, 18 July 1983, in Fonds Conseil du statut de la femme, E99 1995-11-003/1, file: Congres des femmes noires du Canada, BANQ.

183 Stasiulis and Bakan, *Negotiating Citizenship*, 157.

184 "Editorial: Fourth National Congress of Black Women," *Contrast*, 25 August 1977, 6.

185 Small and Thornhill, "Harambec!" 434, 440.

186 RG 6-F, ATIP Division, interim container 92, file 0901-H, Citizenship Sector – National Congress of Black Women of Canada – Founding Conference of the NCBWC, 15 September 1980.

187 See, for example, "Minutes of Meeting Held on 20 November 1982 of the Regional Committee of the National Congress of Black Women – Montreal," in Concordia University Library, Special Collections, series F027/A – Negro Community Centre, box HA04173, file 27, Congress of Black Women minutes.

188 Thornhill, "Selected Awards." See also Thornhill, "Black Women's Studies."

189 Glenda Simms, President of the Congress of Black Women, to Monique Gagnon-Tremblay, Minister Responsible for the Status of Women, 22 December 1986, in Dorothy Wills Fonds, MG 31 H179, vol. 6, file 6-18, Thornhill, Esmeralda, copies of her reports.

190 McKeown, dir., *Désirs de liberté*; Sandoval, "U.S. Third World Feminism."

191 For example, in a 1975 article published in the *Black Scholar*, Sekou Touré outlined the role of African women in the revolution. As the first president of independent Guinea, he asserted the mutually constitutive nature of two social movements taking place all over the Black diaspora: "If African women cannot possibly conduct their struggle in isolation from that our people wage for African liberation, African freedom, conversely, is not effective unless it brings about the liberation of African women." Touré, "Role of Women," 32.

CHAPTER THREE

1 "Table ronde: Front de libération des femmes, le 16 novembre 1982," in O'Leary and Toupin, eds, *Québécoises deboutte!*, vol. 2, 329.

2 S. Mills, *Empire Within*, 119–20.

3 Quoted in Solange Chalvin, "Le Front commun des Québécoises descendra dans la rue, ce soir," *Le Devoir*, 28 November 1969, in O'Leary and Toupin, eds, *Québécoises deboutte!*, vol. 1, 57.

4 O'Leary and Toupin, eds, *Québécoises deboutte!*, vol. 1, 26.

5 Dumont, "La culture politique." The organizers invited only forty-one women's organizations, for 6 per cent of the total participants. They included the by then defunct Fédération nationale Saint-Jean-Baptiste but failed to invite the more active, larger, and more relevant women's organizations.

6 Dumont, "La culture politique."

7 Quoted in Tanguay, "La page féminine du *Devoir* 50."

8 Lanthier, "L'impossible réciprocité," 2.

9 For an explanation of the French Canadian elite's understanding of Indigenous history prior to the 1960s, see Gélinas, *Les autochtones*, 57–77.

10 McCarthy, *In Divided Unity*, 43.

11 Tuck and Yang, "Decolonization Is Not a Metaphor."

12 Michaud, *Frontiers of Feminism*, 35–40.

13 Dua, "Exclusion through Inclusion," 448–9.

14 Sangster, *Demanding Equality*, 48. Morgan's interest in the Haudenosaunee Confederacy was largely fetishistic. McCarthy, *In Divided Unity*, 44–53.

15 Lacelle, *Entretiens avec Madeleine Parent et Léa Roback*.

16 Larochelle, "Émanciper l'histoire."

17 O'Leary and Toupin, eds, *Québécoises deboutte!*, vol. 1, 27.

18 "F.L.F.Q. Historique: Été 1970," in O'Leary and Toupin, eds, *Québécoises deboutte!*, vol. 1, 65–6.

19 Evans, *Personal Politics*, 24.

20 Ibid., 100.

21 Ibid., 205.

22 "F.L.F.Q. Historique: Été 1970," in O'Leary and Toupin, eds, *Québécoises deboutte!*, vol. 1, 66.

23 S. Mills, *Empire Within*, 122.

24 Péloquin, *En prison pour la cause*, 29.

25 S. Mills, *Empire Within*, 124.

26 *Montreal Women's Liberation Network Newsletter*, June 1970, 1.

27 S. Mills, *Empire Within*, 124.

28 "Monday Night Classes," *Montreal Women's Network Newsletter*, March 1970, 3.

29 S. Mills, *Empire Within*, 124. During the 1960s, an estimated 30,000 to 100,000 American resisters came to Canada, of which many were women, following their husbands, their boyfriends, or "their own political conscience into an uncertain exile." Churchill, "Draft Resisters," 227.
30 O'Leary and Toupin, eds, *Québécoises deboutte!*, vol. 1, 40.
31 Thompson, "Multiracial Feminism," 44.
32 Henretta, "Oppression of Women in Canada," 1.
33 hooks, *Ain't I a Woman*, 8.
34 Mary Porter, "Some Reflections on the Problem of Female Sexual Oppression: Prepared for the Women's Liberation Study Group," in box 139, Women's Liberation Study Group, Canadian Women's Movement Archives Collection, Morisset Library Special Collections, University of Ottawa.
35 "Karate," *Montreal Women's Liberation Newsletter*, June 1970, 4.
36 Cherniak and Feingold, *Birth Control Handbook*, 3.
37 Ibid., 43.
38 Ibid., 1.
39 Wynn, "Pill Scare," 5.
40 See, for example, Dubinsky, *Babies without Borders*, 75.
41 Simon, *Translating Montreal*, 90.
42 Lévesque, "Les midinettes de 1937."
43 Sethna, "Evolution of the *Birth Control Handbook*," 96.
44 Troper, *Defining Decade*, 191, quoting one of the "red-diaper babies," a term used in reference to the children of 1930s Jewish radicals.
45 Ibid., 197, quoting Gorny, *State of Israel*. This contestation included strong support for feminism, as exemplified by the high percentage of Jewish women involved in the women's liberation movement in the United States and Canada. Antler, "We Were Ready," 211.
46 See, for example, "Notes biographiques sur les administrateurs de la FFQ," *Bulletin de la FFQ*, June 1970, 7; and "National Council of Jewish Women," *Bulletin de la FFQ*, December 1970, 9.
47 Troper, *Defining Decade*, 24, 84.
48 Thompson, "Multiracial Feminism," 45.
49 Cherniak and Feingold, *Birth Control Handbook*, 3.
50 S. Mills, *Empire Within*, 138.
51 Sethna, "Evolution of the *Birth Control Handbook*," 109.
52 Girourd, *Pour un contrôle de naissances*, 3. See also Sethna, "Evolution of the *Birth Control Handbook*," 107–9; and S. Mills, *Empire Within*, 126.

53 S. Mills, *Empire Within*, 126.

54 O'Leary and Toupin, eds, *Québécoises deboutte!*, vol. 1, 45.

55 Ibid., 137.

56 "Septembre 1970: Un bilan de parcours," in O'Leary and Toupin, eds, *Québécoises deboutte!*, vol. 1, 76.

57 Ibid.

58 Péloquin, *En prison pour la cause*, 259, 260.

59 Ibid., 28.

60 "Le sexisme dans les groupes mixtes," *Bulletin de liaison* FLFQ, August 1971, in O'Leary and Toupin, eds, *Québécoises deboutte!*, vol. 1, 119; O'Leary and Toupin, eds, *Québécoises deboutte!*, vol. 1, 31.

61 "Le sexisme dans les groupes mixtes," *Bulletin de liaison* FLFQ, August 1971, in O'Leary and Toupin, eds, *Québécoises deboutte!*, vol. 1, 119; "Bilan du Centre des femmes de Montreal, November 1974," in O'Leary and Toupin, eds, *Québécoises deboutte!*, vol. 1, 158.

62 "Exploitation spécifique des femmes," *Bulletin de liaison* FLFQ, August 1971, in O'Leary and Toupin, eds, *Québécoises deboutte!*, vol. 1, 107.

63 "Origine de cette exploitation," *Bulletin de liaison* FLFQ, August 1971, in O'Leary and Toupin, eds, *Québécoises deboutte!*, vol. 1, 107–10.

64 Quoted in "Table ronde: Centre des femmes, le 18 novembre 1982," in O'Leary and Toupin, eds, *Québécoises deboutte!*, vol. 2, 349.

65 Quoted in "Table ronde: Front de libération des femmes, le 16 novembre 1982," in O'Leary and Toupin, eds, *Québécoises deboutte!*, vol. 2, 329.

66 "F.L.F.Q. Fonctionnement: Été 1970," in O'Leary and Toupin, eds, *Québécoises deboutte!*, vol. 1, 67.

67 Ibid.

68 S. Mills, *Empire Within*, 55.

69 O'Leary and Toupin, eds, *Québécoises deboutte!*, vol. 1, 129.

70 Ibid., 100.

71 "Cellule X," *Bulletin de liaison* FLFQ, July 1971, in O'Leary and Toupin, eds, *Québécoises deboutte!*, vol. 1, 101.

72 O'Leary and Toupin, eds, *Québécoises deboutte!*, vol. 1, 22.

73 Ibid., 47.

74 "Mouvement des femmes," *Bulletin de liaison* FLFQ, August 1971, in O'Leary and Toupin, eds, *Québécoises deboutte!*, vol. 1, 113.

75 Lanthier, "L'impossible réciprocité," 39; S. Mills, *Empire Within*, 46–7.

76 "Cellule II," *Bulletin de liaison* FLFQ, July 1971, in O'Leary and Toupin, eds, *Québécoises deboutte!*, vol. 1, 105, original emphasis.

77 "Cellule I," *Bulletin de liaison* FLFQ, July 1971, in O'Leary and Toupin, eds, *Québécoises deboutte!*, vol. 1, 104.

78 Péloquin, *En prison pour la cause*, 85.

79 "Cellule II: Pourquoi un FLF," *Bulletin de liaison* FLFQ, August 1971, in O'Leary and Toupin, eds, *Québécoises deboutte!*, vol. 1, 107.

80 "Quelques conditions de la libération des femmes," *Bulletin de liaison* FLFQ, August 1971, in O'Leary and Toupin, eds, *Québécoises deboutte!*, vol. 1, 111–21, quote at 113.

81 On Québécois women, see O'Leary and Toupin, eds, *Québécoises deboutte!*, vol. 1, 40. On French women, see Duchen, *Feminism in France*, 69.

82 Quoted in "Table ronde: Centre des femmes, le 18 novembre 1982," in O'Leary and Toupin, eds, *Québécoises deboutte!*, vol. 2, 349.

83 Delphy, "L'ennemi principal"; "Septembre 1970. Un bilan de parcours," in O'Leary and Toupin, eds, *Québécoises deboutte!*, vol. 1, 76; "Été 1971: publication de deux bulletins de liaison: Le FLF: Pourquoi? Pour qui? Comment?" in O'Leary and Toupin, eds, *Québécoises deboutte!*, vol. 1, 100.

84 "Cellule I," *Bulletin de liaison* FLFQ, July 1971, in O'Leary and Toupin, eds, *Québécoises deboutte!*, vol. 1, 104.

85 Maillé, "French and Quebec Feminisms," 52, quoting Collectif Clio's *L'histoire des femmes du Québec* (1982).

86 Ibid., 51–6, quote at 52.

87 "Table ronde: Centre des femmes, le 18 novembre 1982," in O'Leary and Toupin, eds, *Québécoises deboutte!*, vol. 2, 328.

88 O'Leary and Toupin, eds, *Québécoises deboutte!*, vol. 1, 40.

89 Vallières, *White Niggers of America*, 13, 17.

90 Ibid., 13.

91 Ibid., 214–15.

92 Ibid., 13.

93 Ibid., 234–6.

94 Girourd, *Pour un contrôle de naissances*.

95 As Sean Mills explains, "Aimé Césaire initially laughed at the prospect of a white population employing the concept of negritude, but he eventually came to see that Vallières and other Quebecers had understood the concept at a profound level." S. Mills, *Empire Within*, 74.

96 S. Mills, *Empire Within*, 60.

97 Memmi, *Portrait du colonisé*, 139.

98 Ibid., 138–45.

99 Ibid., 103.

100 Austin, *Fear of a Black Nation*, 59, 60.

101 Vallières, *White Niggers of America*, 21.

102 Cornellier, "Struggle of Others," 35, 40.

103 Wu, *Radicals on the Road*, 211.

104 Austin, *Fear of a Black Nation*, 45.

105 "F.L.F.Q. Fonctionnement: Été 1970," in O'Leary and Toupin, eds, *Québécoises deboutte!*, vol. 1, 66.

106 Ibid., 67.

107 Nicolas, "Maîtres chez l'Autre," 42–6.

108 Austin, *Fear of a Black Nation*, 51–70 ; Maillé, "Réception de la théorie postcoloniale."

109 McClintok, "Family Feuds," 77–8.

110 Robinson, *Black Marxism*, 2, 24–8, 121.

111 "Canadian Feminists Fight for Change." See also Fédération des femmes du Québec, *La participation politique*, 1; and "F.L.F.Q. Historique: Été 1970," in O'Leary and Toupin, eds, *Québécoises deboutte!*, vol. 1, 66.

112 D. Lamoureux, "Nationalisme et féminisme"; Sethna, "Evolution of the *Birth Control Handbook*," 109.

113 O'Leary and Toupin, eds, *Québécoises deboutte!*, vol. 1, 31, 69.

114 L. Desmarais, *La bataille de l'avortement*, 57.

115 Hewitt and Sethna, "Sex Spying," 134.

116 "Abortion Caravan (1970)," in box 1-8, Abortion Caravan (May 1970): proposals, brief, clippings, and other material, 1970–88, Canadian Women's Movement Archives Collection, Morisset Library Special Collections, University of Ottawa.

117 Ibid. This demand refers to Trudeau's oft-cited assurance that "there is no place for the state in the bedrooms of the nation."

118 Sethna, "Evolution of the *Birth Control Handbook*," 93.

119 Delorme, "Gaining a Right to Abortion."

120 "Abortion Caravan," *Montreal Women's Liberation Newsletter*, June 1970, 9–10.

121 Quoted in "10 mai 1979, jour de la fête des mères: Le FLF manifeste en

faveur de l'avortement," in O'Leary and Toupin, eds, *Québécoises deboutte!*, vol. 1, 70–1, quote at 71.

122 L. Desmarais, *La bataille de l'avortement*, 74.

123 "Avortement libre, gratuit, et sur demande," *Québécoises deboutte!*, November 1971, in O'Leary and Toupin, eds, *Québécoises deboutte!*, vol. 1, 144.

124 Ibid.

125 "Abortion Caravan," *Montreal Women's Liberation Newsletter*, June 1970, 9–10.

126 O'Leary and Toupin, eds, *Québécoises deboutte!*, vol. 1, 32.

127 Ibid.

128 Ibid., 33.

129 "Table ronde: Front de libération des femmes du Québec, le 16 novembre 1982," in O'Leary and Toupin, eds, *Québécoises deboutte!*, vol. 2, 332.

130 Quoted in Péloquin, *En prison pour la cause*, 51.

131 Quoted in S. Mills, *Empire Within*, 128.

132 Péloquin, *En prison pour la cause*, 27.

133 Péloquin, *En prison pour la cause*, 13, 11, 21–2, 44, 175, 231.

134 Anne Cools, Marlene Dixon, Estelle Dorais, Susan Dubrofsky, Vickie Tabachnik, and Eileen Nixon, "Memorandum to the Interim Work Committee," 19 December 1970, in Women's Movement Collection, F-166, file 2, Indochinese Women's Conference, Montreal International Collective, Simon Fraser University Archives. I was able to order only one of the three files in the Simon Fraser University Archives.

135 "Décembre 1970: Lettre à des féministes américaines," in O'Leary and Toupin, eds, *Québécoises deboutte!*, vol. 1, 79–80.

136 Ibid.

137 "Conference?" *Montreal Women's Liberation Newsletter*, June 1970, 3.

138 Wu, *Radicals on the Road*, 198, 205–12, 259, 218.

139 Sangster, *Demanding Equality*, 262.

140 Moreover, Gerry Ambers, for example, recalled how she and her counterparts wanted to include First Nations men in their struggles, whereas white women drew a "hard line at gender" earlier. Wu, *Radicals on the Road*, 239.

141 Third World Women's Caucus, Los Angeles, California, "Untitled document," in Women's Movement Collection, F-166, file 2, Indochinese Women's Conference, Montreal International Collective, Simon Fraser University Archives. According to historian Judy Wu, drawing on the estimates

of the Voix des femmes/Voice of Women, 109 women from six states and five provinces attended the Vancouver conference, and 388 women from nineteen states, three provinces, and Australia attended the Toronto conference. Wu does not specify whether there was a Quebec delegation or whether francophone women attended the conference. The delegation from Southeast Asia consisted of three teams of two women and one male translator each for North Vietnam, South Vietnam, and Laos. Wu, *Radicals on the Road*, 388, 244.

142 Wu, *Radicals on the Road*, 198, 205–12, 218, 259.

143 This book was originally published in Italian as *Dalla Cina: Dopo la rivoluzione culturale* by Feltrinelli in 1971.

144 Liu, "Au pays de l'avenir radieux," 152.

145 "Les femmes en Chine," *Québécoises deboutte!*, September 1973, in O'Leary and Toupin, eds, *Québécoises deboutte!*, vol. 2, 256.

146 "Les Algériennes," *Québécoises deboutte!*, July 1973, in O'Leary and Toupin, eds, *Québécoises deboutte!*, vol. 2, 227–38.

147 Gluck, "Shifting Sands," 101.

148 "Histoire d'une oppression: Les Amérindiennes," *Québécoises deboutte!*, December 1972, in O'Leary and Toupin, eds, *Québécoises deboutte!*, vol. 2, 41.

149 For the Black Power movement's cultivation of revolutionary images of women see Spencer, "Engendering the Black Freedom Struggle," 99. See also the compelling ideas in Gunn Allen, *Sacred Hoop*, 209–21.

150 Sangster, *Demanding Equality*, 276.

151 O'Leary and Toupin, eds, *Québécoises deboutte!*, vol. 1, 34; O'Neill, "Y aura-t-il toujours des pauvres."

152 Milot, "Histoire du mouvement."

153 O'Leary and Toupin, eds, *Québécoises deboutte!*, vol. 1, 129–30; "Table ronde: Front de libération des femmes, le 16 novembre 1982," in O'Leary and Toupin, eds, *Québécoises deboutte!*, vol. 2, 368.

154 O'Leary and Toupin, eds, *Québécoises deboutte!*, vol. 2, 23.

155 L. Desmarais, *La bataille de l'avortement*, 93.

156 "Bilan du Centre des femmes de Montréal, janvier 1972 à septembre 1974," in O'Leary and Toupin, eds, *Québécoises deboutte!*, vol. 1, 159.

157 L. Desmarais, *La bataille de l'avortement*, 49.

158 Ackerman and Stettner, "'Public Is Not Ready,'" 243, 244.

159 L. Desmarais, *La bataille de l'avortement*, 71.

160 "Perquisition au Centre des femmes," *Québécoises deboutte!*, March 1973, in O'Leary and Toupin, eds, *Québécoises deboutte!*, vol. 2, 114.

161 "Table ronde: Front de libération des femmes, le 16 novembre 1982," in O'Leary and Toupin, eds, *Québécoises deboutte!*, vol. 2, 361.

162 "Bilan du Centre des femmes de Montreal, janvier 1972 à septembre 1974," in O'Leary and Toupin, eds, *Québécoises deboutte!*, vol. 1, 165.

163 D. Lamoureux, "La lutte pour le droit," 83.

164 Quoted in Milne, "Creating Change," 18.

165 Ackerman and Stettner, "'Public Is Not Ready,'" 244, 240. As the two historians explain, "These developments in Quebec underscore the importance of approaching abortion history in Canada as many ongoing and competing histories instead of a single national story." Ibid., 244.

166 D. Lamoureux, "La lutte pour le droit," 85.

167 Ibid., 84.

168 "Le PQ: Espoir ou illusion," *Québécoises deboutte!*, April 1973, in O'Leary and Toupin, eds, *Québécoises deboutte!*, vol. 2, 127–31, quote at 129.

169 Ibid., 130.

170 Yuval-Davis, *Gender and Nation*, 2.

171 Praud, "La seconde vague féministe."

172 Quoted in Yanacopoulo, *Regroupement des femmes québécoises*, 24.

173 Ibid., 23–6.

174 Palmer, *Canada's 1960s*, 333.

175 Yanacopoulo, *Regroupement des femmes québécoises*, 23–6. As Yanacopoulo explains, Aquin supported her initiatve in fouding the RFQ, writing on the first official minutes, "I want you to know that I support you." Quoted in ibid., 26n13.

176 Quoted in ibid., 30–1, original emphasis.

177 L. Desmarais, *La bataille de l'avortement*, 147.

178 Ibid., 148; D. Lamoureux, "La question lesbienne," 171, 173. See also Rodriguez-Arbolay Jr, "Connecting Fragments," 49.

179 Hildebrun, "Genèse d'une communauté lesbienne," 208.

180 Millward, *Making a Scene*, 21–2, 178, 209.

181 Podmore and Chamberland, "Entering the Urban Frame," 199.

182 Quoted in Yanacopoulo, *Regroupement des femmes québécoises*, 97.

183 Yanacopoulo, *Regroupement des femmes québécoises*, 99.

184 D. Lamoureux, "Les ambivalences du féminisme québécois."

185 L. Desmarais, *La bataille de l'avortement*, 186.

186 Yanacopoulo, *Regroupement des femmes québécoises*, 89.

187 L. Beaudry, "Les groupes d'extrême gauche."

188 S. Mills, *Empire Within*, 136; Delorme, "Gaining a Right to Abortion," 109.

189 Baillargeon, *Brief History*, 179.

CHAPTER FOUR

1 Neptune-Anglade, "Les conférences internationales," 166.

2 Comité ad hoc des femmes haïtiennes, *La femme haïtienne en diaspora*, 22.

3 Charles, "Gender and Politics," 148.

4 Dejean, *Les Haïtiens au Québec*, 101.

5 Sanders, "La voix des femmes." The LFAS is referenced, for example, in Merlet, *La participation politique*, ix; Zéphir, ed., *Haitian Women*, 1; *Femmes et démocratie en Haïti*, 13; Myriam Chancy, *Framing Silence*, 40–5; and Neptune-Anglade, *L'autre moitié du développement*, 24–6.

6 Labelle et Therrien, "Le mouvement associatif haïtien," 72.

7 Interviewed in Sanders, "La voix des femmes," 62, 107.

8 Magloire, "L'antiféminisme en Haïti," 205.

9 Fouron and Glick Schiller, "All in the Family," 547.

10 S. Mills, *Place in the Sun*, 7.

11 Antrobus, *Global Women's Movement*, 1.

12 Antrobus, "Caribbean Journey," 144.

13 Robinson, *Black Marxism*, 144.

14 West, "Afterword," 258.

15 See, for example, Bouchereau, *Haïti et ses femmes*, 231; and Merlet, "Women in Conquest."

16 Smith, *Red and Black in Haiti*, 1.

17 Charles, "Gender and Politics," 146; Myriam Chancy, *Framing Silence*, 42; Sanders, "La voix des femmes," 36.

18 Smith, *Red and Black in Haiti*, 188.

19 Ligue féminine d'action sociale, *Femmes haïtiennes*, 9, 23.

20 Ibid., 1.

21 Ibid., 200.

22 Garoute, "Suprême appel de notre président," 36.

23 "Exposé d'introduction: Par Madeleine Sylvain Bouchereau: Présidente du Comité d'Organisation," in LFAS, *Le féminisme en marche*, 7–9.

24 "Discours d'Ouverture de Mme Lucienne Heurtelou Estimé," in LFAS,
    Le féminisme en marche, 6–7.

25 "Discours de Madame Lakshmi N. Menon à la séance du Premier congrès
    national des femmes haïtiennes," in LFAS, *Le féminisme en marche*, 9.

26 Ibid., 9–10.

27 "Premier congrès national des femmes haïtiennes du 10 au 15 avril 1950,"
    in LFAS, *Le féminisme en marche*, 1–2.

28 Charles, "Gender and Politics," 147; Myriam Chancy, *Framing Silence*, 40–5;
    Magloire, "L'antiféminisme en Haïti."

29 Magloire, "L'antiféminisme en Haïti."

30 Quoted in Cléante Desgraves Valcin, "La manifestation aux Gonaïves," and
    Lydia Jeanty, "Campagne pour les droits de la femme haïtienne," in LFAS,
    Le féminisme en marche, 31–9.

31 Sanders, "La voix des femmes," 162.

32 S. Mills, "Quebec, Haiti," 411.

33 Sanders, "La voix des femmes," 188–9; Charles, "Gender and Politics,"
    139–41.

34 S. Pierre, ed., *Ces québécois venus d'Haïti*, 257–60.

35 Lévy, *Espace d'une génération*, 17; S. Pierre, *Ces québécois venus d'Haïti*, 3–5.

36 Lévy, *Espace d'une génération*, 17, 26.

37 RAFA, *Femmes haïtiennes*, 45; A. Chancy, *Profil*, 19.

38 Quoted in A. Chancy, *Profil*, 25.

39 Ibid., 22.

40 For more on Marxism and Haiti's intellectual elite, see Montas, "Sur la
    diffusion." See also A. Chancy, *Profil*, 14.

41 "Études: Les caractéristiques sociodémographiques de l'immigration des
    femmes haïtiennes au Québec," *Collectif paroles*, March-April 1984, 3–4.

42 Rochat, "Archiving Black Diasporic Activism," 71.

43 Congress of Black Writers, *Towards the Second Emancipation*. Interestingly,
    the first page of the conference proceedings was bilingual, and the eminent
    Haitian poet and communist activist René Depestre was a speaker at the
    Montreal gathering.

44 Rochat, "Archiving Black Diasporic Activism," 162.

45 Ibid., 84, 87.

46 Paul, "Women and the International Division," 178.

47 Dejean, *Les Haïtiens au Québec*, 29, 31.

48   "Études: Les caractéristiques sociodémographiques de l'immigration des femmes haïtiennes au Québec," *Collectif paroles*, March-April 1984, 3–4.

49   Rochat, "Archiving Black Diasporic Activism," 87.

50   S. Pierre, *Ces québécois venus d'Haïti*, 350; Paul, "Women and the International Division," 200.

51   S. Mills, *Place in the Sun*, 176.

52   Quoted in ibid., 176–7.

53   Rochat, "Archiving Black Diasporic Activism," 159.

54   Ollivier, "Étude"; A. Chancy, "Éducation: La lettre à la famille."

55   A. Chancy, "L'alphabétisation des immigrants."

56   Estimable, "L'intégration des jeunes immigrants."

57   Moise, "Dans la diaspora"; "French and the Black Student," *Contrast*, 24 November 1977, 4.

58   A. Chancy, "L'alphabétisation des immigrants," 24.

59   A. Chancy, *L'analphabétisme*.

60   Ibid., 105.

61   N'Zengu-Tayo, "Fanm se poto mitan," 132; Lamour, "Partir pour mieux s'enraciner."

62   A. Chancy, *L'analphabétisme*, 105, 115.

63   Maison d'Haïti, *Mémoire de la Maison d'Haïti*.

64   A. Chancy, "Lagrame."

65   Rateau, "Mireille Neptune."

66   After some debate, its founders settled on the name Point de ralliement des femmes d'origine haïtienne. They deemed "d'origine" most appropriate and inclusive given that some of its members were born in Montreal.

67   Namaste, "Les infirmières haïtiennes."

68   Marlène Rateau, interview with author, Montreal, 13 June 2014.

69   Rateau, "*Pawòl fanm*," 178–9. Rateau reiterated many of these ideas when interviewed by the author. Also, when asked which texts the group read, Rateau could not remember, saying that the group studied some of the more well-known feminist texts. Marlène Rateau, interview with author, Montreal, 13 June 2014.

70   Marlène Rateau, interview with author, Montreal, 13 June 2014.

71   "Entrevue avec Point de ralliement des femmes d'origine haïtienne," *Collectif paroles*, March-April 1984, 10–12.

72   For more on how Haitian men responded to feminism, see Hector, "Rapport sur quelques états d'âme."

73 Marlène Rateau, interview with author, Montreal, 13 June 2014.

74 Quoted in Ravix, "Entrevue avec Nègès vanyan," 11.

75 Merlet, *La participation politique*, 14.

76 Rochat, "Archiving Black Diasporic Activism," 92, 103, 242.

77 Ravix, "Entrevue avec Nègès vanyan."

78 "Entrevue avec Point de ralliement des femmes d'origine haïtienne," *Collectif paroles*, March-April 1984, 10–12.

79 Both Marlène Rateau and Amanthe Bathalien, for example, stated that personal networks played the largest role in determining membership of their respective women's groups. Marlène Rateau, interview with author, Montreal, 13 June 2014; Amanthe Bathalien, interview with author, Montreal, 19 February 2014.

80 Olcott, *International Women's Year*, 248; *Documents of the World Congress for International Women's Year*, 40, 500–1.

81 Donert, "Women's Rights," 201, 202; *Documents of the World Congress for International Women's Year*, 28.

82 de Haan, "Eugénie Cotton," 174.

83 Clergé, "Pour en finir."

84 "1975 – Année internationale de la femme: Conseil québécois de la paix (sous-comité) réunion du 11 février 1975," in Fonds Huguette Lapointe-Roy, P656, 1998-04-002/15, file: Année internationale de la femme, Procès-verbal, BANQ.

85 "Rapport de table-ronde I.20: Les femmes d'autres origines," in Reports of Round Table Discussions, Carrefour '75, Québec-Canada, in RG 106, vol. 14, file: Canada-Québec Carrefour '75, LAC.

86 "Évaluation de la femme," minutes of the 7th Annual Conference of the FFQ, held at l'Hôtel Chanteclerc, Ste-Adèle, Quebec, 24–26 May 1974, in Fonds Huguette Lapointe-Roy, P656, 1998-04-002/15, file: FFQ Congrès 1974, BANQ.

87 Lapointe-Roy, "Comité des Affaires Internationales (FFQ)," 8.

88 Huguette Lapointe-Roy, president of the Comité des affaires internationales, "Rapport du comité des affaires internationales (C.A.I.)," in fonds Huguette Lapointe-Roy, P656, 1998-04-002/15, file: C.A.I, affaires courantes, BANQ.

89 *Documents of the World Congress for International Women's Year*, 121, 129.

90 RAFA, *Femmes haïtiennes*, 3.

91 Ibid., 4, 43.

92 Ibid., 55–7.

93 Ibid., 4

94 Quoted in *Documents of the World Congress for International Women's Year*, 103.

95 Ibid., 57, 58.

96 Ibid., 47.

97 Ibid., 58–9.

98 Ibid., 12, 13.

99 Ibid., 13.

100 Holly, Labelle, and Larose, "L'émigration haïtienne"; Lévy, *Espace d'une génération*, 26, 17.

101 Max Chancy, "Chain Must Be Broken."

102 See, for example, "Nouvelle optique," *Nouvelle optique*, January 1971, 5; "Symposium-Haiti 70," *Nouvelle optique*, January 1971, 115–18; G. Pierre, "Bilan économique duvaliériste"; Hector, "Fascisme et sous-développement"; Ollivier, "Le rachitisme"; Ollivier, "Lire Paulo Freire"; Joachim, "Sur l'esprit de couleur"; and Pierre-Charles, "La complémentarité des stratégies."

103 Castor, "L'occupation américaine en Haïti."

104 RAFA, *Femmes haïtiennes*, 12.

105 Gabaccia, *Foreign Relations*, 179, 72.

106 "Conférence des femmes latino-américaines, Montréal, 25 September 1983," in Fonds Conseil du statut de la femme, E99 1995-11-003/1, file: Femmes latino-américaine, Troisième conférence, BANQ.

107 Dejean, *Les Haïtiens au Québec*, 54.

108 D. Brand and Stikeman, dirs, *Sisters in Struggle*.

109 Amanthe Bathalien, interview with author, Montreal, 19 February 2014.

110 Stroka, *Femmes haïtiennes*, 46.

111 Marlène Rateau, interview with author, Montreal, 13 June 2014.

112 Rateau, "*Pawòl fanm*," 178.

113 Lee and Cardinal, "Hegemonic Nationalism," 216–17.

114 See, for example, Thornhill, *La discrimination raciale*; Bataille, *Situation du logement*; Mouvement québécois pour combattre le racisme et al., *Mémoire présenté à la Commission parlementaire*; and Dejean, *Communauté haïtienne et racisme*.

115 Charles, "Gender and Politics," 150.

116 E.M. Greenway (Miss), Membership Committee, National Congress of
    Black Women, to Mrs N. Walker, National Congress of Black Women
    of Canada, Winnipeg, Manitoba, 27 March 1987, in Concordia University
    Library, Special Collections, series F027/A – Negro Community Centre,
    box HA04173, file 29, Congress of Black Women (1 of 3).

117 Dejean, *Les Haïtiens au Québec*, 99–102. The position taken by the organiza-
    tion, as Dejean specified, was the English-speaking Black community's only
    official intervention during the ordeal.

118 A. Chancy, *Profil*, 23, 25.

119 S. Mills, "Quebec, Haiti," 434.

120 Mugabo, "Black in the City," 632.

121 Quoted in Gipson, ed., *Impetus*, 21.

122 Ibid., 51.

123 Ruth Knights to Esther Marks, Secretary of State Department, Women's
    Program, Complex Guy-Favreau, 25 August 1987, in Concordia University
    Library, Special Collections, series F027/A – Negro Community Centre,
    box HA04173, file 29, Congress of Black Women (1 of 3).

124 A. Chancy, *Faut-il nommer le racisme?*, 1–8.

125 Razack, *Race, Space, and the Law*, 3.

126 A. Chancy, *Faut-il nommer le racisme?*, 2.

127 Canadian Negro Women's Association, "Report of the First National
    Congress."

128 Vergès, *Le ventre des femmes*, 116.

129 A. Chancy, "Médecine, politique."

130 Rojas, *Women of Color and Feminism*, 34.

131 A. Chancy, "Médecine, politique."

132 Amanthe Bathalien, interview with author, Montreal, 19 February 2014.

133 Dawn Williams, *Who's Who in Black Canada*, 215–16; McDougall, "Lives
    Lived."

134 S. Mills, *Empire Within*, 178–9.

135 Jumelle, "Les structures sociales," 246, 253–5.

136 Thornhill, "Focus on Black Women!"; Thornhill, "Black Women's Studies."

137 Charles, "Haitian Life in New York."

138 Comité ad hoc des femmes haïtiennes, *La femme haïtienne en diaspora*, 2.

139 Ibid., 5.

140 A. Chancy, *Profil*, 31.

141 Merlet, "More People Dream," 217.

142 Merlet, *La participation politique*, vii. See also "Myriam Merlet (1956–2010)."

143 Charles, "Gender and Politics," 153.

144 Ibid., 152.

145 Burton, "Transmigration of Rights," 785.

146 A. Chancy, "L'éducation: Une bataille idéologique."

147 Castor, "Femme et participation sociale."

148 A. Chancy, "L'éducation: Une bataille idéologique," 8, 25–30; Merlet, "Les droits économiques."

149 Magloire, "L'antiféminisme en Haïti."

150 Fontaine, "La lutte des femmes," 47.

151 Midy, "Dossier Canada-Haïti."

152 A. Beaudry, "Jouons-nous les impérialistes?" The editorial was reprinted in *Collectif paroles*, July–August 1980, 22.

153 "Dans la diaspora: La revue *Relations* et les six millions haïtiens," *Collectif paroles*, July–August 1980, 21–2.

154 See, for example, Neptune-Anglade, "Du travail domestique."

155 Stroka, *Femmes haïtiennes*, 67.

156 See Rateau, "Violence, AIDS, and Education," 95–100.

157 Rateau, "*Pawòl fanm*," 185.

158 Marlène Rateau, interview with author, Montreal, 13 June 2014.

159 Niosi, "Marjorie Villefranche"; Beauséjour, "Personnalités La Presse."

160 Rochat, "Archiving Black Diasporic Activism," 188, 172, 178.

161 Bannerji, *Dark Side of the Nation*, 9–10.

CHAPTER FIVE

1 Baillargeon, *Brief History*, 161–8.

2 D. Lamoureux, "Paradoxes of Quebec Feminism," 315.

3 "Centre de femmes: La soupe bout," *La vie en rose*, May 1984, 10–11, quote at 10.

4 Quoted in ibid., 10.

5 Cormier, "Mot de la présidente"; Moisan, "Dix ans après l'Année de la Femme."

6 Here is a list of the Centro Donne's founders: Isa Iasenza, Giuseppina Barbusci, Sabina Lanzolla, Loretta Mazzocchi, Domenica Venetico, Marie-Antoinette Simoncini, Vittoria Nucciarone, Margherita Morsella, Assunta

Sauro, Marta Bonato, Tiziana Carafa, and Roberta Giorgetti. Here is a list of women who joined the organization in the months following its founding: Iva Salerio, Renata Flor, Graziella Di Pace, Anna Silvestri, Anna Caputo, Matilda Mossa, Antonella Perzia, Lucia Carbone, Antoinette Melchiore, Gina Mavica, and Maria Angela. See Iasenza, "Une histoire d'engagement."

7 Iacovetta, "Ordering in Bulk," 53. The American historiography is also instructive in this regard. See Guglielmo, *Living the Revolution*, ch. 3; Roediger, *Working toward Whiteness*; and Jacobson, *Whiteness of a Different Color*. See also Giuliani and Lombardi-Diop, *Bianco e nero*; and Lombardi-Diop and Romeo, *Postcolonial Italy*, 2–6.

8 Gabaccia and Iacovetta, "Women, Work, and Protest," 177. For more on Italian women's transnational activism, see Gabaccia and Iacovetta, *Women, Gender and Transnational Lives*.

9 Guglielmo, *Living the Revolution*, 3.

10 Ibid., 4.

11 Quoted in Centro Donne Italiane di Montreal, *Il coraggio di sognare*, 34.

12 See the inner flap of the January–February 1980 edition of the periodical *Quaderni culturali: Pubblicazione dell'associazione di cultura popolare italo-quebecchese*.

13 Iasenza, "Une histoire d'engagement."

14 Del Negro, *Looking through My Mother's Eyes*, 37–40.

15 Quoted in Centro Donne Italiane di Montreal, *Il coraggio di sognare*, 36.

16 "Femmes italiennes," *Des luttes et des rires de femmes: Bulletin de liaison des groups autonomes de femmes*, October–November 1978, 33–4, reprinted in Dumont and Toupin, eds, *La pensée féministe au Québec*, 645–8, quote at 647.

17 Quoted in Centro Donne Italiane di Montreal, *Il coraggio di sognare*, 36.

18 Lombardi-Diop and Romeo, "Italy's Postcolonial 'Question,'" 370.

19 Iacovetta, *Such Hardworking People*, xviii–xxi. As southern Europeans, Italians had long been considered less desirable than British, white American, and northwestern European immigrants. Equating hot climates with darker populations and cultural backwardness, nativist thinking resurfaced after the Second World War. Iacovetta, *Such Hardworking People*, 22.

20 Iacovetta, *Such Hardworking People*, xxii–xxiii.

21 Germain and Rose, *Montréal*, 225.

22 Assunta Sauro, interview with author, Montreal, 26 February 2015.

23 On Italians dying in workplace accidents, see, for example, Ciamarra, "Gli

emigranti"; "Un'altra vittima del lavoro: Salvatore Barbadoro perisce in un incidente," *Il Cittadino Canadese*, 18 December 1959, 1; and "Ancora vittime per la 'metropolitana': Le autorità locali apriranno gli occhi?" *Il Cittadino Canadese*, 18 December 1965, 12.

24 "La rubrica gentile," *Il Cittadino Canadese*, 23 November 1951, 3.

25 "An Interview with Francesco di Feo," *Ovo Magazine*, nos 27–8 (1977): 14–15.

26 "La donna italiana è la più sfruttata," *Il Lavoratore*, May 1971, 1.

27 Quoted in Del Negro, *Looking through My Mother's Eyes*, 40.

28 "La donna italiana è la più sfruttata," *Il Lavoratore*, May 1971, 1.

29 "CFMB: Radio italiana," *Il Lavoratore*, 16 May 1970, 5.

30 "La scuola contro i figli di operai?" *Quaderni culturali*, January-February 1980, 5.

31 "Emigrazione e cultura: La scuola e i figli degli emigrati," *Il Lavoratore*, June 1971, 5–6.

32 Carnevale, *New Language*, 36.

33 Iacovetta, "Trying to Make Ends Meet," 9.

34 "La puntata," *Il Lavoratore*, February 1971, 5–6.

35 Renée Rowan, "Féminin Pluriel: Portraits: Isa Iasenza," *Le Devoir*, 20 August 1984, reprinted in "Noi e il femminismo," *Il Bollettino*, October 1984, 14, 16.

36 "Gli immigrati nel Québec," *Il Lavoratore*, May 1970, 1.

37 "Il problema linguistico nel Québec," *Il Lavoratore*, December 1971, 4.

38 "Gli immigrati nel Québec," *Il Lavoratore*, May 1970, 1.

39 Ibid.

40 For mentions of the involvement of Italian immigrants in unions, see Bucci, "La vostra posta"; Bucci, "Gli operai italiani"; Bucci, "Sulla scena sindacale"; and "Attenzione: Membri dei Locali 205, 262, 439, 485 e 521: Unione internazionale dei lavoratori di abbigliamento femminile," *Il Cittadino Canadese*, 26 August 1966, 19.

41 See Andrade, "La commission des écoles catholiques," 476.

42 Caccia, *Sous le signe du phénix*, 261–2.

43 Lacombe, dir., *Artisans de notre histoire: Marco Micone*.

44 "L'emigrante italiano," *Il Lavoratore*, January 1971, 2.

45 "Editoriale: *Parti Québécois*," *Il Lavoratore*, December 1971, 2; "Il problema linguistico nel Québec," *Il Lavoratore*, December 1971, 4.

46 "CFMB: Radio italiana," *Il Lavoratore*, 16 May 1970, 5. For more on Italian Montrealers' trilingualism, especially their tendency to mix and confuse

languages, see Tardif, Beaudet, and Labelle, *Question nationale et ethnicité*, 17–19.

47 "Emigrazione e cultura: La scuola e i figli degli emigrati," *Il Lavoratore*, June 1971, 5.

48 Robinson, *Black Marxism*, 2, 24–8, 121.

49 Villata, *Bilinguisme et problématiques*, 183–91.

50 Quoted in Renée Rowan, "Féminin Pluriel: Portraits: Isa Iasenza," *Le Devoir*, 20 August 1984, reprinted in "Noi e il femminismo," *Il Bollettino*, October 1984, 14, 16.

51 Pirone, "Parità di sessi e nudismo"; Istria, "12.000 'Yvette' al Forum."

52 Pirone, "Parità di sessi e nudismo," 4.

53 Antonelli, "L'anti-fallocratico"; Antonelli, "Le femministe propongono."

54 Centro Donne Italiane di Montreal, *Il coraggio di sognare*, 7, 36; Assunta Sauro, interview with author, Montreal, 26 February 2015.

55 "CFMB: Radio italiana," *Il Lavoratore*, 16 May 1970, 5.

56 "Femmes italiennes," *Des luttes et des rires de femmes: Bulletin de liaison des groups autonomes de femmes*, October–November 1978, 33–4, reprinted in Dumont and Toupin, eds, *La pensée féministe au Québec*, 645–8, quote at 645–6.

57 Ibid., 646.

58 Ibid., 647.

59 Michaud, *Frontiers of Feminism*, 171.

60 Collectif des femmes immigrantes du Québec, *Êtres immigrantes au Québec*.

61 Iasenza, "Une histoire d'engagement."

62 Quoted in Centro Donne Italiane di Montreal, *Il coraggio di sognare*, 33, 36, 37.

63 "Domenica, 27 Gennaio 1985, alle ore 13.00," *Il Bollettino*, January 1985, 5.

64 Centro Donne Italiane di Montreal, *Il coraggio di sognare*, 27.

65 "Comunicato: Integrazione alfa verso l'autonomia," *Il Bollettino*, November 1983, 6; "La donna e il lavoro," *Il Bollettino*, September 1985, 12.

66 "Sessione di menopausa al Centro Donne," *Il Cittadino Canadese*, 12 March 1980, 15; "Conferenza organizzata dal Centro Donne," *Il Cittadino Canadese*, 21 May 1980, 18; "Taccuino sociale: Centro Donne Montreal," *Il Cittadino Canadese*, 15 October 1980, 18; "Il programma della salute preparato dal Centro Donne," *Il Cittadino Canadese*, 5 November 1980, 18; "Attività del

Centro Donne: La violenza fatta alle donne," *Il Cittadino Canadese*, 4
February 1981, 9.

67 Centro Donne Italiane di Montreal, *Il coraggio di sognare*, 27.

68 D. Lamoureux, "Paradoxes of Quebec Feminism," 315.

69 Dessureault, "Centre des femmes de Verdun"; Assunta Sauro, interview
with author, Montreal, 26 February 2015.

70 Claude Belanger and Annik Lescop, "Rapport sur les cours de français of-
ferts aux femmes immigrantes dans le cadre du programme des 'cours sur
mesure' et 'perspectives d'avenir,'" Ministère de l'immigration du Québec,
Direction de formation, Montreal, August 1980, in Fonds Huguette
Lapointe-Roy, P656, 1998-04-002/9, file: Femme immigrante (Table de
concertation), BANQ.

71 Iacovetta, *Such Hardworking People*, 8.

72 Claude Belanger and Annik Lescop, "Rapport sur les cours de français of-
ferts aux femmes immigrantes dans le cadre du programme des 'cours sur
mesure' et 'perspectives d'avenir,'" Ministère de l'immigration du Québec,
Direction de formation, Montreal, August 1980, in Fonds Huguette
Lapointe-Roy, P656, 1998-04-002/9, file: Femme immigrante (Table de
concertation), BANQ.

73 "Care Lettrici," *Il Bollettino*, October 1983, 2.

74 "La donna italo-canadese," *Il Bollettino*, October 1983, 9.

75 Dubinsky and Iacovetta, "Murder, Womanly Virtue, and Motherhood," 531.

76 "La donna italo-canadese," *Il Bollettino*, October 1983, 9.

77 "Riceviamo," *Il Bollettino*, October 1983, 11.

78 "La Donna e la salute: La solitudine," *Il Bollettino*, November 1983, 7.

79 "Riceviamo … Parliamoci," *Il Bollettino*, November 1983, 13.

80 di Domenico, "Il lavoro casalingo"; Perzia, "La ripartizione dei compiti."
The International Wages for Housework Campaign came up in Assunta
Sauro, interview with author, Montreal, 26 February 2015.

81 "Care lettrici," *Il Bollettino*, October 1984, 3.

82 "La posizione del Centro Donne Italiane di Montreal sul contraccezione
e sull'aborto," *Il Bollettino*, October 1984, 10.

83 Perzia, "Lo scopo del sesso?" 11.

84 "La donna e la chiesa," *Il Bollettino*, October 1984, 5.

85 Perzia, "Le due 'F'?" 7.

86 "La violenza coniugale," *Il Bollettino*, September-October 1987, 5.

87 "Violenza familiare," *Il Bollettino*, November-December 1987, 11.

88 Assunta Sauro, interview with author, Montreal, 26 February 2015.
89 "Attività del Centro Donne: Violenza coniugale nella comunità italiana," *L'altra faccia della luna*, Summer 1997, 5.
90 "Mot de la directrice," *L'altra faccia della luna*, Autumn 2002, 6.
91 "Progetto per ragazze italiane di Montreal-Nord," *Il Bollettino*, October 1983, 10.
92 "Café rencontre," *Il Bollettino*, October 1987, 8.
93 "Colloquio federazione," *Il Bollettino*, February 1988, 2.
94 Eleazzaro, "Seconda generazione."
95 Di Lullo, "Riflessione sul Centro Donne," 12.
96 Morabito, "Madre e figlia."
97 Baldassar and Gabaccia, "Home, Family," 12. For more on Italian Canadian attitudes stemming from emigration, feelings of threat and disrespect, and the resulting trend toward social conservatism, see "Così la penso, se vi pare! Differenza tra gli italiani in Canada e gli italiani in Italia," *Il Bollettino*, March–April 1988, 14.
98 Centro Donne Italiane di Montreal, *Il coraggio di sognare*, 29.
99 "Le donne italiane e la marcia contro la povertà," *L'altra faccia della luna*, October 1995, 6; "Marcia mondiale delle donne 2000," *L'altra faccia della luna*, October 2000, 4; "La pagina del Centro: Manifestazione à Québec," *L'altra faccia della luna*, Spring 2003, 15.
100 Perzia, "L'America ancora."
101 Casola, "Freedom to Fly," 7.
102 "Isa Iasenza, membro C.A.," *Il Bollettino*, September 1984, 16–17.
103 Sauro, "Cos'è il Centro Donne?" 2.
104 Iannazzo, "Testimonia," 12.
105 Centro Donne Italiane di Monreal, *Il coraggio di sognare*, 49.
106 Gabaccia, *Italy's Many Diasporas*, 191.
107 Ibid., 9, 60.
108 For a counter-example, see Franca Iacovetta's article on an anti-fascist activist. Iacovetta, "Betrayal, Vengeance."
109 "Notizie dall'Italia: Un partito di quali donne?" *Il Bollettino*, April 1985, 15.
110 Perilli, "'Sexe' et 'race.'"
111 Marco Micone, interview with author, Montreal, 26 January 2015; Choate, *Emigrant Nation*.
112 Morsella, "Femminismo e comunità."
113 "Documento finale della II Conferenza."

114 Dalla Costa, "Reproduction et émigration."

115 Pardo, Das, and Gauthier, *Development of Intercultural Modalities*, 14.

116 Colloque femmes immigrées, à nous la parole, *Femmes immigrées, à nous la parole!*, 52.

117 Iacovino and Sévigny, "Between Unity and Diversity," 250.

118 "Rencontre des participantes à la Table de concertation sur les femmes immigrantes du 23 avril 1981," in Fonds Huguette Lapointe-Roy, P656, 1998-04-002/9, file: Femme immigrante (Table de concertation), BANQ.

119 "Rencontre des participantes à la Table de concertation sur les femmes immigrantes du 6 avril 1981," in Fonds Huguette Lapointe-Roy, P656, 1998-04-002/9, file: Femme immigrante (Table de concertation), BANQ.

120 "Document de travail du colloque," in Fonds Huguette Lapointe-Roy, P656, 1998-04-002/9, file: Femmes immigrantes (Table de concertation), BANQ.

121 "Compte rendu de la réunion du 18 décembre 1981 de la Table de concertation," in Fonds Huguette Lapointe-Roy, P656, 1998-04-002/9, file: Femmes immigrantes (Table de concertation), BANQ.

122 "Compte rendu de la réunion sur la Table de concertation des femmes immigrées du 26 avril 1982," in Fonds Huguette Lapointe-Roy, P656, 1998-04-002/9, file: Femmes immigrantes (Table de Concertation), BANQ.

123 Colloque femmes immigrées, à nous la parole, *Femmes immigrées, à nous la parole!*, 9.

124 Blouin, "Comment briser l'isolement?"

125 Danae Savides, interview with author, Laval, 11 December 2014.

126 Colloque femmes immigrées, à nous la parole, *Femmes immigrées, à nous la parole!*, 27.

127 Ibid., 26–30.

128 Baillargeon, *Brief History*, 162.

129 Colloque femmes immigrées, à nous la parole, *Femmes immigrées, à nous la parole!*, 52, 53.

130 Ibid., 53–7.

131 Ibid., 59, 60, 63

132 Ibid., 64.

133 Ibid., 65–6.

134 Ibid., 68, 69, 73.

135 Ibid., 70, 72.

136 Renée Rowan, "Les immigrées veulent une autre rencontre, avec des Québécoises," *Le Devoir*, 8 June 1982, reprinted in Colloque femmes immigrées, à nous la parole, *Femmes immigrées, à nous la parole!*, 173.

137 Colloque femmes immigrées, à nous la parole, *Femmes immigrées, à nous la parole!*, 58.

138 Lapointe-Roy, "Femmes immigrées, à nous la parole!" 17.

139 "A l'ombre des Québécoises," *La vie en rose*, September-October 1982; "Femmes immigrées, à nous la parole!" *Communiqu'elles*, July-August 1982, reprinted in Colloque femmes immigrées, à nous la parole, *Femmes immigrées, à nous la parole!*, 190–5.

140 Colloque femmes immigrées, à nous la parole, *Femmes immigrées, à nous la parole!*, 67. See, for example, "Une place pour les femmes des communautés culturelles," *La gazette des femmes*, September-October 1983, 27; "Le Collectif des femmes immigrants de Montréal," *La gazette des femmes*, July-August 1985, 31.

141 Simoncini and del Balso, "Colloque sur les femmes immigrantes," 20.

142 Association féminine d'éducation et d'action sociale, *Femmes d'ici, femmes d'ailleurs*.

143 Da Rosa and Poulin. "Espaces ethniques."

144 del Balso et al., "Dossier," 4.

145 Labelle, *Histoires d'immigrées*, 168, 210, 222.

146 Labelle, Goyette, and Paquin, *Intégration économique*, 47.

147 Dorothy Williams, *Road to Now*, 168.

148 "Il lavoro del Centro Donne per l'anno 1995–1996: Un bilancio," *L'altra faccia della luna*, October 1996, 5. For more on the Greek women's organization the Hellenic Women's Association, see "Tassia Helen Giannakis: Mieux intégrer les Québécoises d'adoption," *La gazette des femmes*, November-December 1989, 24.

149 McKeown, dir., *Désirs de liberté*.

150 "Les femmes domestiques: Esclaves des temps modernes," *L'R des centres de femmes du Québec: Bulletin de liaison*, October 1987, 8. In fact, the network voted unanimously to endorse the campaign of the Association pour la défense des droits du personnel domestique to ensure that domestic workers benefited from Quebec labour laws, specifically minimum wage and paid vacation.

151 David, "Congrès 1988," 2.

152 I am following Pierre Anctil's terminology for discussing relations among
     Jewish and francophone Quebecers. Anctil, *Le rendez-vous manqué*, 319.

153 D. Lamoureux, "Paradoxes of Quebec Feminism," 316.

154 Collectif des femmes immigrantes du Québec, *Êtres immigrantes au
     Québec*.

155 Ibid.

156 Collectif des femmes immigrantes du Québec, *Au Québec pour bâtir
     ensemble*.

157 Collectif des femmes immigrantes du Québec, *À la recherche de l'équité
     raciale*, 8, 12; Tousignant, "À propos des femmes immigrantes," 13.

158 Véronique O'Leary, "Disparaitre: Les vieilles souches," *Le Devoir*, 14 Febru-
     ary 1989, reprinted in *L'R des centres de femmes du Québec: Bulletin de
     liaison*, March 1989, 11–12.

159 "D'un signe de feu au bûcher des préjugés," *L'R des centres de femmes
     du Québec: Bulletin de liaison*, June 1991, 4.

160 Rouleau, "Madeleine Parent," 122.

161 Salutin, "Iron Will," 123.

162 Mulay, "Importance of Being Madeleine," 113–14.

163 David, "Tribute to a Valiant Lady," 118.

164 Beauchamp, Côté, and Paquerot, *Forum pour un Québec*, 13.

165 Centre de documentation sur l'éducation des adultes et la condition
     féminine, Un Québec féminin pluriel, box 1.

166 Ibid.

167 Beauchamp, Côté, and Paquerot, *Le Forum pour un Québec*, 58, 63.

168 Mulay, "Importance of Being Madeleine," 115.

169 "Femmes autochtones," *Le féminisme en bref*, December 1993, 6.

170 St-Amand, *Stories of Oka*, 26.

171 Ibid.

172 Kettenbeil and Centre de femmes d'ici et d'ailleurs, "Crise d'indifférence,"
     4–6; L. Turcotte, "Itinéraire d'un courant politique," 383; St-Amand, *Stories
     of Oka*, 80.

173 L. Turcotte, "Itinéraire d'un courant politique," 383.

174 L'R des centres de femmes du Québec, *Actes du colloque*, 5.

175 Ibid.

176 J. Lamoureux, "L'unité par le SPM?," 12.

177 D. Lamoureux, "Paradoxes of Quebec Feminism," 316.

178 Quoted in ibid.

179 LeClerc and West, "Feminist Nationalist Movements," 239.

180 D. Lamoureux, "Paradoxes of Quebec Feminism," 316.

181 Government of Quebec, *Réponse du Québec*.

182 Pâquet and Savard, *Brève histoire*, 11.

183 D. Lamoureux, "Paradoxes of Quebec Feminism," 314–15. In response to this situation, some grassroots organizations formed noncompetitive, Quebec-wide coordinating structures to acquire leverage with the government. This approach helped women's groups to avoid competing with one another for piecemeal funding, leaving more time for activism and service provision.

184 D. Lamoureux, "Paradoxes of Quebec Feminism," 310.

185 Ibid., 317.

186 Collectif des femmes immigrantes du Québec, *À la recherche de l'équité raciale*, 8, 12.

187 Tousignant, "À propos des femmes immigrantes," 13; Asselin, "Les Centres de femmes," 13.

188 Robert, "Le mot de la présidente," 1.

189 Bannerji, *Dark Side of the Nation*, 10.

190 Rouleau, "Madeleine Parent."

CONCLUSION

1 *Tremblay v Daigle*, [1989] 2 SCR 530. See Caouette, "L'affaire Daigle contre Tremblay."

2 Kyong, "Case of Mistaken Identity?" 117.

3 Baillargeon, *Brief History*, 187.

4 Kyong, "Case of Mistaken Identity?"

5 Faludi, *Backlash*, 11.

6 Ibid., 12.

7 Povitz, *Stirrings*, 198–239. See, for example, Petitclerc and Robert, "Les lois spéciales."

8 Sangster, *Demanding Equality*, 276.

9 "Le mouvement des femmes à l'aube de l'an 2000," *L'R des centres de femmes du Québec: Bulletin de liaison*, October 1991, 5; "Canada: Draft Resolution. Indigenous Women" and "Resolution on Minority and Indigenous Women: Prepared by Indigenous Women," both in R-1407, box 48, file 48-2, Status of Women, Nairobi Conference, Briefing in Nairobi and Other Information, 1985, LAC.

10 Maillé, "Réception de la théorie postcoloniale."

11 Collectif des femmes immigrantes du Québec, *Êtres immigrantes au Québec.*

12 See, for example, Collectif des femmes immigrantes du Québec, *Je ne suis pas raciste.*

13 Collectif des femmes immigrantes du Québec, *Au Québec pour bâtir ensemble*, 1, emphasis added.

14 Government of Canada, Royal Commission on Bilingualism and Biculturalism, "Submission of Miss Kahn-Tineta Horn," emphasis added. See also AFAQ, *Mémoire.*

15 Villefranche, "Pourquoi une féministe immigrante?"

16 Quoted in "Le mouvement des femmes à l'aube de l'an 2000," *L'R des centres de femmes du Québec: Bulletin de liaison*, October 1991, 5.

17 Pâquet and Savard, *Brève histoire*, 79–82.

18 Government of Quebec, *Réponse du Québec.*

19 Véronique O'Leary, "Disparaitre: Les vieilles souches," *Le Devoir*, 14 February 1989, reprinted in *L'R des centres de femmes du Québec: Bulletin de liaison*, March 1989, 11–12.

20 Fédération des femmes du Québec, *Déclaration solennelle de solidarité.*

21 LeClerc and West, "Feminist Nationalist Movements," 239.

22 Lamoureux, "Paradoxes of Quebec Feminism," 316.

23 Increasingly, scholars are turning to trying to historicize Black-Indigenous solidarities. See, for example, Néméh-Nombré, *Seize temps noirs.* Certainly, much of Quebec immigration history remains to be written.

24 Morgensen, "Settler Homonationalism."

25 Pâquet and Savard, *Brève histoire*, 176–7.

26 N. Fraser, "Feminism, Capitalism." I am aware that philosopher Nancy Fraser's article provoked a great deal of debate, namely over her generalizations regarding "second-wave" feminism, but I think that her article is worth reading nonetheless.

27 See, for example, Maynard and Le-Phat, "Accommodate This!" 24; A. Pierre, ed., *Empreintes de résistance*; and Lanctôt, *Les libéraux.*

28 Néméh-Nombré, *Seize temps noirs*, 101; A. Pierre, ed., *Empreintes de résistance*, 27.

Bibliography

Interviews

Bathalien, Amanthe, interview with author, Montreal, 19 February 2014.
Micone, Marco, interview with author, Montreal, 26 January 2015.
Patry-Buisson, Ghislaine, interview with author, Laval, 5 February 2015.
Rateau, Marlène, interview with author, Montreal, 13 June 2014.
Sauro, Assunta, interview with author, Montreal, 26 February 2015.
Savides, Danae, interview with author, Laval, 11 December 2014.

Archives

Bibliothèque et Archives nationales du Québec (BANQ), Montreal

Fonds Conseil du statut de la femme, E99 1995-11-003/1, file: Congres des femmes noires du Canada; and file: Femmes latino-américaine, Troisième conférence.
Fonds Huguette Lapointe-Roy, P656, 1998-04-002/9, 1998-04-002/15.

Canadian Women's Movement Archives Collection, Morisset Library Special Collections, University of Ottawa

Box 1-8, Abortion Caravan (May 1970): proposals, brief, clippings, and other material, 1970–88.
Box 139, Women's Liberation Study Group.
Journal: *Montreal Women's Liberation Newsletter*.

Centre de documentation sur l'éducation des adultes et la condition
féminine, Montreal

Un Québec féminin pluriel, box 1.

Concordia University Library, Montreal, Special Collections, series F027/A –
Negro Community Centre

Box HA04173, file 6, Congress of Black Women, Montreal Committee, 1986.

Box HA04173, file 20, Brief National Congress of Black Women.

Box HA04173, file 27, Congress of Black Women minutes.

Box HA04173, file 29, Congress of Black Women (1 of 3).

Box HA04173, file 30, Congress of Black Women (2 of 3).

Box HA04810, RC 5921, file 32, Second National Congress of Black Women,
History of the Coloured Women's Club Inc.

Library and Archives Canada (LAC), Ottawa

Dorothy Wills Fonds, MG 31 H179, vols 1–16.

R-1407, box 47, file 47-12, Status of Women, Nairobi Conference.

R-1407, box 48, file 48-2, Status of Women, Nairobi Conference, Briefing in
Nairobi and Other Information, 1985.

RG 6, 1986-87/319, box 96, file CB-9-390-34, Native Council of Canada.

RG 6-F, ATIP Division, interim container 92, file 0901-H, Citizenship Sector –
National Congress of Black Women of Canada – Founding Conference of the
NCBWC.

RG 6-F-4, 1986-87, box 96, file CB-9-390-45, National Steering Committee on
Native Women, National Native Women's Conference, Edmonton, Alberta.
22–3 March 1971.

RG 22, vol. 88, file 6-10-3, part 1.

RG 10, vol. 7143, file 1/3-8-2, part 1, Complaints and Petitions Received from
Kahn-Tineta Horn, vol. 1, October 1963 to May 1964.

RG 106, vol. 14, file: Canada-Québec Carrefour '75.

Simon Fraser University Archives, Vancouver

Women's Movement Collection, F-166, file 2, Indochinese Women's Conference, Montreal International Collective.

Newspapers and Periodicals

Akwesasne Notes
L'altra faccia della luna: Revue du centre des femmes italiennes
  de Montréal
Black Scholar
Il Bollettino Centro Donne di Montreal
Bulletin de la FFQ
Bulletin/Ligue des femmes du Québec
Il Cittadino Canadese, 1943–82
Collectif paroles: Revue culturelle et politique haïtienne
Communiqu'elles
Contrast, 1969–78
Il Corriere Italiano
Expression
La gazette des femmes, 1979–90
Habari Kijiji (*Village News*)
Il Lavoratore: Organo del movimento progressista italo-quebecchese
Montreal Women's Liberation Newsletter
The Nation
Nouvelle optique
Petite presse (FFQ)
Quaderni culturali: Pubblicazione dell'associazione di cultura popolare italo-
  quebecchese
L'R des centres de femmes du Québec: Bulletin de liaison, 1986–92
Les têtes de pioche
UHURU: *Black Community News Service*
Umoja: Black Dialogue
La vie en rose

Other Sources

Ackerman, Katrina, and Shannon Stettner. "'The Public Is Not Ready for This':
    1969 and the Long Road to Abortion Access." *Canadian Historical Review* 100,
    no. 2 (2019): 239–56.

AFAQ (Association des femmes autochtones du Québec). *Document d'informa-
    tion préparé par Carole Lévesque pour la Commission royale sur les peuples
    autochtones.* Montreal: INRS-Culture et société, 1993.

– *Mémoire: Assemblée Nationale.* Mémoire déposé à la Commission permanente
    de la présidence du conseil, de la constitution et des affaires intergouvernemen-
    tales. Montreal: AFAQ, 1983.

– *Mémoire présenté le 20 août 1980 au ministère de la santé et du bien-être Canada.*
    Montreal: AFAQ, 1980.

– *Primauté de l'intérêt de l'enfant: Adoption.* Mémoire déposé à la Commission
    parlementaire permanente de la justice sur la réforme du droit de la famille.
    Montreal: AFAQ, 1979.

– *Rapport final de la recherche socio-culturelle présenté aux groupes de l'*AFAQ *et*
    DEFI. Montreal: AFAQ, 1982.

Affan, Samah. "Ethical Gestures: Articulations of Black Life in Montreal's 1960s."
    MA thesis, Concordia University, 2013.

Agnew, Vijay. *Resisting Discrimination: Women from Asia, Africa, and the
    Caribbean and the Women's Movement in Canada.* Toronto: University of
    Toronto Press, 1996.

Aks, Judith. *Women's Rights in Native North America: Legal Mobilization in the
    United States and Canada.* New York: LFB Scholarly Publishing, 2004.

Aladejebi, Funké. *Schooling the System: A History of Black Women Teachers.*
    Montreal and Kingston: McGill-Queen's University Press, 2021.

– "'We've Got Our Quota': Black Female Educators and Resistive Pedagogies,
    1960s–1980s." *Ontario History* 107, no. 1 (2015): 113–31.

Alexis, Darline, Denyse Coté, and Sabine Lamour, eds. *Déjouer le silence: Contre-
    discours sur les femmes haïtiennes.* Montreal: Éditions du remue-ménage, 2018.

Alfred, Gerald Taiaiake. *Heeding the Voices of Our Ancestors: Kahnawake Mohawk
    Politics and the Rise of Native Nationalism.* Toronto: Oxford University Press,
    1995.

Anctil, Pierre. *Le rendez-vous manqué: Les Juifs de Montréal face au Québec de
    l'entre-deux-guerres.* Montreal: Institut québécois de recherche sur la culture,
    1988.

Anderson, Kim. "An Interview with Katsi'tsakwas Ellen Gabriel of the Kanien'kehá:ka Nation, Turtle Island." *Canadian Woman Studies* 26, nos 3–4 (2008): 52–8.

Andrade, Miguel Simao. "La commission des écoles catholiques de Montréal et l'intégration des immigrants et des minorités ethniques à l'école française de 1947 à 1977." *Revue d'histoire de l'Amérique française* 60, no. 4 (2007): 455–86.

Antler, Joyce. "'We Were Ready to Turn the World Upside Down': Radical Feminism and Jewish Women." In *A Jewish Feminine Mystique? Jewish Women in Postwar America*, ed. Hasia Diner, Shira Kohn, and Rachel Kranson, 210–34. New Brunswick, NJ: Rutgers University Press, 2010.

Antonelli, Claudio. "L'anti-fallocratico, ovvero l'inversione dei sessi: I nuovi educatori." *Il Cittadino Canadese*, 28 June 1978, 1, 10.

– "Le femministe propongono: Una società senza sessi." *Il Cittadino Canadese*, 22 November 1978, 1, 4.

Antonin, Arnold, ed. *Femmes et démocratie et Haïti*. Port-au-Prince. Forum libre, 1989.

Antrobus, Peggy. "A Caribbean Journey: Defending Feminist Politics." In *Developing Power: How Women Transformed International Development*, ed. Arvonne Fraser and Irene Tinker, 138–48. New York: Feminist Press, 2004.

– *The Global Women's Movement: Origins, Issues, and Strategies*. Black Point, NS: Fernwood, 2004.

Asselin, Michèle. "Les centres de femmes: Un lieu de rencontre avec les femmes des différentes communautés culturelles." *L'R des centres de femmes du Québec: Bulletin de liaison*, March 1989, 13.

Association féminine d'éducation et d'action sociale. *Femmes d'ici, femmes d'ailleurs*. Montreal: Association féminine d'éducation et d'action sociale, 1986.

Austin, David. "All Roads Led to Montreal: Black Power, the Caribbean, and the Black Radical Tradition in Canada." *Journal of African American History* 92, no. 4 (2007): 516–39.

– "An Embarrassment of Omissions, or Rewriting the Sixties: The Case of the Caribbean Conference Committee, Canada, and the Global New Left." In *New World Coming: The Sixties and the Shaping of Global Consciousness*, ed. Karen Dubinsky, Catherine Krull, Susan Lord, Sean Mills, and Scott Rutherford, 368–78. Toronto: Between the Lines, 2009.

– *Fear of a Black Nation: Race, Sex, and Security in Sixties Montreal*. Toronto: Between the Lines, 2013.

– "Narratives of Power: Historical Mythologies in Contemporary Québec and Canada." *Race Class* 52, no. 1 (2010): 19–32.

Baillargeon, Denyse. *A Brief History of Women in Quebec*. Trans. W. Donald Wilson. Waterloo, ON: Wilfred Laurier University Press, 2014.

– *To Be Equals in Our Own Country: Women and the Vote in Quebec*. Trans. Käthe Roth. Vancouver: UBC Press, 2020.

Baldassar, Loretta, and Donna Gabaccia. "Home, Family, and the Italian Nation in a Mobile World: The Domestic and the National among Italy's Migrants." In *Intimacy and Italian Migration: Gender and Domestic Lives in a Mobile World*, ed. Loretta Baldassar and Donna Gabaccia, 1–22. New York: Fordham University, 2011.

Bannerji, Himani. *The Dark Side of the Nation: Essays on Multiculturalism, Nationalism, and Gender*. Toronto: Canadian Scholars' Press, 2000.

Barker, Joanne, ed. *Critically Sovereign: Indigenous Gender, Sexuality, and Feminist Studies*. Durham, NC: Duke University Press, 2017.

Bataille, Joseph J. *Situation du logement des Haïtiens à Montréal-Nord*. Montreal: Maison d'Haïti, 1984.

Beal, Frances. "Slave of a Slave No More: Black Women in Struggle." *Black Scholar*, March 1975, 2–10.

Beauchamp, Colette, Rosette Côté, and Sylvie Paquerot. *Forum pour un Québec féminin pluriel*. Montreal: Éditions Écosociété, 1994.

Beaudry, Albert. "Jouons-nous les impérialistes?" *Relations*, July-August 1980, 200.

Beaudry, Lucille. "Les groupes d'extrême gauche au Québec et la question des femmes: De l'opposition à la conciliation." *Bulletin d'histoire politique* 13, no. 1 (2004): 57–63.

Beauséjour, Martin. "Personnalités La Presse: Marjorie Villefranche." *La Presse*, 23 April 2012.

Bell, Beverly, ed. *Walking on Fire: Haitian Women's Stories of Survival and Resistance*. Ithaca, NY: Cornell University Press, 2001.

Bertley, June. "The Role of the Black Community in Educating Blacks in Montreal, from 1910 to 1940, with Special Reference to Reverend Dr. Charles Humphrey Este." MA thesis, McGill University, 1982.

Bertley, Leo. "The Universal Negro Improvement Association of Montreal, 1917–1979." PhD diss., Concordia University, 1980.

Bevien, Janice. "Seminar: Women under Apartheid." *Black Scholar*, September-October 1980, 88.

Blain, Keisha N. *Set the World on Fire: Black Nationalist Women and the Global Struggle for Freedom*. Philadelphia: University of Pennsylvania Press, 2018.

Blain, Keisha N., and Tiffany M. Gill, eds. *To Turn the Whole World Over: Black Women and Internationalism*. Urbana-Champaign: University of Illinois Press, 2019.

Blouin, Jacqueline. "Comment briser l'isolement des immigrantes? Entrevue avec Danae Theodorakopoulos, membre du CSF." *La gazette des femmes*, February 1982, 8–9.

Bouchereau, Madeleine Sylvain. *Haïti et ses femmes: Une étude d'évolution culturelle*. Port-au-Prince: Presses Libres, 1957.

Brand, Dionne. "'We weren't allowed to go into factory work until Hitler started the war': The 1920s to the 1940s." In *"We're Rooted Here and They Can't Pull Us Up": Essays in African Canadian Women's History*, ed. Peggy Bristow, Dionne Brand, Linda Carty, Afua Cooper, Sylvia Hamilton, and Adrienne Shadd, 171–92. Toronto: University of Toronto Press, 1994.

Brand, Dionne, and Ginny Stikeman, dirs. *Sisters in Struggle*. DVD. Montreal: National Film Board of Canada, 1991.

Brand, Jennifer, and Kim Anderson, "Indigenous Mothering: New Insights on Giving Life to the People." In *Maternal Theory: Essential Readings*, 2nd ed., ed. Andrea O'Neilly, 713–33. Bradford, ON: Demeter, 2021.

Bristow, Peggy, Dionne Brand, Linda Carty, Afua Cooper, Sylvia Hamilton, and Adrienne Shadd, eds. *"We're Rooted Here and They Can't Pull Us Up": Essays in African Canadian Women's History*. Toronto: University of Toronto Press, 1994.

Brooks, Lisa. *The Common Pot: The Recovery of Native Space in the Northeast*. Minneapolis: University of Minnesota Press, 2008.

Brooks, Pamela. *Boycotts, Buses, and Passes: Black Women's Resistance in the US South and South Africa*. Amherst: University of Massachusetts Press, 2008.

Brown, Rosemary. *Being Brown: A Very Public Life*. Toronto: Random House, 1989.

Brown, Wayne. "Mary Two-Axe Earley – Footprints." *Windspeaker*, November 2003.

Bucci, Mario. "Gli operai italiani ed il sindacalismo nel Quebec: 'L'ora delle decisioni importanti!'" *Il Cittadino Canadese*, 9 April 1965, 17.

– "Sulla scena sindacale: Necessaria la partecipazione attiva di voi tutti!" *Il Cittadino Canadese*, 16 April 1965, 17.

– "La vostra posta: La parola ad un sindacalista." *Il Cittadino canadese*, 25 February 1965, 2.

Burton, Barbara. "The Transmigration of Rights: Women, Movement, and the Grassroots in Latin America and the Caribbean." *Development and Change* 35, no. 4 (2004): 773–98.

Caccia, Fulvio. *Sous le signe du phénix: Entretiens avec quinze créateurs italo-québécois.* Montreal: Éditions Guernica, 1985.

"Canadian Feminists Fight for Change in 1967." Video. CBC *Newsmagazine*, 28 March 1967. https://www.cbc.ca/player/play/1402753109.

Canadian Negro Women's Association. "Report of the First National Congress of Black Women, 6–8 April 1973, Westbury Hotel, Toronto, Canada." In Dorothy Wills Fonds, MG 31 H179, vol. 9, file 9–23, Library and Archives Canada.

Cannon, Martin. *Men, Masculinity, and the Indian Act.* Vancouver: UBC Press, 2019.

Caouette, Marilyne. "L'affaire Daigle contre Tremblay: Le temps comme moteur du débat social au Québec à la fin des années 1980." *Revue d'histoire de l'Amérique française* 72, no. 3 (2019): 73–95.

Carby, Hazel V. "White Women Listen! Black Feminism and the Boundaries of Sisterhood." In *The Empire Strikes Back: Race and Racism in 70s Britain*, ed. Centre for Contemporary Cultural Studies, University of Birmingham, 212–35. London: Hutchinson and Co., 1982.

Cardinal, Harold. "Indian Women and the Indian Act." In *Two Nations, Many Cultures: Ethnic Groups in Canada*, ed. Jean Leonard Elliot, 44–50. Scarborough, ON: Prentice-Hall of Canada, 1979.

– *The Unjust Society.* Vancouver: Douglas and McIntyre, 1969.

Carmichael, Stokely, and Charles V. Hamilton. *Black Power: The Politics of Liberation in America.* New York: Vintage Books, 1967.

Carnevale, Nancy. *A New Language, A New World: Italian Immigrants in the United States, 1890–1945.* Urbana-Champaign: University of Illinois Press, 2009.

Casola, Domenica. "Freedom to Fly." *L'altra faccia della luna*, March 2005, 7.

Castle, Elizabeth. "'The Original Gangster': The Life and Times of Madonna Thunder Hawk." In *The Hidden 1970s: Histories of Radicalism*, ed. Dan Berger, 267–83. New Brunswick, NJ: Rutgers University Press, 2010.

Castor, Suzy. "Femme et participation sociale." In *Théories et pratiques de la lutte des femmes*, ed. Adeline Chancy and Suzy Castor, 11–17. Port-au-Prince: Centre de recherche et de formation économique et sociale pour le développement, 1988.

– "L'occupation américaine en Haïti." *Nouvelle optique*, January 1971, 27–43.

Centro Donne Italiane di Montreal. *Il coraggio di sognare, 1978–2003*. Montreal: Centro Donne Italiane di Montreal, 2004.

Chancy, Adeline. "L'alphabétisation des immigrants: Un problème spécifique ancré dans la société québécoise." *Collectif paroles*, April-May 1981, 23–5.

– *L'analphabétisme chez les femmes immigrantes haïtiennes*. Montreal: Librairie de l'Universite de Montreal, 1981.

– "Éducation: La lettre à la famille: Une situation d'apprentissage pour les immigrants haïtiens analphabètes." *Collectif paroles*, March 1980, 33–6.

– "L'éducation: Une bataille idéologique." In *Théories et pratiques de la lutte des femmes*, ed. Adeline Chancy and Suzy Castor, 25–30. Port-au-Prince: Centre de recherche et de formation économique et sociale pour le développement, 1988.

– *Faut-il nommer le racisme?* Montreal: Éditions du CIDICHA, 1984.

– *Lagramè: Grammaire créole par Adeline Chancy avec la collaboration de l'équipe Maison d'Haïti*. Montreal: Maison d'Haïti, 1982.

– "Médecine, politique, et l'année internationale de l'enfant à Port-au-Prince: La vision de l'UNICEF de la situation de l'enfant haïtien." *Collectif paroles*, September 1979, 40–1.

– *Profil: Max Chancy (1928–2002)*. Pétion-Ville, Port-au-Prince: Fondation Gérard Pierre-Charles, 2007.

Chancy, Adeline, and Suzy Castor, eds. *Théories et pratiques de la lutte des femmes*. Port-au-Prince: Centre de recherche et de formation économique et sociale pour le développement, 1988.

Chancy, Max. "The Chain Must Be Broken." *Ovo Magazine*, nos 27–8 (1977): 88–9.

Chancy, Myriam. *Framing Silence: Revolutionary Novels by Haitian Women*. New Brunswick, NJ: Rutgers University Press, 1997.

Charles, Carolle. "Gender and Politics in Contemporary Haiti: The Duvalierist State, Transnationalism, and the Emergence of a New Feminism (1980–1990)." *Feminist Studies* 21 (1995): 135–64.

– "Haitian Life in New York and the Haitian-American Left." In *The Immigrant Left in the United States*, ed. Paul Buhle and Dan Georgakas, 289–301. Albany: State University of New York Press, 1996.

Cherniak, Donna, and Allan Feingold. *The Birth Control Handbook*. 4th ed. Montreal: n.p., 1970.

Child, Brenda. *Holding Our World Together: Ojibwe Women and the Survival of Community*. New York: Viking, 2012.

Choate, Mark. *Emigrant Nation: The Making of Italy Abroad*. Cambridge, MA: Harvard University Press, 2008.

Churchill, David. "Draft Resisters, Left Nationalism, and the Politics of Anti-imperialism." *Canadian Historical Review* 93, no. 2 (2012): 227–60.

Ciamarra, Nicola. "Gli emigranti, queste povere vittime: Sempre più numerosi i 'martiri del lavoro.'" *Il Cittadino Canadese*, 2 October 1959, 2.

Claude, Judy. "Some Personal Reflections on the Sixth Pan-African Congress." *Black Scholar*, Winter 2008, 48–9.

Clément, Dominique. *Human Rights in Canada: A History*. Waterloo, ON: Wilfred Laurier University Press, 2016.

Clergé, Natacha. "Pour en finir avec une historiographie héroïsante: Critique de l'historiographie féministe traditionnelle." In *Déjouer le silence: Contre-discours sur les femmes haïtiennes*, ed. Darline Alexis, Denyse Côté, and Sabine Lamour, 224–35. Montreal: Éditions du remue-ménage, 2018.

Collectif Clio. *L'histoire des femmes au Québec depuis quatre siècles*. Montreal: Quinze, 1982.

Collectif des femmes immigrantes du Québec. *À la recherche de l'équité raciale: Compte-rendu du colloque tenu les 19 et 20 mai 1990 à l'Université du Québec à Montréal*. Montreal: Collectif des femmes immigrantes du Québec, 1991.

– *Au Québec pour bâtir ensemble: Mémoire: Remis au Secrétariat de la Commission de la culture relativement à l'énoncé de politique en matière d'immigration et d'intégration, Janvier 1991*. Montreal: Collectif des femmes immigrantes du Québec, 1991.

– *Êtres immigrantes au Québec: Des femmes s'organisent*. Montreal: Collectif des femmes immigrantes du Québec, 1985.

– *Je ne suis pas raciste, mais … Cahier de réflexion et de sensibilisation sur les relations interculturelles*. Montreal: Collectif des femmes immigrantes du Québec, 1994.

Collectif l'insoumise, ed. *Le foyer de l'insurrection: Textes sur le salaire pour le travail ménager*. Geneva: Collectif l'insoumise, 1977.

Colloque femmes immigrées, à nous la parole. *Femmes immigrées, à nous la parole! Actes du colloque, Montréal, 4, 5, et 6 juin 1982*. Montreal: Direction des communications du Ministère des communautés culturelles et de l'immigration, 1983.

Comité ad hoc des femmes haïtiennes. *La femme haïtienne en diaspora*. Montreal: Centre international de documentation et d'information haïtienne, caribéenne, et afro-canadienne, 1986.

Congress of Black Writers. *Towards the Second Emancipation: The Dynamics of*

Black Liberation. Proceedings of a conference at the Students Union and Leacock Building, McGill University, Montreal, 11–14 October 1968.

Conseil du statut de la femme. *Pour les québécoises: Égalité et indépendance.* Quebec City: Conseil du statut de la femme, 1978.

Cooper, Afua. *The Hanging of Angélique: The Untold Story of Canadian Slavery and the Burning Down of Old Montréal.* Toronto: Harper Collins, 2006.

Cormier, France. "Mot de la présidente." *L'R des centres de femmes du Québec: Bulletin de liaison*, May-June 1986, 1.

Cornellier, Bruno. "The Struggle of Others: Pierre Vallières, Québécois Settler Nationalism, and the N-Word Today." *Discourse* 39, no. 1 (2017): 31–66.

Cott, Nancy F. "What's in a Name? The Limits of 'Social Feminism,' or Expanding the Vocabulary of Women's History." *Journal of American History* 76, no. 3 (1989): 809–29.

Coulthard, Glen. *Red Skin, White Masks: Rejecting the Colonial Politics of Recognition.* Minneapolis: University of Minnesota Press, 2014.

Cull, Randi. "Aboriginal Mothering under the State's Gaze." In *"Until Our Hearts Are on the Ground": Aboriginal Mothering, Oppression, Resistance and Rebirth*, ed. D. Memee Lavell-Harvard and Jeannette Corbiere Lavell, 141–56. Toronto: Demeter, 2006.

Dalla Costa, Mariarosa. "Reproduction et émigration." In *Le foyer de l'insurrection: Textes sur le salaire pour le travail méneger*, ed. Collectif l'insoumise, 44–85. Geneva: Collectif l'insoumise, 1977.

Da Rosa, Victor M.P., and Richard Poulin. "Espaces ethniques et questions linguistiques au Québec: À propos des communautés italienne et portugaise." *Canadian Ethnic Studies* 18, no. 2 (1986): 143–9.

David, Françoise. "Congrès 1988 de L'R des centres de femmes du Québec." *L'R des centres de femmes du Québec: Bulletin de liaison*, June 1988, 2–3.

– "A Tribute to a Valiant Lady." In *Madeline Parent: Activist*, ed. Andrée Lévesque, 118–19. Toronto: Sumach, 2005.

Davis, Angela. "Racism, Birth Control and Reproductive Rights." In *Feminist Postcolonial Theory: A Reader*, ed. Reina Lewis and Sara Mills, 353–67. Edinburgh: Edinburgh University Press, 2003.

de Haan, Francisca. "Eugénie Cotton, Pak Chong-ae, and Claudia Jones: Rethinking Transnational Feminism and International Politics." *Journal of Women's History* 25, no. 4 (2013): 174–89.

Deiter, Walter, and Walter Currie. *Presentation to Senate Committee on Poverty.* Winnipeg: National Indian Brotherhood, 1970.

Dejean, Paul. *Communauté haïtienne et racisme*. Montreal: Centre international de documentation et d'information haïtienne caribéenne et afro-canadienne, 1984.

– *Les Haïtiens au Québec*. Montreal: Presses de l'Université du Québec, 1978.

del Balso, Benedetta, Michele del Baso, Giovanna Spadafora, Sylvie Taschereau, and Maria Triguerio. "Dossier: Tra lavoro e disoccupazione: Operaie italiane nell'industria dell'abbigliamento." *Quaderni culturali* 1, nos 3–4 (1982): 3–8.

Del Negro, Giovanna. *Looking through My Mother's Eyes: Life Stories of Nine Italian Immigrant Women Living in Montreal*. Toronto: Guernica, 1997.

Deloria, Vine, Jr. *God Is Red*. New York: Grosset and Dunlap, 1973.

Delorme, Lisa. "Gaining a Right to Abortion in the United States and Canada: The Role of Judicial Capacities." *Berkeley Journal of Sociology* 36 (1991): 93–114.

Delphy, Christine. "L'ennemi principal." In *Libération des femmes, année zéro*, 2nd ed., ed. Les Partisanes, 112–39. Paris: Éditions Maspero, 1971.

Demczuk, Irène, and Frank Remiggi, eds. *Sortir de l'ombre: Histoires des communautés lesbienne et gaie de Montréal*. Montreal: VLB Éditeur, 1998.

de Sève, Micheline. "Féminisme et nationalisme au Québec, une alliance inattendue." *International Journal of Canadian Studies* 17 (2007): 157–76.

Desmarais, Danielle. "Violence familiale, pauvreté et autonomie politique: Défis des femmes autochtones québécoises: Entrevue avec Michèle Rouleau." *Nouvelles pratiques sociales* 6, no. 1 (1995): 15–31.

Desmarais, Louise. *La bataille de l'avortement: Chronique québécoise*. Montreal: Éditions du remue-ménage, 2016.

Dessureault, Lyne. "Centre des femmes de Verdun: Rôle en santé mentale." *L'R des centres de femmes du Québec: Bulletin de liaison*, March 1989, 5–7.

di Domenico, Mariangela. "Il lavoro casalingo: Prospettive di analisi." *Il Bollettino*, July-August 1984, 5–6.

Di Lullo, Emilia. "Riflessione sul Centro Donne." *Il Bollettino*, September 1984, 12.

"Documento finale della II Conferenza Nazionale dell'Emigrazione." In *Consiglio Generale degli Italiani all'Estero: I Documenti*, ed. Marco Villani, 29–36. Rome: Consiglio Generale degli Italiani all'Estero, 2014.

Documents of the World Congress for International Women's Year Held in Berlin 20–24 October 1975. Berlin: National Organizing Committee of the GDR for the World Congress for International Women's Year, 1975.

Donert, Celia, "Women's Rights in Cold War Europe: Disentangling Feminist Histories." *Past and Present* 218, suppl. 8 (2013): 176–202.

Douglas, Rosie. "Canadian Racism and Sir George." *UHURU*, 2 February 1970,
4–5.

Downey, Allan. *The Creator's Game: Lacrosse, Identity, and Indigenous Nationhood*. Vancouver: UBC Press, 2018.

– "Engendering Nationality: Haudenosaunee Tradition, Sport and the Lines of
Gender." *Journal of the Canadian Historical Association* 23, no. 1 (2012): 319–54.

Drake, St Clair. "The Black Diaspora in Pan-African Perspective." *Black Scholar*,
September 1975, 2–13.

Dua, Enakshi. "Exclusion through Inclusion: Female Asian Migration in the
Making of Canada as a White Settler Nation." *Gender, Place, and Culture* 14,
no. 4 (2007): 445–66.

Dubinsky, Karen. *Babies without Borders: Adoption and Migration across the
Americas*. Toronto: University of Toronto Press, 2010.

Dubinsky, Karen, and Franca Iacovetta, "Murder, Womanly Virtue, and Motherhood: The Case of Angelina Napolitano, 1911–1922." *Canadian Historical Review*
72, no. 4 (1991): 505–31.

Duchen, Claire. *Feminism in France: May '68 to Mitterand*. London: Routledge
and Kegan Paul, 1986.

Dumont, Micheline. "La culture politique durant la Révolution tranquille: L'in-
visibilité des femmes dans Cité libre et l'Action nationale." *Recherches féministes*
21, no. 2 (2008): 103–25.

– *Le féminisme québécois raconté à Camille*. Montreal: Éditions du remue-
ménage, 2008.

– "Politique active et féminisme: Les députées de l'Assemblée nationale." *Bulletin
d'histoire politique* 20, no. 2 (2012): 247–60.

Dumont, Micheline, and Louise Toupin, eds. *La pensée féministe au Québec:
Anthologie, 1900–1985*. Montreal: Éditions du remue-ménage, 2003.

Eleazzaro, Carolina. "Seconda generazione." *L'altra faccia della luna*, September
2006, 4.

Erhagbe, Edward O. "The African-American Contribution to the Liberation
Struggle in Southern Africa: The Case of the African Liberation Support
Committee, 1972–1979." *Journal of Pan African Studies* 4, no. 5 (2011): 26–56.

Este, David. "The Black Church as a Social Welfare Institution: Union United
Church and the Development of Montreal's Black Community, 1907–1940."
Journal of Black Studies 35, no. 1 (2004): 3–22.

Este, David, Christa Sato, and Darcy McKenna. "The Coloured Women's Club of Montreal, 1902–1940: African-Canadian Women Confronting Anti-Black Racism." *Canadian Social Work Review* 34, no. 1 (2017): 81–99.

Estimable, Lamarre. "L'intégration des jeunes immigrants haïtiens au système scolaire qéuébécois: L'exemple du quartier Saint-Michel." MA thesis, Université du Québec à Montréal, 2006.

Evans, Sara. *Personal Politics: The Role of Women's Liberation in the Civil Rights Movements and the New Left*. New York: Random House, 1979.

Fahrni, Magda. "Reflections on the Place of Quebec in Historical Writing on Canada." In *Contesting Clio's Craft: New Directions and Debates in Canadian History*, ed. Michael Dawson and Christopher Dummitt, 1–20. London: Institute for the Study of the Americas, 2009.

Faludi, Susan. *Backlash: The Undeclared War against American Women*. 1991. Reprint, New York: Crown, 2006.

Fanon, Frantz. *Les damnés de la terre*. Paris: Éditions Maspero, 1961.

Farmer, Ashley. *Remaking Black Power: How Black Women Transformed an Era*. Chapel Hill: University of North Carolina Press, 2017.

Fédération des femmes du Québec. *Déclaration solennelle de solidarité entre la Fédération des femmes du Québec et Femmes autochtones du Québec*. 1 October 2004. https://www.ffq.qc.ca/fr/protocole-de-solidarite-avec-faq.

– *La participation politique des femmes du Québec*. Ottawa: Information Canada, 1971.

Femmes et démocratie en Haïti. Pétion-Ville, Port-au-Prince: Forum de jeudi, 1989.

Finestone, Sheila. "Une journée à la Commission des droits à la personne." *Bulletin de la FFQ*, April-May 1978, 8–13.

Fiske, Jo-Anne. "Political Status of Native Indian Women: Contradictory Implications of Canadian State Policy." In *In the Days of Our Grandmothers: A Reader in Aboriginal Women's History in Canada*, ed. Mary-Ellen Kelm and Lorna Townsend, 336–66. Toronto: University of Toronto Press, 2006.

– "Spirited Subjects and Wounded Souls: Political Representations of an Im/moral Frontier." In *Contact Zones: Aboriginal and Settler Women in Canada's Colonial Past*, ed. Katie Pickles and Myra Rutherdale, 90–108. Vancouver: UBC Press, 2005.

– "The Womb Is to the Nation as the Heart Is to the Body: Ethnopolitical Discourses of the Canadian Indigenous Women's Movement." *Studies in Political Economy* 51, no. 1 (1996): 65–95.

Flynn, Karen. "'Hotel Refuses Negro Nurse': Gloria Clarke Baylis and the Queen Elizabeth Hotel." *Canadian Bulletin of Medical History* 35, no. 2 (2018): 278–308.

Fontaine, Suzanne. "La lutte des femmes au Québec." In *Théories et pratiques de la lutte des femmes*, ed. Adeline Chancy and Suzy Castor, 47–53. Port-au-Prince: Centre de recherche et de formation économique et sociale pour le développement, 1988.

Fouron, Georges, and Nina Glick Schiller. "All in the Family: Gender, Transnational Migration, and the Nation-State." *Identities: Global Studies in Culture and Power* 7, no. 4 (2001): 539–82.

Fraser, Arvonne, and Irene Tinker, eds. *Developing Power: How Women Transformed International Development*. New York: Feminist Press, 2004.

Fraser, Nancy. "Feminism, Capitalism, and the Cunning of History." *New Left Review*, no. 56 (2009): 97–117.

Gabaccia, Donna. *Foreign Relations: American Immigration in Global Perspective*. Princeton, NJ: Princeton University Press, 2012.

– *Italy's Many Diasporas*. Seattle: University of Washington Press, 2000.

Gabaccia, Donna, and Franca Iacovetta. *Women, Gender and Transnational Lives: Italian Women Workers of the World*. Toronto: University of Toronto Press, 2002.

– "Women, Work, and Protest in the Italian Diaspora: An International Research Agenda." *Labour/Le Travail* 42 (1998): 161–81.

Gabriel, Ellen. "Aboriginal Women's Movement; A Quest for Self-Determination." *Aboriginal Policy Studies* 1, no. 1 (2011): 183–8.

Garoute, Alice. "Suprême appel de notre président, Alice Garoute, à la constitution de 1950." In Ministère à la condition féminine et aux droits de la femme, with Le musée du panthéon national Haïtien, *Femme, notre histoire: Un panorama des femmes haïtiennes, héroïnes de notre Independence et figures politiques contemporaines*, 36. Port-au-Prince: Government of Haiti, 1998.

Gélinas, Claude. *Les autochtones dans le Québec post-confédéral, 1867–1950*. Sillery, QC: Septentrion, 2007.

Germain, Annick, and Damaris Rose. *Montréal: The Quest for a Metropolis*. New York: Wiley, 2000.

Gipson, Joella H., ed. *Impetus – The Black Woman: Proceedings of the Fourth National Congress of Black Women of Canada*. Windsor, ON: Congress of Black Women of Canada, 1977.

Girourd, Lisette. *Pour un contrôle de naissances*. 2nd ed. Montreal: Journal Offset, 1971.

Giuliani, Gaia, and Cristina Lombardi-Diop. *Bianco e nero: Storia dell'identità razziale degli italiani*. Florence: Le Monnier, 2013.

Glen, Colleen, with Joyce Green. "Colleen Glen: A Métis Feminist in Indian

Rights for Indian Women, 1973–1979." In *Making Space for Indigenous Feminism*, 1st ed., ed. Joyce Green, 233–40. Black Point, NS: Fernwood, 2007.

Gluck, Sherna Berger. "Shifting Sands: The Feminist-Nationalist Connection in
the Palestinian Movement." In *Feminist Nationalism*, 2nd ed., ed. Lois A. West,
101–29. New York: Routledge, 1997.

Goeman, Mishuana, and Jennifer Nez Denetdale. "Native Feminisms: Legacies,
Interventions, and Indigenous Sovereignties." *Wicazo Sa Review* 24, no. 2
(2009): 9–13.

Goodleaf, Donna. *Entering the War Zone: A Mohawk Perspective on Resisting
Invasions*. Penticton, BC: Theytus Books, 1995.

Gorny, Yosef. *The State of Israel in Jewish Public Thought*. London: Macmillan,
1994.

Government of Canada, Royal Commission on Bilingualism and Biculturalism.
"Submission of Miss Kahn-Tineta Horn." *Transcripts of Public Hearings*, 1 December 1965, 4316–45.

Government of Quebec. *Réponse du Québec au questionnaire de l'ONU sur les
réalisations de la décennie en matière de condition féminine (1976–1985)*. Quebec
City: Secrétariat à la condition féminine, 1985.

– *Some Missing Pages: The Black Community in the History of Quebec and
Canada*. Quebec City: Ministry of Education, 1985.

Green, Joyce, ed. *Making Space for Indigenous Feminism*. 1st ed. Black Point, NS:
Fernwood, 2007.

– ed. *Making Space for Indigenous Feminism*. 2nd ed. Black Point, NS: Fernwood,
2017.

Guglielmo, Jennifer. *Living the Revolution: Italian Women's Resistance and Radicalism in New York City, 1880–1945*. Chapel Hill: University of North Carolina
Press, 2010.

Gunn Allen, Paula. *The Sacred Hoop: Recovering the Feminine in American Indian
Traditions: With a New Preface*. 1986. Reprint, Boston: Beacon, 1992.

– "Who Is Your Mother? Red Roots of White Feminism." *History Is a Weapon*,
1986. https://www.historyisaweapon.com/defcon1/allenredrootsofwhite
feminism.html.

Gzowski, Peter. "How Kahn-Tineta Horn Became an Indian." *Maclean's Magazine*, 16 May 1964, 175–81.

– "Portrait of a Beautiful Segregationist." *Maclean's Magazine*, 2 May 1964, 169–74.

Hampton, Rosalind, and Désirée Rochat, "To Commit and to Lead: Black

Women Organizing across Communities in Montreal." In *African Canadian Leadership: Continuity, Transition, and Transformation*, ed. Tamari Kitossa, Erica S. Lawson, and Philip S.S. Howard, 149–69. Toronto: University of Toronto Press, 2019.

Harewood, John. "NBCC Leaders: Bayne, Wills, Clarke." *Contrast*, 24 October 1975, 6–7.

Harris, Aroha, and Mary Jane Logan McCallum. "Assaulting the Ears of the Government: The Indian Homemakers' Clubs and the Maori Women's Welfare League." In *Indigenous Women and Work: From Labour to Activism*, ed. Carol Williams, 225–39. Urbana-Champagne: University of Illinois Press, 2014.

Hauptman, Laurence M. *The Iroquois Struggle for Survival: World War II to Red Power*. Syracuse, NY: Syracuse University Press, 1986.

Hector, Cary. "Fascisme et sous-développement: Le cas d'Haïti." *Nouvelles optique*, January-March 1972, 48–9.

"Rapport sur quelques états d'âme de males haïtiens face au féminisme. Confidences, inquiétudes, interrogations et … espoirs." *Collectif paroles*, double issue, November-December 1984 and January-February 1985, 10–14.

Henretta, Marie. "The Oppression of Women in Canada." *Montreal Women's Liberation Newsletter*, March 1970, 1–2.

Henry, Frances. "The West Indian Domestic Scheme in Canada." *Expression*, n.d., 14–24.

Herr, Ranjou Sedou. "The Possibility of Feminist Nationalism." *Hypatia* 18, no. 3 (2003): 135–60.

Hewitt, Nancy A., ed. *No Permanent Waves: Recasting Histories of U.S. Feminism*. New Brunswick, NJ: Rutgers University Press, 2010.

Hewitt, Steve, and Christabelle Sethna. "Sex Spying: The RCMP Framing of English-Canadian Women's Liberation Groups during the Cold War." In *Debating Dissent: Canada and the Sixties*, ed. Gregory Kealey, Lara Campbell, and Dominique Clément, 134–51. Toronto: University of Toronto Press, 2012.

Higginbotham, Evelyn Brooks. "African-American Women and the Metalanguage of Race." *Signs* 17, no. 2 (1992): 251–74.

High, Steven. *Deindustrializing Montreal: Entangled Histories of Race, Residence, and Class*. Montreal and Kingston: McGill-Queen's University Press, 2022.

– "Little Burgundy: The Interwoven Histories of Race, Residence, and Work in Twentieth-Century Montreal." *Urban History Review* 46, no. 1 (2017): 23–44.

Hildebrun, Andrea. "Genèse d'une communauté lesbienne: Un récit des années

1970." In *Sortir de l'ombre: Histoires des communautés lesbienne et gaie de Montréal*, ed. Irène Demczuk and Frank Remiggi, 207–33. Montreal: VLB Éditeur, 1998.

Hill, Susan. *The Clay We Are Made Of: Haudenosaunee Land Tenure on the Grand River*. Winnipeg: University of Manitoba Press, 2017.

Hill Collins, Patricia. "Intersectionality's Definitional Dilemmas." *Annual Review of Sociology* 41 (2015): 1–20.

– "It's All in the Family: Intersections of Gender, Race, and Nation." *Hypatia* 13, no. 3 (1998): 62–82.

Holly, Daniel, Micheline Labelle, and Serge Larose. "L'émigration haïtienne, un problème national." *Collectif paroles*, October-November 1979, 18–26.

hooks, bell. *Ain't I a Woman: Black Women and Feminism*. New York: Taylor and Francis, 1981.

Horn-Miller, Kahente. "Distortion and Healing: Finding Balance and a 'Good Mind' through the Rearticulation of Sky Woman's Journey." In *Living on the Land: Indigenous Women's Understanding of Place*, ed. Nathalie Kermoal and Isabel Altamirano-Jiménez, 19–38. Edmonton: Athabasca University Press, 2016.

– "My Mom, the 'Military Mohawk Princess': Kahintinetha Horn through the Lens of Indigenous Female Celebrity." In *Indigenous Celebrity: Entanglements with Fame*, ed. Jennifer Adese and Robert Alexander Innes, 80–101. Winnipeg: University of Manitoba Press, 2021.

– "Otiyaner: The 'Women's Path' through Colonialism." *Atlantis: A Women's Studies Journal* 29, no. 2 (2005): 57–68.

Hudson, Peter James. "Imperial Designs: The Royal Bank of Canada in the Caribbean." *Race and Class* 52, no. 1 (2010): 33–48.

Iacovetta, Franca. "Betrayal, Vengeance, and the Anarchist Ideal: Virgilia D'Andrea's Radical Antifascism in (American) Exile, 1928–1933." *Journal of Women's History* 25, no. 1 (2013): 85–110.

– "'In the case of a woman' or 'the headache': Married Women's Nationality and Canada's Citizenship Act at Home and Europe, 1946–50." *Women's History Review* 28, no. 3 (2019): 396–420.

– "Ordering in Bulk: Canada's Postwar Immigration Policy and the Recruitment of Contract Workers from Italy." *Journal of American Ethnic History* 11, no. 1 (1991): 50–80.

– "'Primitive Villagers and Uneducated Girls': Canada Recruits Domestics from Italy, 1951–52." *Canadian Women's Studies* 7, no. 8 (1986): 14–18.

– *Such Hardworking People: Italian Immigrants in Postwar Toronto*. Montreal and Kingston: McGill-Queen's University Press, 1992.

– "Trying to Make Ends Meet: An Historical Look at Italian Women, the State and Family Survival Strategies in Postwar Toronto." *Canadiana* 8, no. 2 (1987): 6–11.

Iacovino, Raffaele, and Charles-Antoine Sévigny. "Between Unity and Diversity: Examining the 'Quebec Model' of Integration." In *Quebec Studies: Quebec Studies for the Twenty-First Century*, ed. Stéphan Gervain, Christopher Kirkey, and Jarrett Rudy, 249–66. Toronto: Oxford University Press, 2011.

Iannazzo, Maria Grazia. "Testimonia." *L'altra faccia della luna*, September 2005, 12.

Iasenza, Isa. "Une histoire d'engagement et de passion: La création du Centro Donne Montréal." Centre des femmes solidaires et engagées, 5 February 2019. https://cfse.ca/it/2019/02/05/40-anni-femminismo.

Indian Chiefs of Alberta. *Citizens Plus*. Edmonton: Indian Association of Alberta, 1970.

Indians of Quebec Association. *Our Land, Our People, Our Future*. Caughnawaga: Indians of Quebec Association, 1974.

Ishiguro, Laura. *Nothing to Write Home About: British Family Correspondence and the Settler Colonial Everyday in British Columbia*. Vancouver: UBC Press, 2019.

Istria, Italo. "12.000 'Yvette' al Forum: Il femminismo ha stancato." *Il Cittadino Canadese*, 16 April 1980, 1–2.

Jacobson, Mathew Frye. *Whiteness of a Different Color: European Immigrants and the Alchemy of Race*. New York: Routledge, 1995.

Jamieson, Kathleen. *Indian Women and the Law in Canada: Citizens Minus*. Study sponsored by the Advisory Council on the Status of Women, Indian Rights for Indian Women. Ottawa: Ministry of Supply and Services Canada, 1978.

– "Multiple Jeopardy: The Evolution of a Native Women's Movement." *Atlantis: A Women's Studies Journal* 4, no. 2 (1979): 157–78.

Janovicek, Nancy. "'Assisting Our Own': Urban Migration, Self-Governance, and Native Women's Organization in Thunder Bay, Ontario, 1972–1989." *American Indian Quarterly* 27, nos 3–4 (2003): 548–65.

– *No Place to Go: Local Histories of the Battered Women's Shelter Movement*. Vancouver: UBC Press, 2007.

Joachim, Benoît. "Sur l'esprit de couleur en Haïti: À propos d'un article de René Piquoin." *Nouvelle optique*, January-March 1973, 149–58.

Jumelle, Yolène. "Les structures sociales de la famille haïtienne." In *African*

Continuities/L'heritage africaine, ed. Simeon Waliaula Chilungu and Sada Niang, 245–55. Toronto: Terebi, 1989.

Kapesh, An Antane. *Je suis une maudite sauvagesse: Eukuan nin matshimanitu Innu-Iskueu*. Trans. José Mailhot, with Anne-Marie André and André Mailhot. Ottawa: Leméac, 1976.

Kettenbeil, Anne, and Centre de femmes d'ici et d'ailleurs. "Crise d'indifférence." *L'R des centres de femmes du Québec: Bulletin de liaison*, November 1990, 4–6.

Kolish, Evelyn. "Note critique: L'incendie de Montréal en 1734 et le process de Marie-Josèphe Angélique: Trois oeuvres, deux interprétations." *Revue d'histoire de l'Amérique française* 61, no. 1 (2007): 85–92.

Kouka-Ganga, Jane. "Femmes noires au Canada." *Cahiers de la femme* 4, no. 2 (1982): 29–30.

Kyong, Wendy Hui. "A Case of Mistaken Identity? Bearing Witness to the Montreal Massacre." *Critical Matrix* 9, no. 2 (1995): 117–26.

Labelle, Micheline. *Histoires d'immigrées: Itinéraires d'ouvrières Colombiennes, Grecques, Haïtiennes et Portugaises de Montréal*. Montreal: Boréal, 1987.

Labelle, Micheline, Marin Goyette, and Martine Paquin. *Intégration économique: Le discours de leaders d'origine italienne de la région de Montréal*. Montreal: Centre de recherche sur les relations interethniques et le racisme, Département de sociologie, Université du Québec à Montréal, 1993.

Labelle, Micheline, and Marthe Therrien. "Le mouvement associatif haïtien au Québec et le discours des leaders." *Nouvelles pratiques sociales* 5, no. 2 (1992): 65–83.

Lacelle, Nicole. *Entretiens avec Madeleine Parent et Léa Roback*. Montreal: Éditions du remue-ménage, 1988.

Lacombe, Pierre, dir. *Artisans de notre histoire: Évelyn O'Bomsawin*. DVD. Montreal: Ciné Fête, 2002.

– dir. *Artisans de notre histoire: Marco Micone*. DVD. Montreal: Ciné Fête, 2002.

Lagacé, Thérèse. *Historique de l'Association des femmes autochtones du Québec, 1974–1980*. Quebec City: Association des femmes autochtones du Québec, 1980.

Lamour, Sabine. "Partir pour mieux s'enraciner ou retour sur la fabrique du poto mitan en Haïti." In *Déjouer le silence: Contre-discours sur les femmes haïtiennes*, ed. Darline Alexis, Denyse Côté, and Sabine Lamour, 96–105. Montreal: Éditions du remue-ménage, 2018.

Lamoureux, Diane. "Les ambivalences du féminisme québécois face au discours postcolonial." Paper presented at the Congrès national de l'Association Française de Science Politique, Strasbourg, 31 August to 2 September 2011.

– *L'amère patrie: Féminisme et nationalisme dans le Québec contemporain.* Montreal: Éditions du remue-ménage, 2001.

– "La lutte pour le droit de l'avortement, 1969–1981." *Revue d'histoire de l'Amérique française* 37, no. 1 (1983): 81–90.

– "La question lesbienne dans le féminisme montréalais: Un chassé-croisé." In *Sortir de l'ombre: Histoires des communautés lesbienne et gaie de Montréal,* ed. Irène Demczuk and Frank Remiggi, 167–85. Montreal: VLB Éditeur, 1998.

– "Nationalisme et féminisme: Impasse et coïncidences." *Possibles* 8, no. 1 (1993): 43–59.

– "The Paradoxes of Quebec Feminism." In *Quebec Questions: Quebec Studies for the Twenty-First Century,* ed. Stéphan Gervais, Christopher Kirkey, and Jarrett Rudy, 307–23. Toronto: Oxford University Press, 2011.

Lamoureux, Jocelyne. "L'unité par le SPM?" *L'R des centres de femmes du Québec: Bulletin de liaison,* October 1991, 12–13.

Lanctôt, Aurélie. *Les libéraux n'aiment pas les femmes: Essai sur l'austérité.* Montreal: Lux Éditeur, 2015.

Lanthier, Stéphanie. "L'impossible réciprocité des rapports politiques et idéologiques entre le nationalisme radical et le féminisme radical au Québec, 1961–1972." MA thesis, Université de Sherbrooke, 1998.

Lapointe-Roy, Huguette. "Comité des affaires internationales (FFQ)." *Bulletin de la FFQ,* April 1975, 8.

– "Femmes immigrées, à nous la parole!" *Petite presse,* February 1983, 17.

Larochelle, Catherine. "Émanciper l'histoire: Pour une histoire de la Multitude." *Histoire engagée,* 10 September 2019. http://histoireengagee.ca/emanciper-lhistoire-pour-une-histoire-de-la-multitude.

Laughlin, Kathleen A., Julie Gallagher, Dorothy Sue Cobble, Eileen Boris, Premilla Nadasen, Stephanie Gilmore, and Leandra Zarnow. "Is It Time to Jump Ship? Historians Rethink the Waves Metaphor." *Feminist Formations* 22, no. 1 (2010): 76–135.

Lawrence, Bonita, and Kim Anderson. "Introduction to Indigenous Women: The State of Our Nations." *Atlantis: A Women's Studies Journal* 29, no. 2 (2005): 1–8.

LeClerc, Patrice, and Lois A. West. "Feminist Nationalist Movements in Québec: Resolving Contradictions?" In *Feminist Nationalism,* 2nd ed., ed. Lois A. West, 220–47. New York: Routledge, 1997.

Lee, Jo-Anne, and Linda Cardinal. "Hegemonic Nationalism and the Politics of Feminism and Multiculturalism in Canada." In *Painting the Maple: Essays on Race, Gender, and the Construction of Canada,* ed. Veronica Strong-Boag,

Sherrill Grace, Avigail Eisenberg, and Joan Anderson, 215–41. Vancouver: UBC Press, 1998.

Leslie, Richard E. "The Negro Citizenship Association Inc. Philosophy and Objectives." *Expression*, February 1965, 3–6.

Les Partisanes, ed. *Libération des femmes, année zéro*. 2nd ed. Paris: Éditions Maspero, 1971.

Lévesque, Andrée. ed. *Madeleine Parent: Activist*. Toronto: Sumach, 2005.

– "Les midinettes de 1937: Culture ouvrière, culture de genre, culture ethnique." In *1937: Un tournant culturel*, ed. Yvan Lamonde and Denis St. Jacques, 71–8. Quebec City: Presses de l'Université Laval, 2009.

Lévesque, Carole, Viviane Michel, and Carole Bussières. *Our Vision, Our Mission, Our Trajectories, Our Battles: Quebec Native Women, 1974–2019*. Kahnawake: n.p., 2018.

Lévy, Joseph. *Espace d'une génération: Entretiens avec Georges Anglade*. Montreal: Éditions Liber, 2004.

LFAS (Ligue féminine d'action sociale). *Le féminisme en marche: Bulletin dédié à la mémoire de Alice Garourte*. Port-au-Prince: Eben-Ezer, 1951.

– *Femmes haïtiennes*. Port-au-Prince: Éditions Fardin, 1953.

Lightfoot, Sheryl. "Indigenous Global Politics." PhD diss., University of Minnesota, 2009.

Liu, Yuxi. "Au pays de l'avenir radieux: Voyages des Québécois en Chine populaire (1971–1975)." *Revue d'histoire de l'Amérique française* 71, nos 3–4 (2018): 133–56.

Lombardi-Diop, Cristina, and Caterina Romeo. "Italy's Postcolonial 'Question': Views from the Southern Frontier of Europe." *Postcolonial Studies* 18, no. 4 (2015): 367–83.

– eds. *Postcolonial Italy: Challenging National Homogeneity*. New York: Palgrave MacMillan, 2012.

Loo, Tina. "Africville and the Dynamics of State Power in Postwar Canada." *Acadiensis* 39, no. 2 (2010): 23–47.

L'R des centres de femmes du Québec. *Actes du colloque: Femmes différentes et semblables, 10 et 11 juin 1993*. http://bv.cdeacf.ca/bvdoc.php?no=2002_17_0105 &col=CF&format=htm&ver=old.

Luxton, Meg. "Feminism as a Class Act: Working-Class Feminism and the Women's Movement in Canada." *Labour/Le Travail* 48 (2011): 63–88.

Magloire, Danièle. "L'antiféminisme en Haïti." In *Déjouer le silence: Contre-*

discours sur les femmes haïtiennes, ed. Darline Alexis, Denyse Côté, and Sabine Lamour, 199–212. Montreal: Éditions du remue-ménage, 2018.

Maillé, Chantal. "French and Quebec Feminisms: Influences and Reciprocities." In *Transatlantic Passages: Literary and Cultural Relations between Quebec and Francophone Europe*, ed. Paula Ruth Gilbert and Milena Santoro, 50–9. Montreal and Kingston: McGill-Queen's University Press, 2010.

– "Réception de la théorie postcoloniale dans le féminisme québécois." *Recherches féministes* 20, no. 2 (2007): 91–111.

Maison d'Haïti. *Mémoire de la Maison d'Haïti à la Commission d'étude sur la formation des adultes*. Montreal: Maison d'Haïti, 1980.

Maltais-Landry, Aude. "Un territoire de cent pas de côté: Récits de la création d'une réserve indienne en territoire innu au milieu du XXe siècle." *Revue d'histoire de l'Amérique française* 69, nos 1–2 (2015), 19–50.

Manuel, George, and Michael Posluns. *The Fourth World: An Indian Reality*. Don Mills, ON: Collier-MacMillan Canada, 1974.

Manulak, Daniel. "'An African Representative': Canada, the Third World, and South African Apartheid, 1984–1990." *Journal of Imperial and Commonwealth History* 49, no. 2 (2021): 368–99.

Mar, Lisa Rose. *Brokering Belonging: Chinese in Canada's Exclusion Era, 1885–1945*. Toronto: Oxford University Press, 2010.

Marano, Carla. "'Rising Strongly and Rapidly': The University Negro Improvement Association, 1919–1940." *Canadian Historical Review* 91, no. 2 (2010): 234–59.

Martel, Marcel. "'Riot' at Sir George Williams: Giving Meaning to Student Dissent." In *Debating Dissent: Canada and the Sixties*, ed. Lara Campbell, Dominique Clément, and Gregory S. Kealey, 97–114. Toronto: University of Toronto Press, 2012.

Mathieu, Sarah-Jane. *North of the Color Line: Migration and Black Resistance in Canada, 1870–1955*. Chapel Hill: University of North Carolina Press, 2010.

Maynard, Robyn, and Sophie Le-Phat. "Accommodate This! A Feminist and Anti-racist Response to the 'Reasonable Accommodation' Hearings in Quebec." *Canadian Women's Studies* 27, nos 2–3 (2009): 21–6.

McCallum, Mary Jane. "Indigenous Labour and Indigenous History." *American Indian Quarterly* 33, no. 4 (2009): 523–44.

McCarthy, Theresa. *In Divided Unity: Haudenosaunee Reclamation of the Grand River*. Tucson: University of Arizona Press, 2016.

McClintok, Anne. "Family Feuds: Gender, Nationalism, and the Family." *Feminist Review*, no. 44 (1993): 61–80.

McDougall, Mary. "Lives Lived: Yolène Jumelle, 68." *Globe and Mail*, 11 February 2013.

McDuffie, Erik S. "The Diasporic Journey of Louise Little: Grassroots Garveyism, the Midwest, and Community Feminism." *Women, Gender, and Families of Color* 4, 2 (2016): 146–70.

– *Sojourning for Freedom: Black Women, American Communism, and the Making of Black Left Feminism*. Durham, NC: Duke University Press, 2011.

McKeown, Paula, dir. *Désirs de liberté*. DVD. 1996. Reprint, Quebec City: Vidéo Femmes, 2008.

McKercher, Asa. "Sound and Fury: Diefenbaker, Human Rights, and Canadian Foreign Policy." *Canadian Historical Review* 97, no. 2 (2016): 165–94.

McKittrick, Katherine. *Demonic Grounds: Black Women and the Cartographies of Struggle*. Minneapolis: University of Minnesota Press, 2006.

Memmi, Albert. *Portrait du colonisé, précédé du portrait du colonisateur, suivi de Les Canadiens français sont-ils des colonisés?* Montreal: L'Étincelle, 1972.

Meren, David. "Crisis of the Nation: Race and Culture in the Canada-Quebec-France Triangle of the 1960s." In *Dominion of Race: Rethinking Canada's International History*, ed. Laura Madokoro, Francine McKenzie, and David Meren, 229–46. Vancouver: UBC Press, 2017.

Merlet, Myriam. "Les droits économiques et sociaux des femmes." In *Femmes et démocratie et Haïti*, ed. Arnold Antonin, 31–7. Port-au-Prince: Forum libre, 1989.

– "The More People Dream." In *Walking on Fire: Haitian Women's Stories of Survival and Resistance*, ed. Beverly Bell, 217–20. Ithaca, NY: Cornell University Press, 2001.

– *La participation politique des femmes en Haïti: Quelques éléments d'analyse*. Port-au-Prince: Éditions Fanm Yo La, 2002.

– "Women in Conquest of Full and Total Citizenship in an Endless Transition." In *Engendering Social Justice, Democratizing Citizenship and Women's Activism in Latin American and the Caribbean*, ed. Elizabeth Maier and Nathalie Lebon, 127–39. New Brunswick, NJ: Rutgers University Press, 2010.

Michaud, Jacinthe. *Frontiers of Feminism: Movements and Influences in Quebec and Italy, 1960–80*. Vancouver: UBC Press, 2021.

Midy, Franklyn. "Dossier Canada-Haïti: Présence canadienne et québécoise en Haïti." *Relations*, April 1973, 102–7.

Mills, Alexandra, Désirée Rochat, and Steven High. "Telling Stories from Montreal's Negro Community Centre Fonds: The Archives as Community-Engaged Classroom." *Archivaria* 89 (2020): 34–68.

Mills, Jennifer. "Conferencing as a Site for the Mobilization of Black Feminist Identities in the Congress of Black Women of Canada." *Journal of Black Studies* 46, no. 4 (2015): 415–41.

Mills, Sean. *The Empire Within: Postcolonial Thought and Political Activism in Montreal.* Montreal and Kingston: McGill-Queen's University Press, 2010.

– *A Place in the Sun: Haiti, Haitians, and the Remaking of Quebec.* Montreal and Kingston: McGill-Queen's University Press, 2016.

– "Quebec, Haiti, and the Deportation Crisis of 1974." *Canadian Historical Review* 94, no. 3 (2013): 405–35.

Millward, Liz. *Making a Scene: Lesbians and Community across Canada, 1964–84.* Vancouver: UBC Press, 2015.

Milne, Nora. "Creating Change to Maintaining Change: The Fédération du Québec pour le planning des naissances and the Pro-choice Movement." MA thesis, McGill University, 2011.

Milot, David. "Histoire du mouvement marxiste-léniniste au Québec, 1973–1983: Un premier bilan." *Bulletin d'histoire politique* 13, no. 1 (2004): 11–15.

Mina, Noula. "Taming and Training Greek 'Peasant Girls' and the Gendered Politics of Whiteness in Postwar Canada: Canadian Bureaucrats and Immigrant Domestics, 1950s–1960s." *Canadian Historical Review* 94, no. 4 (2013): 514–39.

Mitchell, Michael Kanentakeron, dir. *You Are on Indian Land.* DVD. Montreal: National Film Board of Canada, 1969.

"Myriam Merlet (1956–2010)." L'Orégand, 21 January 2010. https://www.oregand.ca/veille/2010/01/myriam-merlet.html.

Mohanty, Chandra Talpade. "'Under Western Eyes' Revisited: Feminist Solidarity through Anticapitalist Struggles." *Signs: Journal of Women in Culture and Society* 28, no. 2 (2003): 499–535.

Moisan, Lise. "Dix ans après l'Année de la Femme: Où nous mènent les féministes d'État?" *La vie en rose*, February 1985, 32–5.

Moise, Claude. "Dans la diaspora: Ici, la Maison d'Haïti." *Collectif paroles*, January-February 1980, 11–13.

Montas, Yves (Jean Luc). "Sur la diffusion du marxisme en Haïti." *Nouvelle optique*, April-September 1972, 89–101.

Montour, Courtney, dir. *Mary Two-Axe Earley: I Am Indian Again.* DVD. Montreal: National Film Board of Canada, 2021.

Morabito, Maria. "Madre e figlia: Due generazioni in conflitto." *L'altra faccia della luna*, October 1996, 3.

Morgensen, Scott. "Settler Homonationalism: Theorizing Settler Colonialism within Queer Modernities." GLQ: *A Journal of Lesbian and Gay Studies* 16, nos 1–2 (2010): 105–31.

Morsella, Margherita. "Femminismo e comunità, le origini del Centro Donne Italiane di Montréal." *Il Corriere Italiano*, 1 February 2022. https://www.corri ereitaliano.com/comunita/attivita/16199/femminismo-e-comunita-le-origini-del-centro-donne-italiane-di-montreal.

Morton, Suzanne. *Black McGill*. 2021. https://www.mcgill.ca/antiblackracism/ files/antiblackracism/black_mcgill_may_2021.pdf.

– *Indigenous McGill*. 2019. https://www.mcgill.ca/indigenous/files/indigenous/ indigenous_mcgill_october_2019_0.pdf.

Mouvement québécois pour combattre le racisme et al. *Mémoire présenté à la Commission parlementaire sur la Charte des droits et libertés de la personne.* Montreal: Mouvement québécois pour combattre le racisme, 1981.

Mugabo, Délice. "Black in the City: On the Ruse of Ethnicity and Language in an Anti-Black Landscape." *Identities: Global Studies in Culture and Power* 26, no. 6 (2019): 631–48.

– "On Haunted Places: Encountering Slavery in Quebec." In *Black Writers Matter*, ed. Whitney French, 89–101. Regina: University of Regina Press, 2019.

Mulay, Shree. "The Importance of Being Madeleine: How an Activist Won the Hearts of Quebec's Immigrant and Minority Women." In *Madeleine Parent: Activist*, ed. Andrée Lévesque, 112–17. Toronto: Sumach, 2005.

Nadasen, Premilla. "Expanding the Boundaries of the Women's Movement: Black Feminism and the Struggle for Welfare Rights." *Feminist Studies* 28, no. 2 (2002): 271–301.

Namaste, Viviane. "Les infirmières haïtiennes comme catalyseurs de changement social: Le cas de l'histoire du sida à Montréal." *Haïti Perspectives* 6, no. 1 (2017): 62–71.

Nash, Jennifer. "The Political Life of Black Motherhood." *Feminist Studies* 44, no. 3 (2018): 699–712.

National Indian Brotherhood. *Declaration on Indian Housing Policy Paper.* Ottawa: National Indian Brotherhood, 1974.

– *Indian Control of Indian Education*. Ottawa: National Indian Brotherhood, 1972.

– *Statement on the Economic Development of Indian Communities*. Ottawa: National Indian Brotherhood, 1973.

– *The Strategy for Socio-economic Development of Indian People: National Report*. Ottawa: National Indian Brotherhood, 1977.

Nelson, Charmaine. *Slavery, Geography, and Empire in Nineteenth-Century Marine Landscapes of Montreal and Jamaica*. New York: Routledge, 2016.

Nelson, Jennifer. *Women of Color and the Reproductive Rights Movement*. New York: New York University Press, 2003.

Néméh-Nombré, Philippe. *Seize temps noirs pour apprendre à dire kuei*. Montreal: Mémoire d'encrier, 2022.

Neptune-Anglade, Mireille. *L'autre moitié du développement: À propos du travail des femmes en Haiti*. Paris: Éditions des Alizés, 1986.

– "Les conférences internationales sur les femmes et leur impact en Haïti." *Recherches féministes* 8, no. 1 (1995): 165–73.

– "Du travail domestique comme deuxième journée de travail des Haïtiennes." *Recherches féministes* 1, no. 2 (1988): 39–52.

Nickel, Sarah. *Assembling Unity: Indigenous Politics, Gender, and the Union of BC Indian Chiefs*. Vancouver: UBC Press, 2019.

– "Introduction." In *In Good Relation: History, Gender, and Kinship in Indigenous Feminisms*, ed. Sarah Nickel and Amanda Fehr, 1–22. Winnipeg: University of Manitoba Press, 2020.

– "Reconsidering 1969: The *White Paper* and the Making of the Modern Indigenous Rights Movement." *Canadian Historical Review* 100, no. 2 (2019): 223–38.

Nicolas, Émilie. "Maîtres chez l'Autre: La naïveté originelle dont se réclame le Québécois nourrit-elle le déni d'un colonialisme bien de chez nous?" *Liberté* 326 (2020): 42–6.

Niosi, Laurence. "Marjorie Villefranche: Le pouvoir de changer des choses." *Journal de St-Michel*, 1 March 2011.

N'Zengu-Tayo, Marie-José. "'Fanm se poto mitan': Haitian Women, the Pillar of Society." *Feminist Review*, no. 59 (1998): 118–42.

O'Leary, Véronique, and Louise Toupin, eds. *Québécoises deboutte!* Vol. 1, *Une anthologie de textes du Front de libération des femmes (1969–1971) et du Centre des femmes (1972–1975)*. Montreal: Éditions du remue-ménage, 1982.

– eds. *Québécoises deboutte!* Vol. 2, *Collection complète suivie de deux tables rondes avec des femmes du Front de libération des femmes (1972–1975)*. Montreal: Éditions du remue-ménage, 1983.

Ollivier, Émile. "Étude: L'alphabétisation des immigrants haïtiens à Montréal."
    Collectif paroles, June 1980, 19–24.

– "Lire Paulo Freire." *Nouvelle optique*, April-September 1972, 187–92.

– "Le rachitisme: L'objectif pédagogique dans le système d'enseignement en
    Haïti." *Nouvelle optique*, January-March 1972, 162–74.

O'Neill, Stéphanie. "Le soleil de la prospérité actuelle ne luit pas pour tout le
    monde: Les exclus de la société de consommation à Montréal, 1945–1975."
    Revue d'histoire de l'Amérique française 70, no. 4 (2017): 55–70.

– "Y aura-t-il toujours des pauvres: Les transformations des discours sur la
    pauvreté en période de prospérité." *Labour/Le Travail* 79 (2017): 157–84.

Olcott, Jocelyn. *International Women's Year: The Greatest Consciousness-Raising
    Event in History*. New York: Oxford University Press, 2017.

Palmer, Bryan. *Canada's 1960s: The Ironies of Identity in a Rebellious Era*. Toronto:
    University of Toronto Press, 2009.

Papillon, Martin. "Aboriginal Peoples and Quebec: Competing or Coexisting Na-
    tionalisms?" In *Quebec Questions: Quebec Studies for the Twenty-First Century*,
    ed. Stéphan Gervais, Christopher Kirkey, and Jarrett Rudy, 109–22. Toronto:
    Oxford University Press, 2011.

Pâquet, Martin, and Stéphane Savard. *Brève histoire de la Révolution tranquille*.
    Montreal: Boréal, 2021.

Pardo, Fabiola, Kalpana Das, and Fernand Gauthier. *Development of Intercultural
    Modalities for Community Cooperation: Report on Focus-Group Discussions*.
    Montreal: Intercultural Institute of Montreal, 2000.

Patry-Buisson, Ghislaine. "La FFQ: Une présence qui s'affirme." *Bulletin de la
    FFQ*, March 1976, 2–3.

Paul, Deborah Ann. "Women and the International Division of Labour: The
    Case of Haitian Workers in Montreal." MA thesis, Queen's University, 1992.

Pelletier, Clotilde, with Claude Laurin. *États des lieux: Violence et santé mentale
    chez les autochtones du Québec*. Montreal: Association des femmes autochtones
    du Québec, 1993.

Péloquin, Marjolaine. *En prison pour la cause des femmes: La conquête du banc
    des jurés*. Montreal: Éditions du remue-ménage, 2011.

Perilli, Vincenza. "'Sexe' et 'race' dans les féminismes italiens." *Les cahiers du
    CEDREF* 14 (2006): 105–43.

Perkins, Margo V. *Autobiography as Activism: Three Black Women of the Sixties*.
    Jackson: University Press of Mississippi, 2000.

Perry, Adele. *Colonial Relations: The Douglas-Connolly Family and the Nine-teenth-Century Imperial World.* Cambridge, UK: Cambridge University Press, 2015.

Perzia, Antonella. "L'America ancora non è delle donne." *Il Bollettino,* September 1985, 18.

– "Le due 'F' – femminismo e fede – alleate o nemiche?" *Il Bollettino,* October 1984, 7.

– "La ripartizione dei compiti." *Il Bollettino,* July-August 1984, 11.

– "Lo scopo del sesso è 'solo' la procreazione?" *Il Bollettino,* October 1984, 11.

Petitclerc, Martin, and Martin Robert. "Les lois spéciales, le droit de grève et la transformation néolibérale de la société québécoise." In *L'État du Québec 2013–2014: Le pouvoir citoyen,* ed. Miriam Fahmy, 387–92. Montreal: Boréal, 2013.

Pierre, Alexandra, ed. *Empreintes de résistance: Filiations et récits de femmes autochtones, noires et racisées.* Montreal: Éditions du remue-ménage, 2021.

Pierre, Guy. "Bilan économique duvaliériste." *Nouvelle optique,* December 1971, 33–9.

Pierre, Samuel, ed. *Ces québécois venus d'Haïti: Contribution de la communauté haïtienne à l'édification du Québec moderne.* Montreal: École Polytechnique de Montréal, 2007.

Pierre-Charles, Gérard. "La complémentarité des stratégies du développement en Afrique et en Amérique latine." *Nouvelle optique,* January-March 1973, 159–64.

Pirone, Michel. "Parità di sessi e nudismo." *Il Cittadino Canadese,* 6 April 1978, 4.

Podmore, Julie, and Line Chamberland. "Entering the Urban Frame: Early Lesbian Activism and Public Space in Montréal." *Journal of Lesbian Studies* 19, no. 2 (2015): 192–211.

Porter, Marilyn. "Transnational Feminisms in a Globalized World: Challenges, Analysis, and Resistance." *Feminist Studies* 33, no. 1 (2007): 43–63.

Povitz, Lana Dee. *Stirrings: How Activist New Yorkers Ignited a Movement for Food Injustice.* Durham: University of North Carolina Press, 2019.

Praud, Jocelyne. "La seconde vague féministe et la féminisation du Parti socialiste français et du Parti québécois." *Politique et sociétés* 17, nos 1–2 (1998): 71–90.

Quebec Native Women's Association. "Statement by the Quebec Native Women's Association on Aboriginal Self-Government." Presented at the "Federal-Provincial Conference: Aboriginal Constitutional Matters," Toronto, 5–6 June 1985.

RAFA (Rassemblement des femmes haïtiennes). *Femmes haïtiennes.* Montreal: Maison d'Haïti and Carrefour International, 1980.

Randolph, Sherie M. *Florynce "Flo" Kennedy: The Life of a Black Feminist Radical.* Chapel Hill: University of North Carolina Press, 2015.

Rateau, Marlène. "Mireille Neptune, la militante féministe." *La Nouvelliste,* 16 August 2011.

– "*Pawòl fanm*: Des femmes haïtiennes de Montréal au micro de Radio Centre-Ville." In *Interrelations femme-medias dans l'Amérique française,* ed. Josette Brun, 177–85. Quebec City: Presses de l'Université Laval, 2009.

– "Violence, AIDS, and Education." In *Haitian Women: Between Repression and Democracy,* ed. Clorinde Zéphir, 95–100. Port-au-Prince: ENFOFANM Éditions, 1991.

Ravix, Raymonde. "Entrevue avec Nègès vanyan." *Collectif paroles,* March-April 1984, 10–12.

Razack, Sherene. *Race, Space, and the Law: Unmapping a White Settler Society.* Toronto: Between the Lines, 2002.

Rebick, Judy. *Ten Thousand Roses: The Making of a Feminist Revolution.* Toronto: Penguin Canada, 2005.

"The Regroupement." *Solidarity with Native People,* April 1991.

Report of the First Alberta Native Women's Conference. Mayfair Hotel, Edmonton, 12–15 March 1968. Edmonton: n.p., 1968.

Report of the First National Native Women's Conference. MacDonald Hotel, Edmonton, 22–23 March 1971. Edmonton: n.p., 1971.

Ricci, Amanda. "Un féminisme inclusif? La Fédération des femmes du Québec et les femmes immigrantes ou racialisées, 1966–1992." *Bulletin d'histoire politique* 25, no. 3 (2017): 102–23.

– "Making Global Citizens? Canadian Women at the World Conference of the International Women's Year, Mexico City, 1975." In *Undiplomatic History: New Histories of Canada in the World,* ed. Asa McKercher and Philip Van Huizen, 206–29. Montreal and Kingston: McGill-Queen's University Press, 2019.

Robert, Diane. "Le mot de la présidente." *L'R des centres de femmes du Québec: Bulletin de liaison,* March 1992, 1.

Roberts, Alfie. *A View for Freedom: Alfie Roberts Speaks on the Caribbean, Cricket, Montreal, and C.L.R. James.* Montreal: Alfie Roberts Institute, 2005.

Robinson, Cedric. *Black Marxism: The Making of a Black Radical Tradition.* 1983. Reprint, Chapel Hill: University of North Carolina Press, 2000.

Rochat, Désirée. "Archiving Black Diasporic Activism: How the Shared Praxis of Haitian Activists at La Maison d'Haïti Built a Community." PhD diss., McGill University, 2021.

Rodriguez-Arbolay, Gregory Pablo, Jr. "Connecting Fragments: Solidarity and Fragmentation in Montreal's Gay and Lesbian Communities." MA thesis, Sarah Lawrence College, 2009.

Roediger, David. *Working toward Whiteness: How America's Immigrants Became White: The Strange Journey from Ellis Island to the Suburbs.* New York: Basic Books, 2005.

Rojas, Maythee. *Women of Color and Feminism.* Berkeley: Seal, 2009.

Roth, Benita. *Separate Roads to Feminism: Black, Chicana, and White Feminist Movements in America's Second Wave.* Cambridge, UK: Cambridge University Press, 2004.

Rouleau, Michèle. "Madeleine Parent: An Unfailing Ally of Native Women." In *Madeleine Parent: Activist,* ed. Andrée Lévesque, 120–2. Toronto: Sumach, 2005.

Roy-Campbell, Zaline Makini. "Pan-African Women Organising for the Future: The Formation of the Pan African Women's Liberation Organisation and Beyond." *African Journal of Political Science* 1, no. 1 (1996). 45–57.

Roy Drainville, Cassandre. "'Nous sommes une nation': Emergence de nouvelles structures politiques autochtones au Québec, 1943–1969." MA thesis, Université du Québec à Montréal, 2019.

Rück, Daniel. *The Laws and the Land: The Settler Colonial Invasion of Kahnawake in Nineteenth-Century Canada.* Vancouver: UBC Press, 2021.

Rueck, Daniel. "Enclosing the Mohawk Commons: A History of Use-Rights, Landownership, and Boundary-Making in Kahnawa:ke Mohawk Territory." PhD diss., McGill University, 2012.

– "When Bridges Become Barriers: Montreal and Kahnawake Mohawk Territory." In *Metropolitan Natures: Environmental Histories of Montreal,* ed. Michèle Dagenais and Stéphane Castonguay, 228–44. Pittsburgh, PA: University of Pittsburgh Press, 2011.

Rushforth, Brett. *Bonds of Alliance: Indigenous and Atlantic Slaveries in New France.* Chapel Hill: University of North Carolina Press, 2012.

Rutland, Ted. *Displacing Blackness: Power, Planning, and Race in Twentieth-Century Halifax.* Toronto: University of Toronto Press, 2018.

Ryan, Tiffany. "Community Control of Education: How the Mohawk Community of Kahnawake Is Reclaiming Their Schools." MA thesis, Concordia University, 2005.

Salutin, Rick. "An Iron Will and a String of Pearls." In *Madeleine Parent: Activist,* ed. Andrée Lévesque, 123–5. Toronto: Sumach, 2005.

Sanders, Grace Louise. "La voix des femmes: Haitian Women's Rights, National

Politics and Black Activism in Port-au-Prince and Montreal, 1934–1986." PhD diss., University of Michigan, 2013.

Sandoval, Chela. "U.S. Third World Feminism: The Theory and Method of Oppositional Consciousness in the Postmodern World." In *Feminist Postcolonial Theory: A Reader*, ed. Reina Louis and Sara Mills, 75–92. New York: Routledge, 2003.

Sandwell, Rachel. "The Travels of Florence Mophosho: The African National Congress and Left Internationalism, 1948–1985." *Journal of Women's History* 30, no. 4 (2018): 84–108.

Sangster, Joan. *Demanding Equality: On Hundred Years of Canadian Feminism*. Vancouver: University of British Columbia Press, 2021.

– "Radical Ruptures, Labor, and the Left in the Long Sixties in Canada." *American Review of Canadian Studies* 40, no. 1 (2010): 1–21.

– *Transforming Labour: Women and Work in Postwar Canada*. Toronto: University of Toronto Press, 2010.

– "Words of Experience/Experiencing Words: Reading Working Women's Letters to Canada's Royal Commission on the Status of Women." In *Through Feminist Eyes: Essays on Canadian Women's History*, ed. Joan Sangster. 359–90. Edmonton: Athabasca Press, 2011.

Sauro, Assunta. "Cos'è il Centro Donne?" *L'altra faccia della luna*, October 1996, 2.

Scott, Corrie. *De Groulx à Laferrière: Un parcours de la race dans la littérature québécoise*. Montreal: Éditions XYZ, 2014.

Sethna, Christabelle. "The Evolution of the *Birth Control Handbook* from Student Peer-Education Manuel to Feminist Self-Empowerment Text, 1968–1975." *CBMH/BCHM* 23, no. 1 (2006): 89–118.

Shohat, Ella. "Area Studies, Transnationalism, and the Feminist Production of Knowledge." *Signs* 26, no. 4 (2001): 1269–272.

Simon, Sherry. *Translating Montreal: Episodes in the Life of a Divided City*. Montreal and Kingston: McGill-Queen's University Press, 2006.

Simoncini, Marie-Antoniette, and Benedetta del Balso. "Colloque sur les femmes immigrantes: Changement ou faux espoirs?" *Quaderni culturali* 1, nos 3–4 (1982): 20.

Simpson, Audra. "Captivating Eunice: Membership, Colonialism, and Gendered Citizenships of Grief." *Wicazo Sa Review* 24, no. 2 (2009): 105–29.

– *Mohawk Interruptus: Political Life across the Borders of Settler States*. Durham, NC: Duke University Press, 2014.

– "To the Reserve and Back Again: Kahnawake Mohawk Narratives of Home, Self, and Nation." PhD diss., McGill University, 2003.

Small, Shirley, and Esmeralda Thornhill. "Harambec! Quebec Black Women Pulling Together." *Journal of Black Studies* 38, no. 3 (2008): 427–42.

Smith, Mathew. *Red and Black in Haiti: Radicalism, Conflict, and Political Change, 1934–1957*. Chapel Hill: University of North Carolina Press, 2009.

Spencer, Robyn. "Engendering the Black Freedom Struggle: Revolutionary Black Womanhood and the Black Panther Party in the Bay Area." *Journal of Women's History* 20, no. 1 (2008): 90–113.

Stacey-Moore, Gail. *Amendments Proposed to the New Indian Act by Quebec Native Women's Association*. Ottawa: National Association of Women and the Law, 1989.

St-Amand, Isabelle. *Stories of Oka: Land, Film, and Literature*. Trans. Susan Elizabeth Stewart. Winnipeg: University of Manitoba Press, 2018.

Stasiulis, Daiva "Relational Positionalities of Nationalisms, Racisms, and Feminisms." In *Between Women and Nation: Nationalisms, Transnational Feminisms, and the State*, ed. Caren Kaplan, Norma Alarcón, and Minoo Moallem, 182–218. Durham, NC: Duke University Press, 1999.

Stasiulis, Daiva, and Abigail Bakan. *Negotiating Citizenship: Migrant Women in Canada and the Global System*. New York: Palgrave Macmillan, 2003.

Stewart, Michelle. "The Indian Film Crews of Challenge for Change: Representation and the State." *Canadian Journal of Film Studies* 16, no. 2 (2007): 49–81.

Stroka, Ghila. *Femmes haïtiennes: Paroles de négresses*. Montreal: Éditions de la parole Métèque, 1995.

Tanguay, Marilou. "La page féminine du *Devoir*, un espace public alternatif? Une étude de cas des mécanismes d'exclusion et de contrôle du 'féminin' et du 'féminisme' dans le quotidien (1965–1975)." *Revue d'histoire de l'Amérique française* 72, no. 4 (2019): 29–59.

Tardif, Francine, Gaétan Beaudet, and Micheline Labelle. *Question nationale et ethnicité: Le discours de leaders d'origine italienne de la région de Montréal*. Montreal: Centre de recherche sur les relations interethniques et le racisme, Département de sociologie, Université du Québec à Montréal, 1993.

Taylor, Ula. *The Veiled Garvey: The Life and Times of Amy Jacques*. Chapel Hill: University of North Carolina Press, 2002.

Theobald, Brianna. *Reproduction on the Reservation: Pregnancy, Childbirth, and Colonialism in the Long Twentieth-Century*. Chapel Hill: University of North Carolina Press, 2019.

Thompson, Becky. "Multiracial Feminism: Recasting the Chronology of Second Wave Feminism." In *No Permanent Waves: Recasting Histories of U.S. Feminism*, ed. Nancy A. Hewitt, 39–60. New Brunswick, NJ: Rutgers University Press, 2010.

Thornhill, Esmeralda. "Black Women's Studies in Teaching Related to Women: Help or Hindrance to Universal Sisterhood?" *Fireweed: A Feminist Quarterly* 16 (1983): 97–104.

– *La discrimination raciale dans le logement.* Montreal: Mouvement québécois pour combattre le racisme, 1978.

– "Focus on Black Women!" *Canadian Journal of Women and the Law* 1 (1985): 153–62.

– "Selected Awards, Honours and Pioneering Initiatives." 2022. https://ethornhill. ca/selected-awards-and-honours.

Toupin, Louise. *Le salaire au travail ménager: Chronique d'une lutte féministe internationale (1972–1977).* Montreal: Éditions du remue-ménage, 2014.

Touré, Sekou. "The Role of Women in the Revolution." *Black Scholar*, March 1975, 32–6.

Tousignant, Josée. "À propos des femmes immigrantes." *L'R des centres de femmes du Québec: Bulletin de liaison*, March 1989, 13.

Troper, Harold. *Defining Decade: Identity, Politics, and the Canadian Jewish Community in the 1960s.* Toronto: University of Toronto Press, 2010.

Tuck, Eve, and K. Wayne Yang. "Decolonization Is Not a Metaphor." *Decolonization: Indigeneity, Education and Society* 1, no. 1 (2012): 1–40.

Turcotte, Louise. "Itinéraire d'un courant politique: Le lesbianisme radical au Québec." In *Sortir de l'ombre: Histoires des communautés lesbienne et gaie de Montréal*, ed. Irène Demczuk and Frank Remiggi, 363–98. Montreal: VLB Éditeur, 1998.

Turcotte, Yannick. "L'Association des Indiens du Québec (1965–1977) et le militantisme autochtone dans le Québec des années 1960–1970." MA thesis, Université de Montréal, 2018.

Two-Axe Earley, Mary. "A Brief to the Royal Commission on the Status of Women." 1968.

– "Indian Rights for Indian Women." In *Women, Feminism, and Development*, ed. Huguette Dagenais and Denise Piché, 429–33. Montreal and Kingston: McGill-Queen's University Press, 1994.

Vallières, Pierre. *White Niggers of America: The Precocious Autobiography of a Quebec "Terrorist."* Trans. Joan Pinkham. New York: Monthly Review, 1971.

Van Kirk, Sylvia. *Many Tender Ties: Women in Fur-Trader Society, 1670–1870.* Winnipeg: Watson and Dwyer, 1980.

– "'Marrying-In to Marrying-Out': Changing Patterns of Aboriginal/Non-Aboriginal Marriage in Colonial Canada." *Frontiers: A Journal of Women's Studies* 23, no. 3 (2002): 1–11.

Vergès, Françoise. *Le ventre des femmes: Capitalisme, racialisation, féminisme.* Paris: Albin Michel, 2017.

Vien, Marie Lise. "'Un mélange aussi redouté qu'il est à craindre': Race, genre et conflit identitaire à Kahnawake, 1810–1851." MA thesis, Université du Québec à Montréal, 2013.

Villata, Bruno. *Bilinguisme et problématiques des langues ethniques: Enquête sur le comportement linguistique des jeunes montréalais d'origine italienne.* Quebec: Centre international de recherche sur le bilinguisme, 1985.

Villefranche, Majorie. "Pourquoi une féministe immigrante ou refugiée serait-elle indépendantiste en 2017?" In *Un Québec-pays: Le oui des femmes,* ed. Réseau des citoyennes pour l'indépendance, 158–63. Montreal: Éditions du remue-ménage, 2018.

"Vivian Barbot et la discrimination raciale." Video. Ottawa: Archives de Radio-Canada, 1968. Accessed 14 May 2014. http://archives.radio-canada.ca/sports/immigration/clips/15820.

Walker, Barrington. "The National Black Coalition of Canada, 'Race,' and Social Equality in the Age of Multiculturalism." *CLR James Journal* 20, nos 1–2 (2014): 159–78.

West, Michael O. "Afterword: Quilting the Black-Eyed Pea." In *To Turn the Whole World Over: Black Women and Internationalism,* ed. Keisha N. Blain and Tiffany M. Gill, 257–72. Urbana-Champaign: University of Illinois Press, 2019.

Wilkins, Fanon Che. "'A Line of Steel': The Organization of the Sixth Pan African Congress and the Struggle for International Black Power, 1969–1974." In *The Hidden 1970s: Histories of Radicalism,* ed. Dan Berger, 97–114. New Brunswick, NJ: Rutgers University Press, 2010.

Williams, Dawn. *Who's Who in Black Canada: Black Success and Black Excellence in Canada: A Contemporary Directory.* Toronto: D.P. Williams and Associates, 2001.

Williams, Dorothy. *The Road to Now: A History of Blacks in Montreal.* Montreal: Véhicule, 1997.

Williams, Robert, II. "From Anti-colonialism to Anti-apartheid: African American

Political Organisations and African Liberation, 1957–93." In *African Americans in Global Affairs: Contemporary Perspectives*, ed. Michael Clemons, 65–89. Boston: Northeastern University Press, 2010.

Wills, Dorothy. "The Status of the Black Woman Today." *Contrast*, 13 September 1972, 14.

Wu, Judy Tzu-Chu. *Radicals on the Road: Internationalism, Orientalism, and Feminism during the Vietnam Era*. Ithaca, NY: Cornell University Press, 2013.

Wuerscher, Rose. *Problems with the Legislative Base for Native Child Welfare Services*. Ottawa: Department of Indian and Northern Affairs, 1979.

Wynn, L. "The Pill Scare." *Montreal Women's Liberation Newsletter*, March 1970, 4–6.

Yanacopoulo, Andrée. *Regroupement des femmes québécoises, 1976–1981*. Montreal: Éditions du remue-ménage, 2003.

York, Geoffrey, and Loreen Pindera. *People of the Pines: The Warriors and the Legacy of Oka*. Toronto: Little, Brown and Company, 1991.

Yuval-Davis, Nira. "Belonging and the Politics of Belonging." *Patterns of Prejudice* 40, no. 3 (2006): 197–214.

– *Gender and Nation*. London: Sage, 1997.

– "Women, Citizenship, and Difference." *Feminist Review*, no. 57 (1997): 4–27.

Zellars, Rachel. "Dreams of a Black Commons on Turtle Island." *Studies in Social Justice* 14, no. 2 (2020): 454–73.

Zéphir, Clorinde, ed. *Haitian Women: Between Repression and Democracy*. Port-au-Prince: ENFOFANM Éditions, 1991.

Index